CISTERCIAN STUDIES SERIES: NUMBER FIFTEEN

THE GOLDEN CHAIN

CISTERCIAN STUDIES SERIES

Board of Editors

CISTERCIAN STUDIES SERIES: NUMBER FIFTEEN

THE GOLDEN CHAIN

*A Study in the Theological Anthropology of
Isaac of Stella*

Bernard McGinn

CISTERCIAN PUBLICATIONS
CONSORTIUM PRESS
Washington, D.C.
1972

Cistercain Studies Series ISBN 0–87907–800–6
This Volume ISBN 0–87907–815–4

Cistercian Publications Inc
Spencer Massachusetts 01562

Library of Congress Catalog Card Number: 70–152487

Ecclesiastical permission to publish this book was received from Bernard
Flanagan, Bishop of Worcester, December 12, 1970.

Printed in the Republic of Ireland by
Cahill & Co. Limited, Parkgate Printing Works, Dublin 8

Dedicated to my mother and the memory of my father

CONTENTS

List of Abbreviations

AHDL   *Archives d'histoire doctrinale et littéraire du moyen âge.* Paris: 1926–.

BGPM   *Beiträge zur Geschichte der Philosophie und der Theologie des Mittelalters.* Münster: 1891–.

CC   *Corpus Christianorum. Series Latina.* Turnhout: 1954–.

COCR   *Collectana Ordinis Cisterciensium Reformatorum.* Westmalle: 1934– (Now *Collectanea Cisterciensia*).

CSEL   *Corpus scriptorum ecclesiasticorum latinorum.* Vienna: 1866–.

DTC   *Dictionnaire de théologie catholique.* Paris: A. Vacant, 1902–50.

DS   *Dictionnaire de spiritualité.* Paris: 1937–.

MGH SS   *Monumenta Germaniae Historica. Scriptorum series.* Berlin: 1815–.

PG   *Patrologiae cursus completus, series graeca.* Paris: J. P. Migne, 1857–66.

PL   *Patrologiae cursus completus, series latina.* Paris: J. P. Migne, 1844–64.

RAM   *Revue d'ascétique et de la mystique.* Paris: 1924–.

RSPT   *Revue des sciences philosophiques et théologiques.* Paris: 1907–.

RTAM   *Recherches de théologie ancienne et médiévale.* Louvain: 1929–.

PREFACE

THE FOLLOWING WORK is a study of the theological anthropology of Isaac of Stella, a twelfth-century Cistercian Abbot. While not among the best-known theological figures of that prolific century, Isaac's position has been unfortunately minimized in the past, partly because the character of his theology is not amenable to analysis by the categories of later Scholasticism, and partly because his thought does not fit completely within the usual confines of Cistercian theology as laid down by men like Bernard of Clairvaux, William of St Thierry, and Aelred of Rievaulx. My purpose is to show that Isaac's theology of man is best understood in the light of the Platonic tradition organized about the central symbol of the golden chain of being. Such an understanding will, I hope, expose the true importance of a system which well deserves to take its place along with those of Bernard and William of St Thierry as the most significant contributions of the Cistercians to the theology of the twelfth century.

Since this study is a product of interests both historical and theological, my gratitude is due to many, but especially to Professor Norman Cantor of the State University of New York at Binghampton, whose lectures stimulated my interest in the twelfth century and whose knowledge and encouragement have guided the work to its completion. I would also like to take this opportunity to thank Father Bernard Lonergan sj of Regis College, Toronto, who first awakened my interest in theology and whose thought has always provided a stimulus and a resource in any field of research. Since the Platonic tradition plays such an important role in these investigations, I wish to thank Professor Paul Oskar Kristeller of Columbia University and Professor Alexander Altmann of Brandeis University for the avenues of access into these complex questions which their erudition opened up for me. Many other scholars have been both free with their time and helpful with their suggestions in the development of this topic, especially Mlle Marie-Thérèse d'Alverny, Fr Jean Leclercq and Fr Gaetano Raciti. Finally, a sincere word of thanks to my sister, Mrs Carolyn Frank, for her assistance with the typing and to Mrs Helen Lemay for permission to make use of a text from her projected edition of William of Conches's *Glosses on Macrobius*.

CHAPTER ONE

LIFE AND WORKS OF ISAAC OF STELLA

T HE ATTEMPT TO RECAPTURE the life of a figure like Isaac of Stella in the face of an extreme paucity of evidence is fraught with innumerable difficulties. One can, like Louis Bouyer, admit to an almost total ignorance of the details of Isaac's biography and proceed to an investigation of his thought;[1] or one can attempt to gather the scattered biographical material into some coherent picture, as has been done four times within the past century.[2] Certainly the latter procedure has far more to recommend it, as that which attempts to make full use of all the relevant material; but it involves the danger, especially when the evidence is so fragmentary, of tending to fill in the gaps by more or less unwarranted conjecture. I will attempt to place Isaac the man against the general background of his time in as satisfactory a fashion as possible, given the gaps in the evidence. The increment to knowledge of the twelfth century from such a biographical sketch will

1. L. Bouyer, *The Cistercian Heritage* (Westminster: 1958), p. 161: "Isaac of Stella is a great mystery among the Cistercians. We know only a few scattered facts about his life. Of his works we have only fragments."

2. F. Bliemetzrieder, "Isaac von Stella, Beiträge zur Lebensbeschreibung," *Jahrbuch der Philosophie und Spekulativen Theologie*, XV (1904), 1–34; J. Debray-Mulatier, "Biographie d'Isaac de Stella," *Cîteaux*, X (1959), 178–98; G. Raciti, "Isaac de l'Étoile et son siècle," *Cîteaux*, XII (1961), 281–306, XIII (1962), 18–34, 133–45, 205–16; G. Salet, "L'Homme," in *Isaac de l'Étoile: Sermons, Tome I (Sources Chrétiennes 130*; Paris, 1967), pp. 7–25.

be small, but of value for the study of the thought of Isaac, which is our major concern.

Obscure as he was, Isaac did manage to leave a few traces on the contemporary scene. One charter with his signature (referring to his role in the settling of a quarrel between the Abbey of Merci-Dieu and the Church of La Roche-Posay) still survives.[3] He played an important role in the founding of this same Abbey, as references to him in charters of 1151 and 1164–66 indicate.[4] Three further charters referring to Isaac's part in the foundation of the Abbey of Notre Dame des Châteliers on the island of Ré have come down to us in defective sixteenth-and seventeenth-century copies.[5] There is also a reference to Isaac's efforts on behalf of Thomas Becket in a letter which John Bellesmains, Bishop of Poitiers, wrote to the exiled Archbishop on June 22, 1164,[6] and there exists a late and defective seventeenth-century copy of a charter of 1167 in which the same John Bellesmains patched up a quarrel between Isaac and Hugh of Chauvigny.[7] The full relevance of this material will be discussed later; but these documents do enable us to tie in Isaac's career, not only in a vague way with the Becket controversy, but also with two important figures in the ecclesiastical world of twelfth-century France: Guichard, Abbot of the Cistercian house of Pontigny from 1136 to 1165, Archbishop of Lyon from 1165 to 1181;[8] and John Bellesmains, Bishop of Poitiers from 1162 to 1182

3. Archives de la Vienne (Poitiers), Depot 244 (de Liguge), photographically reproduced in G. Raciti, *op. cit.*, XIII (1962), facing p. 145. Raciti dates it between 1164 and 1165.

4. G. Raciti, *op. cit.*, XIII (1962), 133–4.

5. Reprinted in J. Debray-Mulatier, *op. cit.*, pp. 195–8.

6. ". . . quamvis tam ego quam communis amicus noster, abbas videlicet de Stella Isaac," in J. Robertson, *Materials for the History of Thomas Becket*, V (Rolls Series; London: 1881), Ep. 60 (pp. 112–14).

7. Text in G. Raciti, *op. cit.*, XIII (1962), 209–10, n. 268.

8. P. Pouzet, "La vie de Guichard, abbé de Pontigny (1113–1165) et archevêque de Lyon (1165–81)," *Bulletin de la Société littéraire de Lyon* (1929), pp. 117–50; this is unfortunately unavailable to me at the present time. Cf. A. King, *Cîteaux and Her Elder Daughters* (London: 1954), pp. 153–6.

and Guichard's successor at Lyon from 1182 to 1193.[9] These connections are indicated by the fact that both the signed charter mentioned previously and Isaac's *Epistola de Officio Missae*[10] are addressed to John Bellesmains, and that Guichard is mentioned in two of the charters referring to Isaac's role in the foundation of Notre Dame des Châteliers.

Isaac's own writings provide us with tantalizingly brief notices of biographical interest. As far as references to the events and personages of his time, many are too generic to be of much use;[11] but a few are of greater interest. His Forty-eighth Sermon,[12] for example, contains an attack on a new military order which seems to suggest a date posterior to the association of the Spanish order of Calatrava with the Cistercians in 1164;[13] in another sermon he refers to having seen St Bernard (†1153) in the flesh.[14] There is an impassioned outcry at the end of the *De Officio Missae* against an attack made on his monastery by Hugh of Chauvigny, in which he bewails that English origin of his which seems to have been a contributory factor to the outrage.[15] The reference to a severe famine and pestilence preceded by some kind of sign at the end of the *Epistola*

9. P. Pouzet, *L'anglais Jean dit Bellesmains (1122–1204?) évêque de Poitiers (1162–82) puis archevêque de Lyon (1182–93)* (Lyon: 1927); J. C. Robertson, *Becket Archbishop of Canterbury* (London, 1859), pp. 344–5; "Belmeis or Belesmains, John," *Dictionary of National Biography,* ed. L. Stephen (New York, 1885), IV, 196–8.

10. *PL* 194, 1889B. All references to the works of Isaac are to the edition found in *PL* 194, unless otherwise noted.

11. E.g., criticisms of ecclesiastical and monastic abuses of the day (1694 B–D; 1726B–D; 1816A–D; 1835B–1836B; 1860D–1861B; 1891A).

12. 1853C–1854C.

13. G. Raciti, *op. cit.,* XIII (1962), 21.

14. 1868C–D; G. Raciti, *op. cit.,* XII (1961), 297, conjectures that this took place at the Council of Rheims in 1148 without adducing any real evidence or cogent reason.

15. 1896 A–B; "Super tecta jam loquitur quod in me de omnibus Anglis ulciscetur. Utinam aut Anglus non fuissem, aut, ubi exsulo, Anglos nunquam vidissem." G. Raciti dates the incident described to 1166, for no given reason, *op. cit.,* XIII (1962), 23.

de Anima[16] enabled J. Debray-Mulatier to date this important work
to the year 1162.[17]

We know that Isaac was the Abbot of Stella, a small Cistercian
house about twelve miles northeast of Poitiers; yet a good number
of his Sermons contain references to the difficulties and dangers of
being placed on a small and barren island:

> Therefore, dear brothers, we have led you to this remote,
> desolate, and neglected solitude. We have done this cunningly,
> so that you are where you can be humble, where you cannot be
> rich. So that in this solitude of solitudes, as I say, lying far out
> to sea, having nothing really in common with the world, insofar
> as you are stripped of every worldly and well-nigh human
> solace, you may be completely still to the world. Besides this
> small island, the last point on earth, there is no more world for
> you.[18]

F. Bliemetzrieder presented cogent reasons for identifying the
island in question with the Île de Ré, a few miles off the French

16. 1889A–1890A.

17. *Op. cit.*, p. 188, n. 65. This date seems preferable to the later one of 1167
suggested by G. Raciti, "L'Autore del *De Spiritu et Anima*," *Rivista di Filosofia
Neo-Scolastica*, LIII (1961), 397; or the earlier one (anterior to 1158) argued by
C. H. Talbot, *Ailred of Rievaulx: De Anima. Medieval and Renaissance Studies,
Supplement I* (London: Warburg Institute, 1952), p. 49.

18. "Eapropter, dilectissimi, et vos in hanc semotam, aridam, et squalentem
induximus solitudinem. Callide quidem, ubi humiles esse potestis, divites non
potestis. In hanc, inquam, solitudinem solitudinum, ut in mari longe iacentem,
cum orbe terrarum nihil ferme commune habentem, quatenus ab omni
saeculari, et fere humano solatio destituti, prorsus sileatis a mundo, quibus,
praeter hanc modicam insulam, omnium terrarum ultimam iam nusquam est
mundus."—Sermon 14 (2nd for 4th Sunday after Epiphany), *Hoste, ed.,*
pp. 276–8 (1737A–B). Other clear references: Sermon 15 (1738A); Sermon 18
(1749D–1750A); Sermon 19 (1756B); Sermon 21 (1758A, 1759B); Sermon 22
(1761B); Sermon 24 (1768D); Sermon 27 (1778A); Sermon 29 (1787B);
Sermon 31 (1793B); Sermon 33 (1799D). Since many of these references come
in sermons that form part of a series, we can affirm that at very least Sermons
13–15 and 18–37, i.e., 23 of the 55 Sermons, were delivered at this island
location. M. Debray-Mulatier assumes that Sermons 1–6 for the Feast of All
Saints were delivered on Ré, but the allusions cited seem too general to make
such a definitive judgment (*op. cit.*, p. 192). For opinions on the number of
sermons preached on Ré (from a low of 23 adopted here to a high of 39),
cf. Salet, *op. cit.*, p. 27.

coast near the port of La Rochelle,[19] a judgment that has been confirmed by the charters concerning the foundation of Notre Dame des Châteliers and by more recent studies of Isaac's life. Finally, there are mysterious references in the Sermons to opposition to Isaac within the Order; these culminate in the striking *Apologia* of Sermon 48, which G. Raciti has made the basis of his interpretation of the life of Isaac.[20]

Of secondary importance for the life of Isaac are the traditions of the early history of the Cistercian order, organized systematically for the most part in that great age of historical erudition, seventeenth- and eighteenth-century France, and today made available in the standard source books of monastic history.[21] Included in this material are some early biographical sketches of Isaac and the edition of his works published by B. Tissier in 1662 and reprinted in the *Patrologia Latina*,[22] whose importance can be gauged from the fact that it is still the sole source (along with the earlier printed edition of G. Tilmann in 1551) for six of Isaac's Sermons. Of these early biographical notices, the most important are those of C. de Visch,[23] C. Oudin,[24] J. François,[25] the *Gallia Christiana*,[26] and the

19. *Op. cit.*, p. 6.

20. Besides Sermon 48, there are veiled references in Sermon 38 (1819B; 1820B; 1821B–C) and Sermon 39 (1821D–22B), cf. Raciti, *op. cit.*, XIII (1962), 30–1.

21. Esp. L. Janauschek, *Originum Cisterciensium*, I (Vienna, 1877) (Stella, p. 85; B. Maria in Insula Rea, p. 139); L. H. Cottineau, *Répertoire topo-bibliographique des Abbayes et Prieurés*, 2 vols. (Macon, 1935–37), les Châtelliers, I, col. 737; l'Étoile, I, col. 1081.

22. B. Tissier, *Bibliotheca Patrum Cisterciensium* (Bonnefontaine, 1662), VI, 1–83, 104–7; PL 194, cc. 1689–1890.

23. C. de Visch, *Bibliotheca Scriptorum Sacri Ordinis Cisterciensis* (Coloniae, 1656), p. 265.

24. C. Oudin, *Supplementum de Scriptoribus vel Scriptis Ecclesiasticis a Bellarmino omissis ad annum 1460* (Paris, 1686), p. 456; and *Commentarium de scriptoribus ecclesiasticis* (Leipzig, 1722), 2 vols., II, cc. 1485–6.

25. J. François, *Bibliothèque générale des écrivains de l'Ordre de S. Benoit* (Paris, 1777), II, 8.

26. [D. de Sainte-Marthe], *Gallia Christiana in Provincias ecclesiasticas distributa* (Paris, 1720), II, cols. 1352–6, 1403C–D; especially important because of its listing of the Abbots of Stella and Beata Maria in Insula Rea.

Histoire littéraire de la France.[27] The nineteenth-century notices[28] are largely derivative and therefore of little independent value.

In turning to the four twentieth-century biographical studies of Isaac, it will become evident how difficult it is to evaluate the extant material without being trapped by either the Scylla of saying next to nothing or the Charybdis of unwarranted conjecture. F. Bliemetzrieder was the first in the century to recognize the importance of Isaac for twelfth-century thought;[29] the importance of his pioneering articles is in no way negated by the judgment that they have been largely superseded by subsequent work; hence, his biographical study will be mentioned only in passing. An analysis of the three more recent studies of J. Debray-Mulatier, G. Raciti, and G. Salet is essential to the task in question. Mlle Debray-Mulatier was the first to make full use of the scattered materials available; her account, which in general refrains from unsupported guesses to fill in gaps in the evidence, is weak in attempting to relate Isaac's life to the context of his age and in interpreting several crucial phases in his career. Fr Raciti's articles (like that of Mlle Debray-Mulatier based upon thesis work) present a fascinating and rich biographical study of Isaac. Admirable in its wide acquaintance with all the available evidence and in its ability to interpret this in the light of the twelfth-century background, in its desire to create a coherent picture from problematic evidence, it frequently indulges in flights of conjecture where abstention from judgment would have been the better course. G. Salet, while disassociating

27. [A. Rivet *et al.*], *Histoire littéraire de la France* (Paris, 1733–63), 38 vols. Cf. vols. IX, 190; XII, 678–83 (reprinted in Migne). On the value of the *Gallia Christiana* and *Histoire littéraire*, cf. G. Raciti, *op. cit.,* XII (1961), pp. 281–2, n. 3.

28. R. Cellier, *Histoire générale des auteurs sacrés et écclesiastiques,* 2nd ed. (Paris, 1863), XIV, Part 2, 694–7; J.-F. Dreux-Duradier, *Histoire littéraire du Poitou* (Niort, 1849), II, 154–5; J. A. Fabricius, *Bibliotheca Latina Mediae et Infimae Aetatis* (Florence, 1858), III/IV, 463.

29. "Isaac von Stella, Beiträge zur Lebensbeschreibung," *Jahrbuch der Philosophie und spekulativen Theologie,* XV (1904), 1–34; "Eine unbekannte Schrift Isaaks von Stella," *Studien und Mitteilungen aus dem Benediktiner und Cistercienser-Orden,* XXIX (1908), 433–41; "Isaac de Stella: Sa Speculation Théologique," *RTAM,* IV (1932), 134–59.

himself from some of Raciti's conjectures,[30] has accepted Raciti's judgment on several of the essential points in which he disagrees with Mlle Debray-Mulatier, without necessarily accepting all the reasons which Raciti uses to arrive at these conclusions.

TOWARD A BIOGRAPHY

We have Isaac's own word for his English origin,[31] so here at least is a firm starting point for our inquiry. It is probably unwise to argue from vague references in several Sermons[32] to any assertion of origin from a noble family. On the basis of his becoming Abbot of Stella in 1147 after what must have been more than a few years in the Schools and as a simple monk, it is possible to conjecture that he was born early in the twelfth century, probably closer to 1100 as suggested by Raciti and Salet,[33] than the 1110–1120 of Debray-Mulatier.[34] Like so many other vital spirits of his intellectually curious generation, he came to France to study with the Masters who were engaged in the great intellectual and educational revolution of the twelfth century. When he came and precisely where he studied is difficult to ascertain in any definitive sense;[35] but since many students began their careers at an early age and since a reading of Isaac manifests a wide philosophical and theological background that most probably required many years of study, the weight of conjecture points to an early date rather than a later one, rather before 1130 than after.

30. *Op. cit.*, pp. 10–12.

31. 1896B.

32. 1778B; 1819B; cf. Salet, *op. cit.*, pp. 12–13, n. 5.

33. Raciti, *op. cit.*, XII (1961), 303, n. 70; Salet, *op. cit.*, p. 12.

34. *Op. cit.*, p. 179.

35. A phrase of Fulk, Prior of Deuil, in a letter to Abelard is used by Raciti (*op. cit.*, XII [1961], 303) as indication that Isaac came as early as c. 1122–25 to study at the Paraclete, but the statement is too general and rhetorical for such a specific conjecture: "Anglorum turbam juvenum interjacens et undarum procella terribilis non terrebat; sed, omni periculo contempto, audito tuo nomine, ad te confluebat." (*PL* 178, 371D). Debray-Mulatier, *op. cit.*, p. 183, suggests 1136–38.

B

The question of what Schools he may have attended is more difficult to answer. We can argue from the similarity of his views with those of the noted Masters of the generation of roughly 1120–1150 to reach some approximate conclusions. These possible dependences will be developed in our study of Isaac's thought; but by way of anticipation of what will be suggested there, the most striking affinities seem to tie Isaac in with Hugh of St Victor (teaching in Paris at Mt St Geneviève c. 1120–1141),[36] and with various representatives of the School of Chartres, especially Thierry of Chartres (taught at Chartres up to c. 1135, then at Paris after 1135, returned to Chartres as Chancellor in the 1140's),[37] and William of Conches (taught at Chartres until approximately 1144).[38] It is important to stress at this point that the School of Chartres is a rather generic term whose major importance in intellectual history is to indicate a basic community of approach towards certain problems shared by some Masters of the first half of the twelfth century who taught almost as frequently at Paris as they did at Chartres itself.[39]

Gaetano Raciti has constructed another type of argument for the determination of Schools from the arresting hints contained in Isaac's Forty-eighth Sermon, which several manuscripts entitle "*ysaac abbatis stelle apologia*." The Sermon begins with a criticism of his listeners for their inattention. Isaac shows himself fully aware of the reason for this inattention, viz., the conscious change of his style from a highly original, speculative mode of teaching to a

36. On the School of St Victor, cf. the article of Jean Châtillon, "De Guillaume de Champeaux à Thomas Gallus: Chronique littéraire et doctrinale de l'École de Saint-Victor," *Revue du Moyen Âge Latin,* 8 (1952), 139–62, 247–72.

37. R. L. Poole, "The Masters of the Schools of Paris and Chartres in John of Salisbury's Time," *Studies in Chronology and History* (Oxford, 1934), pp. 242–3.

38. *Op. cit.,* pp. 237–9.

39. The literature on the School of Chartres is extensive. The classic work of A. Clerval, *Les Écoles de Chartres au Moyen Âge du Ve au XVIe Siècle* (Paris, 1895) is still valuable. A modern popular introduction is R. Klibansky, "The School of Chartres," in M. Clagett et al., *Twelfth-Century Europe and the Foundations of Modern Society* (Madison, 1966), pp. 3–14.

more traditional one;[40] he then goes on to defend this change of style by appealing to the difficulties caused by the views of certain unnamed figures who are described as being *"spectabilis ingenii homines et exercitationis mire."*[41] Raciti has argued with great ingenuity and a multitude of textual parallels that Isaac is speaking of Abelard and Gilbert of Poitiers specifically, and thereby affirming that he had followed the lectures of these noted Masters.[42] This is certainly not beyond the realm of possibility; the textual parallels evinced by Raciti between Isaac's description and the contemporary descriptions of Abelard and Gilbert, while individually very general in nature, are convincing in their profusion; Gilbert and Abelard were two of the most important teachers of the generation when Isaac was a student, and we know from the testimony of John of Salisbury in his *Metalogicon* that it was possible for a peripatetic twelfth-century student to hear a large number of Masters over the course of a few years.[43] Finally, the problems raised by the disciples of Abelard and Gilbert were integral to the theological tensions of the mid-1160's when the Sermon may have been delivered.[44] Raciti conjectures that Isaac first studied with Abelard at the Paraclete (c. 1122–25), then at Chartres from c. 1125 to 1142, and finally accompanied Gilbert to Poitiers upon the occasion of his being made Bishop of that city;[45] but there is no real warrant in any documentary source for such precise identifications, which are therefore scarcely legitimate.[46]

40. "Set querimini nos stilum, nescitis qua ratione, mutasse. Et, qui subtiliter solebamus aut inuenire prorsus nova, aut eleganter innouare uetera, nunc comunia tantum terimus et, sermone triuii replicamus." Raciti ed. II, *op. cit.,* XII (1961), p. 288.

41. *Ed. cit.,* V, 289; sections V–IX of Raciti's edition of the Sermon are directly relevant to the issue.

42. *Op. cit.,* XII (1961), 292–6.   43. *Met.* II, 10.

44. Raciti dates it on June 24, 1166 (it was given for the feast of the Nativity of John the Baptist), but no conclusive reason is given why it could not have been delivered in 1165. On the theological quarrels of the 1160's, cf. Raciti, *op. cit.,* XIII (1962), 24–7; and J. de Ghellinck, *Le mouvement théologique du XIIe siècle* (Paris, 1948), pp. 251–63.

45. *Op. cit.,* XII (1961), 303–6.

46. Salet has the same outline as Raciti, but emphasizes its conjectural nature; cf. p. 13.

In conclusion, it seems safe to say that Isaac studied in France in the late 1120's and 1130's, and that he most likely was at Paris and possibly Chartres (after all, it was the thing to do for the bright young student, and these were the places to go). To attempt any further particular chronology of this part of his career, however, seems to go beyond the bounds of a sober attempt to deal with the evidence at our disposal.

Isaac's entry into the monastic life after a career in the Schools is not surprising. Thierry of Chartres, one of the most important figures of the early twelfth-century Schools, ended his life as a Cistercian;[47] two of the most important Masters of the second half of the century, Alan of Lille and Peter Cantor, did the same; among the important Cistercian figures of the period (albeit his reaction to Scholasticism was highly intemperate) we find Geoffrey of Auxerre, a former pupil of Abelard; and Everard of Ypres had been a disciple of Gilbert of Poitiers before joining the white monks.[48] Isaac's case is a *tertium quid* between that of Thierry of Chartres and that of Geoffrey of Auxerre. He did not wait to the end of his life to enter the monastery as a most honorable and efficacious way to prepare for death like Thierry; nor did he reject his training and interests in the violent kind of over-reaction that characterized Geoffrey: Isaac's writings are evidence of his view that, despite the tensions, he could be both open to many of the ideas discussed in the Schools and yet remain monastic to the core.

Two controversies surround Isaac's entry into the monastic order: the place and the date. Isaac, as we know, became Abbot of Stella in 1147. A confusing reference in the *Gallia Christiana* (1720) refers to the event in these terms: "Blessed Isaac of English stock . . . when he had been a monk of Asterciensis was made Abbot of Stella."[49] A marginal correction in later editions reads *"forte*

47. N. Häring, "The Writings against Gilbert of Poitiers by Geoffrey of Auxerre," *Analecta Cisterciensia*, XXII (1966), 35, n. 60.

48. N. Häring, "The Cistercian Everard of Ypres and His Appraisal of the Conflict between St Bernard and Gilbert of Poitiers," *Medieval Studies*, XVII (1955), 143–72.

49. "B. Isaac genere Anglus . . . cum esset monachus Asterciensis factus est abbas Stellae." *Gallia Christiana*, II, cc. 1352–53.

Cisterciensis," for the mysterious "Asterciensis," and since in the
twelfth century *"Cisterciensis"* would refer to the monastery of
Cîteaux and not the Cistercian Order in general, Mlle Debray-
Mulatier proposed that Isaac entered Cîteaux itself and from there
was transferred to Stella.[50] Both Raciti and Salet have denied this,
and with good reason: it would have been against the monastic
customs of the day, is contradicted by other seventeenth- and
eighteenth-century witnesses, and is probably explainable through
copyists' errors.[51] We have no secure information concerning the
date. Isaac thought that one should be in the school of obedience
as a simple monk for a long time before assuming the responsibilities
of the position of Abbot,[52] but this is no firm basis for his own
history. Both Debray-Mulatier[53] and Salet[54] prefer a fairly long
period of novitiate; Raciti, with his customary abruptness, tells us
that the entry took place as late as c. 1144–5;[55] but since this is
based upon the unlikely supposition of a teaching career at Poitiers
when the famous Gilbert became Bishop there in 1142, this seems
an unwarranted conjecture. Isaac's education and that forcefulness
and independence of character that are so evident in his writings
may have considerably shortened the time between his entry and
his accession to the abbatial position; the great Bernard became
Abbot of Clairvaux only three years after his entry into Cîteaux,
but those were more pioneering days.

Stella had been founded in 1124 by Isembaud, a reformer who
had found it impossible to remain Abbot of his original monastery
of Preuilly.[56] From the beginning, then, the Abbey was part of
that reforming movement of which the Cistercians were the
crowning achievement. The second Abbot, Bernard, acceded in

50. *Op. cit.*, p. 184, n. 31.
51. Raciti, *op. cit.*, XII (1961), 304–6; Salet, *op. cit.*, p. 14.
52. 1859D.
53. *Op. cit.*, p. 185.
54. *Op. cit.*, p. 15.
55. *Op. cit.*, XII (1961), p. 306.
56. *Gallia Christiana*, II, c. 1352; the founding charter is given in
"Instrumenta," c. 378.

1140, and placed in motion a request to the Pope to confirm the goods which the Abbey had received and to be joined to the Cistercian Order. Pope Eugene III granted the request to Bernard on February 1, 1147. Bernard must have died shortly thereafter, because the requests were confirmed in a letter to Isaac, now Abbot, dated October 28, 1147. Stella was placed under the motherhouse of Pontigny.[57] The significance of Isaac's entrance into Stella, a house not yet Cistercian, is that his decision was always primarily in terms of the most perfect *monastic* life. In the 1140's this meant cooperation in the expansion of the Cistercian reform; in the 1160's it might mean something a bit different.

The Cistercian movement had reached its high-water mark in 1147. Eugene III, former monk of Clairvaux, sat on the throne of Peter; St Bernard was the religious arbiter of Europe, his authority not yet shaken by the disaster of the Second Crusade; Cistercian houses had sprung up so fast all over Europe that in 1152 the General Chapter would be forced to call a temporary halt to new establishments. In the midst of so much activity, the early part of Isaac's career as Abbot maintains an unusual degree of anonymity. He played an important role in the foundation of the nearby monastery of Merci-Dieu in 1151,[58] and intervened in the affairs of the monastery on the invitation of his friend John Bellesmains in the period c. 1164–66, as the charter reprinted by Raciti indicates. So much of the energy of the twelfth century was involved in quarrels and litigation over land that it is not surprising to find the Abbey of Stella involved in tensions with the neighboring lords of Chauvigny. In 1152 we have record of a quarrel of Isaac with

57. Raciti, *op. cit.*, XII (1961), 306, n. 90; Salet's account, *op. cit.*, pp. 14–15, is confusing on the question of dates. The letters are unfortunately not extant; we know of their existence from the *Gallia Christiana*, II, 1352–3. Debray-Mulatier, *op. cit.*, p. 185, speaks of the first Cistercian monks as entering on July 25, 1145, a date dependent on L. Janauschek, *Originum Cisterciensiam* (Vienna, 1877), p. 85, n. 210, and not having any basis among now extant documents.

58. Raciti, *op. cit.*, XIII (1962), 133–4, citing E. Clouzet, "Cartulaire de Notre-Dame de la Merci-Dieu," in *Archives Historiques du Poitou*, XXXIV (1905), App. I, p. 345 (unavailable to me).

Peter Elias of Chauvigny over some forest lands,[59] and Isaac's reference to the attack made on his monks and cattle by Hugh of Chauvigny has already been mentioned. Isaac's appeal to his friend John Bellesmains was apparently successful in the latter case, since record survives of the Bishop of Poitiers' mediation of the quarrel.[60] The lords of Chauvigny may not have always been so hostile, since there is late record of a grant made by William of Chauvigny to the monastery.[61]

The period after 1160 is the most interesting and significant time in the life of Isaac, but it confronts the historian with many difficulties of interpretation. The main issues in question are three: first, what are the dates and circumstances of Isaac's sojourn on the Île de Ré; second, what was the nature of his activities in the Becket controversy; and third, what was the nature and motivation for the change of style hinted at so mysteriously in Sermon Forty-eight. Fr Gaetano Raciti's study of Isaac's life brilliantly relates all three questions in advancing the hypothesis that it was

59. C. Oudin, *Commentarium*, II, c. 1485. The Peter Elias mentioned is not the Paris master of the same name, as Bliemetzrieder thought (*op. cit.*, p. 29); but is probably the son of the Petrus Elias who appears in the foundation charter of Stella of 1124. Perhaps even the source of the controversy is indicated in this charter, since Guy of Cenius speaks of giving among other things woodland "quae sunt communia inter me et Petrum Eliae libere accipiant" (*Gallia Christiana*, II, Instrumenta, c. 378), and Peter is curiously absent from the attested witnesses. Raciti refers to another charter of Merci-Dieu (c. 1164–6) in which Isaac is mentioned; *op. cit.*, XIII (1962), 134.

60. Text in Raciti, *op. cit.*, XIII (1962), 209–10; notice in *Gallia Christiana*, II, 1180b.

61. "Cum item Abbati Stellae Isaaco dedit quartam partem sylvae Gullielmus de Chauvigny, consentientibus uxore Lucia, et Godefrido filio: et multi alia multa, ad Ecclesiae Stellensis incrementum et utilitatem." Oudin, *op. cit.*, II, c. 1485; on the lords of Chauvigny, cf. H. Beauchet-Filleau, *Dictionnaire historique et généalogique des familles du Poitou*, 1891–5, 2 vols., II, 352–3, according to which "Petrus Helias de Calviniaco" (c. 1050–1120) had a son Petrus Helias (c. 1080–1130), who in turn had four sons: (1) Helias, (2) Hugh, the one who quarreled with Isaac (†1184), (3) Peter Helias, and (4) Andrew. Andrew, who together with his brothers made a grant to Stella in 1184, founded a new family branch, the Barons of Chateauroux. Since the next three members of his line were called William, might it be possible to see William as Andrew's second name, thus making him the donor of 1165?

because of Isaac's political activity in favor of Thomas Becket that forces inimical to the English Archbishop in the Cistercian Order, using Isaac's advanced speculative theology as a handle for attack, silenced him and eventually had him banished to Ré shortly before his death. Any investigator after Raciti, while admitting the tentative character of an hypothesis based upon such fragmentary evidence, must take a stand in relation to this interpretation. It appears that the hypothesis can in general be accepted, even if particular aspects and guesses at motivation must be rejected.

Modern students of the life of Isaac have suggested three possible dates for the foundation of the Abbey of Notre Dame des Châteliers on the Île de Ré and Isaac's sojourn there: 1151–52 (Bliemetzrieder), 1155–56 (Debray-Mulatier), and 1167 (Raciti and Salet). Isaac's own references to his position on the Île de Ré give us no indication of date. When we turn to the other evidence, we are confronted by confusing and contradictory traditions. Of the three documents reprinted by Mlle Debray-Mulatier, the first (no longer extant in its original form) records the original grant made by Eble of Mauléon to Isaac, Abbot John of Trizay,[62] and others. It also gives no date. The next letter, from Eble to the Abbot of Pontigny, mother-house of both Stella and Trizay, indicates a new initiative on his part. The significant section here is the first half:

> Eble of Mauléon sends greetings to the Venerable Father and Lord G, Abbot of Pontigny, and to the whole chapter of the monastery. We thank God in all things, and the venerable members of the Cistercian Chapter, but especially you through whose goodness and diligent inquiry we obtained the goal of our desire, namely, that you might build a monastery of your most holy order in our region. Therefore we grant you for the execution of this the whole wood and all the land. Over and above and in like manner, we grant with their assent all those things unchanged which we had given to Abbot Isaac and Abbot John.[63]

62. Abbot c. 1165, according to *Gallia Christiana*, II, c. 1444C.

63. "Venerando patri et domino G[uichardo] abbati pontiniacensi totique capitulo ejusdem loci, Eblo de Malleone salutem. Gratias agimus Deo per omnia nec non et venerabilibus personis capituli cisterciensis, vobis autem maxime quorum pietate et diligenti perquisitione desiderii nostri impetravi-

The letter indicates an appeal to the Chapter of Cîteaux (or perhaps the General Chapter) and the influence of the Abbot and Community of Pontigny were both necessary before Eble could obtain what he wished, a Cistercian Abbey on Ré; he then reconfirmed his gift. A further problem is raised by the name Guichard in the printed editions of the text, for since Guichard was elevated to the episcopacy in 1165, this would effectively rule out Raciti's date of 1167 for the foundation of the monastery. However, Guichard's successor was Garin (1165–1174) and Raciti has shown that the original text in the Chartulary of Pontigny has only the initial G in the heading and could therefore apply to either of the Abbots.[64] The same may be held to be possible for the mention of Guichard in the third document, which is the definitive charter of establishment in which Eble mentions the visit of the Abbot of Pontigny to the island and the confirmation and indeed extension of his original donations. This took place in the presence of Isaac and John (who are somewhat confusingly called both monks and Abbots), and an Abbot Geoffrey.[65]

The interpretation of these three charters has been as varied as the divergence in dating. Mlle Debray-Mulatier[66] claims that Isaac and John made the original petition to Eble, but needed the authorization of their mother-house and the General Chapter before this could be legally accomplished; the second two documents are the confirmation of this necessary appeal, which is tied to the 1152 prohibition on new foundations.[67] Fr Raciti[68] has a

---

mus effectum, ut scilicet abbatiam sanctissimi ordinis vestri in terra nostra construetis. Concedimus itaque vobis ad hoc perficiendum totum nemus et universam terram insuper et omnia pariter ex integro quaecumque dederamus abbati Ysaac et abbati Johanni, ipsis hoc annuentibus. . . ." *Op. cit.,* p. 197.

64. *Op. cit.,* XIII (1962), 210, n. 273.

65. "Dederamus monachiis [*sic*] suis, videlicet Isaac, abbati Stelle, et Johanni, abbati Trizagii." "Totum hoc similiter dedit et concessit Savaricus nepos Eblonis in manu G[uicardi] abbatis, presentibus et audientibus Goffrido Abbate, Isaac et Iohanne monachis. . . ." Debray-Mulatier, *op. cit.,* pp. 197–8.

66. *Op. cit.,* pp. 190–1.

67. J. M. Canivez, *Statuta Capitulorum Generalium Ordinis Cisterciensis* (Louvain, 1933), I, 45, n. 1.

68. *Op. cit.,* XIII (1962), 210–12, n. 274.

different interpretation of the motivation. Isaac, John, and other Abbots first approached Eble when, threatened by punishment, they were actively seeking a place of exile; the Abbot of Pontigny then graciously regularized their situation. The curious reference to Isaac and John as *monachi* in the final charter is accepted by both Debray-Mulatier and Raciti as evidence that both reverted to the position of simple monks during the Ré sojourn; but once again the interpretation differs, Debray-Mulatier seeing it as a sign of unique humility,[69] and Raciti viewing it as definitive proof of their deposition by the Order because of their part in the Becket case.[70] Neither author seemed to notice that both *monachi* and *abbates* are used of the two during the course of the third charter. Was it possible for the Abbot of a daughter monastery of Pontigny to be referred to as a *monachus* in the presence of his superior Abbot? G. Salet's explanation is more nuanced and complete. Not excluding political motivation for Isaac's choice, he interprets the basic motivation as spiritual: desire for a more arduous monastic life.[71] He rejects the assertion of Debray-Mulatier and Raciti that Isaac was not Abbot of the new foundation: all the evidence of the Sermons suggests that he was, and the third charter is not conclusive on this point.[72] The most interesting suggestion made by Salet is that we are really dealing with two separate foundations here: an unofficial and extra-legal one to which the first charter gives evidence, and a second testified to in the two later charters where the situation was regularized according to the Cistercian customs by Eble's appeal to the Abbot of Pontigny.[73] Salet's suggestion prompts two observations. First, it is difficult to reconcile Isaac's attitude toward obedience as the foundation of the monastic

69. *Op. cit.*, p. 191.

70. *Op. cit.*, XIII (1962), 210–12.

71. *Op. cit.*, pp. 17–18, 20.

72. Cf. p. 20. Later, Salet does note that Isaac would be automatically deposed from the Cistercian point of view for founding a monastery without the consent of the General Chapter (p. 23, n. 2), but he postulates that the situation was regularized by the Abbot of Pontigny.

73. P. 21, esp. n. 2; p. 23.

state[74] with the apparently cavalier way in which he would have flouted the Cistercian customs in performing such an action, unless we see it as part of a dissatisfaction with the Order in relation to the ideal of monasticism.[75] Second, it is also possible that this was a necessary mode of operation in the light of the Statute of 1152 forbidding the foundation of new houses. We know that this rule was not observed in practice (between the end of 1152 and 1167, *fifty-three* houses were founded),[76] but we know little about how the law was circumvented in the practical order.

To introduce a further complicating factor, we need only recall that none of the three documents is dated. There are, however, two traditions for dating the foundation of the Abbey outside these documents, and these traditions in turn do not agree.[77] The tradition of the historians of the Île de Ré gives a wide variety of dates up to as late as 1178;[78] but since this is incompatible with Isaac's activity, and since confirmations of charters are frequently mistaken for the actual unwritten donation or even the original charter,[79] it is safe to reject this tradition along with Debray-Mulatier, Raciti, and Salet. The Cistercian traditions give May, 1156, for the foundation,[80] the date accepted by Debray-Mulatier. Raciti was able to cast grave doubts upon this tradition:[81] the fact

74. Isaac on obedience: e.g., 1859C; 1732D–34A; 1850D–51B; 1739B.

75. Whether Isaac himself adverts to his action as illegal is questionable. Salet mentions several phrases in Isaac's Sermons given on Ré, especially the "quasi conjuratis . . . confugitive" and "induximus . . . callide" of Sermon 14, 1737A–C (*op. cit.,* pp. 17–18): but the words do not necessarily connote any illegal proceeding.

76. F. van der Meer, *Atlas de L'Ordre Cistercien* (Amsterdam, 1965), "Arbre Généalogique," pp. 22–8.

77. Raciti, *op. cit.,* XIII (1962), 207–8.

78. E.g., E. Kemmerer, *Histoire de l'Île de Ré* (La Rochelle, 1868), 2 vols., I, 100–16 (gives dates 1150, 1160, 1178).

79. V. H. Galbraith, "Monastic Foundation Charters of the 11th and 12th Centuries," *Cambridge Historical Journal,* IV (1934), p. 214.

80. A. Manrique, *Cisterciensium seu verius ecclesiasticorum annalium a condito Cistercio* (Lyon, 1642), II, under 1156, Cap. VI, p. 290; *Gallia Christiana nova* XII, c. 442; L. Janauschek, *Originum Cisterciensium,* p. 139, n. 353; L. H. Cottineau, *Répertoire topo-bibliographique des Abbayes et Prieurés,* I, c. 737.

81. *Op. cit.,* XIII (1962), pp. 208–10.

that traditional foundation dates among the Cistercians had become
confused as early as the first half of the thirteenth century;[82] the
appearance of the unidentified *"abbatia de Salereis"* (scribal error for
"Insula Rea"?) in Manrique under the date 1167;[83] the fact that the
traditions of Stella do not indicate an abandonment and return to
his position there on Isaac's part (a thing that would have been
highly irregular under Cistercian customs).[84] To be sure, these
doubts are not probative in themselves. Both dates (1156 and 1167)
have a certain amount of tangential evidence behind them; but the
indication of an unusual, perhaps irregular, situation in which the
fate of Isaac was closely bound to that of the important Abbey of
Pontigny points to the troubled times of the involvement of the
Cistercian Order in the Becket controversy in the 1160's as the more
likely time for the foundation of Notre Dame des Châteliers. Since
this controversy forms the historical background for the last years
of Isaac of Stella, and especially since the letter of John of Salisbury
shows us that he did play some role as a Becket supporter, a sketch
of the early stages of the quarrel (1161–66) and the involvement of
the Cistercian Order in it has been appended to this chapter as an
excursus.

The relevance of the Becket controversy to the problem of
determining the date of Isaac of Stella's arrival on the Island of Ré
may seem rather remote, but the fact that Isaac was an active
supporter of Becket is of great significance. Our *excursus* demonstrates the existence of both a pro- and an anti-Becket party among
the Cistercians during the period 1164–66. The victory of the anti-
Becket party at the General Chapter of 1166 that forced the Archbishop to leave his first refuge at Pontigny was part of the upswing
in Henry II's fortunes that may well have had an effect on Order
policy at the end of 1166 and the beginning of 1167. Henry was
certainly not the type of man to fail to pursue an advantage, but

82. J. B. Mahn, *L'Ordre Cistercien et son gouvernement,* 2nd ed. (Paris, 1951),
pp. 193–4, n. 5.
83. Manrique, *op. cit.,* II, c. 9, p. 451: "eodem anno, Abbatia de Salereis,
alia de Salarius."
84. Mahn, *op. cit.,* p. 206.

our evidence is so fragmentary that we must be reduced to accepting the most coherent hypothesis. G. Raciti has speculated that after forcing Becket to leave Pontigny, Henry pursued a policy of vengeance against the pro-Becket party in the Cistercian Order, but the major piece of evidence he adduces for this, a letter of Henry to Gilbert of Cîteaux complaining of the pro-Becket mission of Abbot Urban of Cercamp, does not date from this period, but from the summer of 1166.[85] Furthermore, the whole of his speculation regarding the role of Geoffrey of Auxerre—that he was responsible for Isaac's silencing and exile, that he was the Abbot Geoffrey mentioned in the third charter for the founding of the Ré Abbey—is most unlikely, given that Geoffrey himself had been at least to some extent the victim of the tensions within the Order during the past two years and was in all likelihood no longer even Abbot of Clairvaux (a house which in any case had no direct control over Stella, which belonged to the line of Pontigny).

There are, of course, negative arguments against any such reaction in the Order, particularly the lack of any evidence in the Cistercian records themselves. This, however, is not as strong an argument as appears at first sight, for when one examines the Cistercian material on the question of Becket's ejection from Pontigny,[86] one finds not only confusion and errors of dating, but an obviously deliberate attempt to prejudice the account in favor of the Order and to avoid the embarrassment entailed in a true narration of the events of 1166.[87] *A fortiori*, such a spirit would also have been at work in distorting or suppressing the less savory aspects of what has been termed Cistercian *Realpolitik*.

In the last analysis, the sources fail to give a conclusive answer to

85. G. Raciti, *op. cit.*, XIII (1962), 143–5. Urban died on August 31, 1166 (*Gallia Christiana*, X, c. 1338), so Henry could scarcely be demanding his punishment in December.

86. The richest source is still Manrique, *op. cit.*, II, under 1166, cap. I (p. 418); under 1167, cap. II (p. 435); and cap. IV (pp. 440–1).

87. E.g., *op. cit.*, 1166, cap. I, n. 5, "Gilberti Abbatis *constantia* adversus regem" (p. 418).

the question of the cause of Isaac of Stella's sojourn on the Île de
Ré, but the evidence does converge to indicate that the Abbot's
active adhesion to the cause of his friend Thomas Becket led to his
sharing in some way in the reversal of the fortunes of the pro-
Becket party at the end of 1166 and the beginning of 1167.Whether
Isaac was forced to leave Stella, or whether he left voluntarily out
of dissatisfaction with the failure of the Order is impossible to
determine. The circumstances of the founding of Notre Dame des
Châteliers indicate departures from the normal Cistercian customs:
an Abbot becoming Abbot of another house without ascending;[88]
the acceptance of parochial revenues, which went against the
Cistercian customs;[89] the refusal to have granges and flocks;[90]
and the evidence of three charters as pointing to a curious kind
of double foundation.[91] But would not these irregularities be
more understandable in the disturbed situation within the Order
resulting from the tensions induced by the Becket affair than in the
more peaceful years of the previous decade? Had Isaac perhaps
undergone enough disillusion with the Cistercian realization of true
monasticism as a result of the Becket affair to be willing to depart
from certain rules to achieve a more perfect realization of his ideal?

Fr. Raciti's proposal of a direct punishment of Isaac engineered
by Geoffrey of Auxerre has all the trappings of high romance, but is
considerably weakened by what we know of Geoffrey's career, and
by the fact that Isaac's immediate superior, Garin the Abbot of
Pontigny, was the center of the now-defeated Becket group within
the Order. Fr Salet's postulation of a somewhat irregular action
by the Abbot of Stella—perhaps because of personal danger, or

88. Cf. Mahn, *op. cit.*, p. 84, which indicates that an Abbot could pass from
one house to another only in the line of promotion, not on the equal or
descending line.

89. Cf. the first charter reprinted by Debray-Mulatier, *op. cit.*, p. 196. The
Instituta No. 5 (*Ed. Turk*, p. 17) forbade this, but Mahn indicates exceptions
made even by the General Chapter, *op. cit.*, p. 175.

90. Salet, *op. cit.*, p. 20, n. 4, sees this as evoking the customs of the Order
of Grandmont, of which Isaac had a high opinion (Sermons, 1694B–D).

91. *Ibid.*

perhaps from a certain disaffection at the failure of the Cistercians to maintain their principles in the case of the Archbishop of Canterbury and an attendant desire to lead a more truly monastic life—an action which was then regularized by the Abbot of Pontigny, has much to recommend it; but no final decision can be given with regard to the particular causes and motivation with any degree of surety. It is to be hoped, however, that putting the disputed question of the foundation date in its historical context has shown that a date early in the year 1167 is the most probable one for Isaac's retirement to Ré.

One further problem remains, the question of Isaac's silencing. As we have seen, Fr Raciti has built up a case to prove that the Forty-eighth Sermon, with its cryptic references to a change of style and to the problems caused by certain theologians, is evidence that Isaac was forbidden to continue his customary highly speculative theological work by forces inimical to him in the Order.[92] In line with his giving such an important place to Geoffrey of Auxerre in the matter of Isaac's exile, and arguing from Geoffrey's well-known antipathy to such controversial thinkers as Abelard and Gilbert of Poitiers,[93] Raciti singles Geoffrey out as the chief agent in this campaign, dating it to the early months of 1166.[94] Admittedly, the hypothesis does not conflict with what we know of the character and capabilities of Geoffrey; but could the Abbot of Clairvaux have had that much direct authority on a son of Pontigny, especially at a time when he himself was apparently fighting for the maintenance of his position? Furthermore, the situation of theological tension would seem to correspond better with 1165 than 1166. Raciti's only reason for the choice of the later date is because he sees political, not theological, motives as dominant in Geoffrey's mind—another unprovable assertion. The reference to the incorporation of the Order of Calatrava dates the Sermon after September 1164, and it was on December 24 of the same year at

92. Raciti, *op. cit.*, XIII (1962), 19–34.

93. N. Häring, "The writings against Gilbert of Poitiers by Geoffrey of Auxerre," pp. 3–83.

94. *Op. cit.*, p. 21.

Sens that Alexander III summoned the theologians to put a halt to unbridled theological speculation.[95] Alexander attempted other such bans without much success;[96] and it seems legitimate, therefore, to suppose that the immediate reaction to the Sens meeting would also be the strongest, and thus there is reason for affirming that Isaac may well have been induced by it to temper the daring of his speculation in 1165 rather than in 1166. There is no real evidence to indicate a concerted effort at silencing. As a matter of fact, Isaac makes a very balanced judgment regarding theological innovations and feels himself restricted only in his more public Sermons,[97] specifically excepting private conferences with the monks.[98] The temporary and partial character of the change of style can be best understood by remembering that Isaac's most profound and bold speculative flight, the Sexagesima Sermons, was given on the Île de Ré.

The life of Isaac of Stella closes with as much mystery as it began. The Cistercian sources mention the next Abbot of Stella, Vaelisius, as appearing in the records before 1169.[99] The charter quoted by Raciti[100] is evidence that Isaac was at Chauvigny some time in 1167 when John Bellesmains finally settled the quarrel with Hugh

95. *Annales Reicherspergenses,* 1164 (MGH. SS. XVII, p. 471). "Ipso anno cum per totam Franciam multae et variae sententiae haberentur de fide inter magistros Francigenas, Alexander Papa convocatis in unum scholasticis et quibusque litteratis in ipsa vigilia nativitatis domini usque ad tria, ut fertur, milia vel ultra, cum assentientibus sibi domnis cardinalibus condemnavit et omnino interdixit omnes tropos et indisciplinatas quaestiones in theologia; Parisiensique episcopo sub obedientia praecipit, ut per totam Franciam eas conpesceret."

96. N. Häring, "The Case of Gilbert of Poitiers," *Medieval Studies,* XIII (1951), 35–9.

97. Such as Sermon 48, given on a major feast day in the vernacular with the *conversi* present.

98. "Praeterea cum simplicibus sermocinatio nostra et maxime in his diebus solemnibus, cum laicorum turba undique cogitur. Non deerit, forsan, familiarior collatio, ubi nobiscum poterimus altius aliquid et subtilius perscrutari" (*ed. Raciti,* XV, 292).

99. *Gallia Christiana,* II, c. 1353 (misspelled as Valisius).

100. *Op. cit.,* XIII (1962), 209–10, n. 268.

of Chauvigny. Raciti also holds that Notre Dame des Châteliers was founded by the end of January, since Sermon Fourteen for the Fourth Sunday after Epiphany (which would have been January 30, 1167) contains an extended reference to the island exile and perhaps to the circumstances of the foundation (1737A–B) which might indicate the very beginnings of the adventure. The chain of dates here (if the appearance at Chauvigny is early in January) would indicate very hurried activity, but would be within the realm of possibility. The Sermon might just as easily have been given in the following year. Beyond this, we know nothing. Some of Isaac's finest Sermons were delivered while on Ré; their complex speculative nature indicates a period of editing and re-working that would demand more time than the months of one winter and spring, which is the unproven supposition upon which Raciti's dating of the beginning of the exile in January 1167 rests; but, on the other hand, Isaac's probable age and the severities of life which he noted in the Sermons would militate against any long survival. The tradition that he died in 1169 is first found in the eighteenth century.[101] In his death, as in his life, Isaac of Stella continues to elude while always managing to intrigue.

THE WRITINGS OF ISAAC

Before turning to the thought of Isaac of Stella, it will be helpful to direct some attention to the questions of the authenticity and literary genera of his writings.[102] The genuine works of Isaac consist of fifty-five Sermons and two treatises in the form of letters. The corpus of Isaac's work has a mixed manuscript tradition: on the whole good for the treatises, but fragmentary for the Sermons. This fact, along with the evidence that most of the texts we have seem to come from the last years of his life (almost half the Sermons from the time of his exile on Ré), have led Fr Raciti to speculate on a

---

101. ". . . cum constet illum anno 1169 esse mortuum." C. Oudin, *op. cit.*, II, c. 1486.

102. Cf. Salet, "L'Orateur," *op. cit.*, pp. 26–35.

C

deliberate campaign to suppress his writings;[103] but the fairly extensive manuscript tradition for the letters rather argues to the disappearance of most of the pre-Ré Sermons through historical accident and the fragmentary tradition for the Ré Sermons as being a result of the poverty and isolation of the new monastery.

Genuine Works

R. Milcamps pioneered the study of the manuscripts and editions of Isaac in his bibliographical article of 1958.[104] In the last ten years work by A. Hoste,[105] G. Raciti,[106] and J. Leclercq[107] have increased our knowledge in this area considerably. Fr Hoste's "Introduction au texte Latin" in the *Sources Chrétiennes* edition of Isaac's Sermons is the best and most recent study;[108] but Fr Leclercq's discovery of a new Sermon induces hope that not only more manuscripts but perhaps even new texts will be uncovered by further research.

Without reproducing the full information of Fr Hoste's listings, it is important to note that only eight extant manuscripts are witnesses to Isaac's Sermons, and none of the eight gives a complete series.[109] As a matter of fact, for six of the Sermons (nos.

---

103. Salet, *op. cit.*, pp. 26–7, citing a private letter of Fr Raciti.

104. R. Milcamps, "Bibliographie d'Isaac de l'Étoile," *COCR*, XX (1958), 175–86.

105. Notice of Milcamps in *Cîteaux*, IX (1958), 302; and "Un thèse inédite sur Isaac de l'Étoile," *COCR* XXV (1963), 256–57.

106. "Isaac de l'Étoile et son siècle," *Cîteaux*, XIII (1962), 216; and his note on Leclercq's article in *Collectanea Cisterciensia*, XXVII (1965), 337–9.

107. "Nouveau sermon de Isaac de l'Étoile," *RAM* XL (1964), 277–88.

108. *Isaac de l'Étoile Sermons*, edd. A. Hoste and G. Salet (Paris, 1967), pp. 69–83.

109. (1) Monte Cassino, ms. 410 LL (13th century)—Sermons 43, 44, 45, 46, 48, 49, 47, 50, 51, 52, 53 (only ms. witness for 49 and 50); (2) Paris, Bibl. Sainte-Geneviève, ms. 45 (13th—14th cent.)—contains 28 of the known 55 sermons; (3) Paris, Bibl. Nat., ms. lat. 3002 (13th cent.)—Sermons 19–26; (4) Paris, Bibl. Nat. ms. lat. 10694 (13th cent.)—incomplete text of Sermons 1–2; (5) Rouen, Bibl. Municipale, ms. 670 (A. 592) (13th cent.)—incomplete text of Sermons 6, 8, 10, 13, 26, 18; (6) Subiaco, Monastery Library, ms.

29, 30, 31, 32, 34, and 54) there are no known manuscript witnesses, thus making the earlier printed editions of great importance. The most important of these earlier editions is that of Bertrand Tissier in his *Bibliotheca Patrum Cisterciensium* (Bonnefontaine, 1662, Vol. VI, pp. 1–77);[110] as far as modern critical work goes, the appearance of the first volume of the Sermons in the excellent edition of the *Sources Chrétiennes* is a milestone in work on the text of Isaac.

The task of recovering the text of Isaac of Stella has been paralleled by research into the literary genre of the monastic Sermons, so that the modern investigator stands in a much better position to evaluate the real intentions of the Abbot of Stella than his predecessors did. While older works are still useful,[111] the extensive writings of Fr Jean Leclercq on the technique and form of the monastic Sermon as summarized in his *The Love of Learning and the Desire for God*[112] are the best introduction to the study of this literary genre.

Like the vast majority of the monastic Sermons that have survived, Isaac's fifty-five Sermons are examples of what Leclercq calls "written rhetoric,"[113] i.e., Sermons never actually delivered in the

---

CCI (15th cent.)—26 Sermons of Isaac, including the "In dedicatione ecclesiae" rediscovered by J. Leclercq and first published in 1964; (7) Subiaco, Monastery Library, ms. CCIII (15th cent.)—Sermon 47; (8) Douai, ms. 391 (14th cent.), indicated by Milcamps, *op. cit.,* p. 180, but not used by Hoste in the preparation of his edition. Hoste also indicates five lost manuscripts, cf. *op. cit.,* pp. 73–4. Finally, fragments of Isaac's Sermons are to be found in a catena of Cistercian texts on the Bible, now known in eleven mss., and printed four times in the sixteenth century, most fully by Geoffrey Tilmann, *Allegoriae simul et Tropologiae in locos utriusque Testamenti* (Paris, 1551). Cf. Milcamps, *op. cit.,* pp. 185–6; T. Käpelli, "Eine aus frühscholastischen Werken exzerpierte Bibelkatene," *Divus Thomas* (Fribourg), IX (1931), 309–19 and especially Hoste, *op. cit.,* pp. 74–7.

110. Reprinted in J. P. Migne, *PL* 194 (Paris, 1855), cc. 1689–1876.

111. L. Bourgain, *La chaire française au XIIe siècle* (Paris, 1879). E. Gilson. "La technique du sermon médiéval," *Les Idées et les lettres* (Paris, 1932), pp. 93 ff.

112. Mentor paperback edition (New York, 1962), Esp. pp. 168–76, resuming themes from "Recherches sur d'anciens sermons monastiques," *Revue Mabillon,* XXXVI (1946), 1–14.

113. *Op. cit.,* pp. 155, 177.

form in which we possess them. Leclercq has buttressed this conclusion by his extensive researches into the Sermons of St Bernard;[114] and while such precise evidence for the complicated process of delivery, editing, and transmission is necessarily lacking in the case of Isaac, there is no reason for disagreeing with G. Salet's judgment that in this respect Isaac is similar to the Abbot of Clairvaux.[115] It is rather improbable that a series of Sermons so intricate, so abstruse, and so carefully organized as the Sermons for Sexagesima Sunday were actually delivered to an audience in anything resembling the form we now have them. Several interesting asides made in the course of the Sermons themselves argue in this direction. First, while it was customary to preach to monks in Latin, Sermons at which others, such as the laybrothers or *conversi*, were present were given in the vernacular, and Isaac's own comments in the midst of three Sermons may be taken to suggest that they were originally delivered in the vernacular.[116] Secondly, in Sermon Forty-eight, which G. Raciti has analyzed in such detail, Isaac remarks that he has spent so much time on his "apologia" that there is little left for reflection on the mystery of the Feast,[117] thus indicating that the present brief autobiographical part of the Sermon is merely a Latin précis of a longer delivery in the vernacular.[118] It is possible to assert, then, that there are two general types of literary Sermons among the fifty-five surviving to us: Sermons that are summaries or literary re-workings of Sermons actually delivered (those that stand individually are more

114. J. Leclercq, "St Bernard et ses secrétaires," *Revue Bénédictine*, LXI (1951), 208–29; *Études sur Saint Bernard et le Texte de ses Écrits, Anal. Sac. Ord. Cist.*, Vol. IX, Parts 1–2 (1953); "Recherches sur les Sermons sur les Cantiques de S. Bernard," *Revue Bénédictine, passim*, LXIV, LXV, LXVI, LXIX.

115. *Op. cit.*, p. 32.

116. Sermon 38: ". . . vulgari sermone breviter narro" (1815B); Sermon 45: "Dicamus simpliciter, maxime propter simplices et illiterato fratres, qui supra sermonem trivii loquentes non intelligunt" (1842D); Sermon 48: "Sermones, uere, isti solemnes simplicibus sinplices sunt, et pedestri sermone effusi" (*ed. Raciti*, p. 292, 1855D).

117. "Modicum istud de tanta uobis hodie solemnitate locuti—in superiore, quippe, apologia horam impendibus" (*ed. Raciti, ibid.*).

118. Raciti, *op. cit.*, XII (1961), 285.

likely to be in this category), and Sermons that are part of a carefully worked-out series and were more likely to have been written out beforehand and read to the monks in more intimate surroundings than those in which formal Sermons were given.[119] These series might be more fairly described as theological treatises which adopt the Sermon form in harmony with commonly accepted monastic practice than as Sermons in the modern sense of the term. It is in them that we can expect to find the Abbot of Stella at his most profound.[120] Assuredly not the least delight of this theological genre is the literary device by which it gives itself a *Sitz im Leben*, even to the assertion that it is being delivered in the fields under the shade of a neighboring tree after the day's toil has been finally brought to a close.[121] To accept Isaac's literary form here in a literal sense would

119. Cf. Leclercq, *Love of Learning*, pp. 172–74. The following Sermons seem to be in the form of series concerning a common theme: (1) Sermons 1–6 (Feast of All Saints)—On The Beatitudes; (2) Sermons 16–17 (Septuagesima)—Conversion; (3) Sermons 18–26 (Sexagesima)—God: One and Three (Sermon 18 here is an introduction, and interestingly not included in Paris Bibl. Nat. ms. lat. 3002, which contains 19–26 only of Isaac's Sermons, thus providing another argument for the treatise character); (4) Sermons 27–29 (Quinquagesima)—Man's Situation and Christian Asceticism; (5) Sermons 33–37 (2nd Sunday of Lent)—Salvation and Predestination (Here the organizational character is less evident and the references to actual interventions in the course of delivery in 1800C and 1811D–12A may indicate Sermons that were once delivered and then re-worked into a more organized form).

There are other series of Sermons for a single Feast which exhibit less unity of content and therefore leave the question open whether they were originally planned as units: (1) Sermons 7–8 (Sunday within the Octave of Epiphany); (2) Sermons 9–10 (1st Sunday after Epiphany); (3) Sermons 14–15 (4th Sunday after Epiphany); (4) Sermons 30–32 (1st Sunday of Lent); (5) Sermons 38–39 (3rd Sunday of Lent). Note that most of these series would be products of the Ré period, when the more organized character might be explained either by the desire to give a full background in theology to a group of monks without library facilities (1761B) or to maintain a teaching role to outsiders (monks of Stella?) through Sermon-treatises.

120. On the theological importance of such Sermons, cf. Leclercq, *Love of Learning*, p. 173; M. M. Lebreton, "Recherches sur les principaux thèmes théologiques traités dans les sermons du XIIe siècle," *RTAM* XXIII (1956), 5–18.

121. Isaac makes reference to delivering Sermons in the open during or after the day's work in 1723A, 1729D, 1768D, 1773D. We know that it was

be to leave the poor monks with the hardest part of the day's work still ahead of them, the effort to come to grips with their Abbot's knotty thought.

Highly literary productions as they are, Isaac's Sermons, like those of Bernard and the other great masters of the rhetoric of monastic theology, bring us close to the author as an individual in a sense that the literary genera of Scholastic theology never do. The rhetoric of the twelfth century, while it could at times degenerate into empty formalism, in its great masters was rather experienced as a unique mode of sensibility and expression, a legitimate style, in the fullest sense of the word. To view it as an insincere and artificial literary convention is to fall into an interpretation based more upon contemporary distrust of rhetoric than upon the classical and Christian educational and cultural roots of twelfth-century monastic style.[122] Isaac's style, while at times falling into abstraction and occasional obscurity due to the nature of the speculation which he loved so much,[123] was for the most part popular with the monks of

the custom to have Sermons in such circumstances (Leclercq, *op. cit.*, p. 169); but since the latter two references at least are in the midst of the Sexagesima Sermons, Isaac's most speculative writing, it seems rather naive to view them as in any way the product of an actual Sermon after a day in the fields. The reference to reclining under the shade of the oak tree ("sub patulae, quam prope cernitis, ilicis tegmine paulisper reclinemus," 1768D), which L. Bouyer accepts as an indication of local color (*op. cit.*, pp. 167–68), is probably a highly sophisticated allusion to Virgil's 1st Eclogue ("tu patulae recubans sub tegmine fagi," *Ecl.* I, 1).

122. On sincerity in twelfth-century rhetoric, cf. Leclercq, *op. cit.*, pp. 177–9. For a broader consideration of the place of the science of rhetoric in the Middle Ages, cf. R. M. McKeon, "Rhetoricism in the Middle Ages," *Speculum,* (1942), pp. 1–8. On the rhetorical style of Bernard, cf. E. Auerbach, *Mimesis* (New York, 1957), pp. 141–7; *Literary Language and Its Public in Late Latin Antiquity and in the Middle Ages* (New York, 1965), pp. 70–5; C. Mohrmann, "Observations sur la langue et le style de Saint Bernard," *Sancti Bernardi Opera,* II (Rome, 1958), ix-xxxiii.

123. Isaac confessed his preference for the allegorical (mystical) sense over the moral, whatever the brethren might like: "Sed video, fratres, exspectationi vestrae non satisfecisse me, qui moralem sensum, quo superaedificemini fundamento, in quo positi estis, avidius bibitis, geremus ergo vobis, pro facultate nobis indulta, morem, sed fateor, contra nostrum morem, quem utique mysteria magis delectant." (1729C–D, *ed. Hoste,* p. 248).

his community[124] for reasons that can still be appreciated today.[125] While capable of great rhetorical power in the building up of sonorous paratactical passages of aural solemnity of an almost liturgical quality—so different from Bernard's lush richness, which strikes a more personal note of religious emotion—it also maintains a unique quality of self-revelation that shines forth in sudden impassioned outbursts, in expressions of a mature self-confidence that somehow are not in conflict with these outbursts, and in the choice of metaphors whose originality and aptness make them immediately memorable.

Isaac's two remaining authentic works belong to another of the well-recognized literary genera of monastic theology, the treatise in letter form.[126] Such letters were not intended to be purely personal communications, but were rather at once personalized and stylized forms of propounding ideas on current questions to a wide audience. Both of these treatises are fairly well represented in the manuscript tradition and seem to have had a much wider influence than the fragmentary collections of Sermons.

The *Epistola de Anima*, addressed to Alcher of Clairvaux, is one of Isaac's best organized and most profound creations. Nine manuscript witnesses are known at present;[127] G. Raciti is at work on a

124. Not only the evidence of the change of style of Sermon 48, but also 1741D and 1750A.

125. On Isaac's style, cf. Salet, *op. cit.*, pp. 30–1; Bouyer, *op. cit.*, p. 161; Raciti, *op. cit.*, XII (1961), 300–303; XIII (1962), 213–15.

126. J. Leclercq, *op. cit.*, pp. 179–82; and "Le Genre épistolaire au moyen âge," *Revue du moyen âge latin*, II (1946), 63–70.

127. (1) Paris, Bibl. Nat., ms. lat. 1252, ff. 5^v–13^v (12th–13th cent.). This important ms. may have come from Stella itself; cf. A. Hoste, *op. cit.*, pp. 73–4; (2) Cambridge, Univ. Lib. ms. KK I 20, ff. 3^r–7^v (13th cent.); (3) Rome, Bibl. Angelica, ms. 70 (A.7.9.), ff. 40^b–42^c (13th–14th cent.); (4) Paris, Bibl. S. Geneviève, ms. 45 (B.I. in fol. 13), ff. 148^r–154^r (13th cent.); (5) Paris, Université de Paris, ms. 584, ff. 92^v–97 (14th cent.); (6) Laon, ms. 412, ff. 41^r–42^r (13th cent.; fragmentary); (7) S. Omer, ms. 119, ff. 5—(13th cent.); (8) Mantua, Bibl. Commun. ms. lat. D.V. 6, ff. 251va–255vb (15th cent.); (9) Erfurt, Bibl. Amplon. ms. 40, ff. 50–51 (14th cent.). Note that a tenth ms. listed by Milcamps, *op. cit.*, p. 183, Rome, Bibl. Vat., ms. Chigi. L. IV, 124, actually contains Italian translations of Isaac of Syria.

critical edition for the *Sources Chrétiennes* whose appearance will supersede the inadequate text of Tissier now available in Migne.[128] Because of the importance of this letter for the study of Isaac's psychology, a corrected text made on the basis of a collation of the first three manuscripts listed in the note will be used during the course of this work. An English translation of this text can be found in *Treatises on the Soul, Cistercian Fathers Series*, volume twenty-four. The division into paragraphs used throughout this study refers to that translation.

By far the most popular work of Isaac, to judge from the manuscripts available, is the work that will probably have the least appeal to the modern reader, the allegorical interpretation of the liturgy in the *Epistola ad Joannem Episcopum Pictaviensem De Officio Missae*. Twenty-two manuscripts of this work are extant,[129] and these seem to include at least three variants in the ending: the text of Tissier's edition as reprinted in Migne, which is clearly defective in sense;[130] a somewhat longer ending found in some Paris manuscripts; and

128. B. Tissier, *Bibliotheca Patrum Cisterciensium*, VI, 78–83, reproduced in *PL* 194, 1875–90. Mlle J. Debray-Mulatier's edition in her thesis *Isaac de Stella et l'Epistola de Anima*, Position de thèse École nationale des Chartes (Paris, 1940), was never published.

129. (1) Paris, Bibl. Nat. ms. lat. 1252 (12th cent.); (2) Paris, Bibl. Nat. ms. lat. 11579 (12th cent.); (3) Paris, Bibl. Nat. ms. lat. 1828 (12th cent.); (4) Paris, Bibl. Nat. ms. lat. 6674 (13th cent.); (5) Paris, Bibl. Nat. nouv. acq. lat. 1791 (12th cent.); (6) Paris, Bibl. Nat. nouv. acq. lat. 2479 (13th cent.); (7) Paris, Bibl. Nat. ms. lat. 1258; (8) Paris, Bibl. Nat. ms. lat. 2474 (13th cent., incomplete); (9) Paris, Bibl. Nat. ms. lat. 812 (13th cent.); (10) Tours, ms. 137 (12th cent.); (11) Cambrai, ms. 259 (249) (13th cent.); (12) Arras, Bibl. Mun. ms. lat. 670 (727) (13th cent.); (13) Rouen, ms. 588 (A542) (13th cent., incomplete); (14) Douai, ms. 391 (14th cent.); (15) Brussels, Bibl. Roy. ms. II 957 (13th cent.); (16) Oxford, Corpus Christi College, ms. XLVIII (13th cent.); (17) Oxford, Bodleian Lib., ms. Auct. F. G. (15th cent.); (18) Cambridge, Univ. Lib. ms. Gg. IV. 16 (13th cent.); (19) Cambridge, Univ. Lib. ms. addit. 3037; (20) Ashburnham Palace, ms. fol. A (13th cent.; present location?); (21) Rome, Bibl. Vat. ms. Reginensis lat. 106 (13th cent.); (22) Vienna, Nat. Bibl. ms. lat. 1068 (Rec. 47) (14th cent.). This list, including the imprecisions of description, is dependent on Milcamps, *op. cit.*, pp. 180–82

130. B. Tissier, *op. cit.*, pp. 104–7, reproduced in *PL* 194, cc. 1889–96. The text was also edited by Dom L. d'Achéry, *Spicilegium* (Paris, 1723), I, 449–51 mistakenly under the name of Isaac, Bishop of Langres.

an even longer ending in the Vienna manuscript which Milcamps considers to be more authentic.[181]

Attributed Works

Like most medieval authors, Isaac of Stella has also had a number of works attributed to him which are at best extremely doubtful. The most important of these, the *Expositio in Cantica Canticorum* found in *Bibliothèque Nationale ms. lat.* 1252 (ff. 13–46), was ascribed to Isaac by Tissier in the seventeenth century and by various later investigators.[132] This attribution has been accepted by a number of scholars in the present century, most recently by Fr Anselm Hoste.[133] R. Collini edited the text in the second volume of his unpublished thesis, *Studi su Isaaco della Stella*,[134] giving the reasons for his acceptance of the authenticity of the commentary. At a first view, there are some arguments for accepting this position: the inclusion of the work in the important ms. 1252, which also contains the indisputably authentic *De Anima* and the *De Canone Missae*, in itself seems to be conclusive for Hoste; but on closer investigation grave doubts arise. First of all, the work itself is of a loose and disconnected character, a kind of *florilegium* (even including fragments of a *Commentary on Ecclesiastes* 12, 1–5 in another hand),[135]

131. *Op. cit.*, p. 182, first discovered by F. Bliemetzrieder, "Isaac de Stella: Sa Speculation Théologique," *RTAM* IV (1932), 135–6. R. Collini discusses the three versions in his unpublished thesis, *Studi su Isaaco della Stella*, Università Cattolica del sacro Cuore (Milan, 1956–7), I, 37.

132. C. Oudin, *op. cit.*, II, c. 1485; J. A. Fabricius, *Bibliotheca Latina Mediae et Infimae Aetatis* (Florence, 1858), III/IV, 463; *Histoire littéraire de la France*, XII, (1869), 683.

133. "Une thèse inédite sur Isaac de l'Étoile," *COCR* XXV (1963), 256–7. Cf. also Milcamps, *op. cit.*, p. 184; F. Stegmüller, *Repertorium Biblicum Mediae Aevi*, 5 vols., Madrid, 1940–55, III, # 5156, 1.

134. *Op. cit.*, II, 362–468.

135. Collini, ed., Vol. II, 463–8. Cf. R. O'Brien, "A Commentary of the Canticle of Canticles Attributed to Isaac of Stella," *Cîteaux*, XVI (1965), 226–8.

thus making it extremely difficult and perhaps illusory to attempt to determine authorship with any degree of accuracy. Collini's internal arguments for ascription to Isaac—style, argument, theme, doctrinal reminiscences of the Sermons[136]—on close investigation, turn out to be so general in nature as to lack definite probative force. It can scarcely be denied that there are affinities with Isaac's thought present;[137] but the differences in terminology,[138] in thematic development,[139] and the generally pedestrian quality of the work make it much more likely that we are dealing with a *florilegium* emanating from Cistercian circles which was influenced by Isaac's thought, but which cannot be said to be his own.[140]

The second of the works attributed to Isaac is an *Expositio in Librum Ruth*, first noticed by F. Bliemetzrieder[141] and also edited by Collini in his thesis.[142] It is found in a manuscript containing other works of Isaac[143] and includes a dedicatory letter to John Bellesmains

136. *Op. cit.*, I, 162–3.

137. The contrast between *nunc* and *tunc* (Ed. Collini, pp. 376, 432–3); the union of *sensus* and *affectus*, i.e., *cognitio* and *dilectio (ibid.)*; the soul as *rationabilis, concupiscibilis* and *irascibilis* (p. 436); the *scala Jacob* image (pp. 393, 432–3); the use of *hyper-* terms (pp. 406, 408); etc.

138. Terms such as *intentio animae, carnalis voluptas,* and *satisfacere,* rare in Isaac, are frequent here. The four fundamental affections are *laetitia, tristitia, desiderium, timor* (pp. 440–45), whereas Isaac always gives *gaudium, spes, timor, dolor* (1747B, 1878D).

139. Many of Isaac's most common themes are lacking at places where they would be expected (e.g., no *cognosce teipsum* theme on p. 409). Isaac's Sermon 52 gives a different interpretation of Cant. 3, 6, than that found in the Commentary (pp. 419–20). The consideration of the effects of original sin, the four cardinal virtues, and four fundamental affections (pp. 440–5) is quite unlike Isaac's classic development of these same themes in Sermon 4 and the *Epistola de Anima*.

140. This is also the conclusion of R. O'Brien, whose judgment on the text is that "it seems too fragmentary to have more than archaeological value" (*op. cit.*, p. 228).

141. F. Bliemetzrieder, "Eine unbekannte Schrift Isaaks von Stella," *Studien und Mitteilungen aus dem Benediktiner und Cistercienser-Orden,* XXIX (1908), 433–41, edited the covering letter to John Bellesmains and the first folio.

142. *Op. cit.*, II, 1–362.

143. Paris, Bibl. S. Geneviève, ms. 45 (B. I. in folio 13), ff. 2ʳ–74ʳ.

couched in friendly terms. These facts have led to its being accepted as authentic by some modern investigators,[144] but on the basis of internal evidence, Fr Hoste expresses doubts that a purely moralizing treatise of such poverty of style should be ascribed to Isaac.[145] In short, there seems to be even less reason for a serious claim to authenticity for this Scriptural commentary than for the previous one.

The final treatise in this category is the *Tractatus de Sacramento Altaris*, which various older authors ascribed to Isaac,[146] and which some identify with a treatise of that name in Douai, ms. 391. Bliemetzrieder sees this treatise, which is largely in the form of an allegorical commentary on the First Book of Kings, as possibly belonging to Isaac;[147] but very few others have followed him in this assertion.[148] Until some adequate analysis or edition of the treatise is published, it seems fair to say that the burden of proof rests with those who assert its authenticity.

Thus, Isaac's writings, while not without involved questions of attribution and the unfortunate situation of still having to depend for the most part on defective seventeenth-century editions, present a solid and manageable corpus for the student of intellectual history. It is puzzling, at times almost astonishing, that a thinker of such originality and power has been accorded such cursory treatment in the past. Fortunately, this neglect is beginning to be cancelled out by the great interest in Isaac evident in the last twenty-five years; it is certain that the new critical edition of the indisputable works will serve as both a corrective for some former work and a stimulus for further investigation.

144. Milcamps, *op. cit.*, p. 185; Stegmüller, *op. cit.*, III, # 5155; Collini, *op. cit.*, I, 170–74.

145. In his note of Collini's thesis, "Une thèse inédite sur Isaac de l'Étoile," *COCR* XXV (1963), 356–7.

146. E.g., C. Oudin, *Commentarius de Scriptoribus ecclesiasticis* (Leipzig, 1722), II, c. 1485.

147. *Op. cit.*, p. 441; cf. Stegmüller, *op. cit.*, III, # 5156.

148. Most authors ignore the treatise; Milcamps places it in a special category of "Oeuvre supposée," *op. cit.*, p. 185.

EXCURSUS

THE PLACE OF THE CISTERCIAN ORDER IN THE EARLY
YEARS OF THE BECKET CONTROVERSY

Modern research into the history of the Cistercians has indicated that it is possible to view the Cistercian activity in the Becket controversy as a pivotal change in the development of the Order.[149] This in turn provides a framework within which the acceptance of 1167 for the foundation of Notre Dame des Châteliers on Ré and the exile of Isaac appears as the most probable dating. For these reasons it seems worthwhile to study the Cistercians' place in the early stages of the Becket controversy in this *excursus*.

In April, 1161, Theobald Archbishop of Canterbury died. By June of the following year, Thomas Becket, whose personal and administrative gifts had already made him Chancellor of the realm at the age of thirty-six and the closest confidant of Henry II, was consecrated as his successor.[150] Thomas's well-known misgivings over accepting the position had already presaged that his role as Archbishop might not be all that Henry had expected, and the storm was not long in coming.[151] By the middle of 1163 the issue

149. For a general account of the period, cf. R. Foreville and J. Rousset de Pina, *Du premier Concile du Latran à l'avènement d'Innocent III*, 2éme partie (Paris 1953), pp. 50–156. For the role of the Cistercians, cf. Martin Preiss, *Die politische Tätigkeit und Stellung der Cisterzienser im Schisma von 1159–1177* (Berlin, 1934; *Historische Studien* 248), pp. 74 seq. (the best study on the topic). Also cf. S. Mitterer, "Die Cistercienser im Kirchenstreit zwischen Papst Alexander III und Kaiser Friedrich I Barbarossa," *Cistercienser-Chronik*, XXXIV (1922), 1–8, 21–6, 35–40; J. B. Mahn, *op. cit.*, pp. 139–47; and M. Seraphin Lenssen, "L'Abdication du Bienheureux Geoffrey d'Auxerre comme l'Abbé de Clairvaux," *COCR* XVII (1955), 98–110; G. Raciti, *op. cit.*, XIII (1962), 133–45.

150. On the problem of Becket the person, cf. D. Knowles, "Archbishop Thomas Becket; A Character Study," in *The Historian and Character* (Cambridge, 1964), pp. 98–128.

151. On the general history of the controversy, cf. A. L. Poole, *From Domesday Book to Magna Carta, 1087–1216* (2nd ed.; Oxford, 1954), pp. 197–231; R. Barber, *Henry Plantagenet* (London, 1964), Chs. 5 and 6; Z. N.

that was to provide the immediate spark for the controversy, the case of the criminous clerks (i.e., whether the Royal or the Ecclesiastical Courts were to have preponderant jurisdiction in the cases of clerics accused of crimes),[152] was already becoming a center of tension between Thomas and Henry. The Archbishop won the first round when he convinced the other Bishops of the kingdom to side with him at the Council of Westminster in October of 1163,[153] but the consciousness of impending danger is already clear in a letter he received from his friend John Bellesmains, Bishop of Poitiers, probably late in the same year. John mentions that little support can be expected from the Roman Curia,[154] since Pope Alexander, now in exile in France, desperately needed to keep Louis VII of France and Henry united in his support against Frederick Barbarossa; significantly, John mentions that he will journey to the Abbey of Pontigny to further Becket's cause with the Cistercians.[155] The reason is obvious: Alexander was deeply indebted to the Cistercians, whose support of his cause, particularly at the General Chapters of 1161 and 1162, had been a significant factor in his survival.[156] Surely if the Cistercians could be brought

---

Brooke, *The English Church and the Papacy* (Cambridge, 1931), pp. 191–214; R. Foreville, *L'Eglise et la Royauté en Angleterre sous Henri II Plantagenet* (1154–1189) (Paris, 1942), Book III; J. C. Robertson, *Becket, Archbishop of Canterbury* (London, 1859).

152. F. W. Maitland, "Henry II and the Criminous Clerks," in *Roman Canon Law and the Church of England* (London, 1898), pp. 132–47.

153. On the role of the Bishops in the controversy, cf. D. Knowles, *The Episcopal Colleagues of Thomas Becket* (Cambridge, 1949).

154. J. C. Robertson and J. B. Sheppard (eds.), *Materials for the History of Archbishop Thomas Becket* (London, 1881), 7 vols. (Rolls Series). Hereafter referred to as *Materials*. Epist. 35, "Excitatus praecurrentis" (V, 55–7): "Nam quod ad humanum auxilium attinet, nihil est quod de curia in aliquo quod regem offendere debeat exspectetis" (p. 56).

155. *Ibid.,* "Ego Pontiniacum proficiscor, ut illius religionis devotioni tam vestram quam nostram commendam intentionem" (p. 57).

156. The often-cited text from Helmhold, *Chronica Slavorum,* I, 90: "Insuper Cisterciensis ordo eidem [Alexander] universus accesserat, in quo sunt archiepiscopi et episcopi quam plures et abbates amplius quam septingenti et monachorum inestimabilis numerus . . . Horem invincibilis sententia vel maximas vires addidit Alexandro" (*MGH SS* XXI, p. 82).

over to the Archbishop's side, they would be able to exert a great influence on Alexander and his Curia, and the powerful Abbot of Pontigny, Guichard, would be an ideal channel for such influence.

If one analyzes the mass of letters relating to the Becket controversy, it becomes evident that John Bellesmains, Bishop of Poitiers, and John of Salisbury, both Englishmen, scholars, and old friends from the days of Archbishop Theobald's court, were among the most important of Becket's advisers and confidants during the period 1163–1170.[157] It is not necessary to hazard the guess that Isaac of Stella accompanied John Bellesmains on the journey to Pontigny mentioned in this letter (as Raciti has done)[158] to recognize that Isaac's close relations with his Bishop—by reason of location, national origin, and scholarly temperament—might involve him in some way in the coming storm.

John's hesitations about the Roman Curia were correct, because Alexander's first legate to England during the crisis, the Cistercian Abbot Philip of Aumône, counseled compliance,[159] and this in part accounts for Thomas's actions at the Council of Oxford in December. It was not until 1164 that the drama moved into its next scene, as Henry pressed home his advantage at the Council of Clarendon (January 25–29, 1164)[160] in presenting the lords spiritual and tem-

---

157. John Bellesmains addressed six long letters to Becket during the early part of the controversy (Robertson, *Materials, V*): #25, "Vix mihi, domine" (1163); #35, "Excitatus praecurrentis" (1163); #60, "Praevenisset tarditatem" (1164); # 105, "Paternitatis vestrae litteras" (1165); and #116, "Supra vires meas" (1165); and in *Materials*, VI: #283, "Ipso die purificationis" (1167). This indicates that John's greatest activity in Becket's behalf was during the Pontigny period of the exile. In 1169 a cooling of the relation is evident. John seems to have thought Thomas's obstinacy was hurting any possibility of settlement (cf. Life of Herbert of Bosham, *Materials*, III, 428), and in Letter 454, *Materials*, VI, 493–4, Thomas complains to John over the latter's role in recent negotiations. The multitude of correspondence between John of Salisbury and Thomas needs no emphasis here, and John of Salisbury and John of Poitiers were in frequent contact, as John of Salisbury's fourteen letters to John Bellesmains between 1166 and 1171 indicate.

158. Raciti, *op. cit.*, XIII (1962), 137–8.

159. Preiss, *op. cit.*, pp. 69–70.

160. The exact dates are obscure; cf. Barber, *op. cit.*, Appendix I, pp. 243–4.

poral with the famous Constitutions of Clarendon. The third clause, which allowed the Royal Courts jurisdiction over a cleric who had been convicted of crime and degraded in an Ecclesiastical Court, was one of five which the Archbishop could scarcely brook; but in a moment of weakness which he later violently regretted, unsure of Papal support, Becket temporized. Henry had overplayed his hand,[161] for issuing the claimed rights in written form produced a Papal condemnation of all but six of the sixteen clauses of the Constitution;[162] thus the Archbishop could openly conduct his campaign under the banner of Papal support.

Henry Plantagenet never lacked persistence; he now resolved that the destruction of the man on whom he had pinned so much hope was the only course to follow. The plans were completed in the spring and summer of 1164, so that by October 6, when the Council of Northampton met, Thomas was confronted by a ring of enemies whose sole determination was to ruin him by the use of any means available. Once again we find John Bellesmains as the confidant and adviser of the Archbishop during this period; and the channels being used are the same—to the Papal Court through the Cistercians, and most particularly through Guichard of Pontigny. Letter 60 (*"Praevenisset tarditatem"*) from the *Materials*, dated by J. Robertson to June 22, 1164,[163] is clear evidence of this activity on John's part. Furthermore, and for our purposes, more importantly, it is also evidence of Isaac of Stella's role in these negotiations:

But I remind your Excellency to become more acquainted with the Abbot of Pontigny mentioned above, either in your own person (if under the excuse of your case you come to France), or certainly by letter (if you do not receive permission to leave); this must be done, even though both I and our common friend, Isaac, the Abbot of Stella, have correctly seen to it that the most holy Abbey of Pontigny has a continual remembrance of your case in its prayers. You will also find the same house prepared

161. Poole, *op. cit.*, pp. 205–7.
162. *Materials*, V, 73–9.
163. *Materials*, V, 110–16.

to serve to even your temporal needs should the necessity arise. . . .[164]

Surely, G. Raciti, on the basis of the final sentence, is correct in seeing here an allusion to active political adhesion to the cause of Becket on Isaac's part,[165] and not only the remembrance in prayers envisaged by Mlle Debray-Mulatier.[166] The lack of any further direct evidence renders suspect imaginative speculation about what forms—visits, letters, etc.—Isaac's work on behalf of Becket may have taken in the period 1164–66; but this does not lessen the assurance that Isaac was an active member of the pro-Becket party in the Cistercian Order whose history fortunately can be traced with some degree of precision.

The group favorable to the Archbishop of Canterbury and willing to use its influence with the King of France and the Pope on his behalf were in the ascendancy in 1165. Among its foremost members, besides Guichard of Pontigny, who was to become Archbishop of Lyons in 1165,[167] Henry, Archbishop of Reims,[168] must be mentioned. Henry, the younger brother of Louis VII, had entered Clairvaux in 1147 and was elected Bishop of Beauvais in 1149. Despite difficulties which seem to have been the result partially of a stern and obdurate attitude toward others and a curious

164. "Commoneo autem sanctitatem vestram, ut cum supradicto abbate Pontiniacensi, vel in persona vestra (si sub praetextu causae vestrae in partes Galliarum veneritis), vel certe per litteras vestras (si exeundi facultatem non acceperitis), ulteriorem initiatis familiaritatem; quamvis *tam ego quam communis amicus noster, abbas videlicet de Stella, Ysaac,* ut continuam vestri habeat sanctissimus ille conventus Pontiniacensis, in orationibus suis, memoriam, recte procuravimus. Invenietis quoque et eandem domum utilitatibus vestris *etiam temporalibus* deservire paratam, si necesse fuerit . . ." (italics added) *Materials,* V, 114.

165. *Op. cit.,* XIII (1962), 137: "Il ne s'agit point la seulement d'une intention de prières, mais aussi d'une adhésion concrète et active à la cause de Thomas Becket."

166. *Op. cit.,* p. 187.

167. Described by John Bellesmains as "industria, etenim, et sanctitate saepedicti abbatis sui omnibus Cisterciensis ordinis abbatiis plus potest" (Ep. 60, *Materials,* V, 114).

168. Mahn, *op. cit.,* pp. 140, 143–5.

vacillation in regard to self,[169] he was advanced to the Archiepiscopal See of Reims in 1162. A personal friend of the new Pope, his usefulness to Alexander, who quickly made him legate in France, was obvious; the immense labors he performed in the Papal cause during these trying early years of the Schism can be judged from a merely cursory glance at the Papal Register for the period. Our knowledge of the other members of the group is scanty: Guichard's successor at Pontigny, Garin (1165–74), and indeed the whole community of Pontigny, were to remain faithful to Becket even after the Order as a whole withdrew from his cause; Isaac, of course, was Abbot of one of the daughters of Pontigny; Abbot Urban of Cercamp (also in the line of Pontigny) played the unenviable role of Becket's messenger to Henry in mid-1166.[170] Finally, Alan, Bishop of Auxerre (1152–67), and former monk of Clairvaux, appears in a role which seems to indicate support of Becket.

King Henry's victory at the Council of Northampton left the Archbishop no choice but flight. Making good his escape on the night of October 13–14, 1164, he landed in Flanders on November 2 and proceeded to France, where he was welcomed by Louis VII and Pope Alexander. The Pope refused Thomas's offer of resignation, but his own precarious situation and the involved diplomacy of which he was such a master militated against any immediate and irrevocable action. A place of exile was chosen; on the basis of the foregoing evidence, it is not at all surprising that it was the Abbey of Pontigny and that the choice was made after consultation with Guichard and other important Cistercians.[171] Here Thomas would

169. Hinted at in John of Salisbury, *Historia Pontificalis,* cap. 35 (*ed. Chibnall,* London, 1956, pp. 69–70).

170. Preiss, *op. cit.,* pp. 94–6; Cercamp in the diocese of Amiens was founded in 1141 from Pontigny; Urban I, the third Abbot, began his rule about 1157, and died on August 31, 1166. Cf. Janauschek, *op. cit.,* p. 66; *Gallia Christiana,* X, c. 1338.

171. "Vir igitur apostolicus [Alexander] ad petitionem *nostram abbatem loci et potiores de fratribus vocat*; et cum abbas et fratres ex ipsius domini papae relatione et (quod tamen prius ex multa famae celebritate audierant) archipraesulis probitatem et virtutem, et praesertim causam ecclesiae quam agebat, certius cognovisset, Domino statim gratias agunt devotissimas, quo in-

D

be safely housed among some of his most powerful supporters and near enough to the Papal Court at Sens (under forty miles) to be able to observe the development of events.

From his arrival at Pontigny early in January of 1165,[172] and indeed throughout the course of that year, Thomas's fortunes seemed to be on the rise. Fr David Knowles has sketched the changes which this period of his exile wrought in the character of the Archbishop;[173] but even during this time one thing he never acquired was a diplomacy equal to that of most of the other players on the scene. The coming of Becket at first served to cement that alliance of Alexander and the Cistercians which had been growing since 1161 and which had thus far largely worked to the advantage of both.[174] On February 2, Alexander wrote to Gilbert, the Abbot of Cîteaux, to confirm all the privileges thus far granted to the Order;[175] on May 17, a special letter of commendation was sent to the Abbot and monks of Pontigny for their kind reception of the exiled Archbishop.[176] On August 8, Guichard, the great protector

---

spirante palaestrita suus talem locum, velut quandam agonis sui palaestram, elegerit. Unde et cum ab adventu nostro circiter septimanas tres in curia fecissemus, apostolica licentia et benedictione accepta Pontiniacum venimus . . ." Herbert of Bosham, *Materials,* III, 357–8. Cf. also William of Canterbury, *Materials,* I, 49–51; Alberic of Trois-Fontaines, *Chronica, MGH SS* XXIII, 847; Roger of Hoveden, *Chronicle,* I, 241 (Rolls Series, Vol. 51, I); Roger of Pontigny, *Vita* (PL 190, 94A); *Manrique,* II, 394.

172. The date usually given for Becket's arrival in Pontigny is November 30, 1164, as indicated by Gervase of Canterbury, *Chronicle,* I, 196 (Rolls Series, Vol. 73, I); but M. Preiss on the basis of careful day-by-day analysis of Becket's progress from Northampton to Pontigny shows that it cannot have been any earlier than the first half of January 1165; cf. *op. cit.,* p. 81, n. 71.

173. *Op. cit.,* pp. 114–17.

174. Cf. Mitterer, *op. cit.,* p. 36, ns. 46 and 47. Preiss's comment for this period deserves mention: "Wenn wir auch über Vermutungen nicht hinauskommen, so ist doch erwiesen, dass die geheimnisvollen Fäden zwischen Alexander III und den Cisterziensern mannigfaltiger und verschlungener waren, als wir im allgemeinen heute erkennen können" (*op. cit.,* p. 75).

175. P. Jaffé, *Regesta Pontificorum Romanorum,* #11151 (PL 200, 340–1).

176. Jaffé, #11192 (PL 200, 368; *Materials,* V, 172–73).

of Thomas Becket, was made Archbishop of Lyons.[177] The most important demonstration of Papal favor toward the Cistercians at this time, however, came in a Bull of Alexander's to Gilbert of Cîteaux, dated August 5, 1165,[178] which once again confirmed all Cistercian privileges and significantly went into detail on the matter of the deposition of Abbots.

Several events of the same year, however, boded ill for any quick victory on the part of the Becket camp. Henry had a most powerful weapon in his armory to forestall any decisive action on the part of the Pope—Alexander needed his support as desperately as Barbarossa desired it in the question of the disputed papal election of 1159. Henry did not have to draw the weapon; it was sufficient to rattle it. Various overtures were made to Barbarossa in early 1165, culminating in May when Henry's envoys at the Diet of Würzburg pledged support to the new anti-Pope, Paschal.[179] The gesture was a diplomatic ploy; Henry never officially recognized the action of his envoys.

Another obscure but significant event indicated that the Archbishop could not count on the total support of the Cistercian Order either. This was the question of the deposition of Geoffrey of Clairvaux. Geoffrey of Auxerre, former secretary of St Bernard and Abbot of Igny, had been promoted to the position of Abbot of Clairvaux in 1162.[180] An Englishman in origin, Geoffrey's life was marked with controversy, as his attacks upon Abelard, Gilbert of Poitiers, and Joachim of Fiora indicate; but he seems to have main-

177. Cf. Becket's Letter of rejoicing to Louis VII, *Materials*, V, no. 105, pp. 199–200.

178. Jaffé, # 11226 (*PL* 200, 390–4); cf. J. Mahn, *op. cit.*, p. 63.

179. *Materials*, V, 183; cf. R. Foreville, *op. cit.*, pp. 171–3.

180. On Geoffrey, cf. M. S. Lenssen, *op. cit.*; H. Grundmann, "Zur Biographie Joachims von Fiore und Rainers von Ponza," *Deutsches Archiv für Erforschung des Mittelalters*, XVI (1962), 510–12; N. Häring, "The Writings against Gilbert of Poitiers by Geoffrey of Auxerre," *Analecta Cisterciensa*, XXII (1966), 3–83; J. Leclercq, "Les écrits de Geoffrey d'Auxerre," *Revue Bénédictine*, LXII (1952), 274–91; J. Leclercq, "Le témoignage de Geoffrey d'Auxerre sur la vie cistercienne," *Analecta Monastica*, II serie (Rome, 1953), pp. 174–201.

tained more amicable relations with his home country, as his presence in 1164 at Rievaulx to witness an agreement between the Cistercians and the Gilbertines indicates.[181] More significantly, Geoffrey was apparently a trusted adviser of Henry II, for even after the incidents that will be our major concern here, he remained in high favor in the Order and was specifically requested as envoy by Henry in 1169.[182] On March 27, 1165, Pope Alexander addressed a letter to Gilbert of Cîteaux advising him to accompany Henry of Reims and Alan of Auxerre, both former Cistercians, to Clairvaux for the purpose of convincing Geoffrey to step down from his position, or, in case of refusal, of removing him without delay. The reason given is a curious one:

> We have learned by the true report of many that as that Abbot rules the monastery who has not deserved the favor and respect which his predecessors knew how to gain in the eyes of princes and rulers, the monastery itself is not only disparaged, but the entire Order has suffered no light inconvenience and detriment from this.[183]

This first attempt must have been an almost immediate failure, because on April 1, Alexander wrote to Henry of Reims, advising a rapid retreat to the Curia *"ne major turbatio propter hoc generetur,"* and called for a conference of Henry, Alan, Cardinal Henry of

---

181. A. King, *Cîteaux and Her Elder Daughters,* p. 249.

182. "Praeterea dilectioni vestre grates uberes exsolvo, quod ad petitionem meam fratrem Gaufridum mihi misistis. Et nunc iterum diligenter peto quatenus eundem quamcitius mihi remittatis; necessarium enim mihi ejus intelligo discretionem et prudentiam, ut mihi presens adsit et aliquamdiu propinqua mihi ejus sit conversatio." L. Delisle and E. Berger, *Recueil des Actes de Henri II,* I, 439 (also *Materials,* VII, 90). Cf. Preiss, *op. cit.,* pp. 106–109. Henry also mentions that the Pope had made use of a Brother Geoffrey to deliver certain letters in 1166 (*Delisle and Berger,* I, 407; *Materials,* V, 362). We cannot be sure, but this may well have been Geoffrey of Auxerre.

183. "Multorum autem veridica relatione didicimus, quod occasione abbatis eidem monasterio praesidentis, qui non eam gratiam et reverentiam in oculis regum et principum promeruit, quam antecessores ejus promeruisse noscuntur, ipsi monasterio non modo derogatur, et totus ordo non minimum exinde incommodum sustinet et jacturam." *Jaffé,* #11169 (*PL* 200, 349 A–B).

Saints Nereus and Achilles, and Geoffrey, former Bishop of Langres, to discuss the issue.[184] Difficulties continued, because on May 25 Alexander denied a request of Henry of Reims that Cardinal Henry be removed from the appointed board.[185] Geoffrey finally was deposed, although there is some obscurity about the date, the *Chronicon Clarevallense* placing it under 1165,[186] and a reference in a letter of John of Salisbury seeming to indicate that it was the result of a new effort by Henry of Reims in 1166.[187] A possible explanation is that the new Abbot Pons was appointed in 1165, but was unable to take up his post until the following year due to the resistance of Geoffrey and his supporters.[188] According to this hint of John of Salisbury, the final ousting of Geoffrey was perhaps made possible by the temporary upswing of Becket's fortunes at Vézeley on June 12, 1166. Whatever the case, the late fifteenth-century reference[189] to Geoffrey remaining as Abbot until 1168 upon which G. Raciti builds his unconvincing case for Geoffrey's part in the exile of Isaac of Stella is almost certainly mistaken.[190]

What was the reason for Geoffrey's deposition? M. Preiss

184. Jaffé, #11171 (*PL* 200, 350–1).

185. Jaffé, #11193 (*PL* 200, 368–9).

186. ". . . abbas Clarevallis domnus Gaufridus, videas [sic] contra se, sive juste, sive injuste, quorumdam odia concitata, abbatiam dimisit, et factus est abbas Claraevallis vir nobilis et religiosus, Poncius Alvernensis, qui erat abbas in Grandisilva" (*PL* 185, c. 1248A).

187. "Quid egeritis Veziliaci, archiepiscopo et Ecclesiae Remensi a multis diebus innotuit, nec operae pretium puto divulgata referre . . . Ipse autem ad Clare-vallem profectus est, accitus, ut aiunt, a majore parte conventus in ruinam abbatis" (*PL* 199, 170D–71A; *Materials*, V, 448).

188. Lenssen, *op. cit.*, p. 102.

189. John de Cirey, *Ex Dialogo de prospero et adverso statu Ordinis*; quoted in J. M. Canivez, *Statuta Capitulorum Generalium Ordinis Cisterciensis*, I (Louvain, 1933), 75–6; also the basis of Manrique's account in II, under 1168, Cap. V, pp. 463–5.

190. *Op. cit.*, XIII (1962), 138–9, n. 207. Most modern investigators suggest 1165–6, e.g., Lenssen, *op. cit.*, 100–102; Grundmann, *op. cit.*, 510–11; Häring, *op. cit.*, 12; Preiss, *op. cit.*, p. 91; Leclercq, "Les écrits de Geoffrey," p. 274. Some of the older literature also suggests the earlier date, e.g., C. Oudin, *op. cit.*, II, c. 1495, "circa annum 1167."

remarks that it is impossible to assert with security, given the obscurity of the sources, but his conjecture of an intimate connection with the stance of the Order in the Becket case has been accepted by Lenssen and Raciti and has much to recommend it.[191] As the events of the year 1166 were to indicate, there was an anti-Becket group among the Cistercians, as well as a pro-Becket one, and it is difficult to imagine that such a group sprang up overnight when Henry II first began to apply pressure on the Order. The famous Aelred of Rievaulx (†1167) had been instrumental in winning Henry over to the cause of Alexander III back in the early 1160's; Geoffrey himself was an Englishman, a trusted adviser to Henry, and a visitor to Rievaulx in 1164 when the great controversy was gathering force. Another Englishman, Gilbert, was the Abbot of Cîteaux from 1163 to 1167.[192] In the complex net of diplomatic intrigue which can be at best partially recovered by the historian, Gilbert's role seems to have been one of attempting to use all the parties involved in the controversy to the best advantage of the Order, thus marking a significant change in the attitude of the Cistercians, the adoption of a spirit of *Realpolitik* that broke with the more idealistic ecclesiastical and political roles of the past. M. Preiss sees the deposition of Geoffrey of Auxerre as indicating a turning point in the history of the Order, in the role which the Cistercians played in the Becket controversy, and in the wider question of the Schism of 1159–1177.[193]

Within this general framework what little we know of Gilbert's activity and the fragmentary evidence for Geoffrey's deposition begin to make sense. Gilbert and Cardinal William of Pavia (former Cistercian and friend of Henry II)[194] had met with Henry in Rouen, probably in March of 1165. Here Gilbert agreed to keep the

191. Preiss, *op. cit.*, pp. 84–92, although he insists on the hypothetical character; e.g., p. 88: "Möglicherweise fällt unter diesen politischen Geschichtspunkt auch die Aktion Alexanders III gegen Gottfried von Clairvaux."

192. Manrique, *op. cit.*, II, 371–2.

193. Preiss, *op. cit.*, pp. 92, 98, 101, 135, 155.

194. John of Poitiers, *Materials*, VI, 146; John of Salisbury, *Materials*, VI, 261.

peace between Henry and the Order.[195] At the same time, Gilbert was willing to reap the benefits that Becket's reception at Pontigny accrued for the Order in the form of Papal approbation and privileges. The first event which brought the split in the Order into the open and betrayed the double game that Gilbert was playing was the Pope's desire to depose Geoffrey, perhaps the most obvious foe of Becket among the Cistercians, from his position as Abbot of Clairvaux. The reference in the Papal letter of March 27 to the loss of confidence of kings and princes in Geoffrey can easily be understood as opposition to the Abbot from Louis VII and his court, who, of course, warmly supported Becket's cause.[196] Alexander could scarcely proceed directly in the matter, since he himself had guaranteed the Cistercians independence from episcopal interference in the matter of depositions in 1160;[197] hence, his desire to have Gilbert accompany his legates on this mission and to induce Geoffrey to step down voluntarily without the formality required for a deposition.[198] Alexander's original attempt seems to have failed, as we have already seen—whether from the refusal of Geoffrey, the lack of cooperation of Gilbert, or a combination of

195. The meeting is referred to in a later letter; cf. *Recueil des actes de Henry II . . . concernant les provinces françaises et les affaires de France*, eds. L. Delisle and E. Berger (Paris, 1909–24), 4 vols., I, 424–5 (*Materials*, V, 365–6): "Quando dominus Willelmus Papiensis et vos nostram apud Rothomagum adiistis praesentiam, conquesti sumus vobis quod quidam monachi ordinis vestri, . . . quaedam verba et mandata adversariorum nostrorum amaritudinum plena nobis deferebant. . . . *Promisit itaque nobis dilectio vestra quod illud corrigeretis* et monachos vestros a talium mandatorum delatione coerceretis" (p. 365).

196. Preiss, *op. cit.*, pp. 88–9.

197. Jaffé, #10635 (*PL* 200, 95). Cf. J.-B. Mahn, *op. cit.*, p. 85.

198. Deposition required consultation with a group of Abbots, cf. *Carta Caritatis*, #24 (ed. *Turk.*, Rome, 1949, p. 111; for the later form, where this is #26, cf. p. 124); cf. Mahn, *op. cit.*, pp. 204, 226. Interestingly enough, the Papal Bull of August 5, 1165 (Jaffé, #11226) confirming the Cistercian *instituta* gives great attention to the question of depositions (*PL* 200, 391C–92B). In one sense, the situation is here more complex, since even voluntary abdication of an Abbacy must be approved by a board of Abbots as well as the Abbot of the mother house (391D–92A); but is it possible to see in this letter an attempt of Alexander to clarify the rules for the deposition of Geoffrey?

both, it is impossible to determine on the basis of presently available evidence. If, as is likely, Geoffrey was finally deposed in 1166, it seems to have been the product of unilateral action on the part of Archbishop Henry of Reims, though probably with the support of the Clairvaux community itself. Such an action would have been technically against the Statutes of the Order, but what we know of Henry's character would indicate that this would not have bothered him greatly were he convinced of the legitimacy of the goal, and if some change of circumstance had now given him the power to achieve this goal. By mid-1166 the two groups in the Order, first clearly defined at the beginning of the controversy over Geoffrey, were apparently out in the open and no longer intent on preserving appearances. Geoffrey himself seems to have retired to Cîteaux,[199] another indication that Gilbert and the Cîteaux community were the focus of the anti-Becket party, just as Pontigny and her line were the chief supporters of Becket.

Thus the state of affairs has polarized in 1166: a year marked by dramatic, almost histrionic, gestures on all sides and increasing tensions between former allies. At the end of the summer of the previous year, Alexander's position in Italy had improved to the point that he ventured to return to Rome. His removal from the immediate scene perhaps contributed to the increasing militancy.

The Archbishop of Canterbury, perhaps partially as a result of his year of meditation at Pontigny, displayed a depth and nobility of character in the early part of the year which was not to be visible again until the last months of his life. A strong desire to achieve a new, but more mature, personal relation with Henry,[200] and the need to give his actions a strong basis in a theory of Christian society, burn through the three important letters he sent to Henry probably in May and June through his personal envoy, Urban, Abbot of Cercamp.[201]

199. Preiss, op. cit., p. 92, n. 28.

200. Knowles, "Archbishop Thomas Becket," pp. 116–17.

201. Herbert of Bosham, Materials, III, 383–5, speaks of three embassies: two by Urban and a final one by a barefoot monk named Gerard. Cf. also Gervase of Canterbury, Chronicle, I, 199 (Rolls Series, Vol. 73, I). The letters

Henry was not to be moved. Perhaps it was this silence, perhaps his own imperious personality, that goaded Thomas into a major escalation of the conflict. In April, Alexander, temporarily feeling more secure now that he was back in Italy, had given the Archbishop legatine powers over England,[202] excepting always the person of the king. On June 12, the Feast of Pentecost, at Vézelay, Thomas took the bold step of using these powers to the fullest in excommunicating Henry's chief advisers and warning the king, an act which came as a surprise even to the closest confidants of his household.[203] Henry could scarcely have accepted the hierocratic implications of the stately letters he had received at the hand of Urban; his reaction to the forceful gesture of Vézelay was to extend the campaign of terror which he had initiated in the previous year with the confiscation of the property and exiling of Becket's friends and relatives.

Henry was determined to separate his friends from his foes, to punish all who adhered to the Archbishop's cause. The Cistercians were among the first to feel the pressure of deciding. Gilbert of Cîteaux had played a waiting game for too long; he must now make the decision to implement his promises of March 1165, or suffer the consequences. The King first dispatched a stinging letter from Chinon to the Abbot, complaining of the embassy which Urban had undertaken in Becket's behalf, and concluding with a scarcely-veiled threat: "But you should know that if you do not punish the outrages of your monks, I will not be able to endure it any longer without seeking a remedy for my injuries."[204] Henry

---

referred to are almost certainly the three letters of *Materials*, V, 266–82; "Loqui de Deo," "Exspectans exspectavi," and "Desiderio desideravi," although it is difficult to say in exactly what order they were sent. R. Foreville discusses Urban's embassy (*op. cit.*, p. 170) and dates it to the end of May or beginning of June (pp. 218–19).

202. Herbert of Bosham, *Materials*, III, 397.

203. Herbert of Bosham, *Materials*, III, 391–2. For Thomas's notification of the excommunication to Alexander, cf. *Materials*, V, 386–8.

204. "Noveritis autem quod, si excessus monachorum vestrorum non correxeritis, ulterius sustinere non poterimus, quin injuriarum nostrarum quaeramus remedium . . ." Edited in Delisle and Berger, *op. cit.*, pp. 424–5;

seems to have widened the attack and may have sent a second letter
to the General Chapter scheduled to meet at Cîteaux in
September.[205] In any case, the meaning was clear, as Becket himself
said in a letter to Bishop Conrad of Mainz:[206] if the Cistercians
were to choose to harbor him any longer, they must be prepared
to suffer the wrath of the most powerful man in Western Europe.
So many of the Chroniclers record the event that it is possible to
surmise that the threat was made frequently and publicly during
the summer of 1166.[207] If we adopt the more probable reading in
a disputed passage of a letter of John of Salisbury, there is also
evidence that Henry summoned Gilbert and other Cistercian
Abbots for a personal warning during the same period.[208]

---

and in *Materials*, V, 365–6. The exact date of the letter is problematic:
Robertson suggests May, but Preiss's suggestion of July 22 seems to fit the
context better (*op. cit.*, p. 95).

205. Preiss, *op. cit.*, pp. 97–8. A letter of the General Chapter is mentioned in Gervase of Canterbury, *Chronicle*, I, 200–201 (Rolls Series), and
Herbert of Bosham, *Materials*, III, 397. The reference in the official Cistercian
records (*Canivez*, I, p. 75, partially taken from *Manrique*, II, 435) is confusing.
First of all, the year is incorrectly given as 1167; then an otherwise unknown
letter to the Abbot of Pontigny, which is probably a confusion of the letter to
Gilbert, is mentioned (". . . rex Angliae mandavit praedicto abbati de Ponti-
gniaco quod si ille ulterius retineret Cantuariensem archiepiscopum in domo sua,
ipse fugaret ab Anglia omnes monachos sui Ordinis"). Finally, the letter sent to
the General Chapter is identified in a note with the letter sent to Abbot Gilbert.

206. Letter to Conrad of Mainz (*Materials*, V, 389), "meamque personam
inexorabili odio persequens, intantum ut abbati Cisterciensi iam scripserit, ut,
sicut abbatias ordinis sui quae in ipsius potestate sunt diligit, ita nos et coexsules
nostros a beneficio et familiaritate ordinis alienet." William of Canterbury,
Materials, I, 50; *Annales de Wintonia*, p. 59 (Rolls Series, vol. 36, 2); Anonymous Life, *Materials*, IV, 65.

207. Edward Grim, *Materials*, II, 414; Gervase of Canterbury, *Chronicle*, I,
200–1; Roger of Hoveden, *Chronicle*, I, 241; Herbert of Bosham, *Vita*,
Materials, III, 397: "Unde et mandavit [Henry] quod, sicut carum habebant
quicquid in terra sua aut cismarina aut transmarina possidebant, ne eum
[Becket] amplius tenerent secum."

208. John of Salisbury, letter 194, *Materials*, V, 385: "Accivit etiam ad se
rex dominum *Cistertiensem* et alios, per quorum prudentiam malitiam consilii
sui adversus Deum posse credit armari; sed profecto, si saperent, vel sibi et
suis parcerent in hac causa, quoniam 'Poena reversura est in caput ista suum.'"
Some mss. read *Cicestrensem* for *Cysterciensem* (i.e., The Bishop of Chichester
instead of the Abbot of Cîteaux).

We are unfortunately once again in the realm of conjecture in trying to analyze the tensions that existed within the Cistercian Order in the summer of 1166. If the deposition of Geoffrey really took place in this period, as is likely on the basis of the evidence cited above, then the pro-Becket group was certainly still able to make its influence felt. Alexander III still warmly supported this faction and sought to forestall the abandonment of the Archbishop in a letter of September.[209] The parties were locked in a struggle from which only one would emerge the victor. The General Chapter which began on September 14 must have been one of the stormiest in the history of the Order; it is a pity that nothing survives of its deliberations. When the dust had settled, it was clear that the anti-Becket party had won. The Order was prepared to risk the displeasure of the Pope rather than the wrath of the king.[210] Thomas must go.

Upon the conclusion of the Chapter, an embassy consisting of Gilbert of Cîteaux, Cardinal William of Pavia (a former Cistercian), and other Abbots were sent to Pontigny to present the Archbishop with the news in as diplomatic a fashion as possible. Herbert of Bosham, Thomas's secretary, recounts the incident in full color, even to the irony with which Becket and his counsellors received the fair speeches of the envoys.[211] King Louis himself came to express his continued support of the exile,[212] and Thomas left Pontigny on November 11 to take up his new refuge at the Benedictine Abbey of Sainte Colombe in Sens.

Many of the sources express the unfeigned sorrow of the Abbot

209. Jaffé, # 11290 (*PL* 200, 414B), ". . . super eo non possumus non mirari, quod vestrum quidam venerabilem fratrem nostrum Cantuariensem archiepiscopum . . . a Pontiniacensi monasterio removeri, sicut audivimus, voluerunt, et eidem ad minas et terrores quorumdum totius vestri ordinis solatium denegari."

210. "Derselbe realpolitische Geist, der Verhandlungen Gilberts mit Heinrich II im Frühjahr 1165 beherrscht hatte, obwaltete auch auf diesem Generalkapitel." Preiss, *op. cit.*, p. 98.

211. *Materials*, III, 397–8.

212. Edward Grim, *Materials*, II, 414; Herbert of Bosham, *Materials*, III, 402–3.

and monks of Pontigny over Becket's forced departure; Thomas
himself paid witness to it with real feeling in a letter that he sent
to the Pope describing the events.[213] Alexander III repaid the
faithfulness of the community of Pontigny with a Bull confirming
the rights and privileges of their Abbey,[214] and it is important to
note that this was the only privilege given to the Order during
the following year.[215] This in itself shows that the incident marked
a real break in the alliance of Papacy and Cistercians, a break that
was not to be permanent, but one which upon healing never quite
effected a return to the idealistic ways of the past.

213. *Materials,* VI, 48–9.
214. Jaffé, # 11295 (PL 200, 423–5) dated Nov. 11, 1166.
215. Preiss, *op. cit.,* p. 100.

CHAPTER II

A PROLEGOMENON TO THE THEOLOGY OF ISAAC OF STELLA: THE *CATENA AUREA*

TO ASSERT THAT THE THEOLOGY of Isaac of Stella is Platonic in character is to begin our investigation in the midst of a problem, for of the great systems of thought, Platonism is among the most protean and difficult to categorize. It is ironic that the thinker whose attention was so much directed beyond the tumultuous realm of history to the ideal realities whose unchanging permanence guaranteed their superior ontological status should have undergone so many sea-changes in the deep places of the history of Western thought. The historian of philosophy may perhaps feel secure in isolating the Platonism of Plato (though even here how many controversies still rage); but once widen the horizon beyond the death of the master of the Academy, and one wonders whether even "varieties of Platonism" and "the Platonic tradition" are terms wide enough to embrace the diversity of views which at some time or other have claimed Plato as their source. Consequently, when the term "Platonic" is used here, it will be employed with the greatest possible extension compatible with a comprehension that still has some meaning. The essential comprehension, as discussed below, will not even attempt to legitimate its relation to the original thought of the *Dialogues*, but will be content to show its relation to what was understood as Platonism in Late Classical thought.

A sense of divisiveness, of separation, of alienation, was at the root of this generalized comprehension of Platonism current toward the end of the classical world. Man's experience of himself and of the world was discontinuous, violently torn apart into a realm where change and imperfection threatened his unquenchable thirst for stability in happiness and a realm of unchanging formal perfection, of ideal order, truth, beauty, and being where such stability was guaranteed. The ideal world of Forms against the historical world of shadows, the world above versus the world below, the here of time as opposed to the there of eternity: in such ways did the Platonic man symbolize his sense of reality and even his very self-understanding, for while his soul pertained to that upper ideal world, in the here of experience it found itself "chained to a dying animal."

But this sense of division or separation was not merely fatalistically accepted or pushed toward some explanation of the world and man framed in total antitheses. The Platonic thought of the first twelve centuries of our era reacted vigorously against essentially dualistic solutions to the experience of alienation and separation, to any Gnostic, Manichaean, or Catharist simplification. Accompanying this sense of the separation of realms at all times, though in an astonishing diversity of forms, was the need for unifying the divergences, for bridging the abyss that yawned between the extremes. The Greek could never abandon his sense of the *cosmos*, the beauty of the order that included even the world of shadows, no more than the Jew or the Christian could abandon his belief that God was the creator and master of the whole of reality. The ideal world of true knowledge did not stand over and apart from the world of sense and opinion in total isolation, nor did it merely wrestle with it in some form of universal struggle; rather it was the pattern and archetype of the world below, the ultimate source and explanation, the vision which could be seen in and through the imperfection that was man's lot. This desire for a pattern of explanation that would redeem separation was as much a crucial component in late antique pagan Platonism as it was of systems of Christian thought deeply influenced by this same world view. The age lived under the spell of the *Timaeus*, that late, obscure, mythic attempt of Plato to account for the unity of man and the universe; as the only Platonic Dialogue readily available to the Western Church Fathers and the Middle Ages, it exercised enormous influence.

In the later forms of Platonism, particularly in those systems of thought which are grouped together under the name of Neo-platonism, this desire for unification was expressed in dynamic fashion through the law of emanation and return. All things came forth from the immeasurably remote realm of the highest principle to descend by carefully graduated stages encompassing the whole of being until the final, most distant and lowest point of this great "downward" path was reached in the quasi non-existence of matter. But the living energy that tied the whole together also made it possible to speak of an "upward" path; rather, the very levels on the downward path were but the static moments whence the process of return began. This ascension by purification and illumination from the confusions of the world below embedded in matter, through the progressively more real levels of the intelligible cosmic structure, to some form of union with the highest principle, had a human resonance as much mystical and religious as purely philo-sophical. Gerard Manley Hopkins expresses something of the totality of such a vision of the world when he writes:

> Thee, God, I come from, to thee go,
> All day long I like fountain flow
> From thy hand out, swayed about
> Mote-like in thy mighty glow.[1]

If such a vision of reality can be said to be in some way common to the Late Classical world, the infinite variety of its expression—philosophical, religious, literary, artistic, political, social—can be merely hinted at here. Our description has been deliberately metaphorical in order to comprehend these categories in their role as symbolic modes of personal and cultural awareness; there is no attempt to do justice to the complexity of issues and difficulties of interpretation raised by their appearance in properly philosophical contexts, particularly in the writings of Plotinus toward the end

---

1. *Poems of Gerard Manley Hopkins*, 3rd ed. (Oxford, 1956), # 116, p. 167.

of the third century.[2] To demonstrate these categories as basic to the world of late pagan antiquity would be a work of immense proportions, but this task would be itself minor in comparison with the difficulty of validating their presence in the patristic authors and in medieval theologians.[3] The oppositions between the *libri Platonici* and the Scriptures were obvious to even the most sanguine of the Fathers, but it would be presumptuous to expect to find in them as clear a sense of the difficulties involved in the program of combining Platonic and Biblical categories as is available to us today.

In the very general way in which the Platonic categories have been described here, it may be possible to give a broad sketch of how they could be viewed from a Christian perspective and thus provide some of the forms within which the Fathers experienced, understood, and structured the world. The category of separation, division, and alienation—the most immediate to man—would be understood, it is true, not only as a necessary determination in the abstract order, but also as a willed historical intrusion into an order whose original intention had been partially perverted. Separation for the Christian thinker was primarily in the will to sin: insofar as this was colored by what might be called the metaphysical sin of matter, it was frequently seen to clash with the strong sense of the importance of the material world in the Scriptures and thus led to viewpoints rejected by the consensus of the theological tradition. The reaction to the views of Origen is a case in point here. The fact that the scriptural sense of sin as separation could interact with and be understood within this Platonic tradition, despite what were judged as aberrations, is what is significant.

2. For a good introduction to the thought of Plotinus, cf. A. H. Armstrong, *The Architecture of the Intelligible Universe in the Philosophy of Plotinus* (Cambridge, 1940; unchanged reprint, Amsterdam, 1967). This should be compared with his later treatment, "Plotinus," in *Cambridge History of Later Greek and Early Medieval Philosophy* (Cambridge, 1967), pp. 195–268.

3. For some interesting remarks on analogous symbolic dimensions in the thought of the Presocratics, especially Heraclitus, cf. W. Jaeger, *The Theology of the Greek Philosophers,* paperback edition (Oxford, 1967), pp. 97–8, 117–20.

The desire for the unification of the separated realms, for salvation in a very undiversified religious sense, common to late paganism in all its manifestations, was also susceptible of a Christian interpretation. Salvation in a Christian context differed from the pagan mode of thought in a manner analogous to the differences evidenced in the sense of separation: the will, active in history, was the means of its realization. Man was redeemed not only through knowledge (merely discovering his true nature and home), but also through right willing; and the original source of this knowledge and desire was not man, but God. Man received it as God's gift. This redemption was not purely flight from history, but was enmeshed in history in some way (as man's sin was), for its realization was through an historical figure, the God-man Jesus Christ. Salvation apart from him was illusion; and even the most a-historical, idealized, Platonizing of theologies had to struggle with that fact.

Finally, the dynamism of the downward and upward path (the metaphorical expression must be used here, since that enables the modal relation to be seen between pagan and Christian understandings), while furthest from common human experience, was also most basic from the systematic point of view, and appeared in the more speculative patristic authors. Again, the viewpoint was changed—how radically, is a judgment that depends upon the later interpretation of this era in the history of theological speculation; but there is no denying that what was primarily a necessary process of emanation and return in Neoplatonism,[4] took on in Christian theology the character of a freely-willed act of creation and the consummation of all things in the kingdom of God. The scriptural insistence on God's absolute dominion over all things was thus interpreted in the light of a doctrine of providence where the dynamism of creation and return established by the will of God was

4. The discussion is deliberately simplified here in order to grasp cultural modes without entering into the problems relating to particular philosophers. For the difficulties of a too simplistic view of the essential character of Plotinian emanation, cf. A. H. Armstrong, *Architecture . . .*, pp. 52–64; *Cambridge History*, pp. 240–1; and A. Altmann and S. M. Stern, *Isaac Israeli* (Oxford, 1958), pp. 154–5.

E

not frustrated by the sin of man. A sacred order had been set up, a hierarchy, and even man's deliberate refusal to accept his role in that order in the end was seen as a part of the order itself.

These homologies of structuring, despite the shifts of perspective noted, are meant to show the harmony between the patristic authors and the pagan intellectual world in which they found themselves. The three aspects have been discussed here in a fashion that hinted at their symbolic character. It is this hint that provides the key for determining the relation of the theological anthropology of Isaac of Stella to the Platonic tradition, for the organizing form of this theology is not a concept or a series of concepts, but a symbolic image, the golden chain of being, the *catena aurea*, which was a Christianized manifestation of the basic Platonic aspects. Before we can turn to the evolution of the symbol of the golden chain, some understanding of the sense in which the word "symbol" is used here must be given.

AN APPROACH TO SYMBOL

The claim that the application of the understanding of symbol in the broadest sense is of value in recapturing certain aspects of twelfth-century theology is not new. It has already been made by such noted scholars as M.-D. Chenu, Mlle M.-T. d'Alverny, Mlle M.-M. Davy and H. de Lubac.[5] In the light of the general interest in such diverse fields as psychology, literature, comparative religion, theology, and philosophy in the nature of the symbol, focusing attention upon the symbolic organization of the thought of Isaac of Stella can be a real contribution to the historical development of symbolism: how symbols worked at a specific time and place. It also may provide some understanding of that quality of twelfth-century intellectual life which was the fertile ground for the

5. M.-D. Chenu, *La théologie au douzième siècle* (Paris, 1957), esp. Chaps. VII and VIII; M.-T. d'Alverny, "Le cosmos symbolique du XIIe siècle," *AHDL*, XX (1954), 31–81; M.-M. Davy, *Initiation à la symbolique romane* (2nd ed.; Paris, 1964) and H. de Lubac, *Exégèse Médiéval*, 2 vols. in 2 parts (Paris, 1959–64), esp. II, 2, Chap. VIII.

renewal of interest in so many fields, especially in questions of anthropology.

For reasons of space no attempt will be made here to discuss the nature of symbol in depth; but perhaps, by making use of some of the recent literature on the question, on the basis of a contrast between the logical and the symbolic mentalities, a general sense of symbol can be arrived at which will provide a basis for the investigation of Isaac's master symbol.

For our purposes, the logical mentality can be taken as that aspect of man's inherent intentionality that produces the concept, the scientific idea which when affirmed as true excludes its contrary as false. It is the operation which creates the scientific world of discourse. But there is another aspect of man's native desire to know, of its nature more diffuse and difficult to describe, present in poetry, in art, in rhetoric, in the world of common experience and expression, and even at times in the heights of philosophical expression, where exactitude is not always necessary and sometimes even undesirable. This is the symbol-making process or mentality.

The most obvious contrast between the two mentalities concerns the relation of word and image in the symbol and concept considered as verbal presentations. The universality of the concept's scientific function tends toward the exclusion of image, picture, or visualizable form in terms of an ideal, i.e., toward an abstraction in which the concept is treated in a purely formal manner.[6] The symbol moves in the opposite direction. As an expression of human intentionality, it is bound to its content, its materiality: the symbol as word of meaning is always in some way tied to an image.[7]

6. In this sense, as Paul Ricoeur has observed in his fundamental book, *The Symbolism of Evil* (New York, 1967), p. 17, symbolic logic as the ultimate formalism is the exact inverse of our use of symbol.

7. Ricoeur has an illuminating discussion of this mutuality in relation to natural things (*op. cit.,* pp. 11–12, 14–15). "The symbolic *manifestation* as a *thing* is a matrix of symbolic meanings as words. We have never ceased to find meanings in the sky (to take the first example on which Eliade practices his comparative phenomenology). It is the same thing to say that the sky *manifests* the sacred and to say that it *signifies* the most high. . . . Thus, the symbol-thing

But a problem emerges as we consider the "imagistic" character of the symbol more closely. Not every image can be called a symbol. A symbol evokes an image which contains diverse levels of meaning. These diverse levels can be roughly described as the *literal, material meaning,* and the *dynamic, open meaning,* or as the prosaic and the obscure meanings.[8] To use the example of the golden chain of being which will be the subject of a textual investigation in this Chapter, we can say that the literal meaning is the chain taken as a sign of the linking together of things, as we speak of a chain of ideas or a chain of causes. The dynamic meaning of the chain is the manifestation that it offers of the unknown inter-relatedness of the totality of things inchoatively grasped through man's constant search for approximations of universal order. The universal order remains a mystery; the symbol does not explain the mystery, but it does manifest it in visual fashion.

Paul Ricoeur notes that in the symbol the literal and dynamic (for him the "opaque") levels of meaning are connected in analogical fashion.[9] This is perhaps reminiscent of the most famous twelfth-century definition of symbol. Hugh of St Victor in his *Commentariorum in Caelestem Hierarchiam* defines *symbolum* as "a comparison, that is, a coaptation of visible forms brought forth to demonstrate some invisible matter."[10] Hugh is not thinking of

---

is the potentiality of innumerable spoken symbols which, on the other hand, are knotted together within a single cosmic manifestation." (p. 11).

8. The following discussion owes much to Paul Ricoeur's distinction between the literal and opaque meanings present in symbols and their analogical relation; cf. *op. cit.,* pp. 14–18; and "Hermeneutique des Symboles et Reflexion Philosophique," *Archivio di Filosofia* (1961), pp. 51–73, esp. p. 53. My development here is also deeply influenced by various aspects of the thought of Bernard Lonergan on symbols, especially "The Sense of the Unknown," in *Insight* (2nd ed.; New York, 1958), pp. 531–4. Lonergan's triple division (p. 533) into *image* (sensible content operative on the sensible level), *symbol* (image as linked with the "known unknown"), and *sign* (image as linked with an interpretation) is twofold in our treatment, because symbol and sign are taken as practical equivalents in their action in cultural history.

9. *Op. cit.,* pp. 15–16.

10. *PL* 175, 960D. ". . . collatio videlicet, id est coaptatio visibilium formarum ad demonstrationem rei invisibilis propositarum."

demonstration in the scholastic sense of a discursive logical process, but rather as a leap in being from a lower to a higher level in line with the thought of the Pseudo-Dionysius.[11] What the medieval author spoke of as an anagogy, or ascent, of meaning, what Ricoeur describes as an analogical donation of secondary intentionality by the primary, and what Bernard Lonergan holds is a paradoxical linking of the image with the "known unknown," are all perhaps different ways of expressing the two essential levels of meaning in the symbol. Neither level can be neglected: the image, considered on the literal, visually-bound, level, is, in a very real sense, the teaching and content. Without it the "unknown," the "opaque" the "anagogic" dimensions of the second level would not be communicated. Thus, truly symbolic thought must be distinguished from allegory, no matter how much the two were intertwined in the medieval period.[12] In allegory, the image masks the teaching or content so that the latter can be translated into a text understood by itself, i.e., a one-level explanation.[13] The symbol must always contain both levels.

The presence of the two intentionalities is at the heart of the difference between symbol and concept. The symbol paradoxically aims in opposite directions: on the one hand, back toward the material image or picture in all its concrete particularity; on the other, out toward the fringes of man's curiosity, the ultimate problems which are so many aspects of the one immense unknown he seeks to know. Yet somehow the symbol manages to yoke the

---

11. Chenu, *La théologie . . .* , pp. 162, 168, 175, 180–1, 185–7. There are, however, differences between the Pseudo-Dionysius and Hugh on the understanding of symbol; cf. R. Roques, *Structures théologiques de la Gnose à Richard de St Victor* (Paris, 1962), pp. 329–30.

12. On the problem of the inadequate distinction between allegory and symbolism in the twelfth century, cf. Chenu, *op. cit.*, pp. 170–3, 188–90. This is allied to another weakness of medieval theory of the symbol, the failure to distinguish between *denominatio* and *significatio; op. cit.*, p. 370.

13. Ricoeur, *op. cit.*, p. 16. A similar treatment may be found in G. Durand, *L'Imagination symbolique* (Paris, 1964), p. 15. For Ricoeur, allegory is a confusion of the true nature of symbolism; Lonergan, on the other hand ("Myth and Allegory," *op. cit.*, pp. 544–6), using the term in a highly individual sense, views it as the first step towards metaphysical thinking.

two in its manifestation of the ultimate in the concrete. The concept, however, makes no attempt to live in such widely diverse realms. Its drive is to free itself from the particularity of the material and the concrete through the process of abstraction; nor is its goal the epiphany of the obscure tendrils of the unknown, but rather the clarity of the universal concept applicable to the totality of a set of particulars. Whatever levels may exist in the concept are not radically opposed as in symbolic presentation, and the manner of their relationship (through inductive or deductive logic) tends to congeal them into a discursive continuum which in comparison with the symbol's unexpected switches may be described as one-dimensional.

Most of the other contrasts between concept and symbol can be seen to flow from the central point of diversity in levels of meaning.[14] Thus the concept, as the product of the logical mentality, intends one thing: either A or not-A; whereas the symbol admits a variety of middle terms in a world that is foreign to the logical principle of contradiction. The universal concept is to be taken in a univocal sense; the symbol has no interest in univocity: enriching accretions or even the joining of logical opposites is the story that the phenomenological study of symbols discloses.[15] Dialectic and syllogistic proofs are the métier of the logical mentality; repetitions, enumerations, rhetorical flourishes, poetic images, etc., are the strength of the symbolic understanding.

Lonergan has remarked on the loss and gain on either side: if the symbol is more efficacious in moving man because of its

14. For an interesting survey of the contrasts, cf. B. Lonergan, *De Verbo Incarnato* (Rome, 1961), pp. 484–6. For a survey of the characteristics of the symbol without explicit contrast with the concept, cf. M. Eliade, *Patterns in Comparative Religion*, Meridian paperback (New York, 1958), pp. 437–56.

15. The multidimensional aspect of the symbol is a favorite theme of many authors: e.g., Lonergan, *De Verbo Incarnato*, p. 484; *Insight*, p. 534; Eliade, *op. cit.*, p. 450; and "Methodical Remarks on the Study of Religious Symbolism," *History of Religions*; *Essays in Methodology* (Chicago, 1959), pp. 99–102. For examples of such multivalence at work, cf. Ricoeur, *op. cit.*, pp. 92–3, on the symbolism of the Exodus; and Eliade, "Methodical Remarks . . . ," pp. 93–5, on the Cosmic Tree.

inclusiveness and concreteness, it is also more ambiguous in its communication of truth.[16] Nevertheless, the symbol does have an ontological direction—it intends to reveal the true.[17] Because of its compactness and inclusion of diverse meanings, though, it can also be a source of confusion. On the level of scientific knowledge, and increasingly on the level of practical decision, as a society becomes more complex and differentiated, the multidimensional character of the symbol makes it difficult to distinguish between opposed meanings. The differentiation that accompanies scientific thought and produces the clarity of the universal concept may appear bloodless in comparison with the symbol, but it represents an immeasurable gain in man's further conquest of his own rationality. It is what he is master of; not merely what in awe he stretches forth his hand to touch. Symbolic thought bows down in the presence of the manifestation of the unknown; conceptual thought moves forward to stake out a claim to some portion of this unknown. Both seem necessary to the functioning of human intentionality.

THE SYMBOL OF THE GOLDEN CHAIN

Toward the end of his *Epistola de Anima,* in speaking of the role of the highest power of the soul, the *intelligentia,* Isaac says:

> The true but not pure incorporeal being [the soul] is therefore some kind of image and likeness of the pure and true incorporeal being [God]; and that which we have called "scarcely-incorporeal" being is an image of the former. That which we said is "almost-bodily" is in turn the image of the "scarcely-incorporeal." The highest body, that is, fire, is joined by a kind of likeness to the almost-bodily, and air to fire, water to air, earth to water. Therefore, in a manner of speaking, by this golden chain of the poet either the lowest realities hang down from the

16. B. Lonergan, *De Deo Trino* (Rome, 1961), pp. 88, 177.

17. S. Langer, *Philosophy in a New Key,* Mentor paperback (New York, 1962), p. 222, notes that presentational symbols can express opposites simultaneously, and therefore prefers to use the terms adequacy/inadequacy of expressiveness rather than truth/falsity in speaking of symbols.

highest, or by the upright ladder of the prophet there is an ascent from the lowest to the highest. Just as Wisdom affects the order of things from one end to the other, that is, from the highest to the lowest, it also, drawing them in strength from the Archetype, sweetly sets all things in order in their proper states so that they are what they should be, directing and ruling through being what he has drawn from nothing into existence. So also the soul, the image of that Wisdom, had it not fallen away, by freely gazing upon him everywhere, would follow Wisdom, admiring and loving, searching out and praising in everything the Power drawing all things from nothing into existence, and the Wisdom ordering all things through being, and the Goodness supporting all things lest they fall back into nothingness.[18]

This "aurea catena poetae," the golden chain of Homer, which is equated with the ladder of the dream of Jacob the prophet, though mentioned expressly only in one other passage in Isaac's writings,[19] is the symbolic key to his theology of man. Furthermore,

18. XVIII. (1885 CD). "Est igitur pure et vere incorporei quedam imago et similitudo vere et non pure incorporeum, et illius, id quod diximus pene incorporeum; et ipsius, id quod diximus pene corpus. Ipsi quoque supremum corpus, id est ignis, quadam similitudine iungitur, et igni aer, aeri aqua, aque terra. Hac igitur quasi aurea catena poete, vel ima dependent a summis, vel erecta scala prophete ascenditur ad summa de imis. Sicut igitur ordinem rerum attingit a fine usque ad finem, id est a summo ad imum, sapientia fortiter ab archetypo quoque trahens in propios status, ut sint quod sunt, et disponit omnia suaviter, moderans ac regens per esse que protrahit de non esse ad esse; sic et anima illius sapientie imago, si non degeneret, eam ubique considerando libenter sequitur, admirans et amans, investigans et laudans in omnibus, et potentiam protrahentem omnia de non esse ad esse, et sapientiam disponentem omnia per esse, et bonitatem continentem omnia ne recedant ad non esse."

19. 1874D–75A. "Anima igitur peregrinatur in tali corpore, et corpus in tali mundo. Ordinatus quippe, ac naturalis status hominis erat, cum spiritus Deo, caro spiritui, mundus carni subjectus fuerat, et in ipso spiritu affectio carni subjacuerat. *Et hic erat primus naturalis mundus, aureum Saturni saeculum, aureaque catena poetae.* Quam cum inobedientia rupisset inter spiritum et Deum, concupiscentia inter carnem et spiritum, ac demum maledictio inter operationem carnis et mundum: apparuit subito exordinata quaedam rerum facies, quae chaos, tenebrae, et abyssus merito dicta est: unde extractum se memoravit, qui per gratiam nova in Christo creatura in novo mundo positus. . . ." Note that this passage is more closely related to the history of salvation. These nuances of meaning should not be seen as contradictory, but as complementary, as will be described below.

the dual symbol of chain and ladder—the one beginning in Homer and having a long history in Greek speculation, the other taken from the account of Genesis—is an admirable vehicle through which to explore the relation of a twelfth-century thinker to those fundamental categories of late Platonism and its Christian use discussed above. In order to indicate the richness of the symbolic tradition which lay behind Isaac's use, we must trace the history of the *catena aurea*, both in the narrow textual sense and in the wider sense of the intellectual world which it manifests.[20]

Ancient Use of the Symbol of the Golden Chain

At the beginning of the Eighth Book of the Iliad, Zeus decides to restore order among the gods and prevent them from taking sides in the Trojan War. He has the power to do so; he expresses it quite unequivocally:

Come, you gods, make this endeavor, that you all may learn this. Let down out of the sky *a cord of gold*; lay hold of it all you who are gods and all who are goddesses, yet not even so can you drag down Zeus from the sky to the ground, not Zeus the high lord of counsel, though you try until you grow weary. Yet whenever I might strongly be minded to pull you, I could drag you up, earth and all and sea and all with you, then fetch the golden rope about the horn of Olympos and make it fast,

20. For the literature on the *catena aurea*, cf. A. O. Lovejoy, *The Great Chain of Being: a Study of the History of an Idea* (Cambridge, 1936); E. Wolff, *Die Goldene Kette. Die Aurea Catena Homeri in der englischen Literatur von Chaucer bis Wordsworth* (Hamburg, 1947); E. Curtius, *European Literature in the Latin Middle Ages* (New York, 1953), pp. 110–11; L. Edelstein, "The Golden Chain of Homer," *Studies in Intellectual History, dedicated to Arthur O. Lovejoy* (Baltimore, 1953), pp. 48–66; P. L'Évêque, *Aurea catena Homeri, une étude sur l'allégorie grecque, Annales Littéraires de l'Université de Besançon,* XXVII (Paris, 1959); Endre von Ivánka, *Plato Christianus* (Einsiedeln, 1964), esp. pp. 73–5, 82–4 136–7; Edouard Jeauneau, "Macrobe, source du platonisme chartrain," *Studi Medievali* (3rd Series), I (1960), 3–24; Henri de Lubac, *Exégèse Médiévale,* Vol. II, Part II (Paris, 1964), pp. 217–21.

so that all once more should dangle in mid-air. So much stronger am I than the gods, and stronger than mortals.[21]

The image is a striking and unusual one, in some ways unique in the Homeric writings. Ludwig Edelstein in his study of the transformation of the golden chain in classical literature and philosophy suggests possible influence from the cult of Hecate as the Great Mother and asserts that in no other passage does Homer come closer to presenting a complete world-view.[22] Thus, from the very beginning, there is a cosmic dimension implicit in the symbol susceptible of increasingly richer accretions and nuances. As in the history of many other symbols, divergences of expressed content tend to have at least analogous relations to an original core of meaning. This cosmic sense, i.e., the symbol as manifestation of the organization of the universe, is even clearer in an Orphic fragment preserved by Proclus:

> And there is the strong bond, as the theologian says, stretching across all things and unifying them by means of the golden chain. Because thus Zeus established the golden chain according to the suggestions of Night—"Moreover while you stretch a strong bond out through all things, the golden chain hanging down from the ether. . . ."[23]

21. Iliad VIII, 18–27 (trans. R. Lattimore, *The Iliad of Homer* [Chicago, 1961]). The Greek text for the central lines 18–20:

εἰ δ' ἄγε πειρήσασθε, θεοί, ἵνα εἴδετε πάντες.
σειρὴν χρυσείην ἐξ οὐρανόθεν κρεμάσαντες.
πάντες τ' ἐξάπτεσθε θεοὶ πᾶσαί τε θέαιναι.

(Loeb ed., p. 338).

22. *Op. cit.*, pp. 56–61.

23. Cf. Otto Kern, *Orphicorum Fragmenta* (Berlin, 1963; 2nd ed.), # 166 from Proclus, *In Platonis Timaeum*, 31c (ed. Diehl, II, 24, 11. 23–9):

καὶ οὗτός ἐστιν ὁ κρατερὸς δεσμὸς, ὡς φησιν ὁ θεολόγος,
διὰ πάντων τεταμένος καὶ ὑπὸ τῆς κρυσῆς σειρᾶς
συνεχόμενος ἐπ' αὐτῷ γὰρ ὁ Ζεὺς τὴν χρυσῆν
ὑφίστησι σειρὰν κατὰ τὰς ὑποθήκας τῆς Νυκτός·
αὐτὰρ ἐπὴν δεσμὸν κρατερὸν περὶ πάντα τανύσσηις
σειρὴν χρυσείην ἐξ αἰθέρις ἀρτήσαντα.

While modern scholarship has minimized the importance once given to the Orphic movement,[24] much of the material in the Orphic texts is of considerable antiquity. In any case, the text is a witness to the essential cosmological expressiveness of the *catena aurea*.

The Greek use of the symbol was by no means restricted to the worlds of poetry and religion, nor to a generalized sense of cosmological order, for almost from the beginning of Greek philosophical reflection, we find it allegorized and incorporated into philosophical discourse in a rich variety of ways.[25] Plato, possibly under the influence of Heraclitus, interpreted it as the necessary motion of the sun preserving the universe from destruction,[26] an interpretation fairly common in later classical texts. Aristotle made use of it in an opposite sense to stress the immobility of the Prime Mover,[27] while the Stoics, who identified the Orphic rope with that mentioned by Homer, in general accepted the sun allegorization or saw in it a symbol of the intertwining of the elements to be destroyed at the end of the world.[28] The continuity in the image itself and the astonishing diversity in the content given it is not surprising. Where the use of a concept would exclude

---

For the role of Night in the Orphic cosmogony, cf. W. K. C. Guthrie, *Orpheus and the Greek Religion,* 2nd ed. (New York, 1952), pp. 102–7; G. S. Kirk and J. E. Raven, *The Presocratic Philosophers* (Cambridge, 1966), p. 40.

24. Kirk and Raven, *op. cit.,* pp. 37–48.

25. The fullest study of the ancient usage of the symbol is to be found in P. L'Évêque, *op. cit.;* cf. also L. Edelstein, *op. cit.*

26. *Theaetetus,* 153c–d. "Need I speak further of such things as stagnation in air or water, where stillness causes corruption and decay, when motion would keep things fresh, or, to complete the argument, press into its service that 'golden rope' in Homer, proving that he means by it nothing more nor less than the sun, and signifies that so long as the heavens and the sun continue to move round, all things in heaven and earth are kept going, whereas if they were bound down and brought to a stand, all things would be destroyed and the world, as they say, turned upside down?" (trans. F. M. Cornford). *Plato: The Collected Dialogues,* ed. by E. Hamilton and H. Cairns (New York, 1961).

27. Aristotle, *The Movement of Animals,* 699 700a, ed. E. S. Forster, Loeb Classical Library, p. 452.

28. Edelstein, *op. cit.,* p. 53.

such diversity of content, the genius of the symbol is to be able to combine a multitude of meanings reaching even to seeming contradiction in one manifestation. Allegory, as an attempt to analyze symbolic images and to give them conceptual content, occupies a shifting middle ground. When vigorously applied by a given author it will tend toward the exclusion of symbolic diversity of meaning; but since the allegorical images are frequently traditional symbols rather than individual creations, the allegorical meaning can shift from author to author and in the long run contribute to the history of symbols gradually accumulating new possibilities of meaning and spiritual and cultural correlatives in the human world.

Such a process is clearly illustrated by the history of the golden chain as it took on further cultural and linguistic dimensions in the ancient world without ever losing its basic cosmic sense. Lucretius introduced the image to Latin literature.[29] The emphasis on the power of Zeus in the Homeric passage was sometimes used by later authors, both pagan and Christian, to prove that Homer was really a monotheist.[30] Ludwig Edelstein has shown that the culmination of this evolution took place when "the *aurea catena Homeri* was established by the Middle Platonists as a figurative expression of the Scale of Being;"[31] he cites a text by Aristides from the middle of the second century AD to the effect that "in the manner of the chain of Homer everything is fastened upon him and everything is suspended from him, a chain much more beautiful than that golden chain [of Aphrodite] or any other chain one might imagine."[32] As in so many comparable areas, part

29. "haud, ut opinor, enim mortalia saecla superne
       aurea de caelo demisit funis in arva
       nec mare nec fluctus plangentis saxa crearunt
       sed genuit tellus eadem quae nunc alit ex se."
                                    De rerum natura II, 1153–6.

30. Ps.-Justin, *Cohortatio ad Graecos, PG* 6, 284; Ps.-Plutarch, *De vita et poesi Homeri,* 114 (ed. F. Dubner, V, 131).

31. *Op. cit.,* p. 59.

32. *In Iovem, 15.* . . . καὶ ἀτεχνῶς κατὰ τὴν Ὁμήρου σειρὰν ἅπαντα εἰς αὐτὸν ἀνήρτηται καὶ πάντα ἐξ αὐτοῦ ἐξῆπται, πολὺ καλλίοων ἅλυσις ἢ κατὰ κρυσῆν τε καὶ εἰ τινα ἄλλων τις ἐπινοήσειει (ed. B. Keil, p. 343).

of this development seems to have been foreshadowed in Philo of Alexandria, who had a fairly evolved notion of the great chain of being.[33]

Thus, when the Neoplatonic thinkers adopted the golden chain of the "original philosopher," Homer, as the symbol for their dynamic sense of the chain of being, they were merely bringing to fulfillment a process of interpretation that was almost as old as Greek thought itself. Interestingly enough, while the rich variety of cosmic themes which the symbol manifests (e.g., the categories of emanation and plenitude of being, the principles of hierarchy, mediation and continuity, and the doctrine of the microcosm) are all present in Plotinus, the image itself is not found. Plotinus does make use of images, symbols, and metaphors, but in a highly individualized and subtle fashion; his successors had no such inhibitions, though the extent of our knowledge is limited because of the loss of many texts of such important earlier Neoplatonists as Porphyry and Iamblichus. The clearest early Neoplatonic reference to the golden chain, and the most influential for the medieval period, is in the celebrated text from Macrobius' *Commentary on the Dream of Scipio*, written c. 400 AD:

> Accordingly, since Mind emanates from the Supreme God and Soul from Mind, and Mind, indeed, forms and suffuses all below with life, and since this is the one splendor lighting up everything and visible in all, like a countenance reflected in many mirrors arranged in a row, and since all follow on in continuous succession, degenerating step by step in their downward course, the close observer will find that from the Supreme God even to the bottommost dregs of the universe, there is one tie, binding at every link and never broken. This is the golden chain of Homer

---

Other Middle Platonic uses, without specific reference to the Homeric image, may be found in Maximus of Tyre, *Oratio XI*, in *Maximi Tyrii Philosophumena*, ed. H. Hobein (Leipzig, 1910), p. 145, and some fragments of Numenius of Apamea, cf. E. von Ivánka, *op. cit.*, p. 136, n. 1.

33. Cf. H. Chadwick, "Philo and the Beginnings of Christian Thought," *Cambridge History of Later Greek and Early Medieval Theology*, ed. A. H. Armstrong (Cambridge, 1967), pp. 142–3.

which, he tells us, God ordered to hang down from the sky to the earth.[34]

Since the golden chain is not found in Plotinus, the source of its appearance in Macrobius's simplified version of the Plotinian universe may be queried. In the absence of any existing earlier Neoplatonic references, final decision is impossible; Edelstein suggested that Iamblichus would be a likely source, since the symbol would have been at home among the richly imagistic and magical elements in Iamblichan thought;[35] but since modern research on Macrobius has tended to stress the importance of the influence of Porphyry on the *Commentary*,[36] the latter would seem the more likely origin for the appearance of the symbol in this particular text.

Aided by "the tendency to multiply the links in the chain of being by the insertion of further hypostases between Plotinus' three and by division of hypostases into further triads,"[37] the symbol of the chain of being as an expression of this multiplication took on an essential role in the growing complexity of late Neoplatonic speculation on the world that reached its culmination in the thought of Proclus toward the end of the fifth century.

34. "Secundum haec ergo cum ex summo deo mens, ex mente anima fit, anima vero et condat et vita compleat omnia quae sequuntur, cunctaque hic unus fulgor illuminet et in universis appareat, ut in multis speculis per ordinem positis vultus unus, cumque omnia continuis successionibus se sequantur degenerantia per ordinem ad imum meandi: invenietur pressius intuenti a summo deo usque ad ultimam rerum faecem una mutuis se vinculis religans et nusquam interrupta conexio *et haec est Homeri catena aurea, quam pendere de caelo in terras deum iussisse commemorat*." *Commentarii in Somnium Scipionis,* I, 14, 15 (*ed. I. Willis*, Teubner, Leipzig, 1963), p. 58. The translation is that of W. H. Stahl, from *Macrobius: Commentary on the Dream of Scipio* (New York, 1952), p. 145.

35. *Op. cit.,* pp. 63–5.

36. Pierre Courcelle, *Les Lettres Grecques en Occident de Macrobe à Cassiodore,* 2nd ed. (Paris, 1948), pp. 3–36. Cf. the excellent summary of the debate on influences on Macrobius in Stahl, *op. cit.,* "Introduction: The Sources," pp. 23–39.

37. A. C. Lloyd, "The Later Neoplatonists," *Cambridge History of Later Greek and Early Medieval Philosophy,* pp. 281–2.

The excessive intricacy of the Proclean series of emanations is frequently described in terms of *seira*—literally "rope, cord, chain"[38]—thus we are not surprised by Proclus's mention of the golden chain of the Orphic fragment in three places in the *Commentary on the Timaeus* and once in the *Commentary on the Parmenides*.[39] The use of the symbol is widespread in late Neoplationism and it is significant that it is found in those two great early sixth-century transmitters of Neoplatonism to the Medieval world: Boethius and the enigmatic Pseudo-Dionysius.[40] In the eighth metrum of the second book of Boethius' *De Consolatione Philosophiae,* it is love that binds together the great chain of being: "And all this chain of things in earth and sky and sea one ruler holds in hand. . . ."[41] In the *De Divinis Nominibus* of the Pseudo-Dionysius the chain hanging down from heaven becomes the symbol of the anagogic value of prayer by which man ascends to God:

> Let us then press on in prayer, looking upwards to the Divine benignant Rays, even as if a resplendent cord were hanging from the height of heaven unto this world below, and we, by seizing it with one hand after the other in steady advance, appeared to pull it down; but in very truth instead of drawing down the rope (the same being already nigh us above and below), we were ourselves being drawn upwards to the higher Refulgence of the resplendent Rays.[42]

38. E.g., *The Elements of Theology,* Prop. 21 *(ed. E. R. Dodds),* pp. 24–5. On the use of σειρά and τάξις in Proclus, cf. R. Roques, *L'Universe Dionysien* (Paris, 1954), p. 74, n. 2; L. J. Rosán, *The Philosophy of Proclus* (New York, 1949), p. 85; P. L'Évêque, *op. cit.,* pp. 61–74.

39. *In Timaeum* 28c *(ed. E. Diehl),* (I, 314, line 12 sq.); *In Timaeum* 34b (II, 112, lines 3 sqq.) and *In Timaeum* 31c (II, 24, lines 23–9). *In Parmenidem,* 2nd ed., V. Cousin (Paris, 1864), c. 1099, line 39–c. 1100, line 10.

40. On the relation of these two thinkers to Proclus, cf. C. J. de Vogel, "Amor quo coelum regitur," *Vivarium,* I (1963), 2–34.

41. "Hanc rerum seriem ligat terra ac Pelagus regens et caelo imperitans amor." *De Consolatione Philosophiae,* II, m. 8, *ed. Rand,* Loeb Library, p. 222; translation of V. E. Watts, Penguin Classics ed., p. 77.

42. *Dionysius the Areopagite on the Divine Names and the Mystical Theology,* trans. C. E. Rolt (London, 1920), p. 82. *De Div. Nom.* III, 3:

These late and it is to be admitted marginal references are not the major source of the twelfth-century usage—the text of Macrobius served admirably in that capacity—but they are a further indication of the importance of the symbol in Neoplatonism and the variety of functions it served. Our brief sketch of the classical history of the symbol now makes it imperative to attempt a more precise determination of its function as a manifestation of the thought world of late antiquity and the contribution of this world to the medieval period.[43]

The Meaning of the Golden Chain of Being

Arthur O. Lovejoy in his celebrated book *The Great Chain of Being: A Study of the History of an Idea* traced the evolution and influence of that "unit idea" of which the *catena aurea Homeri* was one of the central expressions. While his major interest focuses on the later, particularly eighteenth-century, manifestations of the idea, he quite justly begins with an analysis of the influence of Plato as in some way determinative of the entire evolution, for he finds the ambiguity in the use of the idea of the Chain of Being implicit in

'Ημᾶς οὖν αὐτοὺς ταῖς εὐχαῖς ἀνατείνωμεν ἐπὶ τὴν τῶν θείων καὶ ἀγαθῶν ἀκτίνων ὑψηλότερον ἀνάνευσιν. "Ωσπερ εἰ πολυφώτου σειρᾶς ἐκ τῆς οὐρανίας ἀκρότητος ἠρτημέης, εἰς δεῦρο δὲ καθηκούσης, καὶ ἀεὶ αὐτῆς ἐπὶ τὸ πρόσω χεροίν ἀμοιβαίαις δραττόμενοι, καθέλκειν μὲν αὐτὴν ἐδοκοῦμεν, τῷ ὄντι δὲ οὐ κατήγομεν ἐκείνην, ἄνω τε καὶ κάτω παροῦσαν, ἀλλ' αὐτοὶ ἡμεῖς ἀνηγόμεθα πρὸς τὰς ὑψηλοτέρας τῶν πολυφώτων ἀκτίνων μαρμαρυγάς. (*Dionysiaca* I, 124–25.) The use here certainly seems to have the Homeric passage in mind. It is important to note that the force of this passage was muted for the early twelfth century by the poor translations available. Hilduin translates the key phrase as "Quemadmodum si multiluminum syrium," Eriugena as "Veluti multiluminis splendorem"; only Sarrazin in the later twelfth century translates it as "Sicut si multiluminis *catena* . . ." (cf. P. Chevallier, *Dionysiaca, ibid.*). Pseudo-Dionysius's doctrine of prayer here is largely taken over from Proclus, cf. R. Roques, *op. cit.*, pp. 128–30 and 333. This is the only place where the Proclean σειρα appears in the Pseudo-Dionysius.

43. The Golden Chain also appears in St Gregory of Nyssa's *De Anima et Resurrectione* (PG 46, 89A); but since this was not available to the medievals in translation, it need not be considered here.

the unresolved tension between the "other-worldly" and the "this-worldly" aspects of Plato's thought.[44] These two aspects lead to "two irreconcilable conceptions of the good":[45] on the one hand, the *Idea of the Good* as completely self-sufficient and indifferent to the world, the highest Form of the Platonic *Dialogues* and ancestor of Aristotle's Unmoved Mover, the goal of the upward path in which man's true nature is achieved by flight from the world and union in contemplation with this Highest Principle; and on the other, the *Idea of Goodness,* the Highest Principle, as lacking in envy and producing all possible beings from its own fullness, found most clearly in the *Timaeus.*[46] This latter concept enshrines its meaning in the axiom *omne bonum est diffusivum sui;* it is the source of the downward path in which man's perfection consists in his exercise of a creativity analogous to that of the First Principle. For Lovejoy, the Great Chain of Being, the idea through which these two divergent aspects express themselves in the history of Western thought, is a Neoplatonic creation combining the principle or plenitude from Plato's *Timaeus* (i.e., that the Goodness of the Highest Principle demands "that no genuine potentiality of being can remain unfulfilled, that the extent and abundance of creation must be as great as the possibility of existence and commensurate with the productive capacity of a 'perfect' and inexhaustible Source, and that the world is the better, the more it contains")[47] with the principles of continuity and gradation which have their remote origin in Aristotle (i.e., "the idea of arranging [at least] all animals in a single graded *scala naturae* according to their degree of perfection.")[48] The fusion of these ideas is complete in the Neoplatonic theory of emanation; Plotinus is the father of the "Great Chain of Being."[49]

44. *Op. cit.,* pp. 24–35.   45. *Op. cit.,* p. 82.

46. For an analysis of the two concepts of the Good, cf. pp. 82–6; for the origin of the second form in the *Timaeus,* cf. pp. 48–51.

47. *Op. cit.,* p. 52.   48. *Op. cit.,* p. 58.

49. "Though the ingredients of this complex of ideas came from Plato and Aristotle, it is in Neoplatonism that they first appear as fully organized into a coherent general scheme of things. The dialectic of the theory of emanation

F

It is significant to note that Lovejoy's book, originally delivered as a series of lectures in 1933, bears affinities to Ernst Cassirer's attempt to summarize the effect of ancient philosophy on the Middle Ages in his 1927 work, *Individuum und Kosmos in der Philosophie der Renaissance.*[50] For Cassirer the most important legacy of ancient speculation to the medieval world was "the concept and the general picture of a graduated *cosmos*,"[51] an idea implicit in Plotinian emanation and most clearly presented to the medievals in the hierarchical world-picture of the Pseudo-Dionysius. Cassirer sees this as a kind of bastard concept, an eclectic mixture of the Platonic stress on transcendence based on the separation of the sensible and intelligible worlds and the Aristotelian concept of development based upon the assertion that reality is one;[52] his insight into the importance of the "fundamental category of graduated mediation" in the Middle Ages is in many ways similar to Lovejoy's Great Chain, save that his stress is on the "mediational" rather than the "plenitudinal" aspect of the Great Chain.

Without in any way attempting to deny the significance of these two studies in uncovering the importance of the concept of hierarchy as manifested through the image of the chain of being in late antiquity and the Middle Ages, we must confront the question whether Lovejoy and Cassirer provide adequate explanations of the origin of the idea and the implications of its use. In the first place, while their emphasis on the lack of unity in Plotinus' thought is well taken, the simple combination of cate-

---

is essentially an elaboration and extension of the passages in the *Timaeus* which have been cited; it is, in short, an attempt at a deduction of the necessary validity of the principle of plenitude, with which the principles of continuity and gradation are definitely fused" (pp. 61–2). E. Hoffmann goes even further in stressing the dominance of the Aristotelian motif over the Platonic in the formation of a chain of being: "kommt bei Aristoteles der Stufen-kosmos des realen Seins. Die Möglichkeit der kirchlichen Jakobsleiter, die auf der Erde steht und bis in den Himmel reicht, ist grundsätzlich immer nur aristotelisch nie platonisch motivierbar." Cf. "Platonismus und Mittelalter," *Vorträge der Bibliothek Warburg* (1923–24), p. 70.

50. E. Cassirer, translated by Mario Domandi, *The Individual and the Cosmos in Renaissance Philosophy*, paperback ed. (New York, 1963).

51. Cassirer, *op. cit.,* p. 9.   52. *Op. cit.,* pp. 16–19.

gories from Plato and Aristotle to form an eclectic system does not appear to be a satisfactory explanation of the scope and depth of the Plotinian program. A. H. Armstrong in his study, *The Architecture of the Intelligible Universe in the Philosophy of Plotinus,* also sets up as a general presupposition that "the philosophy of Plotinus . . . is not, for historical reasons, a fully consistent philosophy";[53] he admits that Plotinus's system is marked by the tension between a "world-accepting" attitude and a "world-rejecting" one, the tension of the Plato of the *Timaeus* as against the Plato of the *Phaedo*;[54] but he provides a necessary corrective to a simplistic view of Plotinus by analyzing the complexity of the tradition which he had inherited and which he felt that he could not reject. Many of the most important elements of the Plotinian system, such as the doctrine of the One as the ultimate ground, remain somewhat ambiguous to the last because they result from an attempt to combine elements from the whole history of Greek religious and philosophical speculation. In the same fashion, the doctrine of emanation and return should not be seen merely as a fusion of Plato and Aristotle, but rather in terms of faithfulness to a wider tradition. Armstrong and others convincingly demonstrate that the concept is Stoic in origin, indeed, one of the clearest examples of Stoic influence on the Father of Neoplatonism, but that it works within a framework where Platonic and Aristotelian elements are essential.[55] The simple dialectical view of Lovejoy and Cassirer is misleading. Furthermore, this more adequate account of the origins of Neoplatonic emanation raises the basic question of the reason behind the desire to combine such a variety of materials.

To abstract from that particular reverence for antiquity, the

53. Armstrong, *op. cit.,* p. ix.   54. *Op. cit.,* pp. 83–7.

55. *Op. cit.,* pp. 33–4, 50–7. E. von Ivánka in *Plato Christianus* lays even greater stress on the influence of Stoicism in later Platonism and the Middle Ages; e.g., pp. 79–80: "Man kann geradezu sagen, dass der Neuplatonismus (einschliesslich dessen, was man heute 'mittleren Platonismus' zu nennen pflegt) eigentlich nichts anders ist als die Ausfüllung des stoischen, (ürsprünglich materialistischen) Seinsschemas mit platonischem (spiritualistischem) Inhalt."

conviction that old wisdom was the best wisdom, which is one of the chief oppositions between the ancient and the modern temper, and also from the practical correlative of this—the attempt to show the fundamental unity of all inherited wisdom (first of all of Plato and Aristotle, but up to and including such works as the *Chaldean Oracles*)—another characteristic of ancient thought long since discarded must be stressed as the necessary context within which to consider this question: the strong association of religion and philosophy.[56] Plato was both an end and a beginning. Living at a time of political and religious crisis in Greek society, his own thought was a major turning point in the religious experience of that society. A.-J. Festugière has pointed out that Plato, confronted by the crisis of the old civic religion, initiated an age of reflective piety with a twofold religious program: on the one hand, "the desire for union with the ineffable God," a mystical religious goal described in the *Symposium*, parts of the *Republic* and *The Seventh Letter;* and on the other, "the desire of union with the God of the world, the cosmic God," most clearly expressed in the *Timaeus* and leading to a cosmic religion directed towards astral deities.[57] This latter doctrine was developed by Stoicism;[58] the former, gradually refined through the speculations of Middle Platonism on the *agnostos theos,* the unknown God, found its fullest expression in the mysticism of Plotinus.[59]

Such a neat schematization does not do full justice to the immense

56. A. H. Armstrong, "Introductory," *Cambridge History of Later Greek and Early Medieval Philosophy,* p. 5: "Philosophy for most of the ancients, after Plato at any rate, and certainly for the men of our period, was as Markus puts it, speaking of Augustine, 'an all-embracing activity concerned with everything relevant to the ultimate purpose of human life.' This accounts for the strong ethical emphasis and, to the modern mind, disconcertingly close connection between philosophy and religion which we find in nearly all the thinkers of the period, in the Greek pagans just as much as in the adherents of revealed religions."

57. A.-J. Festugière, *Personal Religion among the Greeks* (Berkeley, 1960), pp. 45–52.

58. *Op. cit.,* Chap. VII, pp. 105–21.

59. *Op. cit.,* Chap. VIII, pp. 122–39.

complexity of this philosophico-religious development; many individual elements in Festugière's analysis, such as his denial of any great weight to Eastern influences, especially Gnosticism,[60] are the subject of much debate; but this approach undoubtedly has the advantage of restoring a particular mode of philosophical thinking to its original perspective. It is in accord with Armstrong's evaluation of Plotinus, for he sees the mystical dimensions of the master's experience as the explanation of his ability to hold two divergent conceptions of the Highest Principle, the One, in union.[61] Finally, such a consideration of the wider background completes Lovejoy's explanation of the principle of the continuity of being in Plotinus and the special place given to man within this continuity. Here, once again, the doctrine seems to have as much of the Stoic as the Aristotelian aura about it;[62] and, as will be discussed later, the motivation is as much religious as narrowly philosophical in the modern sense of the word. The association of philosophy and religion is an essential explanatory principle for understanding the chain of being.

The lack of conceptual unity in Neoplatonism which Lovejoy affirmed is at once more profound than his analysis indicates (since it includes more elements than his rather simple Platonic and Aristotelian indications) and more significant for its role as a form of cultural structuration (since its dimensions are religious as well

60. E. von Ivánka, *op. cit.*, pp. 78–9, 134–5, has summarized the positions here where Festugière, who reduces Gnostic influence to a minimum, is opposed by E. Norden and H. Wolfson. A. H. Armstrong also judges Gnostic influence to be minimal, cf. "Preface," *Cambridge History of Later Greek and Early Medieval Philosophy*, p. xiii.

61. "In Plotinus' descriptions of the One we have, as elsewhere, in the *Enneads*, a profound and sensitive, if at times somewhat confused, account of the spiritual life poured into the mould of an already complex metaphysical tradition," *op. cit.*, p. 28. "The only way, I think, . . . in which we can begin to understand the combination of these conflicting ideas in Plotinus's theology is by a consideration of the mystical experience itself," pp. 43–4.

62. "Plotinus' passionate desire to maintain the organic unity of the *cosmos* is the element in his thought which brings him closest to the Stoics; we have already seen how this results in the admission of concealed Stoic materialism into his system in the theory of emanation." Armstrong, *op. cit.*, p. 63.

as philosophical). Perhaps then the kinds of inherent contradictions which Lovejoy frequently points out in the history of the idea of the Great Chain of Being (at least in its ancient and medieval phases) are only inherently contradictory when seen from the narrow viewpoint of a philosophy which does not take into account all the dimensions of the systems of thought under investigation. The fullness of the human background to these various "ideas" must always be kept in mind, especially since this background included religious and mystical elements which would be lacking in the modern understanding of the scope of philosophical systems and ideas; furthermore, it may also be taken as an argument for the assumption made at the beginning of this chapter, viz., that the limiting, exclusive character of conceptual thinking—the ultimate tool which Lovejoy uses—is not the ground from which Neo-platonism as a cultural system operated; but we must rather look to the inclusive, synthetic power of the symbol which enabled divergent manifestations of the real to be held in a single awareness. The unity of Neoplatonism, especially in its more general cultural context, was symbolic rather than conceptual.

This point should become more evident by an analysis of the depth and extent of content manifested in the symbol of the golden chain. Such an analysis, insofar as it dissects what originally was whole, must transpose the symbol into a conceptual framework; but only when one proceeds from that operation to a judgment on contradictory conceptual elements within the symbolic framework is there danger of an illicit operation. The operation becomes illicit when it is insensitive and premature: insensitive, in that it leads to a distortion of the expressed content of the symbol as our texts report it to us; premature, in that it is done from the point of view of a philosophical analysis which does not allow for the specific character of symbolic speech before attempting to interpret it on a higher level. Such an approach rarely allows the social and cultural function of the symbolic system to be taken into account.

As an illustration of the above dangers, certain aspects of Lovejoy's treatment of the Great Chain of Being can be singled out, particularly his consideration of what he terms the two irreconcilable conceptions of the Good.[63] First of all, Lovejoy's continued appeal to the incompatibility of these two notions never passes much beyond the realm of assertion; the one real argument adduced, the fact that these notions broke down at the end of the eighteenth century is not completely probative, since other factors besides supposed internal contradiction possibly operative in this breakdown have not been considered and rejected. That there are two factors in Platonic thought which may be rooted in two conceptions of the Good; that these two conceptions coexist in the tradition in a variety of ways; that frequently one or another was pushed to an extreme in a particular thinker; that the two factors are only with difficulty absorbed into a fully coherent system—all this is true; but that the two are necessarily logically contradictory is very much another case. The question can be pushed one step further, for the assumption upon which Lovejoy would apparently build his case (that questions of value are ultimately governed by logic alone) would be unintelligible to the men of these periods and unacceptable to many today. Pure logical coherency is not the deepest issue at stake here. We are dealing rather with the ways by which men structured their understanding of self and of world, the way in which they found value in human life. To say that they should work in a certain way and to judge them as inconsistent when they do not, can easily blind us to discerning how they actually did work. That the late Platonic and medieval formulation eventually failed, that it did not produce a technological society, that it was capable of absorbing a rather heterogeneous tradition of philosophical and religious material into a symbolic system, is not to be denied; if this be Lovejoy's principle of contradiction, then it is admirably realized in the sketch that he draws. One is allowed to wonder if it is sufficient to recapture historically what was the significance of the thought in question.

The objection might be advanced that the value judgment is not essential to the actual investigation, for the contradictions are explicit in the texts adduced. But here the narrowness of Lovejoy's

63. *Op. cit.,* pp. 82–98.

point of view frequently leads to a deformation of the evidence, a picking and choosing out of context which falsifies interpretation. Many of the nuances, distinctions, more inclusive formulations made by the authors in question, precisely because of their awareness of the difficulty of doing full justice to the depth of the problem, are ignored, misconstrued, or interpreted as "spurious and irrelevant distinctions."[64] Thus, there is a tendency to extreme and dichotomous formulations in which the true position of the author in question is unrecognizable.[65] The most serious consequence of this type of interpretation is the large-scale failure to tell us what Neoplatonism was really all about. Plotinus was certainly aware

64. *Op. cit.*, p. 81.

65. Some examples of this kind of treatment seem to be in order: (1) p. 43: Not all philosophical theologians who admitted that God has no need of a world proceeded to the affirmation that he is indifferent to it. Aristotle may have, but Lovejoy might have read further. (2) pp. 49–50: Is the basis for Plato's assumption of the Idea of Goodness the tacit "assumption that the existence of many entities not eternal, not supersensible, and far from perfect, was inherently desirable . . . ," or is it possible that he was trying to account for the sense world as well as the intelligible world (here neglected) in the light of a conception of the Highest Principle which was perhaps not quite so clearly evolved as Lovejoy would lead us to believe? (3) p. 67: Can we really say: "God's 'love,' in other words, in medieval writers consists primarily rather in the creative or generative than in the redemptive or providential office of the deity"? Do such vague generalities really serve to explain medieval thought? (4) p. 68: Is the "Love which . . . moved itself to creation" in the quotation from the Pseudo-Dionysius really "an expression of the dialectic of emanationism"? (5) pp. 73–82: The entire account of Aquinas fails to do justice to the larger framework within which Aquinas' solution to the problem is to be understood; cf. J. de Finance, *Être et Agir dans la Philosophie de St Thomas,* 2nd ed. (Rome, 1960). (6) p. 84: No medieval thinker (and scarcely anyone before the nineteenth century) would have said that "the God who had from all eternity perfectly possessed the good which is the object of man's quest was held to have found, so to say, his *chief* good in the 'way down.' " (7) p. 89: Nor would they have said (even according to one side of their traditional assumptions) that "no *true* value could be ascribed to any created thing." (8) pp. 96–97: The three possible accounts of the world which can be given by a consistently other-worldly philosophy explicitly exclude the Christian idea of sin and redemption which was the foundation of medieval thought. If, then, the Christian theological system is not consistently other-worldly, what relationship does it have to the consistently this-worldly and the consistently other-worldly.? This is never clarified.

of the necessity of working out the relations of the "downward" and "upward" paths; and whether we find his solution satisfactory or not, his attempt seems to escape Lovejoy's blanket condemnation that "the parallel between the descending and ascending process was little more than verbal."[66] In the Plotinian system the upward and downward ways are intimately related because each stage in the universal chain receives its power of activity in relation to the immediately lower stage by reason of its contemplation of the stage immediately above.[67] Thus contemplation, or the return to the Idea of the Good in Lovejoy's terms, is the ultimate goal; but it is exactly this sharing in the nature of the One by contemplation which enables the lower stages on the scale of emanation to exercise the active role analogous to Lovejoy's Idea of Goodness. Contemplation and action from the deepest point of view are the same reality within this dynamic system.

Lovejoy's continued stress on the plenitude and continuity of the Chain of Being as its most dominant characteristics may be legitimate for eighteenth-century usage, but is less valuable for explaining most of the Neoplatonic and medieval uses. In the twelfth-century texts in which the *catena aurea* appears, other aspects—anthropological, moral, and anagogic—are more to the fore.[68] He does turn his attention to the anagogic or ascensional aspect at the end of Chapter Three, but the predetermination of his

66. *Op. cit.*, p. 90.

67. Armstrong, *Architecture* . . . , pp. 86, 109; "Plotinus," *Cambridge History of Later Greek and Early Medieval Philosophy*, pp. 253–54. (The whole of *Enneads* III, 8, one of the most remarkable of Plotinus's writings, is devoted to this question).

68. As Lovejoy affirms, *op. cit.*, p. 90: "The notion of infinitesimal gradation, which was of the essence of the cosmological Chain of Being, was hardly suitable to a program which was, after all, designed to bring man as speedily as possible to his final supersensible felicity. . . ." It is important to note that Lovejoy's medieval section concentrates on Abelard and Aquinas, and not on the texts which will be our major concern. While certain important weaknesses of his treatment of these great Scholastics have been remarked on in note 65 above, his neglect of these other texts makes his treatment at best one-sided.

point of view does not allow him to do justice to the phenomenon. Once again he finds the whole program contradictory:

> For, in the first place, the parallel between the descending and the ascending process was little more than verbal. The scale of being conceived as a ladder by which man might mount to beatitude was not literally composed of the same steps as the scale of being conceived as a series of natural forms.[69]

The hidden assumption in the latter sentence is that the Aristotelian biological formulation of the "series of natural forms" was still central in the medieval use of the Chain of Being. A study of the texts in which the *catena aurea* appears shows that it was the religious rather than the scientific dimensions of the Chain which were significant during this whole period; the hierarchical structure of the ascent (from sensible being to intelligible to union with the super-intelligible),[70] and not its scientific aspect was what the medievals concentrated upon.[71] Lovejoy invents a "scientific" downward path for the medieval world, which he then finds incompatible with a "religious" upward path. Such dichotomies are anachronistic projections back upon the medieval attitude. A. J. Festugière's appreciation may be overly neat and uncritical of some of the problems raised by the variety of expression of this ascensional process, but at least he does justice to the intent of the program when he says:

> Thus one can elevate oneself by a natural progression from the entities of the physical world to those of the intelligible world,

69. *Ibid.*

70. This is true at least of the tradition influenced by the Pseudo-Dionysius, though Augustine always held for a direct and unmediated relationship of the soul to God.

71. The *reductio ad absurdum* argument for inherent contradiction given on p. 90 of Lovejoy's work is based on this false premise of the supremacy of the scientific aspect. "No one, I think, seriously proposed, as the true method of man's salvation, that he should begin by fixing his thought . . . upon what Macrobius called the 'dregs of being,' and should then proceed from these, by minute transitions, through successively more complex forms of . . . life . . . and so on in detail through the hierarchy of nature as medieval natural history conceived it, and finally through the successive grades of angels."

from thence to the Supreme Genera, from thence to God. God is omnipresent; the world is filled with him; it is possible to seek the imprints which he has set in things, even beginning with the lowest existing things. Thus from Plotinus to St Bonaventure, there exists an *itinerarium mentis ad deum*. It can be said that this itinerary reconciles the two currents of Platonic thought, that of the *Timaeus,* and that of the great dualistic dialogues, the *Phaedo,* the *Symposium,* and the *Republic.*[72]

If Lovejoy's treatment is then inadequate, what was the full range of implications of the symbol of the Chain of Being in the medieval period? While it is difficult to do justice to such variety, certain essential areas can be indicated. The ascensional, dynamic aspect of the law of the *downward* and *upward* path,[73] highlighted in the quotation from Festugière, was only one of the intimately related components. First of all, the sense of separation and alienation noticed earlier as basic to this whole awareness of the world was clearly manifested in the contrast between the two extremes of the Chain, matter and the Highest Principle. Plotinus himself never adequately solved the problem of matter.[74] Though the side of Neoplatonism which regarded matter as the source of evil could not be fully accepted by an orthodox Christian, it had its effect in the stress on the evil of the world and the abysmal unworthiness of the material in comparison to the spiritual which was common in the Christian thinkers of late antiquity and the Middle Ages. But this aura of pessimism must never be taken by itself; for it operated in

72. *Op. cit.,* p. 131.

73. A. H. Armstrong at times speaks of the "static" quality of the Plotinian universe in the sense that it is "eternal and unchanging as a whole." ("Plotinus," *Cambridge History,* p. 223; cf. also *Architecture . . . ,* p. 112). He explicitly notes, however, that this is not to be taken in the sense of "lifeless." Since the analysis here is not specifically concerned with an exegesis of the philosophy of Plotinus, but rather with the way in which the system first clarified by Plotinus was used as an expression of a world-view, and particularly since this world-view when used as an explanatory tool for Christian theology took on dimensions of historicity and change lacking in the pagan formulations, our stress on dynamism and ascensional movement does not seem unwarranted.

74. On Plotinus's views of matter, cf. Armstrong, *Architecture . . . ,* pp. 86–7; on matter as the source of evil, cf. especially *Enneads* I, 8, 15; II, 4, 16.

symbolic harness with a strong sense of the beauty, harmony, and organization of the whole universe—the structural characteristics which made the joining of the opposites possible. This is clear, not only in Plotinus, who, despite the strength of his "world-rejecting" aspect, directed one of the longest of the *Enneads* against the impiety of the Gnostics, who dared consider the material universe as evil,[75] but also among Christian authors, for whom everything that God created was good.

Therefore, despite this awareness of the extremes which is so constant a feature during the periods we are discussing, the radically dualistic solution was rejected by the main line of thought. Plato himself, although he cannot be said to have explained the ontological connection between the different spheres of being,[76] introduced a fundamental idea which was one of the explanatory categories preventing such a strong sense of the separation of the material and spiritual from becoming radical dualism. In the *Timaeus* 31bc, we are told that "it is not possible that two things alone should be conjoined without a third; for there must needs be some intermediary bond to connect the two."[77] This principle, which we may call the principle of mediation, or of concatenation, was to become very important to the late classical and medieval understanding of the Chain of Being. Oppressed by a sense of separation that made them acutely conscious of the distance between grades of being, and especially between the ultimate principle and man, the thinkers of this period fastened upon mediation as the means of affirming the unity of the universe, the existence of a real cosmos. Mediation was the progenitor of hierarchy.

This is not to say that the principle of mediation makes an explicit appearance in the philosophy of Plotinus. Here, as in so many other areas, Plotinus' deeply speculative insights, in this

75. *Enneads* II, 9; cf. A. H. Armstrong, "Plotinus," *Cambridge History*, pp. 230–2.

76. E. von Ivánka, *op. cit.*, pp. 70–3.

77. δύο δὲ μόνω καλῶς ξυνίστασθαι τρίτου χωρὶς οὐ δυνατόν δεσμὸν γαρ ἐν μέσῳ δεῖ τινὰ ἀμφοῖν ξυναγωγὸν γίγνεσθαι. (Ed. and trans. of R. G. Bury, Loeb Classical Library, pp. 58–9.)

case into the meaning of transcendence, led to a weakening of some of the more symbolic principles which bulked much larger in the general history of the system as a cultural form;[78] but the late Neoplatonic tendency to multiply the stages in the process of emanation seems to have been accompanied by an explicit return to Plato's principle of mediation. This is particularly strong in Proclus, as E. R. Dodds notes;[79] and from him it passes over into the Pseudo-Dionysius.[80] The influence of the Pseudo-Dionysius and of the *Timaeus* made it significant for the twelfth-century formulations of the Chain of Being.[81]

With or without the explicit invocation of the principle of mediation (which may be seen as a clarifying and simplifying procedure), the Neoplatonic world-view is nothing if not hierarchical. The notion of hierarchy—the structure of the universe as dependent upon God and consisting of levels of reality arranged in ascending order of value—is found in Plotinus,[82] and is part of

78. Armstrong goes so far as to say: "There can certainly be no place in the mind of anyone who has studied Plotinus for the idea that the dignity of the Highest demands the intervention of intermediaries between it and the material universe." Cf. *Architecture* . . . , p. 117.

79. E. R. Dodds, *Proclus: The Elements of Theology,* 2nd ed. (Oxford, 1963) "Introduction," p. xxii: "Again and again in the *Elements* Proclus justifies his multiplication of entities, like Iamblichus in the same circumstances, by reference to the 'law of mean terms,' viz. that two doubly disjunct terms AB and not-A, not-B cannot be continuous, but must be linked by an intermediate term, either A not-B or B not-A, which forms a 'triad' with them." Cf. also A. C. Lloyd, "The Later Neoplatonists," in the *Cambridge History,* p. 310.

80. E.g., *De Div. Nom.* VII, 3. In the twelfth century this Dionysian usage was frequently expressed by the words *continuitas* and *continuatio* (cf. M.-D. Chenu, *op. cit.,* pp. 291–2, n. 2) and *connexio* (cf. R. Javelet, *Image et ressemblance au douzième siècle* [Paris, 1967], I, 150–57, 451–3).

81. The influence of this principle on Isaac of Stella has been noted by E. Bertola, "La dottrina psicologica di Isaaco di Stella," *Rivista di filosofia neoscolastica,* XLV (1953), 301; and by R. Javelet, "La vertu dans l'oeuvre d'Isaac de Étoile," *Cîteaux,* XI (1960), 256, 262 and *op. cit., passim.* Cf. also K. Werner, *Der Entwicklungsgang der Mittelalterlichen Psychologie* (Vienna, 1876), p. 28.

82. E.g., *Enneads* IV, 4, 36; cf. Armstrong, "Plotinus," *Cambridge History,* p. 250.

the legacy of many of the important patristic writers influenced by Neoplatonism; but it is true to say that it is the Pseudo-Dionysius who makes the concept of hierarchy central to his system and who is the chief influence in most explicit medieval expressions.[83] Since this aspect of the heritage which the medievals absorbed has been admirably dealt with by René Roques, among others,[84] there is no necessity of concentrating upon it here; but it must always be kept in mind when discussing the history and meaning of the Chain of Being.

One further symbolic dimension of the *catena aurea* must be considered, i.e., the anthropological dimension, or the relation between the Great Chain of Being and man as microcosm. The long and diverse history of the microcosm theme has been discussed by Rudolf Allers;[85] our concern here is to show the relation of this particular motif to the Neoplatonic world-view symbolized by the Golden Chain. Neoplatonism was open to rich developments of microcosmic themes from two directions. First of all, in a universe of carefully graded levels stretching from the absolutely spiritual down through the abysmally material, man, as sharing both in the material and the spiritual, served the function of the meeting ground of these two extremes, a "bridge-being."[86] Even Plotinus, for whom the true man was the man above, the upper soul,[87] made use of the theme of man as microcosm, sometimes in the sense of man as occupying the middle ground between worlds and sharing in these different worlds,[88] sometimes in the more pregnant sense

83. E.g., *De Caelesti Hierarchia* III, 1; IX, 2 (*Dionysiaca* II, 785–98, 895–903); *De Ecclesiastica Hierarchia* I, 1 (*Dionysiaca* II, 1071–94).

84. René Roques, *L'Universe Dionysien: Structure hierarchique du monde selon le Pseudo-Denys* (Paris, 1954); "Connaissance de Dieu et théologie symbolique d'après l'*In Hierarchiam coelestem sancti Dionysii* de Hugues de Saint-Victor," *Structures théologiques' de la Gnose à Richard de Saint-Victor*, pp. 294–364 and M.-D. Chenu, "*La théologie . . .* , pp. 116, 129–30.

85. R. Allers, "Microcosmos from Anaximandros to Paracelsus," *Traditio*, II (1944), 319–409. Cf. also M.-D. Chenu, *op. cit.*, pp. 34–43.

86. The expression is Armstrong's; cf. *Architecture . . .* , p. 101.

87. E.g., *Enneads* I, 1, 7; II, 1, 5; III, 8, 5.

88. E.g., *Enneads* III, 2, 8; III, 4, 2.

of the soul as being an intelligible universe in itself.[89] This latter usage brings us closer to a deeper bond between Neoplatonism and speculation on man as microcosm. Plotinus's system has been seen by some as a form of metapsychology, a projection upon the universe of the categories of Greek logic and certain introspective discoveries of great significance.[90] Such a paralleling of psychology and ontology set up the ground within which varying changes rung upon the theme of microcosm were an important manifestation of the intense desire for the harmony of all things—man and the universe, material and spiritual, the above and below, "all things in everything, but appropriately"—which we have postulated as essential to an understanding of the interactions between Christianity and the Platonic tradition.

The same Macrobius who was the intermediary for the *catena aurea Homeri* was also instrumental in spreading knowledge of the microcosm theme,[91] though the concept was also filtered through a more general tradition. The great florescence of these ideas in the twelfth century which has been pointed out by so many investigators was due to their suitability as a means of symbolically manifesting man's relation to the cosmos; in this connection, man as microcosm, though the more common theme, may be considered as another face of Homer's image. One final note might be added. The continuity of microcosm as a symbolic cultural form also

89. "For the soul is many things, and all things, both the things above and the things below down to the limits of all life, and we are each of us an intelligible universe, making contact with this lower world by the powers of soul below, but with the intelligible world by the powers above and the powers of the universe. . . ." *Enneads* III, 4, 3 (trans. Armstrong, Loeb Classical Library ed., Vol. III); cf. also II, 4, 11; III, 4, 6; IV, 4, 36.

90. Cf. Armstrong, *Architecture* . . . , p. 113: "Nothing is real which is not also soul, and there is a stage of universal soul to correspond to every level of human experience. The structure and divisions of reality are determined not so much by cosmological considerations as by the need to bring it into exact correspondence with the structure of the human soul and mind as determined by the Platonic-Aristotelian tradition and by Plotinus's own introspection."

91. "ideo physici mundum magnum hominem et hominem brevem mundum esse dixerunt. . . ." *In Somn. Scip.* II, 12, 11 (*ed. Willis*, p. 132); cf. Allers, *op. cit.*, p. 321.

highlights a serious weakness in Cassirer's presentation of the shift from the medieval to Renaissance periods, for in laying strong emphasis on the Renaissance use of the microcosm concept as a factor distancing it from the Middle Ages, he fails to realize that although Renaissance authors naturally selected different aspects for emphasis from the vast possibilities of the microcosm symbol, Allers is correct in asserting that "The philosophy of the 'Platonists' [of the Renaissance] does not contain any essentially new contribution to microcosm whatever other originality may have been theirs."[92] While it cannot be denied that there is a negative, "world-rejecting," side of the medieval resumption of microcosmic themes, it has been the point of this analysis of the content of the *catena aurea* and its relation to these microcosmic themes to demonstrate that it also allowed a Christian author to bring to speech in a meaningful, if imperfect, manner a positive attitude toward the world.[93]

The Medieval Use of the Golden Chain

In one sense the long digression on the content of the symbol has put us ahead of ourselves, since we have had to make reference to the medieval as well as classical period, but it would have been impossible to do justice to the discussion of content and to point out some of the shortcomings of earlier investigations in this area without a consideration of the late classical materials in their medieval form. It is now necessary to complete our survey of the textual history of the *catena aurea* to demonstrate the presence of

92. Allers, *op. cit.*, p. 391.

93. E.g., Cassirer, *op. cit.*, pp. 40, 64–6, emphasizes the break in the case of Nicholas of Cusa. Allers, *op. cit.*, pp. 386–7, admits that Cusa's use of microcosm differs from the twelfth-century use, but his treatment indicates that the radical difference emphasized by Cassirer is illusory. Man's redemption as expressed through the microcosm motif included the ascension of the *whole universe* to God just as much for the medieval author as it did for Cusa. To cite Isaac of Stella alone, this is surely clear from the *catena aurea* passage in 1875A–76A, especially the phrase "qui per gratiam nova in Christo creatura *in novo mundo* positus."

these dimensions among medieval authors down to the end of the twelfth century.

Despite the influence of Macrobius on some of the Latin patristic authors, such as Boethius,[94] and the knowledge of the *Commentary on the Dream of Scipio* in the early Middle Ages,[95] there seems to be no clear reference to the Golden Chain in the Latin West before the twelfth century. That springtime of the European intellect which we associate with the School of Chartres in the early twelfth century saw the reintroduction of the symbol. This is not surprising, considering the use that the Chartrain authors made of Macrobius as a source for their particular brand of Platonism.[96] The earliest appearance of the symbol is in the works of the noted Norman master, William of Conches. Born toward the end of the eleventh century, a teacher at Chartres for many years, where he numbered John of Salisbury among his pupils, tutor to the future King Henry II of England in the late 1140's, William was still alive in 1154 when Alberic of Trois-Fontaines noted: "At the time Master William of Conches was a philosopher of great repute."[97] William's inquisitive and far-ranging mind makes him an admirable example of the spirit of Chartres; and the fact that some of his most original thought is found in his numerous glosses on the great texts of the tradition (Plato, Priscian, Boethius, and Macrobius) is most revealing for the relation of the twelfth century to antiquity. In the twelfth century the spark of genius was enkindled by contact with the past.

94. P. Courcelle, "La Posterité Chrétienne du Songe de Scipion," *Revue des études latines,* XXXIV (1958), 205–34.

95. P. M. Schedler, *Die Philosophie des Macrobius und ihr Einfluss auf die Wissenschaft des christlichen Mittelalters, BGPM,* XIII 1 (Münster, 1916), 104–14.

96. Cf. the excellent study of E. Jeauneau, "Macrobe, source du platonisme chartrain," *Studi Medievali,* 3rd series, I (1960), 3–24.

97. "Huius tempore magister Guilelmus de Concis philosophus magni nominis habitus est." *Chronica, MGH SS* XXIII, p. 842. For the sparse materials on the life of William, cf. R. L. Poole, "The Masters of the Schools at Paris and Chartres in John of Salisbury's Time," *Studies in Chronology and History* (Oxford, 1934), pp. 237–9; T. Gregory, *Anima Mundi: La Filosofia di Guglielmo di Conches e la Scuola di Chartres* (Florence, 1955), pp. 1–40; E. Jeauneau, *Guillaume de Conches: Glosae super Platonem* (Paris, 1965), pp. 9–10.

G

William's *Glosses on the Timaeus,* recently edited by Edouard Jeauneau, are a work of his maturity and therefore probably date from some time in the late 1130's or 1140's.[98] In commenting on *Timaeus* 34c from Chalcidius's translation (*Itaque tertium animae genus excogitauit hoc pacto*),[99] he identifies the Platonic World Soul with the Holy Spirit and proceeds to place the Holy Spirit in a carefully described cosmic framework:

> For the Holy Spirit is not made nor created nor generated but proceeds. Since he wished to devise such a soul, he did just that. And this is the text: "Therefore God devised a third kind of soul, that is, a soul which is a certain kind of thing, that is a certain manner of things." It is "third" in the Golden Chain of Homer. For the divine essence exists so that it is from nothing, but Divine Wisdom is from him, the Soul of the World is from both, the heavenly bodies from the three, and the earthly from the four.[100]

As Jeauneau points out in a footnote to this passage and describes at greater length in his article on the influence of Macrobius on the School of Chartres, this is not the first appearance of the *catena aurea* in the writings of William.[101] In the still unedited *Glosae super Macrobium,* which are a work of his youth and therefore probably date to the first years of his teaching career in the early 1120's,[102] we

---

98. *Op. cit.,* p. 14.

99. *Timaeus a Chalcidio Translatus,* ed. J. H. Waszink (Leiden, 1962), p. 27.

100. "Non enim a Deo factus est nec creatus nec genitus sed procedens est Spiritus Sanctus. Quandoquidem talem voluit animam excogitare, ergo excogitavit. Et hoc est: *Itaque Deus excogitavit tercium genus anime* id est animam que est quoddam genus rei, id est quedam maneria rerum. *Tercium* in aurea catena Homeri. Divina enim essentia ita est quod a nullo, divina vero sapientia est ab illo, anima mundi ex utroque, celestia corpora ex illis tribus, terrestria ex quatuor." Ms. M. (Munich, Clm 540B—late twelfth or thirteenth century) contains the interesting addition "qui dicit hanc protendi a celo ad terram in qua sunt ista quinque." A diagram on the margin shows a chain containing "Deus pater—filius—anima mundi—celestia corpora—terrestria corpora—terra." *Ed. Jeauneau,* pp. 148–9.

101. *Ibid.*; and "Macrobe, source du platonisme chartrain," p. 9.

102. Jeauneau, *Glosae,* pp. 10, 14–15.

find the theme exposed at greater length and very significantly associated with the ladder of Jacob as we have already seen it in Isaac of Stella. Since this important text is still unavailable except for the brief fragment quoted by Jeauneau, my thanks are owed to Mrs. Helen Lemay, at present preparing an edition of these *Glosses*, for permission to translate the passage as she had edited it from two of the six known manuscripts.[103]

"Therefore according to this." Since *Togaton* begets *Nous, Nous* Soul, Soul creates bodies, and the order in earthly things is as we have said, if anyone then wishes to make a close consideration, he will find a kind of connection of created things to each other, a connection that is even joined to God himself. The Soul is joined to God in many ways, inasmuch as it is immortal and incorporeal by intellect and reason and in many other ways. Likewise it is joined to the angels by reason, to brute beasts by sense and the power of growth. Brute beasts are joined to grass and trees by the power of growth; grass and trees to inanimate bodies by existence. "One splendor." Whatever splendor and beauty is in man is present in the body from the soul; but lest anyone think that this is wonderful or impossible that one and the same Soul should be in different bodies, he shows that it is no marvel. "As in many mirrors even to the last created beings." "Even to the last created being," because there is no creature which does not have some similarity with God. This is the joining together of all things. "The golden chain of Homer." For Homer, in order to describe this joining together of things, says that Jove lets a kind of chain down from heaven that hangs without interruption to the earth. This is also the ladder of which Jacob dreamed.[104]

Three things deserve to be noted about this text. The first is the highly significant transposition of Macrobius's version of the

103. K = Copenhagen, Kgl. Bibliothek, GI. Kgl.S. 1910 (twelfth century); U = Vatican, Urbinus Lat. 1140 (fifteenth century). K is the basic manuscript used for the edition, though in the opinion of the editor the text is interpolated; esp. lines 10–15. Cf. Jeauneau, *Glosae,* p. 12, n. 3, for list of manuscripts, as well as his article "Gloses de Guillaume de Conches sur Macrobe. Note sur les manuscrits," *AHDL,* XXVII (1960), pp. 17–28.

104. The Latin text and apparatus are given in the Appendix, pp. 239–40.

Plotinian emanations into the Christian Trinity. The possibility of such a procedure, as uncomfortable and unhistorical as it may appear to later theology, was grounded in a view of the unity of truth, a reverence for antiquity and the possibility of the acquaintance of Platonic philosophers with the Scriptures that goes back to the patristic period.[105] This was facilitated for twelfth-century thinkers by the use of the notion of *integumentum* or *involucrum*, a kind of pre-critical medieval demythologizing technique, which grew out of classical pagan allegorization.[106] The history of classical allegory is much too complex to be discussed at length, but a few indications of Neoplatonic attitudes are important to understand the background to this unusual twelfth-century notion.

The poets were the original philosophers; the philosophers themselves, especially the pre-eminent Plato, made use of myths and stories in the course of their philosophic work. Hence the Neoplatonists were confronted with the problem of absorbing poetic and symbolic texts into philosophical systems. Macrobius gives one of the fullest investigations of the legitimacy of the use of such material in philosophy in the second chapter of the first book of his *Commentary*. Most types of fiction are always to be excluded from philosophy—*fabulae* which only serve to please the listener, and even those which have a moral purpose when the stories are completely fictitious, or when, although true in intent, they relate something unworthy about the gods.[107] But one fiction does have a legitimate place. That type described as "a decent and dignified conception of holy truths, with respectable events and

105. St Augustine had affirmed this of Plato himself in *De Civ. Dei*, VIII, 11.

106. On *integumentum* and *involucrum*, cf. E. Jeauneau, "L'usage de la notion d'*integumentum* à travers les gloses de Guillaume de Conches," *AHDL*, XXIV (1957), 35–100; and *Guillaume de Conches: Glosae super Platonem*, pp. 19–21; M.-D. Chenu, "*Involucrum*, le myth selon les Théologiens médiévaux," *AHDL*, XXII (1955), 75–9; E. Curtius, *European Literature and the Latin Middle Ages* (New York, 1963), Chap. 11: "Poetry and Philosophy," pp. 202–13; H. de Lubac, *Exégèse Médiévale*, Vol. II, Part 2, Chap. VIII, 3: "Allégorie non biblique," pp. 182–208 and F. J. E. Raby, "*Nuda Natura* and 12th-Century Cosmology," *Speculum*, XLIII (1968), 72–7.

107. I, 2, 7–11 (ed. *Willis*, pp. 5–6).

characters, presented beneath a modest veil of allegory"[108] can be admitted, not when speaking about the Highest God, but when speaking of the World Soul and lower spirits, including the soul of man. These veils and fictions are necessary because Nature does not wish to expose her secrets indiscriminately to those who lack prudence.[109]

The men of the twelfth century, with their strong interest in classical texts and confidence in the large measure of truth to be found in the pagan philosophers, expanded the program beyond the narrow confines set down by Macrobius. No attempt will be made here to describe the full range and complexity of twelfth-century usage of the terms *integumentum, involucrum,* and *involumentum;*[110] its wide-ranging and careful use by William of Conches, however, was clearly the instrument which prompted him to uncover Christian truth beneath the allegorical covering of the old philosophers in a manner which, though we may judge it naive and uncritical, is a divining rod for the deeper concerns at work behind this façade: the desire to order the universe and all human knowledge, even that of the poets and philosophers of pagan antiquity, into something both beautiful and coherent.[111] While William does not mention *integumentum* specifically in the passage from the *Glosae super Macrobium*, the parallel passage from the *Glosae super Platonem* provides the clue for the startling inclusion of

108. "sacrarum rerum notio sub pio figmentorum velamine honestis et tecta rebus et vestita nominibus," *ibid.,* 11 (trans. W. H. Stahl, *op. cit.,* p. 85).

109. I, 2, 17: "de dis autem (ut dixi) ceteris et de anima non frustra se nec ut oblectent ad fabulosa convertunt, sed quia sciunt inimicam esse naturae apertam nudamque expositionem sui, quae sicut vulgaribus hominum sensibus intellectum sui vario rerum tegmine operimentoque subtraxit, ita a prudentibus arcana sua voluit per fabulosa tractari" (*ed. Willis,* p. 7).

110. de Lubac, *op. cit.,* pp. 188–97.

111. As early as 1916 Clemens Baeumker recognized two motives as essential to the Platonic tradition in the Middle Ages: "der ästhetische Sinn für die Natur und die Vorstellung von einem die ganze Natur durchziehenden Zusammenhang," in "Der Platonismus im Mittelalter," *BGPM, XXV,* 1–2, (Münster, 1927), 165. This was the essential Platonic legacy which William and others were attempting to preserve through their use of *integumentum.*

the Christian Trinity in Homer's Golden Chain.[112] In this text there is a recognition of the Macrobian program, for the *Deus* of Chalcidius's translation of Plato is obviously taken in the sense of God the Father and is not described as *integumentum*, but when the text speaks of the *tercium genus anime*, or World Soul, which William here identifies with the Holy Spirit,[113] he tells us that Plato is *"more suo per integumenta loquens."*[114] This involves an ambiguous relation to the Macrobian position, for in order to accommodate the Holy Spirit to the World Soul, *integumentum* is used to discern truths about the divine essence (in the person of the Holy Spirit) and not just lower spirits; but such ambiguity was an integral part of trying to find the Trinity in pagan philosophy. That such a program and point of view is operative in the case of the text from the *Glosae super Macrobium* is evident from the substantial identity of the two passages, despite the lack of specific mention of the *integumentum* in the earlier work; and, of course, the dimension of meaning implicit in both texts—that under poetic figures, myths and symbols are hidden deep philosophical truths— is part of the motive force, whether conscious or not, for the twelfth-century fascination with the *catena aurea Homeri*.

A second important point that becomes evident in a reading of these texts from William of Conches is that the emphasis is neither on the plenitude principle of Lovejoy (the universe must contain all possible beings), nor on the ascensional character that we spoke of earlier as being so important to the twelfth century; but is rather on the fundamental cosmic sense, that all things are bound together in a perfect order. The words *ordo, connexio, coniunctio* provide the leitmotif for an exposition that leads up to the central affirmation *"nulla est creatura que cum deo non obtineat aliquam similitudinem*

112. According to E. Jeauneau *integumentum* is so essential for William that "Ignorer la philosophie et ignorer la signification des *integumenta* ne sont donc, au fond, qu'une seule et même ignorance" (*Glosae,* p. 20).

113. As did Abelard, *Introductio in Theol.* I, 17 (*PL* 178, 1014A), who also found *integumentum* a valuable tool; cf. *Introductio* I, 20 (*PL* 178, 1022B). Cf. L. Ott, "Die Platonische Weltseele in der Theologie der Frühscholastik," *Parusia: Festgabe J. Hirschberger* (Frankfort, 1965), pp. 307–31.

114. Ed. *Jeauneau,* p. 156.

qualemcumque, et hec est rerum coniunctio," the *coniunctio* for which Homer's Golden Chain is the figure or *integumentum*. If the ascensional context is not explicit, and it is rather the sense of hierarchy and connection with God that William stresses in these first appearances of the theme in the twelfth century, it is nonetheless obvious that the wealth of the symbol implicitly hints at some of the future dimensions which were to become clear as the century progressed. The first of these is the anthropological dimension. In the *Glosae super Platonem*, William identifies the *tercium genus anime* only with the Holy Spirit,[115] and it seems that this holds true for the earlier *Glosae super Macrobium*.[116] Much of what William says in the latter text about the Holy Spirit was later seen to be incompatible with traditional notions of the third Person of the Trinity,[117] but could easily be applied to the human soul and become another symbol to express the microcosmic aspect of man, i.e., that his soul is the Golden Chain in sharing something with all the levels of the hierarchical universe. This is exactly what Isaac of Stella was to do in the passage from the *Epistola de Anima* which began our discussion. The other major hint at development, the combination of the *scala Jacob* with the *catena aurea*, appears in both passages, and to the best of my knowledge seems to be original with William; the appearance of this unique combination of symbols in Isaac is a convincing sign of his influence. Most importantly, the *scala Jacob* was an important influence in introducing the dynamic ascensional values of an ancient and complex Christian symbolic theme into the Macrobian image.

The significance of themes of ascent in general, and the ladder as a particular example, are well known in the history of religions and

115. This is why he is at such pains to explain that Plato's description of the Soul's (Holy Spirit's) formation from all kinds of natures and substances (a position unacceptable to a Christian) is *per integumenta* to be understood as "Deum fecisse animam aptam ad dividuum et individuum genus substantie vivificandum et discernendum et ad ea que in alique sunt eiusdem nature et in aliquo diverse, dicit Deum fecisse eam ex omni genere nature et substantie" (*ed. Jeauneau*, p. 150).

116. E.g., "anima *creavit* corpora," in line 2 of the text.

117. Especially ll. 4–9.

have been considered with specific relation to the twelfth century by several authors.[118] While the ladder of heaven is a common religious symbol, the story of the ladder of Jacob in the twenty-eighth chapter of Genesis gave it a special meaning for Christians.

The specific case that we are investigating here, the combination of the ladder of Jacob with a Platonic theme containing ascensional dimensions, may have had an important antecedent in the patristic period, if P. Courcelle is correct in asserting that one of the Greek Fathers (perhaps Gregory of Nyssa) may have compared the heavenly ladder of Plato's *Symposium* 211c with either the ladder of Jacob or the Gradual Psalms.[119] If such a passage did exist and survived into the twelfth century, it could have had an important effect on the stress on anagogic values that becomes strong in the later use of the *catena aurea* symbol. Such stress, as we have seen, was not prominent in William of Conches, though it was he who introduced the comparison; it is strong in the texts of Isaac, where the symbol is used of the five powers of the soul, always viewed in a highly anagogic way.[120] The double conjecture involved in the existence of such a text and knowledge of it in the twelfth century is not necessary, however, to explain the rapid growth of the ascensional aspect. There are two reasons why such stress should have come to the fore in the monastic circles of the twelfth century: the first was the influence of the anagogic world of the Pseudo-

118. E.g., G. de Champeaux and S. Sterckx, *Introduction au monde des symboles* (Paris, 1966), pp. 161–207, esp. p. 199; M.-M. Davy, *Initiation à la Symbolique Romaine (XIIe Siècle)* (Paris, 1964), pp. 223–4 and especially R. Javelet, *Image et Ressemblance,* I, 145–57, 371–6; II, cf. "Échelle" under "Table des Idées," p. 351.

119. P. Courcelle, "Tradition Neo-Platonicenne et traditions Chrétiennes de la 'region de dissemblance'," *AHDL,* XXXII (1957), 23. Courcelle notes the two passages are combined in Augustine, *Enarr. in Ps. 119, 2,* 3 (*CC* XL, 1777–8).

120. These dimensions are present, though not overt, in the passage quoted previously: e.g., "sapientia fortiter, ab archetypo quoque *trahens* in proprios status, ut sint quod sunt, et disponit omnia suaviter . . . [downward way], sic et anima illius sapientiae imago, si non degeneret, eam ubique libenter considerando *sequitur,* admirans et amans, investigans et laudans in omnibus [upward way]." *Epistola de Anima,* XVIII (1885 CD).

Dionysius on twelfth-century monasticism, as providing the milieu in which such patterns of emphasis would be natural; the second more traditional reason was specifically related to our symbol: the use of the ladder of Jacob by St Benedict as an image for the life of the monk.

Patristic exegesis of Gen 28:12 had been in general quite varied: the *scala Jacob* could signify the two testaments by which man ascends to God,[121] or be interpreted in a moral sense as the virtues or beatitudes,[122] or signify the evangelists and preachers of the Gospel, who ascend to God in contemplation in order to descend with the message of salvation to mankind,[123] or even be taken as the descent of Christ to man so that man might ascend to God.[124] The most significant patristic text occurs in the seventh chapter of the *Rule of St Benedict*, which, while remaining within the moralizing framework, in this case of the fundamental virtue of humility,[125] is open to anthropological and systematic dimensions that were to have great influence on the twelfth century.[126] Above all, in giving

---

121. E.g., Zeno of Verona (*PL* 11, 428A). Found in the twelfth century in Abelard, Sermo XXVIII (*PL* 178, 553 A–C).

122. E.g., Chromatius of Aquileia (*PL* 20, 328A); St Jerome, *Epist.* 98, 2 (*CSEL* 55, 186); St Basil, *Homilia in Ps.* I, 4 (*PG* 29, 218CD); while Rabanus Maurus interprets it as charity (*PL* 112, 1043B). The moral interpretation is still found in the twelfth century in Philip of Hervengt, who says that the two sides of the ladder are faith and hope (*PL* 203, 501D), and in Bruno of Asti, *In Gen.* 28 (*PL* 164, 208D–209A). Honorius Augustodunensis uses the fifteen steps of the Gradual Psalms as a moral *scala* in an analogous fashion (*PL* 172, 869–76; 1239–42).

123. The interpretation of Gregory the Great, *Registrum* I, 24 (*PL* 77, 748D), and Isidore of Seville (*PL* 83, 258B–D). Also found in the *Glossa ordinaria* (*PL* 113, 134A–D).

124. Augustine, *Enarr in Ps. 119*, 2, 3 (*CC* 40, pp. 1777–8).

125. "Unde, fratres, si summae humilitatis volumus culmen attingere et ad exaltationem illam caelestem, ad quam per praesentis vitae humilitatem ascenditur, volumus velociter pervenire, actibus nostris ascendentibus scala illa erigenda est, quae in somno Jacob apparuit, per quam ei descendentes et ascendentes angeli monstrabantur," *Regula* VII, 5–6 (ed. R. Hanslik, *CSEL* 75, 40).

126. "Latera enim eius scalae dicimus nostrum esse corpus et animam, in qua latera diversas gradus humilitatis vel disciplinae evocatio divina ascendendo inseruit," *Regula* VII, 9 (*op. cit.*, p. 41).

this text such an important place in his *Rule*, Benedict made it a part of the daily life of monasticism—something which the monk would continually hear, reflect upon, and seek to make meaningful in an intellectual way—thus assuring it a significant future. St Bernard's reaffirmation of this theme as central to the monastic life in his treatise *De Gradibus Humilitatis et Superbiae* is the best known fruit of this process of reflection,[127] though here the expression of the ascensional symbol is unaffected by the infusion of the special Platonic and Dionysian interests which influenced Isaac of Stella.

The use of the *scala Jacob* alone, without any specific identification with the *catena aurea,* is found in several of the most important mystic theologians of the mid-twelfth century with many of the same cosmic, anthropological, and anagogic shades of meaning that the combined symbol has in Isaac. Hugh of St Victor uses it in a passage in the *De Unione Corporis et Spiritus* that has many affinities to the passage from Isaac's *Epistola*;[128] and it is found in Godfrey of Admont, who, although he adopts it as a figure of the Blessed Virgin, also stresses its individual anagogic application to man.[129] Richard of St Victor bears the palm, however, for the most frequent use of the *scala Jacob*. His interpretation is invariably mystical; the ladder manifests the ascent to God from the visible things of this world to the invisible realities of contemplation. The goal is above, but the things of this world serve the important role which St Paul had already pointed out:

We are warned what we ought to seek in the question of divine things outside our experience from the things we know through

127. *Sancti Bernardi Opera,* III, 13–59, eds. J. Leclercq and H. M. Rochais (Rome, 1963), Chap. II, 3, refers to the *scala Jacob* in the terms of Benedict as the virtue of humility (*ed.,* p. 18), and IX, 24–7, does the same in an extended passage of great rhetorical power (*ed.,* pp. 35–7). For another use of the *scala* in Bernard, cf. J. Leclercq, "Nouveaux témoins de la *regio dissimilitudinis*," *Studia Anselmiana,* LIV (Rome, 1965), 141. On the cosmic picture and importance of ascension in Bernard, cf. W. Hiss, *Die Anthropologie Bernhards von Clairvaux* (Berlin, 1964), pp. 85–7; and G. B. "Burch, Introduction," *St Bernard: The Steps of Humility* (Notre Dame, 1963), pp. 101–7.

128. *PL* 177, 285B–86B.

129. *PL* 174, 1011A–D.

experience: "For the invisible things of God are beheld through
the understanding of created things." We who are men and
cannot fly are accustomed to use a ladder when we want to
climb up to high things. Let us then use the likeness of visible
things so that the things which we are not able to see in themselves through looking we may deserve to see from a mirror of
this kind and as it were through a mirror.[130]

Late twelfth-century usage of the *scala* tends to be somewhat more
fragmented in meaning and less frequent in occurrence: Joachim
of Fiore uses it in his *Concordia* as referring to the *Rule of Benedict,*[131]
and Alan of Lille in order to signify the ascent of the Catholic man
from the beginning of faith to its consummation in preaching.[132]

The use of the *catena aurea*, on the other hand, alone or in tandem
with the *scala Jacob*, is our main concern. Bernardus Silvestris
(c. 1150) in his famous cosmographic poem, the *De Mundi Universitate,* is the earliest witness outside that of William of Conches;[133]
as might be expected from his Chartrain spirit, he is most interested
in the symbol's power to manifest cosmic order and the relation of

130. "Ex rebus quas per experientiam novimus, admonemur quid circa
inexperta et divina quaerere debeamus: Invisibilia enim Dei per ea quae facta
sunt intellecta conspiciuntur (Rom 1:20). Ubi ad alta conscendere volumus,
scala quidem uti solemus, nos qui homines sumus et volare non possumus.
Rerum ergo visibilium similitudine pro scala utamur, ut que in semetipsis per
speciem videre non valemus, ex ejusmodi specula et velut per speculum videre
mereamur." *De Trinitate,* V, 6 (*ed. J. Ribaillier,* p. 201; *PL* 196, 952D). That
this comment is to be seen in the light of the *scala Jacob* from Gen 28, 12,
becomes clear from comparable passages where specific reference is made to
that text; cf. *PL* 196, 1111C–1112C; 1219B–C. Compare with *Benj. Min.* II,
12 (*PL* 196, 89D–90A) and *De Trinitate* I, C. 10 (*ed. Ribaillier,* p. 95; *PL* 196
895D), where again no mention is made of the Genesis passage. On the use,
of *scala* images in Richard, cf. A.-M. Ethier, *Le 'De Trinitate' de Richard de
St Victor* (Paris, 1939), pp. 57–8; H. de Lubac, *Exégèse Médiévale,* II, 11,
175–6, who ties in these passages with a long tradition of exegesis of
Rom 1:20.

131. *Concordia,* Chap. 48 (Venice ed. 1519, f. 83A–B).

132. *Summa de Arte Praedicatoria,* Praefatio (*PL* 210, 111A–C.).

133. Dedicated to Thierry of Chartres during the pontificate of Eugene III
(1145–53); cf. J. de Ghellinck, *L'Essor de la Littérature latine au XIIe Siècle*
(Brussels, 1955), p. 64. Cf. also E. Curtius, *op. cit.,* pp. 110–11.

microcosm and macrocosm. His is also the strongest witness to Lovejoy's principle of continuity in the twelfth century, as the stress on *"nihil vel dissipabile vel abruptum"* in the Chain indicates.[134] The *aurea catena* is also used in an anonymous medieval *Cosmographia* which is clearly dependent on William's interpretation, and may come from the mid-twelfth century.[135] Isaac's texts, dating from the 1160's, return to William of Conches's combination of the two symbols to draw out the richness of implications which attempt to fit the renewed Platonic tradition into the framework of medieval monasticism.[136] The fullness of these implications will only be evident after our analysis of Isaac's theology of man. A number of interesting texts from the latter part of the twelfth century show that the symbolic theme maintained its vitality, if not the central position it had in Isaac, during this period. Simon of Tournai (†1201) witnesses to the combination of the biblical and Hellenic images within a strongly Dionysian-Erigenean framework where the ladder or chain signifies the grades of angels by which

134. "In Deo, in noy scientia est, in caelo ratio, in sideribus intellectus. In magno vero animali cognitio viget, viget et sensus causarum praecedentium fomitibus enutritus. Ex mente enim caelum, de caelo sidera, de sideribsu mundus, unde viveret, unde discerneret, linea continuationis excepit. Mundus enim quiddam continuum et in ea catena nihil vel dissipabile vel abruptum." *De mundi universitate libri duo, sive Megacosmos et Microcosmos,* I, 4, edd. C. S. Barach and J. J. Wrobel (Innsbruck, 1876), p. 31. Bernard uses it elsewhere: "In lunari enim limite, ubi aureae Homeri quasi medietas est catenae, superioris inferiorisque mundi videlicet umbilicus, spirituum numerus ad milia circumfusus populosae more civitatis laetabundus occurrit." II, 7 (*ed. Barach-Wrobel,* p. 47, corrected according to A. Vernet's unpublished edition cited by E. Jeauneau, *"Integumentum* chez Guillaume de Conches," p. 68, n. 1). William had adverted to the principle of continuity (Appendix ll. 9–13), but not given it much emphasis.

135. *Cosmographia* contained in Munich, CLM 331 (F.8ᵛ): "Assignat Homerus auream catenam quam dicit de celo pendere, et in principio et summitate catene ponit Deum, et in secundo loco ponit noym id est mentem, in tertio loco ponit animam mundi, in quarto loco ponit quattuor elementa et omnes res temporales." (Cited in E. Jeauneau, *ibid.*)

136. The *scala* theme alone appears clearly in other passages of Isaac, e.g., Sermo IX (1722D); Sermo XI (1730C), and with reference to Jacob, in the *Epistola de Officio Missae* (1894 C–D).

divine knowledge comes to man and man ascends to God.[137] Alexander Neckham (1157–1217), an Englishman with that taste for scientific observation, encyclopedic curiosity and wide knowledge of the classics which characterized many medieval Englishmen,[138] made use of the *aurea catena* in his *De Naturis Rerum*.[139] The most interesting of these appearances, however, is in a curious passage in Absalom of St Victor (†1203)[140] where Homer's Golden Chain is joined to the Golden Bough of Virgil in a felicitous passage which, if it lacks any great intellectual depth, is at least suffused with that particular humanist coloring that was so characteristic of the twelfth century.[141]

137. "Hee ergo trium specierum theophanie tres diffinitiones IX concludunt ordines angelorum. Hac distinctione angelorum texitur aurea catena hominum, sive scala Jacob in qua vidit angelos ascendentes et descendentes, id est sanctos qui instinctu angelorum promoti primo prophetant minora, secundo, ulterius ascendentes, instinctu archangelorum praedicant maiora; tertio, ulterius provecti, instinctu Virtutum faciunt signa et miracula, et sic Ypophanie gradibus transcursis ascendunt ad Yperphaniam," *Sententiae,* ed. M.-Th. d'Alverny, *Alain de Lille: Textes inédites* (Paris, 1965), p. 312; cf. also H. Dondaine, "Cinq citations de Jean Scot chez Simon de Tournai," *RTAM,* XVII (1950), pp. 303–11.

138. J. de Ghellinck, *op. cit.,* pp. 150–155.

139. "Nolo tamen ut opinetur lector me naturas rerum fugere volentes investigare velle philosophice aut physice, moralem enim libet instituere tractatum. *Auream igitur Homeri catenam* aliis relinquo, quo in libertatem proclamo de qua in Evangelio dicitur, 'Si vos Filius liberavit, vere liberi eritis.' " A marginal note (whether by Alexander or not, the editor does not indicate), adds: "Aurea catena Homeri dicitur philosophica eruditio, quae nunc in diffinitiva speculatione ad generalissima ascendit, nunc per divisiones ad singularia descendit." Ed. T. Wright, *Alexandri Neckham De naturis rerum* (London, 1863; Rolls Series, vol. 34), pp. 2–3.

140. On Absalom of St Victor, cf. C. Oudin, *Commentarius de Scriptoribus ecclesiasticis* (Leipzig, 1722), II, cc. 1713–14; V. Rouzies, *DTC,* I, c. 133; H. de Lubac, *Exégèse Médiévale,* II, 1, p. 371.

141. "Unde et duo philosophorum peritissimi, cum mundi gloriam et sanctam conversationem, quae est in Christo Jesu vellent typice figurare, alter earum inferni ingressu arborem habentem ramum aureum descripsit: alter vere catenam auream de caelo in terras dependentem somniavit. Quid aliud, quaeso, per ramum illum aureum, quam mundi hujus decor et gloria significatur? quae et in introitu inferni ideo esse dicitur, quia per amorem huius mundi ejus amatores ad infernum transmittuntur. Timeat ergo omne semen

The later use of the Golden Chain of Homer lies outside the ambit of our consideration; its role in philosophy and theology, as well as in literature, was to be a long and varied one, though the nuances were never quite the same as they were in the twelfth century.[142] In the thirteenth century the term *catena aurea* came to be widely used for the collections of biblical texts and commentaries popular at the time; in the same century, we find it used by Boethius of Dacia in a more philosophical sense.[143] Finally, Meister Eckhart combines the *aurea catena* and *scala Jacob* in a text from one of his sermons that indicates an acquaintance with the hierarchical aspect of the twelfth-century use.[144]

Arthur O. Lovejoy's account of the Great Chain of Being fastened upon an eighteenth-century conception as an essential idea in the history of Western thought. In exposing the importance of the Great Chain, in tracing it back to its roots in the Golden Age of Greek philosophy, and in discerning the key position of Neoplatonism in its evolution, Lovejoy's book was of real significance. Our textual study of the symbol of the *aurea catena Homeri*, one of the expressions of the Great Chain of Being, however, highlights two grave weaknesses in Lovejoy's approach, at least as applied to the medieval period. The texts we have studied indicate that Lovejoy's conceptual patterns of plenitude and continuity do not exhaust the twelfth-century manifestations of the Chain of Being. The first appearances of the *catena aurea* in William of Conches and

---

Israel hanc arborem contingere, quia facilis descensus Averni. Sed revocare gradum, superasque evadere ad auras, hic labor, hic gemitus. Sed et alter per catenam auream vitam sanctorum voluit significare, quae in terris constituta coelestibus tantum jungitur sancta meditatione, pia devotione, sicut dicit Apostolus: Nostra autem conversatio in coelis est. Et si enim viri religiosi in terra sunt positi, virtutum tamen gradibus et bonis operibus quasi per catenam sunt connexi." Sermo IV (*PL* 211, 36D–37A.)

142. Cf. Lovejoy, *The Great Chain of Being,* and E. Wolff, *Die Goldene Kette,* for the later history.

143. Boetius de Dacia, *Tractatus de mundi aeternitate* (2nd ed.), ed. Geza Sajo (Budapest, 1964), p. 53, l. 569. Here it is used as referring to God's conservation of all things in a distinctly Platonic setting.

144. In *Lib. Parab. Gen.,* from Cod. Cus. 21, f. 39^v, cited in V. Lossky, *Théologie negative chez Maître Eckhart* (Paris, 1960), p. 351, n. 53.

Bernardus Silvestris are variations on the cosmic sense basic to the symbol since Homer, the *aurea catena* as an expression of the order of the world. In the second half of the century, William of Conches's fusing of the *catena aurea* and the *scala Jacob* is the source of Isaac of Stella's combination of the Greek cosmic sense with the ascensional, anagogic dimensions of traditional monasticism (here influenced by Dionysian theology), and for his development of the anthropological and microcosmic aspects implicit in the traditional symbol. This also indicates that the value of the *catena aurea-scala Jacob*, either as a key to the theology of Isaac,[145] or in its more general aspects as a form of twelfth-century thought, cannot be measured by a narrow conceptual yardstick, but rather must be seen as a symbolic mode which helped to manifest the sense of separation, the desire for unification, and the dynamic manner of the realization of this which were essential contributions of the thought of late antiquity—both pagan Neoplatonism and patristic theology—to the twelfth century. Only by paying close attention to the variations in historical context and by recognizing the symbolic nature of the operation of the Great Chain can we hope to do justice to its role in twelfth-century intellectual history.

The twelfth-century symbol, a synthetic force within its own cultural and religious world, fragmented in later historical contexts. But our concern is not in attempting to demonstrate some kind of perennial validity for this particular symbolic form, but rather in tracing the long and involved history of its use. In the face of

145. The central importance of the *aurea catena* in Isaac's theology has been recognized by R. Javelet, *Image et Ressemblance,* I, 152–7, 453. "Hugues complète donc les chartrains en ce qu'il double le dynamisme causal de la création de son dynamisme final. D'autre part, il introduit en ce cycle une axiologie des êtres où la 'proximite' est participation à l'Être et affinité vers lui, ou parenté. C'est la notion commune au XIIe siècle. Celui qui l'enseigne avec le plus d'originalité est Isaac de l'Étoile dont les 'connexions' manifestent un univers où toute s'enchaine, où tout 'tuile.' Souvent on rencontre la comparaison de l'échelle de Jacob, frémissante de la descente et de la montée des anges. Elle exprime l'intercommunication des hiérarchies, le procès de Dieu jusqu'aux confins de son oeuvre et le procès inverse de cette oeuvre au Créateur" (p. 453).

history's sublime indifference, the symbol is important not for what it said but for what it did. In enabling man to feel at home in the world, in giving him a sense of the unity of all being with God, in inviting him to the arduous ascent to which his nature called him, and in allowing him to unify the intellectual tradition to which he was heir, Homer's Golden Chain played a not unworthy role on the brilliant stage of twelfth-century intellectual life.

CHAPTER III

THE UNDERSTANDING OF MAN IN
ISAAC OF STELLA

IF OUR STUDY OF THE *CATENA AUREA* has indicated the complexity of the background of this symbol and something of the originality of Isaac's use of it, the necessity still remains of demonstrating the claim that it serves as the best interpretive tool for grasping all the dimensions of the Abbot of Stella's thought on the mystery of man. Such a demonstration should indicate that the dimensions of manifestation uncovered in our analysis of the symbol—cosmic order, continuity, microcosm, anagogy, and the like—are the essential themes of Isaac's theological anthropology. If this be the case, then the explicit appearance of the symbol in his works, especially in the all-important *Epistola de Anima,* cannot be viewed as a mere passing illustration, but must be understood as at the core of his entire doctrine. This is not to deny that Isaac's works have a coherent logical order, a conceptual development which demonstrates the rigor and clarity of the Abbot's mind. What is proposed here is rather that the underlying ground that offered the themes and insights for such organization was the symbolic understanding of man, rooted in the history of Platonism, whose riches are manifested in the *catena aurea Homeri.*

ORIGINS OF THE TWELFTH-CENTURY INTEREST IN ANTHROPOLOGY

Before turning to this analysis of Isaac's anthropology, it may help to make a few tentative suggestions concerning the origins of

H

the intensive concern of the twelfth century with the mystery of man.

The metaphors that come to mind upon even a cursory acquaintance with the twelfth-century world are those of "vitality," "creativity," "expansiveness," "variety," "openness," and even the overused term "Renaissance." The problem with such terminology is enhanced by the difficulty of forging more adequate explanatory tools, even after a wider knowledge of the period. Rather than using any variations upon the traditional metaphors of "the twelfth-century Renaissance,"[1] "the passage from Epic to Romance,"[2] "the open society of the twelfth century,"[3] "the contrast between monastic and scholastic theology,"[4] or even the "creativity of the twelfth century," I should like to introduce the

1. First popularized by H. Haskins, *The Renaissance of the 12th Century* (Cambridge, 1927), it was adopted by G. Paré, A. Brunet, and P. Tremblay in their 1933 work, *La Renaissance du XIIe Siècle: Les Écoles et L'Enseignement.* Since then it has remained popular among French scholars, e.g., the first chapter of M.-D. Chenu's classic, *La Théologie au douzième siècle,* and the most recent twelfth-century study edited by M. de Gandillac and E. Jeauneau, *Entretiens sur la Renaissance de 12e Siècle* (Paris, 1968). Greater reservations about the value of the term have been expressed in the English-speaking world, cf. W. A. Nitze, "The So-Called 12th Century Renaissance," *Speculum,* XXIII (1948), 464–71; E. M. Sanford, "The Twelfth Century—Renaissance or Proto-Renaissance?", *Speculum,* XXVI (1951), 635–42; and especially the strictures of N. F. Cantor, *Medieval History* (New York, 1963), pp. 367–70 and K. F. Morrison, "Church, Reform, and Renaissance," *Life and Thought in the Early Middle Ages* (Minneapolis, 1967), pp. 143–59. For a confused reaction in favor to the term, cf. U. T. Holmes, "The Idea of a Twelfth Century Renaissance," *Speculum,* XXVI (1951), 648–51. The whole topic should be considered in light of E. Panofsky's famous essay, "Renaissance and Renascences," *Kenyon Review,* VI (1944), 201–36.

2. The title of the last chapter of R. W. Southern's perceptive *The Making of the Middle Ages,* Yale paperback ed. (New Haven, 1963), esp. pp. 221–2. It is taken from W. P. Ker's 1896 work on Medieval literature, *Epic and Romance.*

3. The interpretation of F. Heer, *The Medieval World: Europe 1100–1350,* Mentor paperback ed. (New York, 1963), cf. Chap. I.

4. This is an admittedly over-simplified way of expressing the point of J. Leclercq's *The Love of Learning and the Desire for God,* Mentor paperback ed. (New York, 1962).

tension between concept and symbol discussed in Chapter II as an admittedly general, but still useful way of understanding the era and its renewal of interest in anthropology.

Both the logical and the symbolic mentality are necessary expressions of human intentionality; their cohabitation, mutuality, and interdependence are essential to the intellectual life of a society. As man advances to a clear, rational, conceptual, differentiated knowledge of himself and the world around him, he at the same time experiences the need to keep some form of contact with the mysterious and the unknown by a return to the symbolic images which manifest what he cannot conceptualize. As Bernard Lonergan puts it: "Though the field of mystery is contracted by the advance of knowledge it cannot be eliminated from human living."[5] In fact, the very increase of knowledge demands a return to the sensitive level, for "even adequate self-knowledge and explicit metaphysics may contract but cannot eliminate a 'known unknown,' and . . . cannot issue into a control of human living without being transposed into dynamic images which make sensible to human sensitivity what human intelligence reaches for or grasps."[6] That both modes of intentionality are found throughout the history of human culture in some way or other is obvious; the important point is the manner and proportion in which they are found.

The importance of the revival of logic in the late tenth century, its gradual growth through the eleventh, and its magnificent flowering in the twelfth, does not need to be stressed here.[7] "Logic was an instrument of order in a chaotic world;"[8] it was the tool which gave men hope of improving a stagnant and confused society; it differentiated, clarified, organized, rationalized, not only theology, but law and government as well. The flowering of the logical mentality was a momentous event in the history of theology:

5. *Insight*, p. 546.

6. *Op. cit.*, p. 548. I am indebted here to the section on "The Notion of Mystery," pp. 546–9.

7. For a broad cultural appreciation, cf. R. W. Southern, *op. cit.*, Chap. IV, "The Tradition of Thought," pp. 170–84.

8. Southern, *op. cit.*, p. 179.

the posing of the question of the possibility and desirability of a separate and differentiated, properly scientific, theological context distinct from the patristic context where dogmatic statement, theological speculation, and religious experience coexisted in a largely undifferentiated manner. So many of the new theological concepts of the twelfth century are obviously the fruit of this mentality that for many scholars—especially those who reduce the theology of the period to the development of Early Scholasticism —virtually nothing else of importance exists.

But the world of conceptual knowledge is not the only face of twelfth-century theology. The researches of the last generation, beginning from the investigation of what Jean Leclercq called "monastic theology,"[9] broadening through research into the theology of the Clerks Regular, particularly of the important School of St Victor, and of such significant episcopal schools as that of Chartres, have disclosed a dimension of twelfth-century theology that cuts across the simple separation of monastic from scholastic theology, and can best be understood as a form of theology in which symbolic intentionality is dominant. M.-D. Chenu's remark: *"Dans toute sa culture, le moyen âge est l'âge du symbole, autant et plus que celui de la dialectique,"*[10] is especially true of the twelfth century.

The dimensions of the symbol as cultural form provide us with a better understanding of both the continuity and the novelty of twelfth-century thought in relation to its classical and patristic inheritance than does the overused concept of "Renaissance." Granted that the basic categories used by twelfth-century authors are those which the patristic legacy made available to them, there is newness, not only in the conceptional movements spurred on by the fascination with logic, but also on the symbolic side of the twelfth-century effort. In the *Epistola de Anima* of Isaac of Stella,

9. Cf. *The Love of Learning and the Desire for God* and "St. Bernard et la théologie monastique du XII^c siècle," *Saint Bernard Théologien, Analecta Sacri Ordinis Cisterciensis*, IX (1953), 10–16. E. Gilson's *The Mystical Theology of St Bernard*, first published in 1934, was an early classic of this interest.

10. *La Théologie au 12e Siècle*, p. 161.

we see a new religious experience attempting to bring itself to speech in the traditional symbols, an experience that demonstrates its specific character at times by new combinations and enrichenings of the old themes, at times by transformations and transvaluations in terms of a new historical context. It is a form of originality difficult to recover, because its richest fruit is achieved as a result of the process that cannot be penetrated by the traditional tools of analysis: along with differentiations leading to clarification of particular issues, we have combinations leading to synthesis of themes; along with analytical procedures working within a conceptual framework, we have images and allegories that organize in a manner analogous to the symbolic modes studied by comparative religion; finally, along with conclusions which attempt to specify what can be known and said about a particular problem in the context of the scientific world, we have rhetorical, poetical— but still theological—statements which aim at making present the unknown dimensions of the experience that is attempting to bring itself to speech.

The tension between concept and symbol helps us to recapture the fullness of the twelfth-century theological world; it also helps to clarify what usually goes under the vague heading of its "vitality" and "creativity," too. The increment to theological effort from the application of logical systematization does not need to be emphasized here. Many excellent studies of this movement already exist. Stimulated in part by a new interest in the classics of the symbolic tradition (e.g., the influence of the Dionysian tradition), but most of all by the perennial need for mystery to be made present in the world of human meaning—especially when new concepts, differentiations, schematizations, and a logic that promised answers for so many questions confronted it with the threat of elimination— the symbolic mentality was stimulated to produce achievements in a wide variety of fields. The process of rediscovery, challenge and fertilization of the two modes of intention, and the accompanying bewildering richness of achievement, are what give the twelfth century its unusual fascination and its resistance to simple classification.

At the center of these currents was the mystery of man. The vigor of the logical mentality gave the men of the twelfth century a self-confidence, an *élan* that moved them to prodigious efforts, from the practical adventure of organizing governments, guilds, legal systems, and wholly new educational institutions, to the intellectual effort of ordering their traditional heritage and giving it a new form. New conceptual insights into the problems of men in society were complemented by similar insights into philosophical and theological anthropology, e.g., the problem of human knowing (the famous discussions about universals), the composition of the human body (the medical and scientific interest) and such controverted questions as the origin of the human soul (one of the earliest triumphs of conceptual theology was the clear affirmation of creationism, a step beyond the hesitations of the patristic era). At the same time, the gap between these conceptual conquests and the full human world of expression was intense. Lonergan notes that when new ideas are coming to speech, "the tension between meaning and expression will be at its maximum at the beginning of the movement;"[11] such a gap, along with the age-old consciousness of the mysterious dimensions of human existence, heightened by the intellectual and social advances of the period, provided an ideal milieu for an anthropology with a sharp awareness of the symbolic dimension of the human mystery. M.-D. Chenu has already drawn attention to the existence of such an anthropology in the twelfth century.[12] It is against this background that Isaac of Stella's *Epistola de Anima* must be viewed.

AN INTRODUCTION TO THE ANTHROPOLOGY OF
ISAAC OF STELLA: SERMON TWO

What were the forms in which the twelfth-century symbolic tradition, and Isaac of Stella in particular, expressed this under-

11. *Insight,* p. 592.
12. Chenu, *op. cit.,* pp. 37–43, 164–6.

standing of man? One of the most common—of special interest in demonstrating the heritage from which the twelfth century sprang —Isaac puts in the following way:

> If you wish to know yourself, to possess yourself, go within to yourself, and do not seek yourself without. You are one thing, what is yours is another, what is around you yet a third. Around you is the world, the body is yours, you have been made within to the image and likeness of God. Return, therefore, "sinner, within, to where you really are, to the heart." Outside you are an animal made according to the image of the world, so that man is said to be a world in miniature; within you are a man made to the image of God so that you are able to be made divine. Therefore, brothers, is not a man who has returned to himself like that younger son, the prodigal, who only found himself in a distant country, in the region of unlikeness, "in the foreign land," where he would sit and weep while he remembered his father and his homeland?[13]

"Know Thyself"

This rich passage from the Second Sermon for the Feast of All Saints introduces a group of themes and reminiscences which are at the heart of Isaac's anthropology. The human situation expressed, the desire for self-knowledge, is common to men of all ages; but here it takes a uniquely Hellenic-Christian form: the appearance of the maxim fallen from heaven and inscribed on the temple of Delphi—*cognosce teipsum, know thyself*! The history of the Delphic

---

13. "Si vis teipsum cognoscere, te possidere, intra ad teipsum nec te quaesieris extra. Aliud tu, aliud tui, aliud circa te. Circa te mundus, tui corpus, tu ad imaginem et similitudinem Dei factus intus. Redi igitur, *praevaricator, intus, ubi tu es, ad cor*. (Is 46:8) Foris pecus es ad imaginem mundi, unde et minor mundus dicitur homo; intus homo ad imaginem Dei, unde et potes deificari. Itaque in semetipsum homo, fratres, reversus, sicut iunior ille prodigus filius, quo se invenit, nisi in regione longinqua, in regione dissimilitudinis, *in terra aliena* (Ex 2:22; Ps 136:4), ubi sedeat et fleat, dum recordetur patris et patriae?" Sermon II, 13, *ed. Hoste*, p. 106 (1695c).

maxim has been ably treated by a number of scholars;[14] through them we can trace the background of the combination of themes which this particular passage illustrates.

The original meaning of the maxim is purely Hellenic: a warning against *hubris* and a plea for moderation, the recognition that man is but a man and the gods are jealous.[15] Socrates begins the development of the theme by turning the maxim toward an investigation of the nature and ethical conduct of man. Plato, theologian of the Gentiles, rises to the higher viewpoint which determines the future of the saying; for him if the soul sees the Divine, it will acquire a better knowledge of itself, since it resembles the Divine in its most noble part.[16] The relation of the knowledge of God to the knowledge of self becomes standard in the late Hellenistic period,[17] and remains so throughout the tradition, whether the direction is from knowledge of self to knowledge of God, or vice versa. Philo is the first to begin to bring the maxim into the biblical milieu,[18] a practice that is continued by the more philosophical of the Fathers,

14. Especially A. Altmann, "The Delphic Maxim in Medieval Islam and Judaism," *Biblical and Other Studies* (Cambridge, 1963), pp. 196–232 and P. Courcelle, "Nosce Teipsum du Bas-Empire au haut Moyen-Âge. L'Heritage Profane et les Developpements Chrétiens," *Il Passagio dall' Antichita al Medioevo in Occidente,* Settimane di Studio del Centro Italiano sull'alto Medioevo IX (Spoleto, 1962), 263–95. For the medieval use, also L. de Bazelaire, "Connaissance de Soi," *DS,* fasc. XIII (Paris, 1950), cc. 1511–43; E. Gilson, *The Spirit of Medieval Philosophy,* Chap. XI, "Self-Knowledge and Christian Socratism," (New York, 1940), pp. 209–28; E. Bertola, "Il Socratismo Christiano nel XII Secolo," *Rivista di Filosofia Neo-Scolastica,* LI (1959), 252–64; R. Javelet, *Image et Ressemblance,* I, 368–71 and M.-M. Davy, *Initiation à la Symbolique Roman,* pp. 42–6.

15. Altmann, *op. cit.,* p. 199. Cf. *Charmides* 164d; Xenophon, *Memorabilia* IV, 11, 24–9 (*Loeb ed.,* pp. 286–8).

16. *First Alcibiades* 132c–33c (*Loeb ed.,* pp. 208–12). I am presuming that the *First Alcibiades* reflects the teaching of Plato, if not being actually from the pen of Plato himself. As Altmann observes, *op. cit.,* p. 200, the usage implies the Empedoclean idea of like being known by like.

17. Stoic doctrine (as represented by Cicero following Posidonius, e.g., *Somn. Scip.* VIII, 2) tends to stress the dignity of man as a partaker of the divine. Cf. Altmann, *op. cit.,* pp. 200–1; Courcelle, *op. cit.,* p. 266.

18. Courcelle, *op. cit.,* pp. 266–7; Altmann, *op. cit.,* p. 223.

such as Clement of Alexandria, Origen, and the Cappadocians among the Greeks, Ambrose, and especially Augustine among the Latins, and Boethius and the Pseudo-Dionysius at the end of the patristic era.[19] The picture is complicated, because, as A. Altmann has pointed out, two further series of motifs combine with the soul's-likeness-to-God understanding of the Delphic maxim. Microcosmic themes, with a long history of their own, are first associated with the maxim in Porphyry;[20] and from Plotinus comes the notion that the soul knows itself by withdrawal from the external world and turning to the *nous* that is above.[21] Christian authors tend to stress the spiritual implications of *cognosce teipsum*, without losing sight of the wealth of motifs acquired over the course of the centuries.[22]

The passage in Isaac combines these dimensions in a fashion that makes it a good example of the almost magnetic attraction which such symbolic motifs had for each other. Since the *cognosce teipsum* theme is found in a wide variety of patristic and intermediary sources, and since Isaac's other statements on the necessity of self-knowledge are rather general,[23] it is difficult to be more precise about the exact provenance of his treatment, though the threefold pattern of *"aliud tu, aliud tui, aliud circa te"* is found in

19. Altmann, *op. cit.,* pp. 201–2; Courcelle, *op. cit.,* pp. 270–3, 275–86, 288–9; de Bazelaire, *op. cit.,* cc. 1516–18.

20. On Porphyry's treatise *On 'Know Thyself,'* cf. Altmann, *op. cit.,* pp. 213–22. Cf. also A. Altmann and S. M. Stern, *Isaac Israeli* (Oxford, 1958), pp. 202–8.

21. Altmann, "The Delphic Maxim," pp. 222–3. E.g., *Enn.,* V, 1, 1; V, 3–7; VI, 7, 41; VI, 9, 7.

22. Courcelle, *op. cit.,* pp. 293–4.

23. (a) *"Dum igitur ad seipsum advertitur homo,* sive ad suum sensum, sive ad voluntatem, sive etiam ad rationem, licet eo usque profecerit ut iumentum exuens, hominem induat . . ."* (1745D; *ed. Hoste,* p. 312).

(b) "Quis enim seipsum vidit? *Quis agnovit se?* Dico imaginem et similitudinem Dei, ad imaginem et similitudinem Dei? *Qui similium alterum novit, utrumque novit; et qui alterutrum non novit, neutrum novit.* Itaque anima que per se debuit Deum noscere supra se, perdidit seipsam noscere in se, et angelum iuxta se." (*Epistola de Anima,* XX, 1886C).

the *In Hexaemeron* of St Ambrose.[24] Other aspects of the passage, such as the notion of man returning to himself (*"Itaque in semetipsum homo . . . reversus"*) are more in line with Augustine's use of a theme combining Plotinus, Porphyry, and possibly Philo.[25] The strong stress on the mutuality of knowledge of God and knowledge of self in the *Epistola de Anima* text repeats one of Augustine's favorite themes.[26] Whatever may be the precise sources of his use, the traditional motif of the necessity of self-knowledge is a significant starting point for Isaac's theory of man. He was taking his place in one of the most popular movements in twelfth-century anthropology, the movement that E. Gilson has called "Christian Socratism."[27]

The Themes of Interiorization and the Inner Man

The mere appearance of the theme of self-knowledge is not as significant as the complexity of values and symbols associated with it. Rather than following any strict line of logical argumentation,

24. *"Attende,* inquit, *tibi soli* (Deut, 4, 9): *aliud enim sumus nos, aliud sunt nostra, aliud quae circa nos sunt.* Nos sumus, hoc est, anima et mens; nostra sunt corporis membra et sensus ejus, circa nos autem pecunia est, servi sunt et vitae istius apparatus. Tibi igitur attende et teipsum scito . . ." (*In Hex.* 6. 7, 42 (*PL* 14, 258A). Cf. also *De bono mortis* 7, 27 (*PL* 14, 553C).

25. "Et inde admonitus *redire ad memetipsum* intravi in intima mea, *duce te:* et potui, quoniam factus es, adjutor meus" (*Conf.* VII, 10; ed. *Wangnereck,* p. 239). The characteristic Neoplatonic notion of "returning to oneself" is equated with "receiving oneself back" in *De Ordine* I, 1, 3 (*PL* 32, 479); its source may have been Porphyry, cf. Altmann, "Delphic Maxim . . .," p. 224. Courcelle, *op. cit.,* p. 284, suggests that there was a precedent in Philo, *De migratione Abraham* 174 (*Loeb ed.* IV, 232), for combining the theme of journey of the soul with the idea of God acting as a guide.

26. Courcelle, *op. cit.,* p. 283.

27. No attempt will be made here to list the numerous appearances of the theme of self-knowledge (with or without explicit mention of the Delphic maxim) in twelfth-century authors; exact citations may be found in the relevant works of Gilson, de Bazelaire, Courcelle, Bertola, Javelet, and Davy already mentioned. Some idea of its popularity may be gathered from the fact that among the Cistercians, besides Isaac, it is very important to Bernard, and also found in William of St Thierry, Aelred of Rievaulx, the anonymous *De Anima* of Ms. Vat. Lat. 175, the anonymous *De Spiritu et Anima* (sometimes

the themes suggest and envelop each other. First, the theme of interiorization, i.e., that true self-knowledge must be sought by going within (*"intra ad teipsum nec te quaesieris extra"*), is clearly conditioned by the Christian acceptance of the Greek dichotomy of soul and body. Plotinus had stressed the necessity of movement within, and it must be remembered that metaphorically speaking to move within and to move above are the same in the Plotinian system.[28] Augustine, following Plotinus, is the great witness in patristic literature for the journey within as the only road back to God. Isaac is usually more interested in ascensional imagery; his strongly Dionysian temper and the central symbol of the *catena aurea* conspire to make images and symbols of ascent among the most popular in his writings;[29] but a passage from the *Epistola de Anima,* in true Neoplatonic fashion, identifies moving within and moving above.[30] Augustine is the most likely source for this identification; indeed, in the *Confessions* IV, 12, in combining ascensional and interiorization metaphors, we find him quoting

---

ascribed to Alcher), Thomas of Cîteaux, Garnier of Rochefort, Helinand of Froidmont, and the anonymous *De Cognitione Humanae Conditionis* and *De Interiori Domo* (sometimes ascribed to St Bernard). Among the Victorines it plays an important role in the thought of both Hugh and Richard of St Victor, and in such lesser known Victorines as Hugh of Fouilloy. It is also known to John of Salisbury, Alan of Lille, Wibold, Philip of Harvengt, Martin of Léon, and the anonymous *Vitis Mystica (PL* 184). In passing, it may be mentioned that explicit mention of the maxim as descending from heaven was available to the twelfth century through Macrobius's repetition of a line from Juvenal in *Comm. in Somnium Scip.* I, 9, 2 *(ed. Willis,* p. 40).

28. Cf. P. Henry, "Introduction: Plotinus' Place in the History of Thought," in Plotinus, *The Enneads,* trans. by S. MacKenna (London, n.d.), pp. xiv–xviii, for "ascent" and "interiorization" as two of Plotinus's favorite metaphors of the mystical experience. Two of the most striking passages of the *Enneads* make the identity clear, *Enn.* I, 6, 8–9; V, 8, 10.

29. Taken in the most general sense, ascensional themes and images appear in 1691A-D; 1697B; 1705B; 1706D; 1709A; 1713C-D; 1714D; 1722D; 1724D; 1726D; 1730A-D; 1732C-D; 1737D; 1738D-39A; 1756C-D; 1760B; 1775D; 1778A-C; 1784C; 1786D-87B; 1788A-C; 1790C; 1798B; 1829A-33C (Sermon on Ascension); 1845A-B; 1848B-C; 1862D; 1867D-68B; 1874B; 1880A-B; 1884D-85D; 1890C-91A; 1894C-D; Sermo 55 *(ed. Leclercq),* lines 40, 69–70.

30. Paragraph VIII (1880B).

the same Scripture text for interiorization as Isaac does here, Isaiah 46:8.[31]

Though not explicitly mentioned in this passage, the aura of another theme of the Hellenic-Biblical tradition is manifestly present. Plato had spoken of the interior man, i.e., the soul (e.g., *Rep.* IX, 589a), a statement which provided an opening for the grafting of the Platonic distinction of body and soul upon the differently-intentioned, but easily confused, Pauline contrast between the inner and outer man (e.g., Rom 7:22; II Cor 4:16). Its frequent appearance in Augustine[32] was enough to insure its popularity in the medieval tradition. We find it used at least eight times by Isaac,[33] as well as by a good number of his contemporaries.[34] As one of the strongest Platonic elements in his thought, its

31. "Non enim fecit [God] atque abiit, sed ex illo in illo sunt. Ecce ubi est, ubi sapit veritas. Intimus cordi est, sed cor erravit ab eo. *Redit praevaricatores ad cor* (Is 46:8) et inhaerete illi qui fecit vos. . . . Quaerite quod quaeritis: sed ibi non est ubi quaeritis. Beatam vitam quaeritis *in regione mortis,* non est illic. . . . Nunquid et post descensum vitae, *non vultis ascendere et vivere?* Sed quo ascendistis, quando in alto estis, et posuistis in caelum os vestrum? *Descendite, ut ascendatis, et ascendatis ad Deum"* (ed. *Wangnereck,* pp. 121–3).

32. E.g., *Conf.,* X, 6 (ed. cit., p. 356); *De div. quaest.,* LI (*PL* 40,32); *De Nat. et Orig. An.* IV, 20 (*CSEL* 60, p. 399); *De Trin.* V, 1, 2; XI, 1, 1; XII, 1 and 2 ed. *Bibliothèque Augustinienne,* I, 426; II, 160; 212–14); *De Civ. Dei* XIII, 24 (ed. *Dombart-Kalb,* II, 410). Also found in simple form in Isidore of Seville, *Etymol.* XI, 1 (*PL* 82, 398B); and Rabanus Maurus, *De Univ.* VI (*PL* 111, 139B).

33. 1735D, 1739A, 1748A, 1780B, 1784B, 1847C, 1849A and especially 1783A–D. Cf. F. Mannarini, "La Grazia in Isaaco della Stella," *COCR,* XVI (1954), 142–3.

34. E.g., (a) Hugh of St Victor, *De Unit.* (*PL* 177, 287); *De Arca Noe mor.* (*PL* 176, 674); (b) Richard of St Victor (*PL* 196), *Benj. Maj.* (96A–C; 99A–B; 117D); *Benj. Min.* (50D–51A); *In.Ps.* 30 (310); *De Erud. Hom. Int.* I, 3 (1236A); II, 25 (1324C); III, 37 (1334–5); (c) Bernard, *De Grat. et Lib. Arbit.* IV, 12 (ed. *Leclercq,* III, 175); *Misc. Sermon 116* (*PL* 183, 741B); (d) *De Spiritu et Anima* (*PL* 40), IX (785), XXIV (803), XXXVI (807), XLIX (815), LIV (819), LXV (830B); (e) Arnold of Bonneval, *De Parad. Animae* (*PL* 189, 1530B); (f). *Liber de Stabilitate Animae* (*PL* 213,914D); (g) *De Statibus Hominis Interioris* (ed. *d'Alverny,* p. 280); (h) *De Anima* (*PL* 184, 487C, 513D; *PL* 177, 183C, 185A–B); (i) *Liber Alcidi* (cf. E. Garin, *Studi sull Platonismo Medievali* [Florence, 1958], pp. 109–10, 148); (j) Helinand of Froidmont, *De Cognit. Sui* (*PL* 212, 724B–27B).

effect upon our passage is to dramatize the split between the themes of man (the soul) as the image of God, and man (the body) as microcosm that immediately follows; but a closer investigation of the two will indicate a decisive movement toward overcoming the polarity.

Man, the Image and Likeness of God

"*Tu ad imaginem et similitudinem Dei factus intus*"—the appearance of the motif of the inner man as the image of God could daunt any investigator by the wealth and variety of its use and the abundance of literature concerning it. Fortunately, the fact that two major works on the use of *imago et similitudo* in the twelfth century have appeared in recent years,[35] makes it unnecessary, were it even possible within our scope, to discuss the full twelfth-century background.[36] Instead, we shall restrict ourselves to an investigation of what Isaac understood by these terms.

The first clue which our passage gives is that in line with the weight of the tradition, the *imago* is always within for Isaac, in the interior, not the exterior, man.[37] E. Gilson has remarked that while the medievals almost invariably placed the image in the spiritual nature of man, there were two basic positions available in the twelfth century for a more precise identification, the Augustinian tradition which stressed the intellectual aspects of the *imago*, and the Bernardine tradition which emphasized man's freedom.[38] This may be an oversimplification; but on the basis of such a division, Isaac must be grouped with those who place greatest emphasis on

35. S. Otto ', Die Funktion des Bildegriffes in der Theologie des 12. Jahrhunderts," *BGPM*, XL, 1 (Münster, 1963) and R. Javelet, *Image et Ressemblance.* . . . Cf. also L. Hödl, "Zur Entwicklung der frühscholastischen Lehre von der Gottebendbildlichkeit des Menschen," *L'Homme et Son Destin*, pp. 347–59.

36. For a convenient sketch of the different possibilities of *imago* and *similitudo* as applied to the soul, cf. Javelet, *op. cit.*, I, 212–24.

37. ". . . intus homo ad imaginem Dei, unde et potes deificari." Compare with 1783A, where the *imago Dei* is the *homo interior*.

38. *The Spirit of Medieval Philosophy*, pp. 210–13.

the intellectual image. The *imago* (and/or *similitudo*) is described as being in the *mens*,[39] in the *intelligentia*,[40] in *ratio*,[41] or vaguely as *"in eminentiori parte anime."*[42] Because all the powers of the soul are one, Isaac frequently merely says that the image and likeness are in the *anima*,[43] or the synonymous *spiritus rationalis*.[44] There is only one passage where Isaac is more precise than this. In the first Sermon for Septuagesima (Sermon 16), he tells us:

> Therefore for the sake of these things (reason and love) man was made to the image and likeness of God, and through these he is recreated and reformed to the same image and likeness—*through reason to the image, through life to the likeness.* . . . To know the true God is eternal life, but to love with the whole heart is the true way. Love is the way, truth the life; *love is the likeness, truth the image*; love is the merit, truth the reward; by love one is on the way, by truth one stands at the goal.[45]

Isaac is here speaking about the dynamic function of the image and likeness as the source of man's deification, but his equation of *sensus—imago—veritas* on the one hand, and *vita—similitudo—caritas* on the other is important. *Sensus (ratio)* and *affectus* are the two fundamental powers of the soul for Isaac;[46] their activities, *cognos-*

39. 1719C; 1765D; 1772C; 1774D; 1863C; *Epistola de Anima*, XXI (1887D); Sermon 55, 11. 105–8 (*ed. Leclercq*, p. 287)

40. "Sicut enim supremum anime, id est *intelligentia*, sive mens, de qua post dicetur *imaginem et similitudinem* sui gerit superioris, id est Dei. . . ." *Epistola de Anima*, XI (1881D).

41. *Epistola*, III (1877A).   42. *Epistola*, XXI (1887C).

43. 1716C; 1838D; *Epistola* I (1876B); XIV (1883D); *Sermo* 55, 56–9 (*ed. Leclercq*, p. 286).

44. 1795A-C.

45. Sermon 16, 15–16. "Propter haec enim factus est homo ad imaginem et similitudinem Dei, ac per haec reficitur et reformatur ad easdem, per sensum ad imaginem, per vitam ad similitudinem. . . . Ut cognoscat verum Deum, aeterna est vita, sed ut toto corde diligat, vera est via. Caritas ergo via, veritas, vita; *caritas similitudo, veritas imago;* caritas meritum, veritas praemium; caritate itur, veritate statur" (*ed. Hoste*, pp. 304–6 [1744A-B]).

46. 1703A-D; 1746D-47A; 1774D; 1795B; 1807D-8A; *Epistola de Anima*, V-VI (1878B-79B); XXI (1887C-88A); XXIII (1888A-89A)—the one passage which substitutes *intelligentia* rather than *ratio* for *sensus*.

cere and *diligere*, lead man to God and are fulfilled when he attains that goal.[47] While Isaac does not mention *affectus* in our passage, it is safe to assume that *vita—similitudo—caritas* are to be equated with *affectus*, so that the *imago* is in the generalized intellectual power of *sensus* and the *similitudo* in the generalized volitional power of *affectus*. There is, moreover, a pseudo-patristic source for this use. It first appears in the *De Dignitate Humane Conditionis*, which originated from the School of Alcuin, but was circulated under the name of Augustine or sometimes of Ambrose.[48] With such prestigious backing, this identification achieved some fame in the twelfth century; Isaac may have taken it over from Hugh of St Victor.[49]

Isaac is not really as concerned with the precise location of *imago*

47. 1708B-C; 1723B-C; 1730A-B; 1746D-47A; 1774D; 1808A; 1822D; 1836C; 1843D; *Epistola* XXIII (1888B-89A). This mutuality of *dilectio* and *cognitio* is stressed by Richard of St Victor, e.g., *Benj. Maj.* IV, 10 (*PL* 196, 145C), and throughout the *Benj. Min.*

48. A suggestion I owe to L. Hödl, *op. cit.*, p. 352; cf. *PL* 17, 1105-8, especially: "Ad imaginem ergo suam conditor, ut dictum est, fecit animam hominis, quae tota dicitur anima. Non autem aliud hominis quam animam significo, cum mentem dico . . ." (1107A-B); and "Nunc vero de similitudine aliqua intellige, quae minoribus cernenda est; ut sicut Deus Creator, qui hominem ad similitudinem suam creavit, est caritas, est bonus et iustus . . .; ita homo creatus est ut charitatem haberet, et bonus esset et iustus. . . ." (1018A).

49. Hugh of St Victor: "Fecit autem [God] eam [the rational creature] ad imaginem et similitudinem suam secundum dilectionem; ad imaginem suam secundum cognitionem veritatis; ad similitudinem suam secundum amorem veritatis" (*Except. Prior* I, 1 (*PL* 177,193A). Cf. also *De Sac.* I, VI, 2 (*PL* 176, 264). Similar uses are found in Munich Ms. Clm. 22307, f. 5 (School of Laon), quoted in Hödl, *op. cit.*, p. 352; Bernard of Cluny, *Instr. sac.*, I, 1 (*PL* 184, 774c); Martin of Léon, *Sermo VIII in Sept.* (*PL* 208, 579B); *Sententiae Udonis,* Vienna ms. lat. 1050, 119 ra-rb, quoted in Javelet, *op. cit.,* pp. 217-18; Richard of St Victor, *Liber excerpt.* I, 1, 1 (*ed. Châtillon,* p. 104); [Gilbert of Poitiers or Achard of St Victor?], *De Discretione Animae, Spiritus, et Mentis, n* 33 (*ed. Häring,* p. 181); *De Spiritu et Anima,* X, XXXIX (*PL* 40, 786A, 809B), where it depends on Isaac; Peter Lombard, *Sent.* II, d. 16, 4 (*PL* 92, 684); Robert of Melun, unedited texts quoted in Otto, *op. cit.,* pp. 95, 100; Praepositinus, also in Otto, *op. cit.,* p. 252 and Peter of Poitiers, *Sent.* II, 9 (*ed. Moore,* II, pp. 48-9). Otto's remark is noteworthy: "Die Zuweisung der *cognitio veritatis* an die *imago* und der *dilectio veritatis* an die *similitudo* ist Traditionsgut . . . " (p. 137). Cf. also R. Javelet, *op. cit.,* I, 217-18.

and *similitudo* as he is with exploring the implications of what it means for the interior man to be made to the image and likeness of God. This is one of the most interesting features of his thought on the soul. The Abbot of Stella had available to him through a number of sources from late antiquity and the early medieval periods lists of definitions of the soul. Macrobius, Nemesius of Emesa, Cassiodorus, and Isidore had all provided such material.[50] Yet oddly enough, he never really defines the soul, not even in the *Epistola de Anima*. The closest that he comes to a definition is in a passage which prompted Meuser to declare that he was most in accord with the Aristotelian idea of the soul as the "likeness of all things."[51]

Therefore the soul has the power from which it searches out and knows, for made to the likeness of all wisdom, it bears the likeness of all things in itself. Hence it has also been defined by the philosopher as the likeness of all things.[52]

It is not impossible that Isaac was aware that Aristotle had spoken of the soul in these terms; but since we find it in none of the sources mentioned above, I am much more inclined to think that Isaac, basing himself upon a mysterious reference to Varro in Hugh of St Victor's *Didascalicon*,[53] is referring to the Roman rather than the

50. Macrobius, *Comm. in Somn. Scip.* I, 14, 19–21 (*ed. Willis*, pp. 58–9); Nemesius, *Premnon Physicon* II, 1–7 (*ed. Burkhard*, pp. 23–5); Cassiodorus, *Liber de Anima* IV (*ed. Halporn*, pp. 72–5); Isidore, *Differentiarum libri duo* II, 16–30 (*PL* 83, 77–85).

51. W. Meuser, *Die Erkenntnislehre der Isaak von Stella* (Bottrop, 1934), pp. 67–9. As Meuser notes, at the same time the *Epistola* was being written, John of Salisbury was already calling Aristotle "the philosopher," cf. *Metal.*, II, 16.

52. "Habet itaque anima unde investiget et cognoscat; ad totalis enim sapientie similitudinem facta, omnium in se similitudinem gerit. Unde et a philosopho definita est omnium similitudo." *Epistola*, XIX (1886A); cf. Aristotle, *de Anima*, 431b: εἴπωμεν πάλιν ὅτι ἡ ψυχὴ τὰ ὄντα πώς ἐστι πάντα. (*Loeb ed.* p. 178).

53. *Didas.* I, 1: "nam sicut Varro in Periphysion dicit: 'Non omnis varietas extrinsecus rebus accidit, ut necesse sit quidquid variatur, aut amittere aliquid quod habuit, aut aliquid aliud et diversum extrinsecus quod non habuit

Greek philosopher, an identification made more possible by Augustine's fulsome praise of Varro in the *De Civitate Dei*;[54] furthermore, his preference for this definition, if such we may call it, is for totally un-Aristotelian reasons.[55] Clearly, it is the Christian notion that the soul is made to the image and likeness of the Divine *Imago*, the *Sapientia* who is the Second Person of the Trinity, which is dominant here, as a comparison with other passages shows.[56] The soul is the likeness of all things, the soul has the capacity to know all things, because its exemplar the Divine Wisdom is the cause of all things and contains their forms within itself.[57]

What is the relation between man as *imago et similitudo* and the Second Person of the Trinity? Here again Isaac stands within a long patristic tradition. The passage from the *Epistola de Anima* which, like the passage in Sermon Two, connects the themes of self-knowledge and likeness to God, suggests that Isaac understands this relation in terms of a combination of Pauline texts with the famous

---

assumere' . . . sic nimirum mens, *rerum omnium similitudine insignita, omnia esse dicitur* . . ." (*ed. Buttimer*, pp. 5–6). As J. Taylor remarks in a note to this passage in the *Didascalicon of Hugh of St Victor*, p. 180, no such work of Varro is known, nor is the phrase found in either Eriugena's *Periphyseon* (*De Divisione Naturae*), nor Nemesius's *Premnon Physicon*. The ultimate source remains a mystery, but Isaac could well have been influenced by the passage.

54. E.g., *De Civ. Dei* III, 4; VI, 2; XIX, 1 (*ed. cit.*, I, 67–68; 167–8; II, 657–60).

55. Here I disagree with Meuser: "vor allem aber—und das ist das Entscheidende—ist die Begründung der anima-similitudo-Lehre bei Aristoteles und bei Isaak genau dieselbe: die liegt beide Male in der Aehnlichkeit der Seele mit ihren Erkenntnisobjekten" (p. 69).

56. (a) Sermon 9 (*ed. Hoste*, p. 206; 1719C–D): "Primus *liber Sapientiae* totus scriptus intus, in quo beati, quibus datum est videre et legere, ubi simul et semel Pater omnia scripsit ab aeterno. *Unde omnia quasi transcripta sunt, quae in secundo libro, id est in mente rationali* legi possunt. . . . Ubi simul omnia, hic *similitudo* omnium; in isto si quidem imago illius . . . Sic in mente rationali ad imaginem totalis sapientiae facta, omnis sapientiae forma continetur, ut non esset ei necesse foris addiscere, nisi intus caligaret." (b) *Epistola*, XXI (1887C); "Que quidem anima, *sicut Deus capabilis omnibus, sic est capax omnium.* . . ."

57. On this aspect of Isaac's use of *imago et similitudo*, cf. Javelet, *op. cit.*, I, 416.

text from Genesis 1:26. Paul described the Second Person of the Trinity as the *Imago Dei* in Rom 8:29; I Cor 15:49; II Cor 4:4 and Col 1:15. Many Greek Fathers held that this was the reason for the expression of Genesis *"ad imaginem et similitudinem Dei."* Only Christ is the true *Imago Dei*; man is created *ad imaginem*, according to the *Imago* who is Christ. Augustine also speaks of man as *ad imaginem*, but is careful to say that he is the image of the whole Trinity.[58] Isaac's hint at this understanding in the *Epistola*[59] is strengthened by his use of the Hilarian-Augustinian triad of *"Aeternitas in Patre, Species in Imagine, Usus in Munere"* as a Trinitarian analogy.[60] In the *Sermo in Dedicatione Ecclesie*, recently discovered and edited by Fr Jean Leclercq, he expresses it unequivocally, though along with Augustine asserting that man is the image of the whole Trinity and not just of the Son:

> Hence the bridegroom can appear both as ascending and as descending; but how did the Bride, who is earthly in her origin, appear as descending? Is it not true nevertheless, dearest brothers, that according to her better part, namely the rational soul, according to which she was made to the image and likeness of God, the Bride seems heavenly or rather divine? The Bridegroom is the image; she is according to the image. He is the image of the Father alone; she is according to the image of the whole

58. E.g., *De Gen. imp.* 61 *(PL* 34, 244); *De Trin.* VI, 10, 11; VII, 6, 12 *(ed. cit.,* I, 496, 550). Augustine disagrees with those who restrict the term *Imago* to the Son, and speak of man only as *ad imaginem*; but he admits the legitimacy of the term to express the difference between the perfect image of the Son and man's image. On the use of *ad imaginem* among the Fathers, cf. "Note Complementaire 45: *L'Homme à l'Image*" in *La Trinité,* edd. M. Mellet and T. Camelot (Paris, 1955), I, 589–90. Among the medievals, cf. R. Javelet, "Le Fils, Image du Père" and "Le Christ, Image du Père," *op. cit.,* I, 72–91.

59. "Quis enim seipsum vidit? Quis agnovit se? Dico imaginem et similitudinem Dei, ad imaginem et similitudinem Dei. Qui similium alterum novit, utrumque novit; et qui alterutrum non novit, neutrum novit." *Epistola,* XX (1886C).

60. E.g., *Epistola* XX (1887B), and, of course, in the *Sermones in Sexagesima.* For the use in Augustine, *De Trin.,* VI, 10, 11; XV, 3, 5 *(ed. cit.,* I, 496; II, 428). Cf. Hilary, *De Trin.* II, 1; and, on the *usus* that is the Spirit, II, 33–5 *(PL* 10, 51A; 73–5).

Trinity. Finally, He is the substantial, proper and native image; she is image made to the image.[61]

Such is man as the *imago et similitudo Dei*. Ontologically, in true Platonic fashion, the *imago* is man's participation in the Divine Nature, marking out both his proximity to God and the possibility of his deification on the one hand,[62] and the difference between his nature and that of the Divine Son on the other. To say that the soul in its highest part is the image of God expresses its very essence and gives the ground for its drive towards universal knowledge. Such was the destiny of the soul; its history was more tragic. Wounded by original sin so that it could no longer know God nor even itself, it lost the possibility of gaining the knowledge of all things through self-knowledge.[63] Only by the restoration of the wounded and darkened image through the illumination of Christ can the soul fulfill its original goal.[64] This history of man as the image of God, the core of Isaac's theological anthropology, will be considered in more detail below in our discussion of the *Epistola de Anima*.

Thus far Isaac's anthropology is decidedly Platonic in outlook—self-knowledge of the soul, the high point of the soul as the *imago Dei*, knowledge of things through the external material world as only necessary as a result of the Fall. At this stage we should be inclined to agree with Gilson's statement about the antiphysicism to which Christian Socratism frequently led.[65] Even what Isaac has to say about the exterior man does not at first seem encouraging

---

61. "Unde et ascendens sicut et descendens potest sponsus apparere. Sponsa, que de terra fuit terrena, quomodo descendens apparuit? Illa tamen, dilectissimi, proportione sua meliori, anima videlicet rationali, secundum quam facta est ad ymaginem et similitudinem Dei, nonne videtur celestis aut potius divina? *Ille ymago, illa ad ymaginem.* Ille tamen ymago solius Patris, ista ad ymaginem totius Trinitatis. Ille denique ymago substantialis, propria et nativa; ista ymago ad ymaginem." (*ed. Leclercq*, ll. 55–61, p. 286).

62. *Epistola*, XI (1881CD).

63. E.g., 1783A–D;[1] 1838C–D and the important passage from the *Epistola* to be discussed below—XX (1886C).

64. E.g., 1712A; *Epistola* XXI–XXIII (1887C–89A).

65. *The Spirit of Medieval Philosophy*, pp. 213–14.

here: "Outside you are an animal made according to the image of the world, so that man is said to be a world in miniature," i.e., a microcosm. Just as the interior man, the soul, is *"ad imaginem Dei,"* the exterior man, the body, is *"ad imaginem mundi,"* or *"per simili-tudinem carnis peccati,"*[66] or the *"imago terrena terreni, vetus veteris, in veritate carnis peccati."*[67] These are strongly negative expressions, even though he sometimes tempers them by using the more positive formula consecrated by Augustine of the body as the *vestigium Trinitatis.*[68] The notion of man's body, however, as the *minor mundus*, when investigated in depth, exposes the positive aspects of Isaac's attitude toward the unity of man and the value of the material aspect of creation.

Man as the Microcosm

The appearance of the theme of the exterior man, the body, as the *minor mundus* situates Isaac squarely in the history of one of the most important symbols bequeathed by Greek thought to the Western tradition, that of man as the microcosm. Following the lead of Rudolf Aller's article, "Microcosmos from Anaximandros to Paracelsus,"[69] along with a sampling of material gathered by a number of other scholars,[70] we can reconstruct something of the

66. Sermon 10 (*ed. Hoste*, p. 222; 1723D).

67. Sermon 27 (1779A–B).

68. "In anima quidem alicuius apparet imago; in corpore vere vix invenitur ullius vestigium." *Epistola* II (1876B). For Augustine, cf. especially *De Trin.* XII, 11, 16 *(ed cit.,* II, pp. 240–2), which shows some similarity to our passage from Sermon 2 by bringing in the question of resemblance to beasts: "Ita cum vult esse sicut ille sub nullo, et ab ipsa sui medietate poenaliter ad ima propellitur, id est, ad ea quibus pecora laetantur: atque ita cum sit honor ejus similitudo Dei, dedecus autem ejus *similitudo pecoris* . . ." On the twelfth-century use, cf. R. Javelet, *op. cit.,* "Nature et Corps, Vestige de Dieu," I, 224–36; and II, 158–60 (n. 234).

69. *Traditio,* II (1944), 319–409.

70. For the older period, I have also used A. Altmann, "The Delphic Maxim," pp. 213–22 and D. S. Wallace Hadrill, *The Greek Patristic View of Nature* (London, 1968), pp. 76–9. For the twelfth century the most important works are Chenu, *La Théologie* . . . , pp. 34–43, 49–51, 122 and P. Delhaye,

background and significance of this rich element in Isaac's anthropology. Due to the variety of ideas which the symbol of microcosm can manifest, and also to the obscurities in our knowledge of the Presocratics, there is some disagreement about the exact origins of the microcosmic theme. Whether it takes its origin from the Pythagorean tradition,[71] or from fragments of Anaximander,[72] or Heraclitus,[73] or of Democritus, or whether it finds uncontestable appearance first in texts of Plato or Aristotle,[74] is not essentially significant; rather, we must see it as implicit in the whole Greek effort at achieving an organized view of the universe and man's place in it. As Allers puts it:

> Microcosmism is one of the great ideas by which man attempts to understand himself and his relation to the totality of being. Insofar one may speak of a relation between microcosmism and 'Humanism,' if the latter term is taken in its widest sense. Whenever and wherever these two lines of human endeavor for understanding reality meet, man tries to unite under one aspect both his view of himself as set over against the universe, and his view of himself as part of the universe. Whenever this happens, microcosmism in one or the other form is apt to reappear.[75]

Yet because this particular motif boldly assays to grasp man's relation to universal order, it is directed toward an impossible task

---

La Microcosmos de Godefrey de Saint Victor, I (Lille, 1951), "Le microcosme dans la littérature psychologique du XIIe siècle," pp. 137–44. Cf. also Chenu "Spiritus: Le vocabulaire de l'âme au XIIe siècle," *RSPT,* XLI (1957), 220–22; M.-M. Davy, *op. cit.,* pp. 40–2, 162–3; R. Javelet, *op. cit.,* I, 135, 183, 231–3; II, 153–4, 200–2; H. de Lubac, *Exégèse Médiévale,* I, 156–7; A. Hoste, "Note Complementaire 2: L'Homme 'microcosme,' " *Isaac: Sermones* I, p. 332 and H. Schipperges, "Einflüsse Arabischer Medizin auf die Mikrokosmos-literatur des 12 Jahrhunderts," *Miscellanea Mediaevalia,* I (Köln, 1962), pp. 129–53.

71. *Vita Anonymi Pythagori,* as cited in Altmann, *op. cit.,* pp. 213–14. Cf. Allers, *op. cit.,* pp. 341–3.

72. Allers, *op. cit.,* pp. 338–40.

73. Allers, *op. cit.,* pp. 340–1.

74. For a survey of the argument, cf. Altmann, *op. cit.,* pp. 213–14.

75. *Op. cit.,* pp. 406–7.

in the conceptual framework; hence the understanding of microcosm, in its direction toward the mystery of the "known unknown," acquires the character of a cultural symbol with all the notes, particularly those of diversity of values and visual presentation, touched upon in our discussion of the symbol. Allers has constructed a typology of the varieties of microcosmic theory which can be of use as an introductory tool for examining Isaac's texts. He uncovers six basic varieties: first, *elementaristic microcosm*, where man contains in his being all the elements of the material world;[76] second, *structural microcosm*, in which man duplicates the context and order of principles in the world;[77] and third, *holistic microcosm*, where the order of the universe is viewed according to the analogy of the orders created by man, e.g., politics or art.[78] The fourth, *symbolistic microcosm*, develops from the second and treats man as symbolic of the laws governing the universe;[79] *psychological or epistemological microcosm*, the fifth, holds man or the soul is the universe in knowing it.[80] Finally, *metaphorical microcosm* treats the theme merely as a figure of speech.[81] As can be seen from this outline, and more clearly from the history of the theme, *elementaristic microcosm* and *epistemological microcosm* tend to be the clearest and best defined; the other four, especially what Allers calls the *structural* and *symbolistic* uses, are difficult to distinguish within the compact world of symbols.

Without attempting a history of microcosmic themes, it is necessary to direct attention to a few of the major stages on the way to the twelfth century in order to understand the significance of the use of the motif in the Abbot of Stella. Plato does not use the term microcosm, but later microcosmic theory continues to hearken back to the *Timaeus* as one of its richest sources. Not only

---

76. *Op. cit.,* pp. 321–2.

77. Pp. 322–3. There are two basic types here: (a) cosmocentric microcosmism, where man is compared to the universe (e.g., pantheism, astrology, magic); and (b) anthropocentric microcosmism, where the universe is viewed according to the primary analogate of man.

78. Pp. 323–6.   79. Pp. 326–30.   80. Pp. 330–1.
81. *Ibid.*

the theory of the World Soul itself (34b–37c),[82] but the parallel between the World Soul and individual souls, each composed from the Circles of Existence, the Same, and the Different (41d), the description of the material universe as a body (30d, 32c–33b) and the location of the various parts of the human soul in the appropriate organs (44d, 69d–72d) were important expressions of the general microcosmic sense that pervades the work. Chalcidius, through whose translations and commentary the *Timaeus* was known to the medieval world, merely made explicit this direction of the *Dialogue* when he said: "Hence I think that man was called a world in miniature by the ancients, and not without reason, because the whole world and even the whole man are from all the same things, with the body having the same elements, and the soul also being of one and the same nature."[83] There is another idea from the *Timaeus*, which at first sight might not seem to contribute directly to the history of microcosm, but is actually of great importance in the later tradition, particularly among the Neoplatonists and their Christian successors, viz., that the soul is the middle-being ranged between God and body, sharing in the nature of each and mediating their differences (35a).[84]

Aristotle, not Plato, was the first to use the word *microcosmos* itself to compare man and the world;[85] and it is evident from the *De Anima* that he was most interested in Aller's epistemological sense of microcosm. Man is in some way all things, the *similitudo omnium* as the medievals would say, because he can know all

82. Compare with *Philebus* 29–30, which stresses the fire-soul concept of the World Soul.

83. "Unde opinor hominem *mundum brevem* a veteribus appellatum; nec immerito, quia totus mundus et item totus homo ex isdem sunt omnibus, corpore quidem easdem materias habente, anima quoque unius eiusdemque naturae." (*Commentarium* 202; ed. *Waszink*, p. 222.)

84. In the translation of Chalcidius (*ed. Waszink*, p. 27): "tertium substantiae genus mixtum locavit medium inter utramque substantiam eodemque modo ex gemina biformique natura . . ." Cf. Allers, *op. cit.*, p. 355, quoting Jaeger on the importance of this idea.

85. *Physics* VIII, 2 (252b, 26–7): ἐι γὰρ ἐν μικρῷ κοσμῷ γίνεται, καὶ ἐν μεγάλῳ (*Loeb ed.* II, 286).

things.[86] Later Greek use of microcosm was particularly marked among the Stoics,[87] as might be expected from their strong attraction to the problem of the unity of the cosmos. The essentially materialistic concept of this unity led to emphasis on the variations of elementaristic aspects of microcosm, and included a pronounced tendency towards astrology in the Hellenistic period.[88]

Due to Philo's place at the juncture of biblical and Hellenic thought, the appearance of the motif in his writings is significant.[89] Subsequently, we find it in Origen,[90] and Clement of Alexandria.[91] The Hermetic movement with its combination of religious, astrological, and philosophical elements found it useful; it occurs in the *Asclepius* tract known in the Middle Ages.[92] Plotinus's *Enneads,* the reservoir of ancient thought and the source of so much of importance in the medieval era, contain a wide variety of uses of microcosm.[93] Plotinus follows the tradition in affirming that the soul is all things;[94] he tells us that it becomes all things by contemplating its true self.[95] He is also a strong witness to the existence of the World Soul, going beyond Plato in seeing individual souls and the World Soul as part of one soul-reality through his sense of the immanence of higher levels in the lower.[96] Like Plato, he sees

86. *De Anima* III, 8 (431b, 21) (*Loeb ed.,* p. 178).

87. Allers, *op. cit.,* p. 347. W. Telfer, *Cyril of Jerusalem and Nemesius of Emesa* (Philadelphia, 1955), pp. 230–1.

88. Altmann, *op. cit.,* pp. 214–15.

89. E.g., *De Opif.* 82 (*Loeb ed.* I, 66); *Quis Rerum Divinarum Heres* XXXI, 155 (*Loeb ed.* IV, 360); *De Migr. Ab.* 39, 220 (*Loeb ed.* IV, 260–62).

90. E.g., *In Gen.,* I, 11 (*PG* 12, 154A–D).

91. *Protrepticus* I, 5, 3 (*Loeb ed.,* p. 12).

92. *Asclepius* 10 (*ed. Nock,* pp. 308–9). Man is the cosmic midpoint and mediator in 6 (ed., pp. 301–3). On microcosm in the Hermetists, cf. Festugière, *Hermes Trismégiste,* I, 92–4.

93. "Microcosmism appears, in fact, historically considered, mostly as a part of a more or less Platonic or especially Neo-Platonic philosophy." Allers, *op. cit.,* p. 331.

94. E.g., *Enn.* II, 4, 11; III, 4, 3; III, 4, 6.

95. *Enn.* III, 8, 6.

96. E.g., *Enn.* II, 3, 7; IV, 3, 1; IV, 4, 36.

the soul as the middle being, both in the symbolic sense, and in a deeper philosophical manner.[97]

Surprisingly enough, the Latin tradition in late antiquity, both pagan and Christian, is more chary than we might suspect in the use of microcosm. Augustine cannot be considered a strong representative of microcosmic theory;[98] and, as M.-D. Chenu has shown, his influence in the twelfth century tends to run contrary to the microcosmic tradition, e.g., in the case of Peter Lombard.[99] Augustine does, however, stress that man is the midpoint between beasts and angels.[100] The most important source in the Latin West is the pagan Macrobius whose *Commentary on the Dream of Scipio* explicitly states:

> The soul moreover, which is the true man, is foreign to every hint of mortality, even to the point that in imitation of God ruling the world, it also rules the body while the body is given life by it. Therefore natural philosophers have said that the world is a large man and that man is a small world.[101]

The *De Diffinitione* of Marius Victorinus (ascribed to Boethius in the Middle Ages) refers to man as a "*minor mundus*" in one place;[102] and in the early Middle Ages Gregory the Great spoke of man as

97. E.g., *Enn.*, III, 2, 8–9.

98. Allers, *op. cit.*, p. 362, n. 112. He is more interested in the general concept of the pervasiveness of order, e.g., *De Civ. Dei* XI, 22 (*ed. Dombart and Kalb* II, 340–41). *Expos. ex Epist. ad Rom.* 53 (PL 35, 2074) and *De div. Quaest.* 83, q. 67 (PL 40, 68) are among the rare references to microcosm in the Bishop of Hippo.

99. *La Théologie au Douzième Siècle*, p. 39.

100. E.g., *De Civ. Dei*, IX, 13 (*ed. Dombart and Kalb*, I, 260–61); *Conf.* VII, 7 (*ed. cit.*, pp. 232–3).

101. "anima autem, qui verus homo est, ab omni condicione mortalitatis aliena est, adeo ut in imitationem dei mundum regentis regat et ipsa corpus, dum a se animatur, ideo physici mundum magnum hominem et hominem brevem mundum esse dixerant." II, 12, 10–11 (*ed. Willis*, p. 132).

102. *De Diffinitione* (PL 64, 907). Boethius himself stresses man's position between God and beast; cf. V. Schmid-Kohl, *Die Neuplatonische Seelenlehre in der Consolatio Philosophiae des Boethius* (Meisenheim-am-Glan, 1965), pp. 45–8.

having something in common with all the levels of creation,[103] while Isidore of Seville referred to him as a microcosm.[104]

More significant for the medieval interest in microcosm was the Greek Patristic tradition.[105] The variety of its appearance in Gregory of Nyssa,[106] though he avoids the elementaristic sense, and in Nemesius of Emesa,[107] might seem surprising were we to forget two important factors. The first is the greater acquaintance of these men with the full classical tradition; more important, though, is the function that microcosm played in the general confluence of Biblical and Hellenic understandings of man. Allers noted:

> The fundamental notions of wholeness, order, proportion, and harmony are perhaps related to a still more fundamental view, one which emphasizes diversity in sameness more than sameness in diversity. . . . Medieval thinkers were struck by the dissimilarity of things, and their problem was therefore to safeguard the unity of the widely different and separated layers of reality. . . . They solved the problem by applying the principle of analogy and by the notion of an intermediary being, or rather by the idea that the highest being in one order somehow participates in the nature of the next higher level. . . .
>
> When one conceives of the world as order in diversity, the microcosmistic view presents definite advantages.[108]

Seen in the light of our discussion in Chapter II on separation, the

103. *Hom. in Evang.* 29 (*PL* 76, 1214 A).

104. *De Natura Rerum* II (*PL* 83, 977).

105. Chenu, *op. cit.*, p. 40. On the positive features of the Greek Patristic view of man, cf. D. S. Wallace-Hadrill, *The Greek Patristic View of Nature* (London, 1968), pp. 66–79.

106. Especially in the *De Hominis Opificio* XVII (*PG* 44, 177–85), which stressed man's communion with all the levels of the universe and his position as midpoint, though avoiding the term microcosm. The body is the image of the world in *De An. et Resurr.* (*PG* 46,28BC); *In Ecc.* (*PG* 44,625B) tells us that man in knowing the universe knows his own nature. For other passages, cf. *De Hom. Opif.* XII (*PG* 44,155–64) and *In Ps.* 3 (*PG* 44, 442). On microcosm motifs in Gregory, cf. E. von Ivánka, *Plato Christianus*, pp. 318–19.

107. Man as microcosm: *Premnon Physicon*, Prologus 16; I, 90 (*ed. Burkhard*, pp. 3–4, 22). The World Soul: II, 88–95 (*ed. Burkhard*, pp. 44–6). Man as the midpoint of the universe: I, 7–11 (*ed. Burkhard*, pp. 6–7).

108. *Op. cit.*, pp. 403–5. Cf. also p. 332.

desire for unification, and the dynamism of this connection as fundamental to the thought-world crystallized in Neoplatonism, the different aspects of microcosmic theory were another means, like the symbol of the *catena aurea,* of manifesting such an understanding of reality. The microcosmic themes, and the related motif of man as the midpoint of the universe, provided an avenue for the expression of the value of the corporeal world and the importance of man's bodily nature which were a means of outflanking the stress on the baseness of man's material nature which was such a significant part of the Platonic heritage of patristic anthropology. This outflanking involved grave ambiguities, inconsistencies, and a tendency towards the creation of two contrasting series of statements and arguments about the material world and the body, one negative in tone, the other positive, which were rarely adequately combined;[109] but the microcosmic theme was at least a serious attempt to synthesize these divergences and to deal with a problem that even today must admit of symbolic overtones: man's sense of belonging to two worlds, of not being capable of easy unification and classification.[110]

It was largely through the influence of Gregory of Nyssa and Maximus the Confessor[111] that microcosm assumed an important role in the thought of John Scotus Eriugena. He avoids the term

109. On the view of the body and the material world in early medieval theology, cf. P. Daubercies, "La théologie de la condition charnelle chez les Maîtres du haut moyen âge," *RTAM,* XXX (1963), 5-54. Daubercies discusses two modes of speaking and the specific early medieval synthesis of these modes. His comments deserve note: "Cependant on relève en même temps des signes nombreaux d'hesitation. De plus en plus souvent, les auteurs soulignent la différence entre leur vocabulaire et celui des Écritures. Ils ne peuvent s'empêcher de signaler la sympathie existant entre le corps et l'âme ou encore l'harmonie régnant au sein de notre être matériel. D'une façon paradoxale, tous s'accordent encore pour juger légitimes des biens désirés par le corps, et Denys se plâit a souligner que le sensible est a l'origine de la contemplation" (p. 6).

110. On the microcosm as symbolic image, cf. Durand, *L'Imagination Symbolique,* p. 73. On microcosm as artistic symbol, de Champeaux and Sterckx, *op. cit.,* pp. 239-46. On its symbolic value in the twelfth century, Chenu, *op. cit.,* pp. 42-3.

111. E.g., *Ambigua* II, 37 (PG 91, 1305A-B).

itself because of a criticism of it in Gregory,[112] but the reality is there, particularly in his many statements about man having something in common with all the levels of reality,[113] and man being the midpoint in the hierarchical world.[114] He also has an epistemological sense similar to Isaac's understanding of man as *similitudo omnium*; the human soul contains the ideas of all things because it is made after the pattern of Divine Wisdom.[115] There is no better sign of the extent of Eriugena's influence on the twelfth century than the new interest taken in man as the microcosm in the first decades of the century.[116] Absent from Anselm of Canterbury, the Erigenean themes are strong in Honorius Augustodunensis.[117] Hugh of St Victor tends to avoid using microcosm except in its epistemological sense,[118] possibly due to the influence of Augustine, though he does speak of man as the midpoint.[119] Later members of the School of St Victor stress microcosm, such as Richard,[120] and Godfrey of St Victor, whose *Microcosmos* is the fullest treatment of the century.[121]

112. *De Div. Nat.* IV, 12 (*PL* 122, 793C).

113. *De Div. Nat.* II, 4; III, 37 (*PL* 122, 503D; 733B); *Hom. in Prologum Evang. Jo.* (*PL* 122, 294).

114. *De Div. Nat.* II, 9; V, 20 (*PL* 122, 536A–B; 893C). On the soul as mid-being in the early Middle Ages, cf. Daubercies, *op. cit.*, pp. 12–13.

115. *De Div. Nat.* IV, 7 (764–5). Compare with II, 13 (541C–D) on the role of the Incarnate Christ in this unification, another affinity with Isaac. On microcosm in Eriugena, cf. M. Cappuyns, *Jean Scot Érigène*, pp. 353–60 and S. Otto, *op. cit.*, pp. 121–2. For other uses, cf. *PL* 122, 531B; 748C; 755B; 760A; 772A; 807A; etc.

116. Chenu, *op. cit.*, pp. 37–8. For listings of use of microcosm in the twelfth century, besides the works already cited, cf. P. Schedler, *Die Philosophie des Macrobius, BGPM*, XIII, 1 (Münster, 1916), pp. 128, 158.

117. E.g., *Eluc.*, I, 11 (*PL* 172, 1116–17); *Sacr. L* (*PL* 172, 773–4); *Liber VIII quaest.* (*PL* 172, 1185–90 and *De Imagine Mundi*, I, 80–2 (*PL* 172, 140). On Honorius, M.-T. d'Alverny, "Le cosmos symbolique du XIIᵉ siècle," *AHDL*, XX (1954), 31–81; Schipperges, *op. cit.*, p. 132.

118. *Didascal.* I, 1 (ed. Buttimer, pp. 5–6). *Homo* as *minor mundus* in Hugh, *Homo. in Eccl.* XII (*PL* 175, 191C).

119. E.g., *De Arca Noe morali* IV (*PL* 176, 666A–B); and *De Vanitate Mundi* II (*PL* 176, 713C).

120. Especially in the *De Stat. Int. Hom.* I, 14 (ed. Ribaillier, p. 78).

121. P. Delhaye, *Le Microcosme de Godefrey de Saint Victor*, I. *Étude Théologique*, II. *Texte* (Lille, 1951); cf. Javelet, *op. cit.*, II, 200–1.

Chenu discerns two major currents in the early twelfth century, a spiritualist one, from Honorius, and a physicist one emanating from Chartres and best seen in Bernard Silvestris' *De Universitate Mundi*, a strange cosmological work stressing the bonds between the macrocosm and the microcosm. These two combined in the second half of the century to produce a rich period of interest in microcosm, evidenced in the works of Godfrey, Hildegard of Bingen and the *Porretani*.[122] That the two were not exclusive in the first half of the century is evident from one of the most interesting treatises of William of St Thierry, the *De Natura Corporis et Animae*.[123] The many affinities between William's work (written about 1140) and Isaac's writings, especially the interest in medical and physiological information testifying to the optimistic anthropology that microcosmic theory abetted,[124] indicate that it is against the background of this mixing of the traditions that Isaac's sense of microcosm must be understood.

To return to the texts of Isaac's use of microcosm, the passage in the Second Sermon is the only one where he uses the term *minor mundus;* here it is quite clear that a sense of separation is to the fore: the body is the image of the world, just as the soul is the image of God.[125] If we study Isaac's other uses of microcosmic themes, we

122. Chenu, *op. cit.,* pp. 38–40. P. Delhaye, *op. cit.,* pp. 138–9, speaks of three kinds of treatment: (1) theologians seeking to explain the place of man in creation and redemption; (2) spiritual authors wishing to find a firm basis for their mystical theories; and (3) special organized treatises like Godfrey's. De Lubac, *op. cit.,* p. 157, distinguishes anthropological and exegetical microcosmic theory. Schipperges discusses the influence of Arabic medical material on a new conception of microcosm, which he finds secondary to the traditional elements, except in such figures as Adelhard of Bath, William of Conches and Daniel of Morley; cf. summary, *op. cit.,* pp. 150–1.

123. *PL* 180, 695–726; cf. esp. 695–96; 711D–712A, for microcosm theme.

124. Chenu, *op. cit.,* p. 41.

125. Such a use is illustrated by Chenu's remark: "L'homme est simultanément, dans une antinomie, image du monde (thème philosophique) et image de Dieu (Genèse). Précisément, c'est la conjoncture du XIIe siècle qui décidera de sa consistance et de son orientation, selon les milieux, hors mis évidemment le milieu augustinien résistant (cf. Hugues de Saint-Victor, Pierre Lombard)" (p. 40).

find that divisiveness of body and soul tends to recede into the background, and the symbolic unifications which the microcosm makes possible are stressed. Isaac's definition of the soul as *similitudo omnium*, already discussed, is a transformation of Aller's epistemological microcosm in a decidedly Christian fashion. In two interesting passages Isaac draws out the parallels between *man* (not just the body) and the cosmos at some length. In the *Epistola de Anima* he uses an image as old as Plato of the universe as a single living body, the *magnum animal*;[126] in a fine passage from Sermon Thirty-two, man's place is described as that of the eye in the body of the universe.[127] The symbolic exchange of images in this Sermon would, if pushed to logical conclusion, reduce man to a part of the cosmos rather than its analogue in miniature; but we are dealing rather with another aspect of the symbol. The passage from the *Epistola de Anima* indicates further dimensions of the symbol of the *magnum animal*; it is a means for manifesting the universal law of the joining of extremes through an apt median term: "For through two most fitting median realities two diverse extremes can be easily and firmly joined: something that is easily seen in the structure of the great animal, as some call it, that is of this world."[128]

As an illustration of the positive value of microcosm, the greatest weight must be given to one of the most important aspects of Isaac's thought, the comparison between the human soul's five stages of ascent to God and the five ascending elements of the material world.[129] Whether we classify this as elementaristic,

126. Isaac probably received the notion from the *Timaeus*, but the term "animal mundus" is also found in *Asclepius*, 29 (*ed. Nock-Festugière*, p. 337). Cf. also Macrobius, *In Somn. Scip.* II, 11-13 (*ed. Willis*, p. 132). Origen spoke of the universe as a great animal in *De prin.* II, 1, 3.

127. 1794D-95D.

128. "Per duas etenim convenientissimas medietates facile et firme due dissidentes extremitates necti possunt, quod in magni ut quidam dicunt animalis id est mundi huius fabrica cernere facile est." *Epistola*, XII (1882c).

129. Appearing in *Sermon* 4 (*ed. Hoste*, p. 134, 1701D-2B), where an at least metaphorical reminiscence of the World Soul of the *Timaeus* is implicit in the phrase "sic et animae *in mundo sui corporis* peregrinanti quinque sunt ad sapientiam progressus." The five-fold comparison is at the heart of the *Epistola de Anima*.

structural, or symbolistic microcosm is not significant; the point is that it is not just the body now which is the image of the world, but the dynamism of human knowing and loving, beginning from the material, proceeding through the various levels up to the *intelligentia,* that joins it with God. The material universe and corporeal man are the symbolic analogues, the images which manifest the teaching that all things are ascending to God in and through man.[130] We will return to this point, particularly to the Dionysian aspect of the ascent, or anagogy, later. This, and Isaac's emphasis on the related theme of man, the midpoint of the spiritual and material worlds, will be examined in our treatment of the *Epistola de Anima.*

Regio Dissimilitudinis

One final anthropological theme makes its appearance in the passage from the Second Sermon. It concerns the effect of sin on the nature of man, and is presented in true symbolic and Platonic fashion under the image of man's wandering in the *regio dissimilitudinis,* the *terra aliena* of separation from God. That the passage closes with this, and that the remainder of the Sermon is largely a development of the effects of original sin, provides an explanation for the strong note given to the more negative features of Isaac's anthropology here. Since its first notice by Gilson in his book *The Mystical Theology of St Bernard,*[131] the provocative image of the *regio dissimilitudinis* has attracted considerable attention from a variety of scholars.[132] If man was made in the image and likeness of

130. Gilson, *The Spirit of Mediaeval Philosophy,* p. 219, notes how the themes of microcosm and midpoint restore the physicism lost in a one-sided stress on knowing the interior man, but his opposition between the "spirituals" and the "philosophers" is too simplified.

131. Chap. II, "Regio Dissimilitudinis," pp. 33–59.

132. A. E. Taylor, "Regio dissimilitudinis," *AHDL,* IX (1934), 305–6; E. Gilson, "Regio dissimilitudinis de Platon à Saint Bernard," *Mediaeval Studies,* IX (1947), 103–30; F. Châtillon, "Regio dissimilitudinis," *Mélanges Podechard* (Lyon, 1945), pp. 85–102 (not seen); P. Courcelle, "Tradition neo-

God, the effect of man's sin is particularly open to such a rendering, especially since many Fathers claimed that the *imago* must remain in fallen man as the source of his redemption, and only the *similitudo* is lost. Plato is the source of the image in a passage from the *Politicus* (273d) describing the adverse effect of the material element on the World Soul as an approach toward the dread region of unlikeness; the metaphor was adopted by Plotinus (*Enn.* I, 8, 13) and Proclus (*In I Alcibiadem* V) and appears in a number of Christian Fathers, most especially Augustine, whose text in the *Confessions* VII, 10, 16 is the chief source of the medieval use and certainly of Isaac's acquaintance.[133] While the symbol could tend to stress a dichotomous view of body and soul, in becoming associated with a number of biblical themes, such as those of Exodus and Exile,[134] and the New Testament parable of the Prodigal Son wandering from his father's home *"in regionem longinquam"* (Lk 15:13), it rather acquired a moral flavor in most Christian authors. There is no point, given the expanse of secondary literature, in discussing the extensive use of *regio dissimilitudinis* in the twelfth century, except to note that it is frequently found among Cistercian authors, especially Bernard, William of St Thierry, and Aelred. So in this, at least, Isaac is very much in harmony with one of the traditional Cistercian themes.

---

platonicienne et traditions chrétienne de la 'région de dissemblance,' " *AHDL*, XXIII(1957), 5–23; "Répertoire des textes relatifs à 'la région de dissemblance' jusqu'au XIVᵉ siècle," *op. cit.*, pp. 24–34; "Témoins nouveaux de la 'région de la dissemblance," *Bibliothèque de l'École des Chartes*, 118 (1960), 20–36; J. Châtillon, "Les régions de la dissemblance et de la ressemblance selon Achard de Saint-Victor," *Recherches Augustiniennes*, 1962, pp. 237–50; R. Javelet, *op. cit.*, I, 266–85; P. Courcelle, "Complement au répertoire des textes relatifs à la région de dissemblance," *Augustinus*, XIII (1968), 135–40; M. Schmidt, "Regio dissimilitudinis," *Freibürger Zeitschrift für Philosophie und Theologie*, XV (1968), 63–108.

133. "Et inveni me longe esse a te in regione dissimilitudinis" (*ed. cit.*, p. 240). P. Courcelle, "Tradition néo-platonicienne et traditions chrétienne la 'région de dissemblance,' " pp. 9–10; *Les Confessions de St Augustin dans la tradition littéraire; Antécédents et Posterité* (Paris, 1963), pp. 287, 290.

134. This is present in Isaac with the mention of "terra aliena" from Ex 2:22 and Ps 136:4. For the theme, cf. Javelet, *op. cit.*, I, 281–5.

The Character of Isaac's Anthropology

In concentrating upon a single brief but rich passage from Isaac's Sermons we have hopefully gained an avenue of access to his theory of man which will enable us to follow the structure and arguments of the *Epistola de Anima* with increased comprehension. The term "Christian Socratism" has disadvantages as a description of this spiritual and theological movement. It is true that E. Gilson, who coined the term, sees that "Christian Socratism" extends far beyond pure moral interest; it leads on through what he describes as initial antiphysicism, to a concentration on the theology of the image of God, rhetorical emphasis on the greatness and misery of man,[135] an opening to microcosmic theory that reintroduces the value of the concrete, and the presentation of the mystical ascent to God as the goal of life.[136] But one wonders if the term keeps more than a verbal connection with the ethical interests originated by Socrates's use of "Know thyself"; rather, the necessity of self-knowledge in the twelfth century expresses a situation both social and traditional, as well as personal and ethical. This concern for self-knowledge has roots in the curiosity of the logical mentality for further knowledge that brought about some of the major advances of the century, but its upper branches are in contact with much older symbolic dimensions of man's awareness of self. In a thinker like Isaac of Stella the ancient symbolic themes of the Platonic tradition express the continued vitality of these dimensions; their presentation was necessary (if only indirectly) to the movement toward the conceptual conquest of greater scientific understanding of man. Thus, it seems also necessary to speak of this movement as a Platonic-Christian symbolic understanding of man.

The key themes found in the Second Sermon—self-knowledge, interiority, the image and likeness of God, microcosm, sin as the

135. This alone of Gilson's themes does not play a major role in Isaac. Despite his rhetorical gifts, his interests remain speculative.

136. Gilson, *op. cit.,* pp. 210–22. E. Bertola also admits a microcosmic as well as a moralistic aspect, *op. cit.,* pp. 253, 260.

K

region of unlikeness—are among the most significant aspects of Isaac's anthropology. The importance of these particular themes and the rich consistency of their interpenetration is what makes this passage an ideal introduction to the *Epistola de Anima;* but the key symbolic image remains the *catena aurea.* It alone will manifest not only the dimensions of the human mystery uncovered in Sermon Two, but also those, like hierarchy and anagogy, which are not explicit in this passage. We must turn to an analysis of the *Epistola* for the fullness of Isaac's teaching on the mystery of man.

AN ANALYSIS OF THE EPISTOLA DE ANIMA

The *Epistola de Anima* (probably written in 1162), along with the *Sermones in Sexagesima,* are the writings of Isaac that have attracted the most attention. A number of descriptions and analyses of the work have appeared in print, but many are quite introductory and none can really be described as adequate.[137] My intention, then, is

137. For the general description of Isaac's epistemology, W. Meuser, *Die Erkenntnislehre der Isaak von Stella,* is extensive but deficient in many respects. G. Webb, *An Introduction to the Cistercian De Anima* (London, 1962; Aquinas Paper 36) is poor. E. Bertola, "La dottrina psicologica di Isaaco di Stella," *Rivista di Filosofia Neo-Scolastica,* XLV (1953), 25–36, is an introductory exposition with no attempt to investigate sources, as is G. B. Burch, *Early Medieval Philosophy,* "Psychology," pp. 115–18. Perhaps the best of the analyses are A. van den Bosch and R. de Ganck, "Isaak van Stella in de Wetenschappelijke Literatur," *Cîteaux in de Nederlanden,* VIII (1957), 203–18 and M. L. Lewicki, *Filozoficzna antropologia Isaaka Stelli* (Lublin, 1955), as reported in "Une double thèse de philosophie sur Alcher de Clairvaux et Isaac de l'Étoile à l'Université de Lublin (Pologne)," *COCR,* XVIII (1956), 247–53. Among the descriptions in general surveys and encyclopedias the old work of K. Werner, *Der Entwicklungsgang des Mittelalterlichen Psychologie,* pp. 25–33, deserves mention. Later and briefer surveys are to be found in H. Siebeck, *Geschichte der Psychologie* (Gotha, 1884), pp. 403–15; M. de Wulf, *Histoire de la Philosophie Médiévale* (Paris, 1934), I, 225–7; B. Geyer, *Die Patristische und Scholastische Philosophie: Grundriss der Geschichte der Philosophie* (von F. Ueberweg; Berlin, 1928), pp. 258–60; E. Gilson, *A History of Christian Philosophy in the Middle Ages* (New York, 1955), pp. 168–9 and A. Forest, *Le mouvement doctrinale du XIe au XIVe siècle* (Paris, 1956), p. 150. I have not been able to obtain Mlle J. Debray-Mulatier's unpublished thesis, *Isaac de Stella et l'Epistola de Anima* (École nationale des Chartes, 1940) and A. J. Cappelletti, *Origen y grados del conocimiento segun Isaac de Stella, Philosophia* (Mendoza) 24 (1961). In general, more valuable suggestions on Isaac's

to comment on the *Epistola* in sufficient detail to indicate the organization, the sources, and the significance of the themes that appear there in the light of the central organizing symbol. My main concern will be with the *Epistola;* but since at least twenty-four of the fifty-five Sermons contain important anthropological and psychological material, reference will be made to them wherever necessary.

The Threefold Comparisons and the Identity of the Soul and Its Powers

The letter is addressed to Alcher, a monk of Clairvaux of whom we know little. For a long time he was thought to be the author of the important work that circulated under the name of St Augustine, the *De Spiritu et Anima;* but modern research has shown the difficulty of this view.[138] Isaac tells us that he was skilled in medicine (XII, 1881D–82C); he was apparently known as a serious inquirer into the fields of psychology and spirituality, since Peter of Celle (†1183) addressed his *Liber de Conscientia* to him.[139] Isaac is responding to Alcher's request for a specifically philosophical, not a Scriptural-based account[140]—we might say he is discussing the soul as nature, and not as history. How far he will be able to keep to this premise remains to be seen. Isaac says that he will concentrate upon the *"natura et viribus"* of the soul. The concern with the *natura animae* is traditional: even before the treatises of Augustine on the soul it was a sign of the depth of the influence of the classical soul-body dichotomy on the biblical view of man. The question of the powers of the soul is more interesting, for this side of his treatment will

---

anthropology and psychology can be found in the books and studies of such scholars as Chenu, Fracheboud, Künzle, Talbot, Michaud-Quantain, Javelet, Reypens, etc., than in many of the above.

138. Especially, G. Raciti, "L'Autore del *De Spiritus et Anima*," *Rivista di Filosofia Neo-Scolastica,* LIII (1954), 385–401.

139. PL 202, 1083–98. Cf. P. Delhaye, "Dans le sillage de S Bernard," *Cîteaux in de Nederlanden,* V (1954), 92–103.

140. I (1875B).

force Isaac back to the history of the soul based upon the biblical account of the Fall and Redemption. In this there is an at least implicit correction of Alcher's request for a purely philosophical treatment; Isaac appears to be saying that the true philosophy of the soul implies what the Scriptures tell us, a view that would be in accord with his undifferentiated conception of *theologia*.[141]

The interest of the medieval theologians, and especially twelfth-century scholars, in the classification of the powers of the soul has long been noted.[142] Lewicki has suggested that among the Cistercians this interest derived from the connection of the various faculties with the exercise of the spiritual life;[143] there were undoubtedly other strong reasons as well. The drive toward the ordering and classifying of inherited knowledge would naturally turn to the task of harmonizing and systematizing the different descriptions of the soul and its faculties that tradition had transmitted; this concern is evident among the so-called "spirituals"—Isaac, William of St Thierry, Aelred, and the *De Spiritu et Anima*—and also among the scholars of the School of Chartres, especially William of Conches. At the same time, another motivation was present in the case of Isaac, for the symbol of the *catena aurea* with its hierarchy of ascent naturally led to an interest in the delimitation of the stages by which that ascent took place: "There are therefore three realities, the body, the soul, and God; but I profess that I do not know their essence, and that I understand less of what the body is than of the soul, and less what the soul is than what God is."[144]

The *leitmotif* of the *Epistola* is introduced: the threefold com-

141. This has been noted by P. Michaud-Quantain, "La classification des puissances de l'âme," *Revue du moyen âge latin,* V (1949), 28.

142. Important in this question is L. Reypens, "Âme (son fond, ses puissances, et sa structure d'après les mystiques)," *DS* (Paris, 1937), I, cc. 433–69 and P. Michaud-Quantain, "La classification . . . ," pp. 15–34. For a general introduction, cf. the latter's "La psychologie dans l'enseignement au XIIᵉ siècle," *L'Homme et Son Destin,* pp. 409–15 and P. Künzle, *Das Verhältnis der Seele zu ihren Potenzen* (Freiburg [Schweiz], 1956).

143. *Op. cit.,* p. 250.

144. "Tria itaque sunt, corpus, anima et Deus; sed horum me fateor ignorare essentiam, minusque quid corpus, quam quid anima, et quid anima, quam quid Deus intelligere." II (1875C).

parison of body, soul, and God will be a frequently recurring theme. Such comparisons of God, soul, and body were present in Augustine;[145] and also in that great Augustinian, Hugh of St Victor;[146] but as a quarrel between Nicholas of Clairvaux and Peter of Celle in the late 1150's or early 1160's indicates, another widely discussed source of the comparison at the time was a passage in the *De Statu Animae* of Claudianus Mamertus.[147] Since the quarrel involved a monk of Clairvaux, and since Alcher, who was known to both Peter of Celle and Isaac, could have acted as middleman, it is possible that Isaac's awareness of this controversy drew his attention to the formula from Claudianus and provided a starting point for his own treatment. The other essential idea of the paragraph, viz., that God is the source of intelligibility, so that understanding decreases as we descend the ladder of being until we reach the radical obscurity of matter, was as old as Plato. As Gilson claims, it is a prime characteristic of any form of metaphysical Augustinianism.[148] There are also affinities here between Isaac and an interesting passage from Eriugena's *De Divisione Naturae*.[149] The

145. E.g., *De Quant. An.* I, 36, 80 (*PL* 32, 1079–80); *Tractatus in Jo.* XXIII. 5–6 (*CC* 36, pp. 234–6).

146. E.g., *De Sac.* I, 10, 2 (*PL* 176, 329C).

147. *De Statu An.* III, 7 (*ed. Engelbrecht*, p. 166): "aliud est vita corporum, aliud vita vitarum, corpus est vivens, anima viva, deus est vita, ita scilicet ut anima quae in se viva est corpori vita sit; ut sic corpus sine ipsa non vivat, sicuti ipsa sine deo." Cf. also II, 2, 6, 12 (*ed. cit.*, pp. 103, 119, 150–1). The quarrel is contained in Letters 63 and 65 of Nicholas of Clairvaux to Peter, and Peter's replies in Letters 64 and 66 (*PL* 202, 491–513). Nicholas's strongly Platonic views are occasionally reminiscent of Isaac, as on God as *simpliciter simplex* (502A–B), and his theology of the One (503C). Isaac does not seem interested in the major point of contention, i.e., whether Nicholas's expansion of Claudianus's dictum was legitimate. On the quarrel, cf. M.-D. Chenu, "Platon à Cîteaux," *AHDL*, XXIX (1954), 99–106.

148. "Here we have a second characteristic of every metaphysical Augustinianism, for in it *the soul is better known than the body.* ... In every Augustinian metaphysics, *the path leading to God must of necessity pass through the mind because God is better known to us than the body.*" *The Christian Philosophy of St Augustine*, p. 244. In Augustine, e.g., *De Gen. ad Litt.* V, 16 (*PL* 34, 333).

149. *De Div. Nat.* II, 27 (*PL* 122, 585A–D), especially in that the truth of every essence is in God, and the appearance of the image theme. There are, however, some pronounced differences.

paradoxical character of Isaac's view will appear in sharper perspective if we recall what the *Sermones in Sexagesima* says about the
impossibility of positive knowledge of God. We cannot know the
essentia that is God; and though we do know *"Omnis enim essentie
in Deo veritas est,"* how much less can we know the real *essentia* of
the soul.[150] Isaac is implicitly asserting that in our present fallen
state we cannot know the *natura-essentia* of the soul. The shift from
the question proposed by Alcher is already evident. We can,
however, by an analysis of the operations of the soul as *imago Dei*
argue to the functional analogy between human and divine natures
which will ground the quasi-definition of the soul as *similitudo
omnium*. First, however, the full range of differences between God,
soul and body must be brought to light by the application of
philosophical categories to the traditional formula.

The starting point of Paragraph III reflects the *Sermones in
Sexagesima* by its repetition of the Augustinian formula that God
is what he has.[151] In fact, we might say that Paragraphs III and IV
are an echo of one of the overriding problems of the *Sermones,*
the advantages and disadvantages of philosophical speech about
divine mysteries. The value of the threefold comparison becomes
evident as Isaac introduces two of the major concerns of his theory
of the soul. The first is the general theme of soul as the midpoint
between God and body. The second major point demonstrates
Isaac's place in a tradition originating in Augustine and continuing
into the thirteenth century: the identity of the soul and its powers.
God can have neither *qualitas* nor *quantitas;* the body has both, but is
neither. In its middle ground the soul cannot have *quantitas*
because it is not a body, but must have *qualitas* since it is not
God.[152] The conclusion is that the soul is to be identified with its

---

150. Isidore, *Sent.* I, 13 (*PL* 83, 564A) and Alcuin, *De An. Rat.* 1 (*PL* 101,
639A), among the early medievals, had also stressed the impossibility of soul
having unaided knowledge of itself.

151. III (1876B). The play on *simplex-compositum* at the end of II is also
reminiscent of the Sermons.

152. III (1876C). "Habet enim vires sive potentias naturales, secundum quas
virtuales sive potentiales dicitur habere partes."

powers. The soul can indeed have "powers or natural potencies, according to which it is said to have virtual or potential parts";[153] however, they must not be understood as quantitative parts, but are of the same nature and essence as the soul. Isaac clarifies what he means through the use of the example of *anima* and *ratio*, basing himself on Augustine:[154] *ratio* is a property or function of the soul not really distinct from it.[155] The reason for this affirmation of identity comes at the end of the paragraph. Everything in the soul must be really identified with soul, because only thus will it have the simplicity requisite for an image of God.[156] The stress on simplicity from the Sexagesima Sermons and the theology of the image and likeness of God combine to enhance what would come to be regarded as one of the hallmarks of Augustinianism in the thirteenth century.

P. Künzle has traced the history of the question of the identity of the soul with its powers.[157] Without ever being clearly asserted by Augustine, this identity is a possible interpretation of some passages in his writings.[158] Later authors were not as ambiguous.

153. *Ibid.* The terminology may go back to Boethius, cf. *Liber de Div.* (PL 64, 888A–C).

154. III (1877A). Isaac's rare quotations are difficult to identify. I have not been able to find these lines *verbatim* in Augustine, and suggest *De Trin.* XV, 17, 28 *(ed. cit.,* II, 502) as the closest parallel.

155. *Ibid.*

156. III (1877AB). Cf. Meuser, *op. cit.,* p. 11.

157. P. Künzle, *Das Verhältnis der Seele zu ihren Potenzen* (Freiburg [Schweiz], 1956). Less successful is M. Ortuzar, "El ser y la accion en la dimension humana (Pedro Abelardo y su gruppo)," *Éstudios* (Madrid), XIII (1957), 219–48, 431–63.

158. E.g., *De Trin.* IX, 4, 5 to 5, 8; X, 11, 18; XV, 17, 28 *(ed. cit.,* II, 82–90, 154–6, 502–4). Cf. Künzle, *op. cit.,* pp. 7–29; Reypens, *op. cit.,* c. 438; M. Schmaus, *Die Psychologische Trinitätslehre des Heiligen Augustinus,* pp. 256, 272–3; Ortuzar, *op. cit.,* pp. 227–34; Gilson, *The Christian Philosophy of St Augustine,* pp. 117, 212, and especially 219: "The constant refusal to admit any real distinction between the soul and its faculties or between the faculties themselves is noticeable throughout the whole history of this school and can be traced to a desire to preserve enough unity in the soul to guarantee that, in spite of the diversity of its parts, it will remain for us a recognizable image of the Trinity."

Claudianus Mamertus,[159] Boethius,[160] Gregory the Great,[161] Isidore of Seville[162] and many of the Carolingian writers have no hesitations about the identification. In the twelfth century we begin to find a divergence: a number of authors, e.g., Aelred,[163] Richard of St Victor,[164] William of St Thierry,[165] Hugh Eterianus,[166] and Peter Lombard,[167] assert the identity; while perhaps beginning with William of Champeaux and Abelard, and strongly supported by Gilbert of Poitiers, we find the contrary claim of a distinction of the soul from its powers that was to be of great importance in the thirteenth century.[168] Some important authors, such as Hugh of St Victor[169] and St Bernard,[170] have either divergent opinions, or are at least still the subject of controversy on this point. The significance of Isaac's assertion of the identity[171] lies mainly in the strong influence that he had upon the pseudo-Augustinian *De Spiritu et Anima*.[172] Problematic as Augustine's own views on the

159. *De Statu An.* I, 24; 26 (*ed. cit.,* pp. 84–7, 94–7).

160. *Lib. de Div.* (PL 64, 888A–C).

161. *Hom. in Ezech.* II, 5 (PL 76, 990A–C).

162. *Etymol.* XI, 1 (PL 82, 399A); *Diff.* II, 29 (PL 83, 84A–C).

163. *De Anima* I (*ed. Talbot,* pp. 79–81, 83, 93, 95, 106).

164. *De Extermin. Mali* III, 18 (PL 196, 1114B–C); *Benj. Min.* 17 (PL 196, 12).

165. *De Nat. Corp. et An.* II (PL 180, 720B–C).

166. *De Anima Corpore iam Exuta* (PL 202, 171D–72A).

167. *Sent.* I, 3, 12 (PL 192, 531).

168. Cf. Ortuzar, *op. cit.,* pp. 432–5. For Aquinas's assertion of the real distinction between the soul and its powers, e.g., *Summa Theol.,* Ia IIae, q. 110, Art. 4, Ad. 1.

169. Compare, for instance, *Did.* II, 4 (*ed. Buttimer,* p. 28) and *De Sac.* I, 3, 25 (PL 176, 227), which seem to assert the identity, with *De Sac.* I, 3, 6–9 (PL 176, 218) and *Spec. Ecc.* IX (PL 177, 377D).

170. Cf. the disagreement between E. van Ivánka, "La structure de l'âme selon S Bernard," *Saint Bernard Théologien: Anal. Sac. Ord. Cist.,* IX (1953), 204 and W. Hiss, *Die Anthropologie Bernhards von Clairvaux* (Berlin, 1964), pp. 89–90.

171. Cf. Reypens, *op. cit.,* c. 444; Künzle, *op. cit.,* pp. 64–6; M. Ortuzar, *op. cit.,* pp. 436–9 and E. von Ivánka, *Plato Christianus,* pp. 366–7, who sees it as an old Stoic theme (e.g., p. 322).

172. *De Spir. et An.* IV; XIII (PL 40, 782; 788D–89B). Cf. Künzle, *op. cit.,* pp. 66–74; Reypens, *op. cit.,* c. 445.

subject were, the circulation of this piece under his name provided a source for identifying the disputed doctrine with the thought of the Bishop of Hippo. Isaac's underground influence was of real moment here in one of the disputed points of thirteenth-century psychology.

"Virtus" in the Epistola

The Fifth Section marks what should be considered as the conclusion of the first major stage of the argument, the comparison of God, soul, and body according to simplicity of nature. The difficulties of this section primarily relate to the introduction of the concept *virtus*. In an enlightening article R. Javelet has discussed the Dionysian roots of the understanding of *virtus* in Isaac's writings;[173] the problem is that the Abbot of Stella seems to have had two views of *virtus*, and that the more important Dionysian one is only clarified in the light of later passages in the *Epistola* and places in the Sermons.

Isaac begins with a distinction of *naturalia*, which are to be identified with the soul, and *accidentalia*, which are not. The *accidentalia* are the *virtutes*, the four cardinal virtues for example, while the *naturalia* are the *vires*, or *facultates* of which we have already been given two lists—*ratio, ingenium, memoria,* and *rationabilitas, concupiscibilitas,* and *irascibilitas.*[174] What is surprising is that these cardinal virtues are described as coming from above, being created in the soul by the divine nature according to the principle: "For the powers are capable of receiving the gifts which by habit become virtues."[175] This descent of *virtus* from the divine Source is emphasized by the use of traditional examples like those of fire

---

173. "La vertu dans l'oeuvre d'Isaac de l'Étoile," *Cîteaux,* XI (1960), 252–67. Cf. also his *Image et Ressemblance,* I, 14, 145, 339; II, 89 (n. 74), 266–7 (n. 254). On Isaac's theory of *virtus,* the older work of T. Graf, *De subjecto psychico gratiae et virtutum* (Rome, 1934), Pars. I, pp. 93–5, is less successful.

174. IV (1877B).

175. "Vires enim sunt susceptivae donorum que habitu virtutes fiunt," IV (1877B).

and light,[176] by a long series of Scripture texts,[177] and by the mention of Jesus as the exemplar and source of all virtue.[178]

Isaac is aware of the ancient—and we might say *anthropocentric*—conception of *virtus* as the *"habitus animi bene instituti,"* originating in the Stoics and passed on by Augustine[179] and Boethius.[180] Popular in the twelfth century, he refers to it three times in the course of his works;[181] but, as Javelet demonstrates, he incorporated this view within a Dionysian conception *virtus*—what we might call the *anagogic* conception—which involves the theory of substance and accidents outlined in the *Sermones in Sexagesima,* and the total ascensional pattern established by the master symbol of the chain of being. As we have seen from the above passage, *virtus* is conceived of as something sent down to man from on high enabling him to ascend the ladder of being to its essential source.[182] This is fully in harmony with everything that has been said thus far about the anagogic dimensions of the *catena aurea.* The distinction between *vires* and *virtutes* is a theological application of the basic metaphysic of *substantia* and *accidens* contained in the Sexagesima Sermons. Briefly put, the doctrine is this: the *facultates* or *vires* fall under the category of *substantiae primae* because they are really identified with the substantial being which is the soul;[183] the *virtutes* are the *accidentia* which Sermon Nineteen has assured us are necessary for the presence of the *substantiae secundae* in the *substantiae primae.*

176. IV (1877C).   177. IV (1877CD).   178. IV (1877D).

179. E.g., *De Div. Quaest.,* 83, XXXI, 1 (*PL* 40, 20), "Virtus, est animi habitus naturae modo atque ratione consentaneus.

180. *De Diff. Top.* II (*PL* 64, 1188C–D)."

181. *Sermo 3* (ed. Hoste, p. 114; 1697C); *Sermo 4* (ed. Hoste, p. 140; 1703C); *Epistola V* (1878D). Cf. G. Engelhardt, *Der Entwicklung der dogmatischen Glaubenspsychologie in der Mittelalterlichen Scholastik vom Abaelardstreit (um 1140) bis zu Philip dem Kanzler (gest. 1236), BGPM.* XXX (Münster, 1933), p. 127.

182. For the anagogic dimension of *virtus,* cf. Javelet, "La vertu . . . ," pp. 260–62, especially the statement: "Le néoplatonisme est sousjacent à cette chaine d'or, et qui voudrait étudier le problème de la grâce chez notre auteur, devrait tenir compte de cette métaphysique." (p. 262).

183. Javelet, "La vertu . . . ," p. 266, n. 110: "La *'premiere substance'* est d'ordre abstrait, ou plûtot indéterminé." This is either a misprint for 'seconde substance,' or a total misunderstanding.

The mutual interdependence of the three are the key to Isaac's program. From the viewpoint of his metaphysic, unless the faculties of man received these formal specifications from above, they could not really exist, nor could man himself exist. Any distinction between natural and supernatural is totally foreign to such thought. While we have to a certain extent extrapolated this theory upon the text given here, two corroborating arguments can be given. First of all, while Javelet does not make explicit appeal to the *Sermones in Sexagesima*, he virtually comes to the same conclusion when he says: *"Pour Isaac, le surnaturel n'est ni une simple actuation d'une nature qui est déjà une grâce d'en haut, ce n'est pas non plus un secours spécial de Dieu favorisant l'extase, c'est l'accident divin qui correspond à la nature, comme une idée platonicienne 'informant' la matière."*[184] Secondly, the dictum, "VIRES *enim sunt susceptiva donorum que habitu* VIRTUTES *fiunt,"* already indicates a mutuality vaguely similar to that of *substantiae* and *accidentia* in the Sermons, but is obscure by reason of the middle term *habitus.* The relation of *habitus* to the solidifying of *dona* into *virtutes* is unexplained— possibly a remnant of the anthropocentric pattern, or, as Javelet asserts, the place for the exercise of human freedom in the divinization of man.[185] A second text removes this obscure intermediate term *habitus* by assuring us that the *naturalia* or *facultates* and the *accidentalia* or *virtutes* are mutually necessary for each other's very existence.[186] Despite the fact that *vires* are identified with the essence of man and *virtutes* are gifts from on high, man as historic being needs both in order to be the man that he is called to be. The passage closes with an aside on the problem of predicating *naturalia* of God (i.e., that the Father has a natural Son and the Son a natural Father)

184. *Op. cit.,* pp. 264–5, n. 96.

185. *Op. cit.,* p. 266.

186. "Virtus in affectu formatur vel potius, affectus ipse in virtute formatur," *Sermo 4 (ed. Hoste,* p. 130; 1701B). If *affectus (vis seu potentia naturalis)* is taken here as identical with *substantia prima,* and *virtus* as identical with *accidens,* then we have a parallel with the statement: "Nihil ergo convincitur esse substantia, si nihil sit accidens," (1755C). Of course, there is a converse to this: the *substantia* can be determined by *vitia* as *accidentia* rather than *virtutes* (cf. *Epistola,* 1879D).

which shows that the proper distance can still be kept between God, soul, and body in such categories.[187]

The Powers of the Soul: Affectus

The fifth paragraph begins the study of the powers of the soul—the topic of major interest for the remainder of the *Epistola*. The traditional Platonic division of the soul into *rationabilitas, concupiscibilitas,* and *irascibilitas*[188] had already been mentioned; Isaac now returns to expand on it.[189] He sees this triad (which was, of course, known to him from a wide variety of patristic and later sources)[190] as another example of the hierarchical structure of the world: just as the soul is the creature in the middle, sharing something with both extremes, the soul itself has an *"imum, medium, summum"* in the Platonic division.[191] This recalls Plato's locating of the divisions of the soul in distinct parts of the body in the *Timaeus;* Javelet remarks that the topographical metaphors frequent in twelfth-century psychology really have an axiological meaning—they signify a situation on the chain of being.[192] Isaac then allegorizes a passage from Isaiah to show that Christ possessed a full human soul, i.e., one having the three Platonic functions, as well as a human body—another testimony to his realization that man is not just the Platonic soul, but the combination of body and soul.

187. IV (1878A). The passage shows Isaac's awareness of more traditional Trinitarian terminology, including the dictum, "quod omnia sua est, excepto quod altera persona ad alteram relative dicitur," than appears in his own use in the *Sermones in Sexagesima.*

188. E.g., *Republic* IV 439–41; VI 504; *Timaeus* 69d, etc.

189. Isaac mentions the triad frequently in his Sermons, e.g., 1726D, 1747B–C, 1773A, 1864A.

190. E.g., Chalcidius, *Commentarium,* Chap. 229 (*ed. Waszink,* p. 244); Macrobius, *Comm. in Somn. Scip.* I, 6, 42–3 (*ed. Willis,* p. 26); Tertullian, *De Anima* 16 (PL 2, 673A); Origen, *In Ezech. Hom.* I, 16 (PG 13, 681B); Jerome, *In Mt.* II, 13; 33 (PL 26, 91B, 94BC); *In Ezech.* I (PL 25, 22–3); Gregory the Great, *In 7 Ps. poenit.* (PL 79, 551C); Isidore of Seville, *DeD iff.* II, 30 (PL 83, 85B); Alcuin, *De An. Rat.* III (PL 101, 639D).

191. V (1878B).

192. *Image et Ressemblance,* I, 130, 267.

How does the Abbot understand the Platonic division? Once again, in dynamic terms; it is the capacity to be illuminated: "through reasonableness the soul is of a nature to be illuminated to know something either below itself, or above itself, or even in itself and beside itself."[193] The formula, "*infra se, supra se, in se, et iuxta se,*" is merely another way of expressing the threefold comparison; Isaac's frequent use of it seems partially due to its ability to be visually conceived in terms of the image of the golden chain.[194] *Concupiscibilitas* and *irascibilitas* exhaust the capacity for movement in the affective order, so that the Platonic triad is identical with Isaac's frequent category of *sensus* and *affectus* as the two fundamental powers of the soul.[195] The source of this doctrine of *sensus* and *affectus*, the rational and affective powers, has caused considerable controversy: Mlle Debray-Mulatier thought it Aristotelian; Lewicki spoke of it as reminiscent of John Damascene; while van den Bosch and de Ganck, without citing any sources, held it for Augustinian.[196] Such a category is almost too general to trace with precision. In the twelfth century, we find it used by Hugh of St Victor,[197] and occasionally by Cistercians;[198] Richard of St Victor is the one whose use is closest to Isaac's.[199]

193. "Itaque per rationabilitatem habilis nature est anima illuminari ad aliquid, vel infra se, vel supra se, vel et in se et iuxta se cognoscendum," V (1878C.)

194. On this formula, which I have been able to trace as far back as Alcuin (*De An. Rat.* 5; *PL* 101, 641B), cf. Gilson, *The Spirit of Medieval Philosophy*, p. 219. Richard of St Victor uses an analogous formula in talking of three kinds of knowledge: *extra nos* [*corporalia*], *intra nos* [*spiritualia*], *supra nos* [*Divina*]; cf. *Benj. Min.* 55 (*PL* 196, 40C–D). For other uses in the *Epistola*, cf. XIV (1884A) and XX (1886C).

195. "De rationabilitate igitur omnis oritur anime sensus, de aliis vero omnis affectus." V (1878D). Sometimes conversely, the Platonic triad is said to arise from *sensus* and *affectus*, cf. 1747B.

196. *Op. cit.,* p. 211.

197. *De Sac.* I, 10, 3 (*PL* 176, 331B–32B); *De Arca No emor.* (*PL* 176, 621); *Hom. in Eccles.* II (*PL* 175, 141B–C).

198. Aelred, *De An.* I (*ed. Talbot,* p. 73); Bernard, *In Ascens.* 3, 1–2 (*PL* 183, 305B).

199. E.g., *Benj. Min.* 3 (*PL* 196, 3A–D); *Benj. Maj.* III, 13 (122D); *De Statu int. Hom.* 34 (*ed. Ribaillier,* pp. 101–2).

Isaac is not interested in *rationabilitas* at this stage. Instead, he turns to a consideration of the kinds of *affectus*[200] and their relation to the virtues, thus bringing out some of the anthropocentric sides of his understanding of *virtus*. Isaac's division of *affectus* on the basis of temporal variation—*gaudium* for thing desired and presently enjoyed, *spes* for one only desired, *dolor* over an evil actually present, and *timor* over a future evil—is part of ancient Stoic moral theory current in late antiquity,[201] and well known among both the Victorines and the Cistercians. Isaac is here merely repeating a theme common among the thinkers of his time. The entire passage is a rearrangement of these traditional anthropological elements: the four *affectus* are the common matter of the virtues, since it is the *affectus* which gives its name to every human action.[202] Reason is what orders the *affectus* to produce the proper virtue, thus justifying the traditional definition of *"virtus est habitus animi bene instituti"* "virtue is the habit of a well-ordered soul."[203]

The traditional anthropocentric treatment of *virtus* is continued in Paragraph VI with the Augustinian theme of the four cardinal virtues as specifications of the supreme Christian virtue of *caritas*. The cardinal virtues, found in Plato[204] and Cicero,[205] were taken

200. On the importance of *affectus* in Victorine theology and in Isaac, cf. J. Châtillon, "Cordis affectus au moyen âge," *DS* I (Paris, 1937), cc. 2288–2300.

201. V (1878D). Compare with the almost word-for-word parallel in *Sermon 17* (ed. Hoste, pp. 316–20, 1746D–47C, and the texts noted there). Important sources here are Chalcidius, *Comm.* 194 (ed. Waszink, pp. 216–17); Lactantius, *Inst.* 6, 16, 1 (*PL* 6, 692–3); Augustine, *Conf.* X, 14, 22 (ed. cit., pp. 371–2); *De Civ. Dei,* XIV, 6 (ed. cit., II, 421); Nemesius of Emesa, *De Nat. Hom.* XVII, 1–6 (ed. Burkhard, pp. 95–6); and especially Boethius, *De Consol. Phil.* I, metr. 7, lines 25–31 (ed, Rand, pp. 168–70), which Isaac cites in the Sermon as the source of his terms. It is also found in such later witnesses as Isidore of Seville, *Diff.* II, 40 (*PL* 83, 95). On the four *affectus,* cf. Bertola, *op. cit.,* pp. 302–3.

202. "Affectus etenim omni operi nomen imponit," V (1878D), a common theme repeated in 1697D, 1703C. 1747D, 1847B, it seems to be taken from Ambrose's *De Off.* I, 30, 147 (*PL* 16, 718).

203. In the *Epistola,* Isaac does not include any of the physiological material on *affectus* and its location in the heart which makes the passage in Sermon 17 so interesting. On this question, compare with 1807D–8A.

204. E.g., *Republic* IV, 427e; 433.

205. *De Fin. Bon. et Mal.,* V, 23, 67 (Loeb ed., pp. 466–70).

up by Augustine as expressions of the supreme virtue of love in a passage in the *De Moribus Eccleslae Catholicae* which is the immediate source of Isaac's treatment here.[206] Almost by way of aside, Isaac concludes with a mention of the various *motus animi* arising from *concupiscibilitas* and *irascibilitas* which may owe something to the discussion of Chalcidius.[207] After this brief, and rather unoriginal, treatment of *affectus*,[208] Isaac turns to *rationabilitas* in all its manifestations, the chief topic of the *Epistola*.

Before we can turn to the question of the stages of *rationabilitas*, however, this transition from *affectus* to *sensus* demands the ventilation of an important problem in Isaac's theory of the soul. Is *sensus* or *affectus* the superior stage in the ascent to God? Robert Javelet in his study of *virtus* in Isaac's writings at times gives a certain superiority to *affectus*,[209] but he does mention that the Pseudo-Dionysius upon whom Isaac depends refuses to separate knowledge and virtue.[210] The *gaudium* which Javelet sees as the ultimate goal of Isaac's spiritual doctrine[211] would then have to be a much richer

---

206. Para. VI (1879A):
"id quod quadripertita virtus dicitur ex amoris vario affectu *formatur, ut temperantia* sit amor Dei se integrum servans et integrum . . . , *fortitudo* amor propter Deum facile omnia preferens, *iustitia* amor Deo tantum serviens . . . , *prudentia* amor ea que iuvant in Deum bona discernans ab his que ab ipso impediunt."

De Mor. Ecc. Cath. I, 15, 25 (*PL* 32, 1322):
"Namque illud quod quadripartita dicitur virtus, ex ipsius amoris vario quodam affectu, quantum intelligo, dicitur . . . ut *temperantia* sit amor integrum se praebens ei quod amatur; *fortitudo*, amor facile tolerans omnis propter quod amatur; *iustitia*, amor soli amato serviens et propterea recte dominans; *prudentia*, amor ea quibus impeditur, sagaciter seligens."

On the identity of the cardinal virtues with *caritas*, cf. Gilson, *The Christian Philosophy of Saint Augustine*, pp. 136, 311; Javelet, "La Vertu . . . ," p. 256.

207. VI (1879AB). Cf. *Commentary* 194 (*ed. Waszink*, pp. 216-17).

208. He recognizes the insufficiency himself: "sed ista iam de affectu tacta potius quam dicta sufficiant," V (1879B).

209. *Op. cit.*, p. 257, and more clearly on p. 267: "C'est ce qui permet di mieux comprendre cette priorité déjà signalée, et qu'Isaac accorde en ce point à l'*affectus* sur la *ratio*."

210. P. 257.

211. *Op. cit.*, p. 267; and *Image et Ressemblance*, I, 141 and 417-18, where, however, he does admit: "Sans doute il insiste particuliérement sur la vertu comme sur l'intelligence au sommet de la connaissance."

thing than just one of the four fundamental *affectus* spoken of
previously. Endre von Ivánka's study of the reassertion of Neoplatonic themes in the twelfth century sees Isaac as the origin of a
mystical schema stressing affectivity over intellectuality.[212] Von
Ivánka contrasts a pattern of spiritual ascent in which there is continuity between the rational and super-rational stages, still evident
in Richard of St Victor, with an affective pattern of ascent in which
principalis affectio as the ultimate stage breaks with any form of
intellectual activity.[213] While Thomas Gallus in the thirteenth
century is the prime representative of the latter view, von Ivánka
sees the crucial point of origin in Isaac's marked differentiation
between *intellectus* and *intelligentia* in the twelfth century.[214]

There are arguments in favor of this supremacy of the affective
aspect in the *Epistola*. The important analysis of the stages of the
ascent to God in Paragraph X (1880D–81A), equates the nine stages
with the nine choirs of angels, implying that the four affective stages
(perhaps the four cardinal virtues) are to be superimposed upon the
five levels of human rationality. Nevertheless, this passage confronts
us with some grave problems. With regard to the *Epistola* itself, we
are permitted to wonder why *affectus* is treated with such brevity,
while *sensus* (*rationabilitas*) is developed at length.[215] Even if we
advert to some special reason for this emphasis in the *Epistola*,
there are still serious arguments for seeing a narrowly affective
interpretation as misleading. The most important of these is the

212. "Zur Überwindung des neuplatonischen Intellektualismus in der
Deutung der Mystik: *intelligentia oder principalis affectio*," *Scholastik*, XXX
(1955), 185–94. Reprinted in *Plato Christianus*, pp. 352–63.

213. *Plato Christianus*, pp. 352–5, 379–83.

214. Pp. 358, 362–3, and 381, especially, "Diese Umdeutung hat Thomas
Gallus—über Isaac de Stella auf die Gedankenmotive bei Proklos zurück-
greifend, die diesen aspekt besonders hervorheben—im wesentlichen voll-
zogen" (p. 363).

215. E.g., *voluntas anime* is mentioned in Par. VIII (1880A); it seems to be
identified with *concupiscibilitas* in Par. XI (1880D). *Liberum arbitrium*, which
plays such a major role in the thought of St Bernard, appears in generally
Bernardine fashion in Isaac's Sermons (e.g., 1726C–D; 1775B; 1808A–B;
1847A–D), but does not appear at all in the *Epistola*.

constant assertion that both *sensus* and *affectus* are equally fundamental to the human soul and both must work together in the
deificatory ascent of man; the union of *cognoscere* and *diligere*, as
has been already noted, is the constant mode in which Isaac expresses the goal of humanity.[216] In this sense, then, it would be
incorrect to think of the stages of the ascent of knowledge as in
some way merely preparatory for a further affective ascent. These
rational stages are not something to be left behind, but are rather
parallel to the ascent of the affective powers. The *caritas* that is the
actuation of affectivity is a *caritas ordinata*, one fully consonant with
reason.[217] Thus it would be a mistake to exalt either *sensus* or
affectus in the ascensional process: both are identical at the summit.
Isaac never uses the popular phrase *"amor ipse intellectus est,"* but it
cannot be said that he would have been adverse to it.

The passage in the *Epistola de Anima* on the nine stages of ascent
should be taken as a symbolic and not as a logical expression. It
does not indicate nine distinct stages, the latter four being considered
as necessarily superior to the first five, but rather the global ascensional process. The fact that this ninefold schema never enters into
the systematic exposition of Isaac's views, and that the nine choirs
of angels play a distinctly minor role in his thought (as compared
with the thought of the Pseudo-Dionysius), is another argument for
this interpretation. Moreover, the distinction that von Ivánka draws
between the radically discontinuous ascension of Isaac which
allowed the invasion of an affective summit as superior to intellect
in later writers and the continuous intellectual ascensional patterns
of Richard of St Victor is much too sharply drawn. While Isaac
does use *intelligentia* in a more sharply defined sense than Richard,
and while his Dionysianism leads to a strong emphasis on its
transcendent character, there is continuity along his chain of being
too, as the descent of the theophanies and ascent of phantasms in
man the mediator and even Isaac's use of light symbolism when

216. Cf. the texts cited on this in note 47 *supra*.

217. On *caritas ordinata*, cf. Javelet, *Image et Ressemblance*, I, 409–27 and
A. Hoste, *Isaac: Sermons* I, pp. 140–1, n. 2. Isaac uses the term frequently, e.g.,
1703C, 1744B, 1805A–D, 1822D, 1837B–D, 1840A–B, 1852C–D.

L

compared with Richard's, indicate.[218] In short, in the question of the absolute superiority of *affectus* or *rationabilitas*, we should accept Isaac's own statement on the necessity of both:

> But the journey must be undertaken as it were on the two feet of reason and affective power. By means of the first, it proceeds from the letter to the spirit; by means of the second, from vice to virtue. Nay more, brother, the journey must be of such a kind that you continually pass from understanding to understanding, and from virtue to virtue, until with perfect knowledge you behold the one whom your soul loves, and embrace the one you behold with the arms of the fullness of love, and joyful for the sake of love you admiringly say, "Such is my well-beloved."[219]

218. Von Ivánka, *op. cit.,* pp. 353, 380-81, places great stress upon the continuity of light from the lowest to the highest stages in Richard of St Victor's schema of ascent. The same is true of Isaac of Stella; there is no real break:

Benj. Maj. V, 9 (*PL* 196, 178D):	*Epistola* XVI (1884D-85B):
Sed in ejusmodi sublevatione, dum mens humana semper ad altiora crescit, dum diu crescendo tandem aliquando *humanae* capacitatis metas transcendit, fit demum ut a semetipsa penitus deficiat, et in supermundanum quemdam transformata affectum, *tota supra semetipsam eat.* Et sicut matutina lux crescendo desinit, non quidem esse lux, sed esse lux matutina . . . ita humana intelligentia ex dilatationis suae magnitudine quandoque accipit ut ipsa jam non sit ipsa, *non quidem ut non sit intelligentia, set ut iam non sit humana* . . .	Sicut ergo sol de subterraneis emergens, aquarum et paludum nebulosa quadam fumositote languens, prius rubet potius quam lucet, deinde in libertatem purioris aeris, calcatis nebulis, evadens serenior splendit, sic nimirum anima, . . . (cf. entire passage).

Von Ivánka's views are based upon an unacceptable hypothesis of Proclean origin for Isaac's fivefold schema (*op. cit.,* pp. 357-61).

219. "Migrandum vero quasi pedibus duobus, sensu et affectu, altero de littera ad spiritum, altero vero de vitio ad virtutem. Quinimmo et transmigrandum, frater, ut semper de sensu in sensum, et de virtute in virtutem migres, usque dum perfecta cognitione cernas quem diligit anima tua; et quasi quibusdam brachiis plenae dilectionis amplectaris, quem cernis, et propter cognitionem laetabundus admirans dicas: *Talis est dilectus meus.*" *Sermon 10* (ed. Hoste, p. 220, 1723B).

The Powers of the Soul: The Two Schemas of Rationality

Isaac has two schemas to describe the functions of man's power of understanding. In Paragraph VII (1879BD) we are introduced to the temporal scheme of *rationabilitas*, consisting in *ratio* (present knowledge), *memoria* (past knowledge) and *ingenium* (future knowledge). The same triad also appears in a parallel passage in the *Sermones in Sexagesima*.[220] P. Künzle was the first to note that this rare triad of faculties appears in the *Ysagoge in Theologiam*, a work of the early 1140's showing both Victorine and Abelardian influence;[221] but Isaac's development of it is unique. We may wonder why Isaac makes use of two separate lists of rational operations. Here issue must be taken with Künzle's view of the lack of an organizing theme in the *Epistola*,[222] for the use of the two schemas has a very definite systematic role. The purpose of the temporal schema is to contrast our way of knowing with God's non-temporal knowledge;[223] the fivefold dynamic pattern of *sensus*, on the other hand, is used to explain how human and divine knowledge are related and joined. Both schemas are necessary in Isaac's system—one to indicate the distance between God and man, the other the possibility of man's ascent to God.[224]

Paragraph VIII (1880AB) introduces us to a most important part

220. 1767A–D. There is another appearance in 1746D.

221. Künzle, *op. cit.*, pp. 65–6. Cf. *Ysagoge I* (*ed. Landgraf*, p. 70). There are, of course, some reminiscences of Augustine, particularly in the mention of the *venter memorie* (VII, 1879C), which we also found in *Conf.* X, 14 (*ed. cit.*, p. 371). The metaphor goes back to Plato. Compare also Cassiodorus, *In Ps.* 30, 11 (*PL* 70, 210D) and Peter Lombard, *In Ps.* 30, 13 (*PL* 191, 305B). On the *Ysagoge*, the most recent work is D. E. Luscombe, *The School of Peter Abelard* (Cambridge, 1969), pp. 236–44.

222. P. 66: "Dem bunten Mosaik der Texte entspricht der Mangel einer einheitlich abgerundeten Gedankenführung."

223. The a-temporal character of God's knowledge is, of course, strongly put in the 5th Book of Boethius's *De Consolatione Philosophiae*.

224. Lacking in the *Epistola* is the physiology of the temporal triad given in *Sermon 17*: "Sensus vero rationalis in tribus existere dignoscitur, ingenio videlicet, ratione, memoria; quae in animalium capite distinctis, et ordinatis cellulis, ancipite, sincipite, occipite vigere et exercere propria creduntur officio" (*ed. Hoste*, p. 316, 1746D).

of Isaac's psychology, the five-tiered schema of the ascent of *rationabilitas*, once again identified with the essence of the soul itself. "There is therefore sense-knowledge, imagination, reason, discernment, understanding. Nevertheless, all these in the soul are nothing other than the soul. Properties are distinguished because of various activities, but there is one rational essence and one soul."[225] Since the source of this schema, and its implications for his theory of man's ascent to God and man's unification with the *cosmos,* are questions of considerable importance and complexity, they will be the subject of a separate study in Chapter IV. Following the actual exposition of the *Epistola,* we will proceed with an analysis of the individual stages beginning in Paragraph IX (1880C), where Isaac first mentions the noetic objects of the single stages. This often-repeated theme highlights a major dimension of the schema: just as the five levels are symbolically likened to the ascent of the five material components of the universe, earth, water, air, aether, and the empyrean; the objects of the levels fully exhaust the types of beings, material or spiritual, which compose the totality of things. *Sensus* perceives bodies; *imaginatio* the likeness of bodies; *ratio* the dimensions or forms of bodies, i.e., universal concepts whose existence depends upon realization in physical bodies; *intellectus* perceives the created spirits of men and angels; and *intelligentia* immediately beholds the sole supreme and pure incorporeal nature of God.[226] These comparisons of the powers of rationality, their objects organized according to the degree of corporeality, the symbolic corresponding elements, and later the sciences ascribed to each, are repeated throughout the *Epistola.* They also appear in a passage in Sermon Four that is a word-for-word parallel to sections from Paragraphs VIII and IX.[227] They can be set down in the form of a chart to simplify our later exposition:

225. "Dicitur ergo sensus corporeus, imaginatio, ratio, intellectus, intelligentia. Hec tamen omnia in anima non aliud sunt quam anima. Alie et alie inter se proprietates propter varia exercitia, set una essentia rationalis et una anima." VIII (1880A).

226. IX (1880C).

227. *Ed. Hoste,* pp. 134–6 (1701D–2C).

Power of Soul[228]	Object	Corporeality	Science[229]	Element[230]
intelligentia (mens– 1881D; acies mentis– 1701C)	Deus	pure incorporeum	theologia	empyreum (ignis)
intellectus	spiritus creatus	vere incorporeum	—	aether (firmamentum)
ratio	dimensiones corporum (1884A– formae incorporeae corporearum: substantiae secundae)	fere incorporeum	(doctrina) mathematica	aer
imaginatio	similitudines corporum (phantasiae –1888B)	fere corporeum	scientia naturalis	aqua
sensus corporeus	corpora	pure corporeum	scientia naturalis	terra

228. For lists of the powers, objects and degrees of corporeality, cf. 1702A; *Epistola* VIII (1880A), IX (1880C), XVI (1885A), XVIII (1885B), XIX (1886B).

229. The corresponding sciences appear in XVI (1884CD) and XX (1886D–87A).

230. Hoste discusses Isaac's list of elements in note 1 on pp. 132–33 of his edition of the Sermons. The doctrine of the four elements of earth, water, air, and fire would have been known to Isaac through *Timaeus* 32b and Chalcidius's *Commentarium,* Chap. 21–2; and especially 129 (*ed. Waszink,* pp. 71–3, 171–2). Plato's addition of the aether between air and fire (*Epinomis* 981c) was a commonplace of classical science accessible through Chalcidius, Chap. 129, and some of the Fathers, e.g., Ambrose, *In Hex.* I, 6; II, 2 (*PL* 14, 132–5, 146–7) and Augustine, *Epist.* 242, III, 5 (*PL* 38, 1140).

The unifying power the five stages give to Isaac's *Epistola* is obvious; not less important is the unification of soul and world which it portends. The spiritual and the material are open to each other as parts of one great order which begins in the corporeality of man and ends in the vision of God.[231] Another side of Isaac's definition of the soul as *similitudo omnium* now appears.[232] One further point is of interest here. A re-entry of the comparison of body, soul and God shows that the fivefold division is to some extent an explication of this theme; but here the comparison takes a form dear to Isaac, of the comparison of God, soul and body in terms of place and time,[233] an idea seemingly based upon a text from Augustine.[234]

Sensus Corporeus

The remainder of the *Epistola* is a methodical treatment of the five powers, beginning with *sensus*,[235] here to be taken in the special sense of sense knowledge, and not as the generalized power discussed

---

231. P. Daubercies has noted the importance of the body as the origin of contemplation in the thought of the Pseudo-Dionysius: "Il n'en reste pas moins intellectualiste de la contemplation, conception dans laquellè le corps peut avoir sa place" (*op. cit.*, p. 23).

232. Clear in XIX (1886A).

233. It will reappear in XV (1884C), XVII (1885BC).

234. IX (1880C):

E.g., Augustine, *Epist.* 18, 2 (ed. Goldbacher; *CSEL* 34, 1, p. 45):

". . . primum videlicet incorporeum [substantia secunda] ad subsistendum tamen indigum corpore, *ac per hoc loco et tempore.*

"est natura per locos et tempora mutabilis, ut corpus,

. . . *spiritum creatum, qui ad subsistendum non eget corpore, ac per hoc nec loco, sed sine tempore minime esse possit, cum nature mutabilis sit.*

et est natura per locos nullo modo, sed tantum per tempora etiam ipsa mutabilis, ut anima,

. . . *ipsum solum summe et pure incorporeum, quid nec corpore ut sit, nec loco ut alicubi, nec tempore ut aliquando eget.*"

et est natura, quae nec per locos nec per tempora mutari potest, hoc deus est."

235. On Isaac's theory of sensation, see Meuser, *op. cit.*, pp. 19–23.

earlier. Isaac's theory of sensation is Augustinian in background, Platonic rather than Aristotelian.[236] Sense is not a passive power acted upon by impressions from exterior bodies—such would be impossible in the hierarchical world where the superior can never be subjected to the action of the inferior level; it is an active power of the soul directed toward perceiving present corporeal forms of bodily realities.[237] It is corporeal only in that its object does not surpass the level of bodies, or insofar as it makes use of corporeal instruments.[238]

Plotinus had asserted that sensation originates in the soul,[239] an analogous doctrine is present in Augustine;[240] he holds with considerable vigor throughout his works that sensation is the awareness in the soul of modifications made on the body.[241] Isaac's doctrine of sensation follows the major lines of Augustine, but in a far more simplified fashion. His treatment revolves around two concerns. First, he is anxious to affirm the interior unity of sensation, necessary for his theory of the identity of rational powers with the nature of the soul. This he does by means of one of the homely examples which we encounter from time to time in his works.[242] Secondly, he wants to maintain, in dependence upon Augustine, that there is a congruence between faculty and object in the act of sensation, since this theory fits in so well with his preference for apt linkages as the means of assuring the unity of the chain of being. Unable or unwilling to follow all the subtleties of Augustine's views on this

236. Sensation is discussed at length in the *Timaeus* 43b–47e, but Isaac's use seems to be more directly related to Augustine.

237. "Est igitur sensus ea anime vis qua rerum corporearum corporeas formas percipit et presentes . . ." X (1880D).

238. *Ibid.*

239. E.g., *Enn.* I, 1, 4; IV, 4, 23; IV, 6, 1–3; V, 3, 2.

240. Cf. E. Gilson, *The Christian Philosophy of St Augustine*, pp. 48, 56–65, 70–6; O'Connell, *St Augustine's Early Theory of Man* (Cambridge, 1968), p. 166, n. 2; 199, n. 4 and R. A. Markus, *Cambridge History*, pp. 374–9.

241. Especially *De Quan. An.* I, 21–30 (PL 32, 1058–69). Also, *De Musica*, VI, 5, 8–10 (PL 32, 1167–9); *De Gen. ad Litt.* IV, 34; VII, 19–20; XII, 24, 51 (PL 34, 319–20; 364–5; 474–5); *De Trin.* XI, 1–3 (ed. cit., II, 160–8).

242. X (1880D–81A).

question, Isaac stresses the congruence of the material components
of the five senses with the four elements present in sense objects in
order to prove his point.[243] Both this and the example used for the
unity of *sensus interior* are fairly close to a passage from Augustine's
De Genesi ad Litteram;[244] what is lacking in philosophical depth is
somewhat compensated for in the stress brought to the connection
of man and the material universe.[245] The polyvalence of Isaac's
symbols can be noted by the fact that the theory of elements is used
both as a symbol of the total process of ascent and as an explanation
of the operation of the lowest stage, *sensus*.

Imagination and the Union of Body and Soul

Imaginatio, the nearest stage of the materially-directed function of

---

243. X (1881A).

244. X (1880D–81A):

"[a] *Sicut enim in lutere aqua recepta,
per plurima foramina radios emittit
varios . . . sic sensus interior . . .*

[b] *Ignis enim micat in oculis . . .*

[c] *Aer vero subtilis . . . sonat in
auribus congruentibus . . .* Nam
[d] *crassus iste et fumosus quodammodo
aer* odoribus fetoribusve affectus
naribus, [e] *et aqua palato sapit.* [f]
Terra autem solidatur in tactu. . . ."

De Gen. ad Litt. XII, 16, 32 (*PL* 34,
319–20):
"Quae cum ita sint, pertinet corporis
sensus ad visa corporalia [a] *qui per
quinque quasi rivulos distanter valentes
distribuitur*: cum illud quod est sub-
tillissimum in corpore et ob hoc
animae vicinius quam cetera; id est
[b] *lux, primum per oculos sola
diffunditur, emicatque in radiis oculorum*
ad visibilia contuenda; deinde mix-
tura quadam, [c] *primum cum aere
puro,* [d] *secundo cum aere caliginoso
atque nebuloso,* [e] *tertio cum corpulen-
tiore humore,* [f] *quarto cum terrena
crassitudine."*

The congruency that Isaac stresses here between the material element in the
object and the material element in the sense organ is strong in *De Gen. ad Litt.*
III, 4–5; IV, 34 (*PL* 34, 281–2; 319–20); *De Gen. ad Litt. Lib. imperf.* 5, 24
(*PL* 34, 228–9); *De Musica* VI, 10 (*PL* 32, 1169). Cf. also Claudianus
Mamertus, *De Statu An.* I, 7 (*ed. Engelbrecht,* pp. 44–6) and Nemesius, *De Nat.
Hom.* VI, 7–10 (*ed. Burkhard,* pp. 76–7).

245. Other passages on the special theory of *sensus* in Isaac are 1775C and
1795A. On theories of sense knowledge in the twelfth century, cf. J. Ebner,
Die Erkenntnislehre Richards von St Viktor, BGPM, XIX, 4 (Münster, 1917),
18–19.

rationabilitas to the purely spiritual realms, as might be expected for one so fascinated with the connections of things, is very important to the Abbot of Stella. *Imaginatio* was an unclear concept in the twelfth century. On the borderline between the physical and the spiritual, it allowed for the absorption of heteronomous material, both physiological and psychological, from a wide variety of traditions.[246] Imagination is the power of the soul which perceives the *absent* corporeal forms of bodily things, just as sensation perceives the present forms; thus, *imaginatio* arises out of *sensus*, for it depends upon true qualities known by sensation for its own images and likeness.[247] Nevertheless, the power never has an incorporeal object; its object is *spiritus corporeus (spiritus pecoris)*, the material principle of life which man shares with animals. Isaac becomes so excited by the hierarchical implications of this that he forgets to mention his usual term for the *"similitudines et imagines"* of real bodies which are produced by imagination; they are called *phantasiae*, a Greek name that smacks of ErIugena.[248] Our suspicions are confirmed by an important text from the latter part of the *Epistola*: "And so just as phantasms rise from below into the imagination, theophanies descend from above into the understanding,"[249] which can be found almost verbatim in the *De Divisione*

246. M.-D. Chenu. "Imaginatio: note de lexicographie philosophique," *Miscellanea Giovanni Mercati*, II, *Studi e Testi* (Vatican City, 1946), pp. 593–602, distinguishes four senses: (1) a generalized Augustinian sense; (2) a Boethian contribution; (3) Avicennan and (4) Aristotelian senses. Chenu's remark on the ascending vocabulary of the Augustinian sense as invoking the metaphysics of participation (p. 596) is close to Isaac's use. Cf. also, Chenu, "Un vestige du stoicisme," *RSPT*, XXVII (1938), 63–68. For Isaac, Meuser, *op. cit.*, pp. 23–5, has the fullest treatment.

247. XI (1881B).

248. In his use of *phantasiae* and its variants some passages (e.g., 1701B) seem Augustinian in flavor; on the other hand, the use of *phantasmate* in 1755B and 1759A may owe something to Eriugena's distinction between the good *phantasiae* that are images of real things, and the *phantasmate* which are merely made up in the mind (*De Div. Nat.* III, 2; *PL* 122, 695B–C).

249. "Itaque sicut in imaginationem desubtus phantasie surgunt, ita in intelligentiam desuper theophanie descendunt." XXIII (1888B). Cf. XVI (1885A), for another passage on the ascension of *phantasiae*.

Naturae.[250] This generalized Augustinianism, now given strong Erigenean overtones,[251] is useful as Isaac turns to what is perhaps the most difficult problem his Platonized psychology had to confront, the explanation of the union of soul and body. Can the unified view of man which Christian anthropology seemed to require be expressed through the medium of Platonic categories?

Isaac's answer to this question cannot be described as a philosophical triumph. Given the material that he had to work with, however, it is not unoriginal, even if it is largely dependent on insights available in Hugh of St Victor. Augustine considered the problem to be beyond solution;[252] the twelfth century did not. Over sixty years ago, Heinrich Ostler, in what is still the best introduction to the twelfth-century treatment of the problem of the unity of man, outlined three solutions: union through number and harmony, union in the personality, and union through a physical medium;[253] but these are by no means to be separated. Isaac has elements of all three within an enveloping theory of Dionysian

250. "Ut enim ex inferioribus sensibilium rerum imagines, quas Graeci *phantasias* vocant, anima recepit; ita ex superioribus, hoc est, primordialibus causis cognitiones, quae a Graecis *theophaniae*, a Latinis divinae apparitiones solent appellari, sibi ipsi infigit, et per ipsas quandam de Deo notitiam percipit . . ." *De Div. Nat.* II, 23 (*PL* 122, 576D–77A). For Eriugena on *phantasiae*, cf. the definitions in *PL* 122, 659B–C; 962–3A; and the two kinds described in 573C (Isaac's use accords with the second).

251. Without having made a detailed study, I would hazard that Isaac's use of *imaginatio* also has interesting relations with Richard of St Victor: e.g., *Benj. Min.* 3–5, 16, 18, 53; *Benj. Maj.* I, 4–6; II, 17 (*PL* 196, 3A–5C; 11B–D; 12C–13B; 39A–D; 67D–72C; 95A–99A).

252. E.g., *De Civ. Dei*, XXI, 10 (*ed. cit.*, II, 776).

253. H. Ostler, *Die Psychologie des Hugo von St Viktor*, BGPM, XV, 1 (Münster, 1906), Chap. VII, pp. 62–89. He discusses Isaac's dependence on Hugh on pp. 74–8. Cf. also Artur Schneider, *Die Abendländische Spekulation des 12ten Jahrhunderts in ihrem Verhältnis zur Aristotelischen und Judisch-Arabischen Philosophie, BGPM*, XVII, 4 (Münster, 1915), 56–8, who sees Isaac as generally in the medium theory. These categories were used by C. H. Talbot, *Ailred of Rievaulx: De Anima, Mediaeval and Renaissance Studies*, Supplement I (London, 1952), pp. 40–4, who also discusses Isaac. G. Webb, *An Introduction to the Cistercian De Anima*, pp. 15–18, is not to be trusted on this question, nor is J. Espenberger, *Die Philosophie des Petrus Lombardus und Ihre Stellung im zwölften Jahrhundert, BGPM*, III, 5 (Münster, 1901), 99.

origin which might be described as union through location on the ascending chain of being.[254] *Imaginatio* is still corporeal, and the corporeal and the spiritual can never cross the unalterable line that divides them, but the necessity of a continuous chain of being comes to the rescue—the highest point of corporeal nature and the lowest point of spiritual nature are so similar that they can be joined in personal union without a confusion of natures. While the chain of being continues to lurk in the background, the phrase "in which [extremes] *without confusion of natures,* nevertheless by a *personal union*"[255] shows that there is a theological motive at work which was also present in Augustine[256] and Hugh:[257] the union of the natures of God and man in the Person of Christ becomes the analogy and exemplar for the union of body and soul in man. Union takes place at the two extreme points of the spheres of being, the *phantasticum animae* which is almost corporeal and the *sensualitas carnis* which is almost spiritual.[258] The principle of like being joined

254. Daubercies, *op. cit.,* p. 39, speaks of the importance of hierarchical solutions to the problem of the union of body and soul in the early Middle Ages and their dependence on the Pseudo-Dionysius.

255. X (1881C): ". . . in quibus sine naturarum confusione personali tamen unione. . . ."

256. Cf. C. Coutourier, "La structure metaphysique de l'homme d'après S Augustin," *Augustinus Magister I,* pp. 549–50; O'Connell, *op. cit.,* p. 274, n. 6.

257. Ostler, *op. cit.,* p. 88.

258. This is a variant of the unity in the medium approach, and is dependent upon Hugh of St Victor's *De Unione Corporis et Spiritus* (PL 177, 285–94):

(a) In the concept of linkings by the near approach of diverse levels reaching out for each other: "Est ergo quiddam quo ascendit corpus, ut appropinquet spiritui, et rursum quiddam quo descendit spiritus, ut appropinquet corpori. . . . Ascendit corpus et descendit spiritus. Ascendit spiritus, et descendit Deus . . . Corpus sensu ascendit, spiritus sensualitate descendit. . . ." (285A–B). Ostler notes Chalcidius, *Comm.* 33 (*ed. Waszink,* pp. 82–3), as a possible source for this doubling of the medium (p. 72).

(b) In describing the physical medium in terms of fire: "Sed ignis qui ipso aere longe subtilior est et mobilior, et non sicut aer, extrinsecus terrena corpora afflando movet, sed interius vegetando vivificat, magis proprie vocatur spiritus . . . [spiritus] nomen pariter et proprietatem illius [ignis] usurpat; non tamen proprie, quia in eo ipso quod spiritus dicitur, corporeae naturae proprietatem nequaquam excedere comprobatur." (286B–D). On Hugh's theories here, cf. also R. Baron, "Situation de l'Homme d'après Hugues de Saint Victor," *L'Homme et Son Destin,* pp. 431–3.

to like is the universal law of the chain of being, explaining the union of the height of the soul with God, and even the vestiges of the Platonic divisions of the soul in animals.[259] Clearly in Isaac's system problems are solved by the multiplication of entities, or at least the modes of operation. The *catena aurea* has little in common with Occam's razor.

Isaac pursues his point by annexing other understandings of this union, logically out of place in a strictly argued presentation, to what has been already established. If what we have seen could be said to be a special adaptation of the medium theory (though not of one medium, but rather of neighboring links in a chain) with hints of a theory of union in person,[260] what follows is an adaptation of the harmony theory. The rational soul has been presented with a fitting bodily dwelling place of its own by the wisdom of the Divine Harpist:[261] its own rational melodies are in control, rather than those of the *spiritus corporeus* which even the beasts possess.[262] The unexpected entry of harmony theories of the union of soul and body betrays an attitude toward the place of music and harmony among the sciences which is difficult to recapture fully. Plato had referred to the Pythagorean idea of the soul as the harmony of the body in *Phaedo* 85e–86d, 93a–c, only to reject it; the theory was discussed in many of the psychological treatises of late antiquity, e.g., Chalcidius, Macrobius, Nemesius, and Gregory of Nyssa.

259. XI (1881CD). For other appearances of the argument, cf. XXIII (1888B); *Sermo* 55, 106–10 (*ed. Leclercq*, p. 287).

260. Most fully developed by Hugh of St Victor, e.g., *De Sac.* II, 1, 11 (*PL* 176, 405–9).

261. ". . . quasi rationabilibus et armonicis eius motibus seu numeris summi cithariste plectro . . ." (1882A). Christ was the true Orpheus for Clement of Alexandria. While we cannot expect twelfth-century writers to have been aware of this, it is noteworthy to see them repeating similarly striking metaphors—for Rupert of Deutz Christ is the *citharum*, not the *citharista*, *In Mt.* IV (*PL* 168, 1389C); for Honorius Augustodunensis, God is the *magnus citharista* who creates the universe as an instrument to play on, *Liber XII Quaestionum*, 2 (*PL* 172, 1179, 1197B). Cf. de Lubac, *Exégèse Médiévale*, II, 2, pp. 98–9.

262. XII (1881D–82A).

Plotinus speaks of the body as a lyre (*Enn.* I, 4, 16; II, 3, 13), though he, of course, also rejected the Pythagorean theory. Two other possible sources for Isaac's acquaintance with the description of the soul as the harmony of the body are Augustine's early treatise, the *De Immortalitate Animae*, where he describes and rejects the *temperatio* theory of the soul's relation to the body;[263] and Boethius's *De Musica*, perhaps the strongest witness to the influence of a Pythagorean notion of harmony of the Middle Ages.[264] These ideas were widely disseminated in the twelfth century, particularly among the Chartrains[265] and William of St Thierry;[266] even Hugh, upon whom Isaac was so heavily dependent in the question of the union of body and soul, has echoes of the harmony theory.[267] We will return to these themes when we treat of the next paragraph.

The rest of Paragraph XII (1882BC) is a reminder of the mine of curious information that a twelfth-century monk could have at his disposal. We are given a brief introduction to the senses of Scripture, as a Scriptural quotation from Proverbs is used to support the harmony theory of the body (here specified to be the head) as the fitting seat of the rational soul.[268] An insight into the medical and

263. II (*PL* 32, 1022, 1029–30). On the ambiguities of these passages, cf. O'Connell, *op. cit.*, pp. 140–2.

264. *De musica* I, 1 (*PL* 63, 1167–71, esp. 1168C–D; 1170D: "Id nimirum scientes [Pythagoreans] quod tota nostrae animae compago musica coaptatione conjuncta est.")

265. E.g., Adelhard of Bath, *De Eodem et Diverso* (ed. *Willner*, p.23); William of Conches, *Dialogus de Subst. Phys.* VI (1567 ed. pp. 304–5); Bernardus Silvestris, *De Mundi Univ.* (ed. *Barach-Wrobel*, pp. 51, 56) and, influenced by the Chartrains, Alan of Lille, *Anticlaudianus* (*PL* 210, 551A).

266. *De Nat. Corp. et An.* (*PL* 180, 712C). Cf. also Gundissalinus, *De Anima* IV (ed. *Muckle*, p. 45).

267. E.g., *Didasc.* II, 12 (ed. *Buttimer*, pp. 32–3); cf. also Richard of St Victor, *De Stat. Hom. Int.* I, 34 (ed. *Ribaillier*, pp. 101–2).

268. Isaac's historical sense here is, of course, really the Platonic idea of the rational soul being situated in the head (*Timaeus* 44d); cf. Chalcidius, *Comm.* 213 (ed. *Waszink*, p. 228). On the senses of Scripture in Isaac, cf. 1690D, 1719B–C, 1721D, 1725D, 1727C, 1729C–D, 1741A–D, 1750A–B, 1777B, 1799B, 1806D, 1870C, and 1872D and A. Fracheboud, "Isaac de l'Étoile et l'Ecriture Sainte," *COCR* XIX (1957), 133–45 and H. de Lubac's fundamental work, *Exégèse Médiévale, passim.*

physiological information of which Isaac was so enamored, and which was undoubtedly a significant part of twelfth-century anthropological speculation, is also present. This is not the place to discuss at length the sources and nature of Isaac's medical information; but this particular description of the six bones composing the head and the seven columns (vertebrae) upon which it rests shows similarities with traditional material from Cassiodorus,[269] and Rabanus Maurus.[270] Other examples of Isaac's interest seem to betray the influence of the Judeo-Arabic material translated in the eleventh and twelfth centuries,[271] especially the *De Differentia Spiritus et Animae* of Costa-ben-Luca,[272] as well as such traditional sources as Augustine's *De Genesi ad Litteram*. The main point is that Isaac takes his place along with Hugh of St Victor, William of St Thierry, Adelhard of Bath, William of Conches, and Alcher (whose expertise in medicine elicits the plea for a treatise at this point)[273] in that movement of medical and physiological interest which showed another side of the century's concern with the whole man as a means of effecting a correction of the Platonic dichotomy of body and soul.[274]

The medical material is only an aside; returning to the real theme of the section, we are given that succinct expression of Isaac's principle of conjunction which we have already noted as so fundamental to his thought: "For through two very apt median realities two diverse extremes can be easily and firmly joined; something

269. *De Anima* XI (*ed. Halporn*, p. 90).

270. *De Anima* V, ix (*PL* 110, 1114A–D; 1119A–B).

271. Cf. 1746D–47D; 1801B; 1808A; 1828C; 1833A–C; 1869A, for other medical information.

272. Edited C. S. Barach (Innsbruck 1878). On the importance of this treatise, cf. E. Bertola, "Le Fonti Medico-Filosofiche della Dottrina dello 'Spirito,' " *Sophia*, XXVI (1958), 55–7.

273. One of Raciti's most telling arguments against the ascription of the *DeSpiritu et Anima* to Alcher is the poverty of its medical material; cf. "L'Autore del 'De Spiritu et Anima,' " p. 388.

274. Isaac's own words here evidence this concern. He wants to learn "quomodo quasi instrumentum operationis et delectationis illud anima et libenter suscipiat, et sollicita custodiat, et invita dimittat, et dimissum desiderabunda exspectet, et in recepta gratulabunda exultet . . ." XII (1882B).

that is easily seen in the structure of the great animal, as some call it, that is, of this world,"[275] Although this expression is close to a text from the Pseudo-Dionysius,[276] the search for sources here is secondary to the recognition of the entire world of thought brought to expression by the principle. The application of the axiom to the perennial problem of the union of soul and body is carried one step further at this stage in a passage that shows Isaac's awareness of Hugh of St Victor's *De Unione Corporis et Spiritus*, and also his acquaintance with the Macrobian influence at Chartres. It is another example of the use of *involucrum*, though here a Latin not a Greek poet is used. The philosophical wisdom uncovered is from Vergil, long the subject, especially among the Neoplatonists, of allegorical and symbolic interpretation.[277] The union affected through the two media, on the one hand the *sensualitas carnis,* or *ignis,* on the other the *phantasticum spiritus,* or *igneus vigor,* is the hidden meaning of a line from the Sixth Book of the *Aeneid*: "*Igneus est illis vigor est celestis origo.*"[278] One may wonder if a poet as deeply influenced by philosophy as Vergil would have been totally adverse to such a philosophical interpretation.

275. "Per duas etenim convenientissimas medietates facile et firme due dissidentes extremitates necti possunt, quod in magni ut quidam dicunt animalis id est mundi hujus fabrica cernere facile est," XII (1882BC).

276. *De Div. Nom.* VII, 3 (*Dionysiaca* I, 407–8).

277. Cf. P. Courcelle, "Les Pères de l'Église devant les enfers virgiliens," *AHDL,* XXX (1955), 5–74 (Isaac's use is mentioned on p. 45, n. 1): and "Interprétations néo-platonisantes du livre VI de l'Eneide," *Recherches sur la Tradition Platonicienne* (Entretiens Hardt), III Geneva. 1955 pp. 95–136. On the, use of Vergil in the Middle Ages in this connection, cf. also H. de Lubac, *Exégèse Médiévale,* II, 2, "Virgile Philosophe et Prophète," pp. 232–62.

278. This particular section from the 6th Book was popular with Macrobius, e.g., *In Somn. Scip.* I, 8, 11; I, 14, 14 (*ed. Willis,* pp. 39, 57–8). The latter, with its mention of the *magnum animal* as the world, and the Homeric *catena aurea,* is the likely source for Isaac's use, though the Abbot's more positive sense indicates dependence upon a Commentary tradition as well (perhaps William of Conches's unedited *Glosa super Macrobium*). Isaac uses the same lines for an *involucrum* in *Sermo* 55, lines 61–6 (*ed. Leclercq,* p. 286), which is very close to the Macrobian passage. For *ignis* and *igneus vigor* in Hugh, cf. *De Unione Corporis et Spiritus* (PL 177, 286B–D).

The Spiritus Vitalis and the Manner of the Soul's Presence

Isaac had earlier distinguished the *spiritus corporeus* (also called *spiritus vitalis, spiritus pecoris, sensualitas carnis*) from the soul: it is the source of the animal life. No other point so succinctly portrays the distance between an Aristotelian view of the relation of the soul to the body and the Platonic tradition within which Isaac is working. The soul is not the form of the body; to say so would be to tie the soul so closely to the body that its immateriality and immortality—two chief advantages the Christian tradition had found in the Platonic theory of man—would be placed in doubt; there must be a separate principle of life for the body itself.[279] An ancient tradition, possibly Stoic in origin, had created such a principle in the *spiritus vitalis*[280] centered in the heart and diffused through the members.[281] Like many of his generation,[282] Isaac used the *spiritus vitalis* both as a fundamental physiological principle and

279. That the soul in itself is not sufficient to vivify the body is evident from 1774A: "Ipsum [corpus] ergo quoniam anima adhuc vivens, et necdum spiritus vivificans, *de se solo vivificare non sufficit* . . . ," and *Epistola* XXII: (1888B): "Sicut autem anima corpori suo non sufficit sola ad vitam. . . ."

280. The doctrine of *spiritus vitalis* is found in Chalcidius, *Comm.* 203, 303, and especially 220 (*ed. Waszink,* pp. 222–3, 304–5, 232–4); and more vaguely in Augustine, *De Gen. ad Litt.* VII, 13 (*PL* 34, 362–3); and, of course, throughout the Judaeo-Arabic medical literature.

281. On the *spiritus vitalis* in Isaac as born in the heart and diffused throughout the body, cf. 1807D–8A.

282. Cf. M.-D. Chenu's article, "Spiritus: Le Vocabulaire de l'âme au XIIIᵉ siècle,'. *RSPT*, XLI (1957), 209–32, esp. pp. 224–25 discussing the biological sense, our *spiritus vitalis*; and especially, E. Bertola, "Le Fonti . . .," pp. 48–61. Among the most important medical-physiological sources here were the *Pantegni* of Ali ibn al-Abbas (10th century, translated by Constantine the African), the *De Differentia Spiritus et Animae* of Costa-ben-Luca and Hunain ben Ishaq's introduction to the *Megategni* of Galen. The treatment of the *spiritus vitalis* in Chap. I of the *De Differentia Spiritus et Animae (ed. S. Barach,* pp. 121–24) is quite close to Isaac's use. For other appearances in twelfth-century authors, cf. William of Conches, *De Phil. Mundi* IV, 22–24 (*PL* 172, 948–95D); Hugh of St Victor, *De Unione Corp. et Spiritus (PL* 177, 285A–C, 288D); William of St Thierry, *De Nat. Corp. et An.* I (*PL* 180, 687C; 700B sqq.); John of Salisbury, *Met.* IV, 16 (*PL* 199, 925B–C); Aelred of Rievaulx, *De Anima* I (*ed. Talbot,* pp. 72–75, 86, 93), II (pp. 124, 130); *De Septem Septennis*

as a means of protecting the immortality of the soul; but he does see that its admission involves a real difficulty—if the *spiritus vitalis*, *corporeus*, or *sensualitas*, gives life to the body, why is it that the body does not go on living after the departure of the soul?[283] Now the real reason for our Abbot's unexpected flirtation with the harmony theory of the union of soul and body comes out, for the harmony of the *sensualitas* of the body itself determines the suitability of the body for the presence of the soul; when this is disturbed, the soul with all its powers of rationality unwillingly departs. A long series of comparisons is used to express the relation between mortal body and immortal soul in this arrangement: e.g., the body is like the musical instrument which when used gives forth the melody, but the melody remains after the instrument is broken and cast aside. The point of the comparisons, including the last between the permanence of numbers and the contingence of numbered things which recalls the Platonic tradition present in the interests of Boethius and the School of Chartres, is to show that the immaterial soul can never be localized: it does not come or go in the strict sense, but is rather immanent like the melody in a page of music.[284] By making the *spiritus corporeus* rather than the soul the harmony of the body, Isaac has used an originally Pythagorean doctrine condemned by Plato to defend the Platonic doctrine of the soul's spirituality and immortal nature. Whether he was the first to use the traditional harmony theory this way, I have not been able to determine.[285]

(PL 199,952D–53A); *De Spiritu et An.* XIV, XXXIII *(PL* 40,790A,803A); Alan of Lille, *Contra Haereticos* I, 28; *Regula* 102 *(PL* 210, 329; 676B–C); Alfred of Sareshal, *De Motu Cordis* X–XII *(ed. Baeumker, BGPM,* 23, 1–2 [Münster, 1923], pp. 37–62).

283. XIII (1882C).

284. XIII (1882D–83A).

285. The closest test to Isaac's use seems to be that of William of Conches in the *Dialogus de Substantiis Physicis (ed. Grataroli* [1587], pp. 304–5), which considers dying as a loss of harmony, but does not make specific mention of the *spiritus vitalis*. Also vaguely similar is Adelhard of Bath, *Quaestiones naturales,* 43 *(ed. Mueller,* p. 44).

M

In conclusion, Isaac's struggle with the problem of the relations of the soul and the body appears as a *mélange* of traditional themes organized in a decidedly unsatisfactory way from the point of view of a strictly logical answer to the problem, but one which testifies to what I have called the symbolic expression of the desire to incorporate man in the cosmos, to see him as a unified existent.[286]

The statements in this paragraph on the impossibility of localizing the soul stimulate the reflection that incorporeality and omni-presence pertain absolutely to God, and to the soul only insofar as it is the image of God.[287] This observation effects a bridge to the following paragraph's comparisons between the manner of God's presence in the world and that of the soul in the body, a theme in which Isaac through some rather careful analysis joins himself to a philosophical tradition of considerable importance since the time of Plotinus. The paragraph revolves around three closely-related problems: the manner of the soul's presence in the body, the in-visibility of the soul consequent upon the immateriality demanded by such a presence, and the way in which the soul is made visible indirectly; but each of these problems is doubled by being shown as analogous to the relation of the divine nature to the world. We have seen that Isaac was aware of the tradition from the *Timaeus* locating the rational soul in the head; that this is nothing more than a metaphor adopted for its value as a symbol of the corresponding hierarchies of man and the world is evident from the stress here on the ubiquity of the essence of the soul despite its use of various bodily instruments.[288] "Just as God is in the whole, and whole

286. Isaac frequently repeats the traditional dictum that the whole man is a creature composed of soul and body (e.g., 1720C–D; 1729D; 1731B; 1742A; 1778D; 1779B; 1847A), but the question is: does he mean it? I hope I have shown that he does. In this, I would concur with Lewicki's judgment: "La solution qu'en donne Isaac s'oppose, au moins partiellement, aux conceptions platoniciennes traditionelles déprécient le corps en tant que matière," (*op. cit.*, p. 249). Meuser has a similar, but more extreme, expression in *op. cit.,* p. 9.

287. XIII (1883B).

288. Succinctly put in *Sermon 34* (1801D): "Sicut etiam cum una sit in hominis corpore anima, tota ubique per essentiam, differenter tamen per virtutem et operationem. . . ."

in each of the parts, but [remains] in himself; so also the soul is in its whole body, and is in itself whole in each of its members."[289] Isaac's summation of the manner of the soul's presence might almost have been taken from Plotinus, who frequently discussed this question.[290] Plotinus, of course, and the Neoplatonists in general, were making use of an Aristotelian insight contrary to the Platonic location of the various powers of the soul within different parts of the body[291]—the kind of combination to which Plotinus' attempt at synthesizing the ancient philosophical tradition naturally lent itself. Augustine was the channel for the knowledge of the concept of the omnipresence and totality of the soul in the whole body and in each single part for the Middle Ages; he returns to the idea frequently as a means for demonstrating that the soul is not corporeal.[292] Claudianus Mamertus's *De Statu Animae,* already noted as an important source of the threefold comparisons of God, soul, and body, is also significant here. The treatise, written against a certain Faustus who held that angels and the souls of men were in some way material and local, leans heavily upon Augustine's demonstrations of the omnipresence of the soul and comparisons of this with the manner of God's presence in the world.[293] While these themes are a recurring feature of the patristic tradition and very popular in the twelfth century, we may suspect that Claudianus was influential in Isaac's handling of the question. Isaac's exposition is clear, so there is no need to discuss it at length,

289. "Sicut vero Deus in toto, et in singulis totus, sed in semetipso: sic et anima in toto suo corpore, et in singulis membris in semetipsa tota." XIV (1883D).

290. E.g., "its [the soul] divisibility lies in its presence at every point of the recipient, but it is indivisible as dwelling entire in the total and entire in any part." *Enn.* IV, 2, 1 (trans. MacKenna, p. 257). Cf. also *Enn.* IV, 3, 3; 7, 5; 9, 1.

291. E.g., *De Gener. An.* I, 19 (726b 22); II, 1 (734b 25) (*Loeb ed.,* pp. 92, 153). The Aristotelian origin is noted by Chalcidius, *Comm.* Chap. 225 (*ed. Waszink,* pp. 238–41). Cf. Schneider, *op. cit.,* p. 58.

292. E.g., *De Immort. An.* 16 (*PL* 32, 1034); *Ep.* 166, 2, 4 (*CSEL* 44, pp. 550–53); and *De Trin.* VI, 6, 8 (*ed. cit.,* I, 488). On the importance of Plotinian omnipresence in Augustine, cf. O'Connell, *op. cit.,* pp. 37–65.

293. Especially in I, 17; III, 2; III, 3 (*ed. Engelbrecht,* pp. 62–4; 155; 158).

except on the interesting point of the manner in which God and the soul in some sense become visible. The soul is invisible and not localized, but it can be seen in the body and through the body, just as the meaning in a piece of writing is seen through the written characters themselves. God is totally invisible, but he can be seen in and through the creatures of this world according to the Scriptures.[294] This thought leads Isaac to a bold expression which brings him close to the spirit of cosmic optimism that pervaded the School of Chartres, another mark of his distance from the supposed world-negating view of which the medievals are sometimes accused—"For the whole of creation is *as it were* the body of the divinity, and the individual parts like individual limbs."[295] This is scarcely pantheism; Isaac's addition of *"quasi"* to indicate the metaphorical nature of his comparison makes that clear, but it is the most daring way in which he puts his positive sense of the cosmos.[296] The passage closes with a reminder that *imaginatio,* the power which began this long series of digressions, must always be described as being on the fringes of the corporeal and localizable, no matter what state it is exercised in. It never transcends the level of the *similitudines corporeae.*[297]

The Power of Ratio in the Special Sense

The *Epistola* now returns to its outline of the powers of *rationabilitas,* beginning the treatment of *ratio* in the special sense in Paragraph XV (1889 AC). This is closely tied in with Isaac's account of abstraction and second substance in Sermon Nineteen of the

294. XIV (1883C).

295. "Universitas etenim creature quasi corpus est divinitatis, singule autem quasi singula membra," XIV (1883CD). Perhaps there is a reminiscence of Claudianus here, who wrote: "illa [anima] quidem non in toto mundo est tota, sed sicut deus ubique totus in universitate, ita haec ubique tota invenitur in corpore," III, 2 *(ed. Engelbrecht,* p. 155).

296. Is it perhaps a last mild form of the identification of the World Soul with the Holy Spirit which had been such a subject of heated controversy in the twelfth century?

297. XIV (1883D–84A).

Sexagesima group.[298] The doctrine here is not Augustinian; the African doctor knows nothing of real abstraction;[299] the source is in the Aristotelian translations and commentaries of Boethius, particularly the *Categories* and the *Commentaries on the Isagoge of Porphyry*. This treatment of *ratio* introduces a note of Aristotelian epistemology which seems to destroy any unity that Isaac's system might have had. This would be true if we were dealing with either a real attempt at creating an epistemology or with an authentic understanding of Aristotle. Neither being the case here, since Isaac's interest is directly psychological, a theory of the soul, and only incidentally epistemological (how the soul arrives at truth), and since his fragmentary knowledge of Aristotle is conditioned by Boethius, who asserted that the Stagirite was in full agreement with Plato, it is possible to understand the source of Isaac's confusion. What this passage on *ratio* and *abstractio* does reveal is the renewed interest in epistemological questions, and particularly the problem of universals, which had entered the world of the Cathedral Schools in the late eleventh and early twelfth centuries and of which the Abbot of Stella had undoubtedly absorbed some knowledge in his years with the Masters. Isaac is no Abelard or Gilbert of Poitiers—the contradiction between his theory of sense knowledge and his theory of the knowledge of reason he seems not to have noticed. As we have already noted, Isaac has a typically Augustinian active notion of sense knowledge—*sensus* perceives the present forms of corporeal things, but *sensus* is a spiritual power (*"cum tamen non sit corpus"*),[300] even though Isaac sometimes uses Aristotelian terminology which seems to contradict this (e.g.,

---

298. 1754A–56A.

299. Agreeing with Gilson, *The Christian Philosophy of St Augustine,* pp. 82–5 and notes, against his opponents in this question. A. Fracheboud in his article, "L'Influence de Saint Augustin sur le Cistercien Isaac de l'Étoile," *COCR,* XI (1949), 13–17, concurs. The fullest account on *ratio* in Isaac is to be found in Meuser, *op. cit.,* pp. 25–31, though I have certain reservations about his treatment, especially the conclusion (p. 31), which fails to stress the dependence of *ratio* on divine action, both before and after Original Sin.

300. X (1880D).

"quia corporeis exercetur instrumentis").[301] While it is an extrapolation upon Isaac's unevolved epistemology, Gilson's comments on Augustine's theory of sensation seem apropos here, for in this system sensations are intelligible impressions, and abstraction of the Aristotelian type has nothing to work on.[302] In a true Aristotelian world, reason in its active aspect would work upon the virtually intelligible phantasms which sense knowledge impresses on the passive intellect to produce universal concepts; Isaac demonstrates his misunderstanding by short-circuiting the system. Since the *phantasiae* of imagination, and the products of *sensus*, are already intelligible as effects of the active soul, there is no place for reason to go but back to the *corpora* themselves. That is why we are told that: "For [reason] abstracts *from a body*, not by an action but by a reflection, those things which are founded in a body."[303] An Aristotelian-based theory of abstraction might use such language, but in its explanation would be careful to show that it must be understood in terms of abstracting from the impressions made upon the intellect by bodies through the senses. Isaac has no such explanation and one doubts if he could have given one, for the incorporation

301. *Ibid.* This phrase could be used, of course, in a more general sense, as it is in Abelard's *Logica ingredientibus*, cf. B. Geyer, *Peter Abelard's philosophische Schriften*, BGPM, XXI, I (Münster, 1933), p. 20: "Cum igitur tam sensus quam intellectus anima sint, haec eorum est differentia, quod sensus per corporea tantum instrumenta exercentur. . . ." But Abelard sees general conceptions as dependent upon sense images in a way that Isaac never does, cf. *op. cit.*, p. 22.

302. *The Christian Philosophy of St Augustine*, p. 294, n. 69, citing Augustine's dependence on Plotinus, e.g., *Enn.* I, 1, 7.

303. "Abstrahit enim a corpore que fundantur in corpore, non actione sed consideratione," XV (1884A). *Consideratio* here is the equivalent of *resolutio* in 1755D. What may be at the basis of "non actione sed consideratione" is an understanding somewhat similar to that of Abelard, who thought of abstraction as a particular kind of attention of the mind directed at things, cf. *Logica ingred. (ed. Geyer*, pp. 25–8), where the same example of the *natura corporis* is used as in Isaac. Like Isaac, too, Abelard holds to a plurality of *formae*. For an introduction to Abelard's logical theories, cf. Gilson, *A History of Christian Philosophy in the Middle Ages*, pp. 155–60; and J. G. Sikes's *Peter Abailard*, pp. 88–112. Geyer, *Die Patristische und Scholastische Philosophie*, p. 259; de Wulf, *op. cit.*, p. 226; and Gilson, *op. cit.*, p. 169, all see Isaac's theory of abstraction as similar to Abelard's.

of these Aristotelian reminiscences within a basically Platonic epistemology could only be accomplished by an assiduous avoidance of such inconsistencies.[304]

A careful analysis of the logical literature of the early twelfth century, and particularly of the work of Peter Abelard, might turn up more precise origins for Isaac's use of abstraction, and for his theories on first and second substances and accidents which appear in this paragraph in a manner similar to that of Sermon Nineteen.[305] This has not been attempted here, basically because Isaac really uses these bits of ultimately Aristotelian material for purposes very different from what they intended in their original contexts. In the Sermons, the interdependence and imperfections of the various forms of *substantia* are intended to demonstrate the necessity of a being *a-se* that cannot really be circumscribed within the language of *substantia*. Here in the *Epistola*, a generalized doctrine of the action of *ratio* is used which in essence is not in conformity with the doctrine of sense knowledge employed, because it serves to introduce the doctrine of the states of knowledge found in the next paragraph, and fits in admirably with the Platonic doctrine of the two directions of knowledge,[306] formulated clearly by Augustine,[307]

304. Perhaps it is significant that the only thing in Isaac's system which might possibly serve the function of a *species impressa*, viz., the *phantasiae* in *imaginatio*, is never spoken of as ascending into the reason, e.g., XII (1888B). The lower three stages of Isaac's epistemological ladder all consider essentially the same object (*corpora* in general), but they do so under the watchful eye of the radical break between the material and the spiritual powers (however much they may be said to be symbolically and anagogically related). Another of the epistemological confusions of Isaac's system may be seen in IX (1880C), where we are told that "ratione [percipit] vero corporum *dimensiones* et similia," something we should rather expect to be said of *sensus* if a careful epistemology were at stake.

305. Compare XV (1884A) with 1754C–55A. The only general work on the subject, J. Gessner, *Die Abstraktionslehre in der Scholastik bis Thomas von Aquin* (Freiburg im-B., 1930), is more expository than explanatory. On Isaac, cf. pp. 42–6.

306. E.g., *Enn.* V, 3, 3; V, 9, 7; also in Chalcidius, *Comm.* 31 (*ed. Waszink*, p. 81). It is a logical conclusion from the nature of the soul as the mid-being in *Timaeus* 35a.

307. E.g., *De Trin.* XII, 3, 3; XIV, 1, 2–3 (*ed. cit.* II, 214–16; 346–50); *De Quant. An.* I, 5, 11 (*PL* 32, 1040). For the history of this important doctrine, cf.

and renewed with vigor by Hugh of St Victor,[308] which provided the general framework for the Abbot's treatment of *ratio*.[309] Thus, the third stage in the ascent is the *ratio inferior* actively directed at bodies and leading to the knowledge that is *scientia*;[310] but above that, the gaze of the soul must be directed toward the true realities unsullied by connection with matter to receive the illumination of *ratio superior* that will lead to the higher truth of *sapientia*.

Divisions of Knowledge in the Ascensional Process

The Abbot now begins the equation of his fivefold schema with the Aristotelian division of sciences into *physica (naturalis)*, *mathematica*, *theologica*, with which he was familiar through Boethius and the discussion of this division among the Masters of Chartres. One interesting note is that Isaac introduces the technical logical term of *status* with a phrase which indicates his acquaintance with the academic debate of his time.[311] In dependence upon

---

R. Mulligan, "*Ratio Superior* and *Ratio Inferior*: The Historical Background," *New Scholasticism*, XXIX (1955), 1–32; and E. von Ivánka, *Plato Christianus*, pp. 215–16; I would disagree with Mulligan's statement (pp. 20–1) that Isaac was familiar with Gundissalinus: there is little reason to suppose that Gundissalinus's writings were widely popular as early as the time Isaac was writing, and the similarities between the two men are better explained in terms of a similar background than direct dependence.

308. E.g., *De Sac.* I, 8, 13 (*PL* 176, 315D); *De Unione Corp. et Spir.* (*PL* 177. 288D–89A) and more problematically in *Didascalicon* I, 8 (ed. Buttimer, p. 15), Cf. J. Kleinz, *The Theory of Knowledge in Hugh of St Victor* (Washington, 1944), pp. 72–3.

309. A suggestion also made by van den Bosch and deGanck, *op. cit.*, p. 216. The two faces appear in a generalized fashion in 1702B–3A, besides their presence throughout the *Epistola*.

310. One difficulty here is that *ratio* is described as "tertius . . . anime ad sapientiam progressus" (1884A), but this can be taken to indicate the influence of the upper stages under God drawing up the whole man—not the goal of *ratio qua* faculty.

311. ". . . status diversi, realis videlicet et rationalis, seu naturalis, *ut quidem malunt*, et doctrinalis . . . ," XVI (1884C). *Status* as a logical term was used by Abelard (e.g., *Logica ingred.*; ed. cit., p. 20), though in a different sense from Isaac's general use here.

Boethius's *De Trinitate* II, he sets up two states or conditions of being, the real or natural, which he equates with the operation of *sensus* and *imaginatio*, and the rational (*doctrinalis*), which is the field of *ratio*. These in turn are equated with the first two divisions of knowledge, *scientia naturalis* (*physica*) and *mathematica*.[312] The equation of the action of *ratio* with the science of *mathematica* (which Isaac significantly feels he has to explain) is an awkward result of trying to combine the passage from Boethius's *De Trinitate* on the divisions of science with the passage from the *De Consolatione Philosophiae* at the root of the fivefold schema of the levels of knowledge, as the following section shows. Isaac's concern is anagogic: he is interested in the way in which the superior powers draw the lower into their ambit; the lower can never move above their appointed bounds by themselves. The world and the soul are hierarchical, and to have the lower act on the higher would contradict the fundamental law of reality. Boethius had made this especially clear;[313] Isaac follows him in pointing out how his division of sciences follows the nature of the powers with which it is identified —the natural sciences always remain below the level of reason, merely pointing to it from afar. The same is true of the relation of reason to *theologia*: Isaac is concerned to preserve true knowledge of God from any contamination from below by *ratio* and its world of *substantiae*.[314] The paragraph closes with what is surely one of the finest passages in Isaac's works. Having established that in the all-important ascent, insofar as we can consider it intellectually, the lower stages do not penetrate beyond their sphere, but are included in a total process of ascent engineered from above, Isaac finds that the best way to express this is by a concrete image drawn with all the resources of his rhetorical style from the natural ascension which begins with sunrise over the marshes, to ascend through all the levels of the elements and culminate in the total fiery reality of

312. XVI (1884C).

313. "In quo illud maxime considerandum est: nam superior comprehendendi vis amplectitur inferiorem, *inferior vero ad superiorem nullo modo consurgit*." *De Cons. Phil.* V, 4, lines 92–4 (*ed. Rand.*, p. 388).

314. XVI (1884D).

the Empyrean. At such a crucial point the symbolic understanding of man returns to visual presentation for renewed strength. It would be as unfeeling to translate this passage as it is curious to note its resemblance to a text of Plotinus himself.[315]

Intellectus

Paragraph XVII (1885B) turns to *intellectus*, the most artificial of the five stages. Isaac seems uncomfortable with it, as his brevity here and his concern in explaining away the lack of a corresponding science for this power in Paragraph XX (1886D–87A) show. *Intellectus* was one of the traditional terms for the higher dimension of the soul, as we shall see in Chapter IV; its appearance in Boethius[316] made it part of a heritage that Isaac did not wish to neglect. Artificial as the category may be in origin, Isaac's identification of it as the power proper to immortal spirits, both *men and angels*, by which they know themselves and other spirits, is not only necessary for the parallel between the grades of being and the stages of knowledge, but also allows him to Augustinianize one of the less acceptable features of the Dionysian anagogic world. Augustine had always claimed that the rational substance of the soul stood in immediate relation to God with no nature intervening. "Therefore the rational substance has also been made through it [Christ as the *imago Dei*], and according to it; for there is no nature placed in between;"[317] but the Pseudo-Dionysius, especially in the *De Caelesti Hierarchia*, had created a hierarchy of ascent where passage through the nine choirs of angels and their attendant virtues was necessary for man's achieve-

315. XVI (1884D–85B) and *Enn.* V, 9, 1–2.

316. *In Isagogen Porphyrii Comm.* I, 1, 2 (*ed. Brandt*, pp. 8–9); *De Trin.* II (*ed. Rand*, p. 8).

317. *De Gen. ad Litt. Lib. imperf.* XVI, 60 (PL 34, 243): "Rationalis itaque substantia et per ipsam facta est et ad ipsam: non enim est ulla natura interposita." Cf. also *Contra epist. Manich.*, XXXVII, 43 (PL 42, 203); *De Quant. An.* XXXIV, 77 (PL 32, 1077–8); *De Immort. An.* XV (PL 32, 1033). This is also stressed by Eriugena (following Augustine) in an important passage on microcosm in *De Div. Nat.* II, 7 (PL 122, 530A–31D). The passage is influenced by Maximus the Confessor.

ment of the goal of divine vision.[318] Isaac's placing of the soul of man on the same level of being and knowledge as the angels, a corollary of the doctrine of the soul as the midpoint between God and the world, is the root of his claim that "the rational soul is purely spirit having above itself the divine nature alone,"[319] and allows him to stress Christ's position as the sole mediator.[320] The place of the angelic hierarchies is mentioned only once in the *Epistola*, and even there it is interiorized in being used as a symbolic illustration of the soul's interior ascent.[321] Augustine's influence here triumphs over the Pseudo-Dionysius.

The Catena Aurea Text and the Principle of Concatenation

The mention of *intellectus* leads Isaac to a repetition of the objects of the five stages listed according to their degree of corporeality in Paragraph XVIII (1885B–86A), as a reminder that *intelligentia* has the highest object of all, the "purely incorporeal . . . which in every way is sufficient to itself."[322] This in turn introduces the symbol of the *catena aurea*, the starting point of our investigation into the thought of the Abbot of Stella. Without repetition of what we have said about the golden chain in Chapter II, we are now in a better position to understand the reason for its appearance here and the constellation of themes which it attracts. Two basic concerns of Isaac's theology are explicitly manifested to us through the symbol in this passage. The first is the theology of the *imago*. In this passage image theology is expanded to form a total theological principle, because we are told not only that the soul (*vere et non pure incorporeum*) is

318. It is true that the influence of the hierarchies of angels could possibly be viewed as merely a symbol of the soul's ascent, but many passages in the *CH* also seem to indicate the necessary action of the angelic hierarchies (always under divine control) in the ascensional process, e.g., *CH*, IV, 2–4 (*ed. Roques*, pp. 94–100).

319. ". . . anima vero rationalis pure spiritus est, habens supra se naturam solam divinam." *Sermon 8 (ed. Hoste*, p. 192; 1716C).

320. Cf. Javelet, "La Vertu . . . ," p. 261; *Image et Ressemblance*, I, 154–5.

321. VIII (1880B).

322. ". . . pure incorporeum . . . quod sibi omnimodis sufficiens est," XVIII (1885C).

the image and likeness of God (*pure et vere incorporeum*), but also that the object of ratio (*pene incorporeum*) is an image of the soul, and that the lowest point of the soul, the *pene corpus* (*phantasticum anime*), is in turn an image of that.[323] The perspective now shifts to the joining together of body and soul through the principle of connection or concatenation,[324] because the *supremum corpus* or *sensualitas* is joined to the *pene corpus*, just as fire is joined to it and the other elements in turn to fire.[325] The text on the *catena aurea* follows. As mentioned in Chapter II, the symbol is interpreted in the light of the verse from the Eighth chapter of the Book of Wisdom describing the ordering activity of divine *Sapientia*, which was used by the Pseudo-Dionysius in precisely the same manner.[326] One unusual feature here is the appearance of the Greek word *archetypus* in this context, since it does not appear in the translations of the Pseudo-Dionysius by Eriugena, but is used in that of John Sarrazin, which is probably slightly posterior in date to Isaac's *Epistola*.[327] It is not necessary to alter our dating of

323. *Ibid.*

324. Thus this passage becomes a commentary on the important passage on the union of body and soul from XI already discussed.

325. XVIII. This all recalls in vague fashion the physics of the *Timaeus* where the four elements are joined together through the geometry of their different shapes, e.g., 31b–33a. There are inconsistencies in the account here that result from the attempt to combine so many dimensions in a single image: (1) *aether* has fallen out of the picture to allow the *empyreum* to be compared with *igneus vigor* according to XII (1882C), rather than *ignis* as it usually is (e.g., XVI [1885A] and 1702B); and (2) if the *pene corpus* (*phantasticum anime*) is in *imaginatio* alone, then sense knowledge gets lost and has no place in the hierarchy. I doubt if Isaac meant to say that; he would rather think of both *senses corporeus* and *imaginatio* as being represented in the *pene corpus*.

326. *De Div. Nom.* VII, 3 (*Dionysiaca* I, 407–8): "Et quidem et ex omnibus (quod quidem dixi) ipsa cognoscenda, ipsa est enim, secundum eloquium, omnium factrix, et semper omnia compaginans, et insolubilis omnium congruentiae et ordinationis causa, *et semper fines priorum connectens principiis secundorum, et unam universitatis conspirantiam et harmoniam pulchram faciens.*"

327. Isaac also uses *archetypus* in 1769B. Eriugena uses *exemplum* or *forma* to translate the Greek ἀρχέτυπος. Cf. M.-T. d'Alverny, "Le cosmos symbolique au XIIᵉ siècle," *AHDL*, XX (1953), 48–9, n. 3. On the translation of John Sarrazin, cf. H. Dondaine, *Le Corpus Dionysien de l'Université de Paris au XIIIᵉ siècle* (Rome, 1953), pp. 28–31; he dates its completion to 1167.

the *Epistola*; the word was available to Isaac from Chalcidius.[328] Isaac's penetration to the core of his vision of God and man provokes a joyful outburst as the soul, which is both part of the chain of being and the chain of being itself because it is the *imago sapientiae*, praises the *potentia*, *sapientia*, and *bonitas* of God[329] in the words of Psalms which the Cistercian Abbot knew so well.[330] The soul's rapt attention to the Wisdom of God spread throughout the world is the cause of the reaction.[331] Isaac's central symbol has led the Abbot to the essential act of the monastic life, the contemplation of the mystery of the Word.

In one of the first lengthy studies of Isaac, W. Meuser noted his fascination with the unity of the universe effected through a series of connections or mediating terms linked together.[332] This observation was seconded by E. Bertola,[333] A. Fracheboud,[334] and especially R. Javelet, who termed it the principle of concatenation.[335] The combination of this principle of the joining of diverse entities through their extremities, which is an expansion of the fundamental Platonic necessity of a mid-term for the unification of the divergent realms of being (*Timaeus* 31bc), here used as the explanatory principle for a theology of the image in its turn based upon a Platonic view of participation, is seen as manifested through a master symbol of the *"aurea catena poete . . . vel erecta scala prophete."* If the influence of the Pseudo-Dionysius is very much to the fore in these passages, it is only because as a faithful follower of the Platonic tradition he

328. E.g., Chalcidius's translation of *Timaeus* 38c; and *Comm.* 329 (*ed. Waszink*, pp. 30, 323).

329. One of the rare appearances in Isaac of the triad of divine attributes so popular and so controversial in the twelfth century.

330. XVIII (1885D).

331. *Ibid.*, ". . . eam ubique considerando."

332. *Op. cit.*, pp. 5, 7–9.

333. "La dottrina psicologica di Isaaco de Stella," pp. 301, 306.

334. "Le Pseudo-Denys . . . parmi les sources . . . Isaac de l'Étoile," *Cîteaux*, X (1948), 26–31.

335. "La vertu dans l'oeuvre d'Isaac de l'Étoile," p. 256; and *Image et Ressemblance*, I, 150-7, 232, 234–5.

had brought the laws of the hierarchical chain of being to a height of development which was particularly influential on twelfth-century Platonists like Isaac of Stella.[336]

This line of thought is continued in Paragraph XIX in a passage we have already considered in our study of the soul as the image of God and the problem of its definition (1886A). Man's sense of wonder over the presence of Wisdom's organizing power and goodness in creation is the source of this search for knowledge. The soul is the likeness of all things because it is made to the image of this total Wisdom.[337] This thought, an apt summary of Isaac's doctrine on the soul, is clarified by three microcosmic themes which drive home the full import of the quasi-definition of the soul as *similitudo omnium*: first, the familiar lineup of the objects of the five powers as exhausting the grades of being;[338] second, the customary comparison with the five elements;[339] and finally, a rather unusual example of elementaristic microcosm which is very close to a famous passage of Gregory the Great.[340]

336. On the influence of the idea of concatenation in the twelfth century, cf. M.-D. Chenu, *La théologie au douzième siècle*, pp. 33, 291–2.

337. XIX (1886A).

338. *Ibid.* One unusual feature here is that the object of *ratio* is described as "corporum dimensiones, et similitudines dissimilium ac dissimilitudines similium." This appears to be a Dionysian theme, and can be compared with Sermon 24 of the *Sermones in Sexagesima* (1771A).

339. *Ibid.*

340. Isaac changes the comparison somewhat to bring it closer to his own patterns:

Isaac:

"vel metallis et lapidibus per essentiam, herbis et arboribus per vitam, animalibus per sensum et imaginationem, hominibus per rationem, angelis per intellectum, Deo per intelligentiam. . . ."

Gregory the Great, Hom. in Evang. 29 (PL 76, 1214A):

"Homini namque commune esse cum lapidibus, vivere cum arboribus, sentire cum animalibus, intelligere cum angelis."

Also cf. Eriugena, *De Div. Nat.* III, 37 (PL 122, 733B); Claudianus Mamertus, *De Statu An.* I, 21 (ed. *Engelbrecht*, p. 71); Nemesius of Emesa, *Premnon Physicon*, I, 8–12 (ed. *Burkhard*, pp. 6–7).

The Effect of Original Sin

Having praised the nature of man and the soul so highly, having exhibited such an optimistic view of the universe, we may be surprised by the sudden pessimistic turn in the Abbot's thought. On the basis of quotations from the Psalms he asserts the impossibility of the soul's attaining to the knowledge which is its destiny: the soul has not the strength to behold what it should. Its iniquities have overwhelmed it; the eye of the soul has been cast awry.[341] The significant use of Scriptural quotations to describe this tragedy gives an explanation for the shift. Isaac is reminding his readers that the soul cannot be discussed *in abstracto*; only the history known through the Scriptures can explain the human condition and provide the answer to the mystery of man. Athwart the threshold of that history is the story of the Fall of Man.

Original sin appears frequently in Isaac's writings,[342] and has been the subject of several discussions in recent years.[343] The Abbot gives no systematic treatment, hence much of his doctrine must be pieced together from asides; when the pieces are collected, what appears is a traditional view based largely upon Augustine and Hugh of St Victor, but having particular nuances of its own within the symbolic world of Isaac's theology. He tells us that: "Therefore only the eyes of concupiscence have been illuminated and opened, namely, [the eyes] of man, that is, of the spirit, to

341. XIX (1886B–C).

342. The more important treatments are italicized: *Sermon 4 (ed. Hoste,* p. 130, 1701B); *Sermon 6 (ed. Hoste,* pp. 162 sq.; 1709A sq.); *Sermon 7 (ed. Hoste,* pp. 180 sqq.; 1713C sqq.); *Sermon 15 (ed. Hoste,* pp. 282–84; 1738B–C); *Sermon 17 (ed. Hoste,* pp. 310–14; 1745B–46B); *Sermon 26* (1777A); *Sermon 28* (1782D–84A); *Sermon 35* (1808A–C); *Sermon 39* (1824A); *Sermon 43* (1834B, 1837A); *Sermon 50* (1858D); *Sermon 54* (1874D–76A). The present passage compares most strongly with that of 1783A–D.

343. F. Mannarini, "La Grazia in Isaaco di Stella," *COCR,* XVI (1954), 137–44, 207–14; L. Gaggero, "Isaac of Stella and the Theology of Redemption," *COCR,* XXII (1960), pp. 21–36; and A. Hoste, *Isaac de l'Étoile; Sermons* I, notes to *Sermons* 6 and 7,, and *"Note Complémentaire 8:* La doctrine du péché originel chez Isaac," pp. 338–9.

curiosity, and of the flesh, that is of the woman, to pleasure."[344] The intimate relation of original sin and *concupiscentia* was one of the least attractive bequests of Augustine to Western theology. Without getting into the difficult question of whether Isaac identified concupiscence with original sin, or only considered it as one of several components,[345] we must determine the way in which the term functions within his system. We are not given very much to work on from this passage; but the hint of the perversion of order which it contains is reminiscent of more explicit passages in the Sermons. Basically, what *concupiscentia* means is *"cor-ruptio,"*[346] the breaking of the hierarchical chain of being. The whole theology that Isaac had carefully built up around the symbol of the *catena aurea*—the themes of the medium, the image, concatenation, illumination, and participation—are destroyed by the sin of man which perverts that order and arrangement. *Concupiscentia*, then, is the state of the broken chain of being manifested in man the microcosm. While this is clearly expressed in several passages,[347] it is most significantly found in the ending of Sermon Fifty-four, the only other explicit appearance in Isaac's writings of the *catena aurea*:

Indeed, it was the ordained and natural state of man,[348] when

344. "Illuminatis igitur tantummodo oculis concupiscentie et apertis, viri videlicet, id est, spiritus ad curiositatem, et carnis, id est, mulieris ad voluptatem," XX (1886C).

345. F. Mannarini judges that of the four current theories in the mid-twelfth century, Isaac's views are closest to those of Hugh of St Victor and the *Summa Sententiarum* that original sin consists in concupiscence with ignorance as an integral part, *op. cit.*, p. 208. Isaac's descriptions of the effects of original sin are seen as largely Augustinian, transmitted through Hugh, pp. 209–12. On the effects of original sin, cf. 1701B, 1714B–C, 1808A–C, 1824A, 1834B. At times Isaac stressed the Bernardine theme of the weakening of *liberum arbitrium* (1808A–C); at times the Augustinian triad of *concupiscentia, ignorantia, difficultas* (1824A, 1834B).

346. Gaggero, *op. cit.*, p. 26, was the first to make this suggestion.

347. E.g., 1783B–84A; 1791D.

348. This is not to be understood in terms of the later distinctions between natural and supernatural. Mannarini notes (p. 139) that Isaac never speaks of the state of man before the fall as *justitia originalis* but always as *elevatio*. This is perhaps due to the symbolic influence of the *catena aurea*.

the spirit was subjected to God, the flesh to the spirit, the world to the flesh, and in the spirit itself the affective power controlled the flesh, This was the first natural world, the golden age of Saturn, and the golden chain of the poet. But when disobedience burst in between the spirit and God, concupiscence between the flesh and the spirit, and finally the curse between the activity of flesh and the world. . . .[349]

Following the intellectual interests of the *Epistola*, the concentration here is on *ignorantia*, the aspect of the broken chain of *concupiscentia* which affects the states of knowledge.[350] Two interesting themes appear at the beginning of Paragraph XX. The first is a strongly anti-feminist one, for the two eyes of concupiscence connote the division of the sexes: the *oculus spiritus*, or the man, has been opened to *curiositas*,[351] while the eye of the flesh, woman, has been opened to *voluptas*.[352] The value judgment implicit here is made stronger by the appearance of a similar, though more traditional, anti-feminist comparison in Sermons Four and Twenty-eight.[353] Secondly, Isaac makes use of the theme of the eye of the

349. "Ordinatus quippe, ac *naturalis status* hominis erat cum spiritus Deo caro spiritui, mundus carni subjectus fuerat, et in ipso spiritu affectio carni subjacuerat. Et hic erat primus naturalis mundus, aureum Saturni saeculum *aureaque catena poetae*. Quam cum *inobedientia rupisset* inter spiritum et Deum *concupiscentia inter carnem et spiritum,* ac demum *maledictio,* inter operationem carnis et mundum . . ." 1874D–75A.

350. Cf. Gaggero's remark, *op. cit.,* p. 29: "Isaac holds the Augustinian conception of the divine image as consisting chiefly in the capacity for intellectual knowledge, the likeness being in the will, the faculty capable of love. Isaac has, in other words, a more intellectual bias than St Bernard, placing more emphasis on man's ignorance and need for illumination from God, while remaining in substantial agreement with the Abbot of Clairvaux as to the essential reasons for man's separation from God . . . ." Also Mannarini *op. cit.,* p. 214: "Gli effetti del peccato originale sono pertanto concepiti come una deformazione psicologica delle facoltà razionali."

351. On *curiositas* as a traditional patristic theme, cf. Hoste, *Sermons,* p. 96, n. 2 and H. de Lubac, *Exégèse Médiévale,* II, I, pp. 309–11. Isaac uses it in the negative sense some twenty times.

352. XX (1886C).

353. The more traditional pattern where *vir* is equated with *ratio* and *mulier* with the *affectio* which ought to be under the control of reason appears in Sermon 4 (*ed.* Hoste, p. 142, 1703D–4A), and in 1783A. For the use of these

N

soul (ultimately reaching back to Plato[354]) popularized in the twelfth century especially through Hugh of St Victor,[355] in explaining the effects of original sin on his fivefold schema: "The eye of sense and of imagination has been clouded so that it sees more obscurely, the eye of reason so that it scarcely sees, the intellect and intelligence so that they see almost nothing."[356] The reduction of the five powers to three eyes is a clear sign of Hugonian influence,[357] but Isaac adapts the theme to his own interests. The blinding of the upper eye (*intellectus* and *intelligentia*) shows the impossibility of man's fulfilling the commandment of self-knowledge. He can know neither God nor himself as *"ad imaginem et similitudinem Dei,"* nor can he know the angelic nature on a par with the soul.[358] The *imago Dei* theme and that of self-knowledge are joined here as they were in Sermon Two. Isaac also feels that this explains the curious fact that there is no special science for *intellectus*. The explanation given here is a rather subtle one, but still has the appearance of being forced, since we know that Isaac is attempting to fit a Boethian division of sciences upon a schema of largely later development. The incorporeal nature of the soul and the angels stands midway between God and the body. It has its *naturalia* which are identified

---

themes in patristic and medieval literature, cf. R. Javelet, *Image et Ressemblance*, I, pp. 236–45; II, p. 209 and H. de Lubac, *Exégèse Médiévale*, II, 11, p. 138. Isaac's use here is closest to that of Abelard (*In Hex.*; PL 178, 763D–64A) in calling woman the *imago viri*, rather than *imago Dei*.

354. It appears most clearly in *I Alcibiades* 132C–33C in association with the Delphic maxim, but is influential in many of the Platonic Dialogues, cf. P. Friedländer, *Plato*, pp. 13–15.

355. E.g., *De Sac.* I, 10, 2 (PL 176, 329–30); *De Van. Mundi*, I (704; 718B–19C); *De Arca Noe mor.*, IV, 5 (670C–71A); *In Hier. Cael.* III (PL 175, 976A); *De Un. Corp. et Spir.* (PL 177, 292B–C); *Miscel.* I, 1 (PL 177, 471B–C).

356. "Oculus sensus et imaginationis turbatus est ut obscurius videat, rationis ut vix videat, intellectus et intelligentia ut fere nil videant." Other references in Isaac are in 1701D, 1719D–20A, 1783B, 1794D–95A.

357. Cf. especially *De Sac.* I, 10, 2 (PL 176, 329C–30A). On this passage, cf. Javelet, *op. cit.*, I, 381–82.

358. XX (1886C).

with it, and therefore cannot be perceived as separate by means of abstraction;[359] and it also has its *accidentalia*, the virtues sent down from God which in their ideal nature, as identified with God, are the object of *intelligentia*. Hence, in fallen man the knowledge of *intellectus* is partially natural (*physica*) and partly theological.[360] The Dionysian understanding of *virtus* discussed earlier comes out very strongly in such a context—the essence of Justice is God; what we call justice is really only a series of participations in the "one . . . essential Justice, not a quality, nor an accident of the soul, subsisting in itself, participated in by just spirits by means of its own sharing, whose participations are the individual justices of spirits which are accidental to them."[261] It would be difficult to find a more succinct presentation of Isaac's Dionysian use of *virtus*.

Man's Participation in the Divine Nature and Augustinian Illumination

The theme of the virtues as participations in the divine nature leads back to a theological concept also found in the *Sermones in Sexagesima*—the triad of *Aeternitas* (*Essentia*), *Species*, *Usus*, introduced by Hilary of Poitiers and adopted by Augustine, as a means to express the proper attributes of the Trinity.[362] Isaac's preference for this triad resides primarily in the opening which it gives him for the expression of the participation of the whole universe in the divine nature.[363] It is an indication of an interest which is constant

359. This is difficult, because while true of the *anima humana*, as incorporated in a body, it is not true in itself of the *angelica natura*. The clue is given by the previous discussion of the blinding of man's highest eye after sin necessitating that the angels use an assumed body or phantasms in the imagination to be perceived. Isaac always speaks of historic man, man after the Fall.

360. XX (1886D).

361. "una . . . essentialis iustitia, non qualitas, nec accidens anime, in semetipsa subsistens, participata a spiritibus participatione ipsius iustis, cuius participationes spiritium iustitie sunt, et illis accidentales," XX (1887A).

362. For the uses of this, cf. R. Javelet, *op. cit.*, I, 88, 200–1; II, 27, n. 28.

363. XX (1887B).

in Isaac, viz., his concentration on Augustine's non-psychological analogies for the Trinity for the sake of their width of application. Even though his major interest is in the soul, the unity of all creation in the *catena aurea* also moves him to search for those themes in the tradition which are most susceptible of showing that God is active throughout the entire compass of being. This he finds in the Hilarian triad, because every existent being must have *esse*,[364] some form, *species*, or image, and a *munus* which gives rise to its activity.[365]

The opening of Paragraph XXI is an explication of the theme of the participation of the universe in the divine nature; it adds nothing to what we have already seen in the *Epistola* or what is present in the *Sermones in Sexagesima*, but does serve as a convenient summary. All created things are *capax divinitatis*, but according to their grade in the scale of being; the image and likeness of God found in the height of the soul is its capacity for all things expressed through the five steps of rationality and the affective power. The intimate relation of the two is stressed as usual.[366] These observations bring the Abbot of Stella back to an idea introduced at the beginning of the *Epistola*, which in turn leads to one also touched upon in the ninth of the *Sermones in Sexagesima* (1774D–75D). The soul has faculties of knowing and loving of its nature, but it only attains to the knowledge of truth and the order of love by grace, or put in the same terms as the Sermon: "Therefore the vessels which creating grace forms that they might exist, assisting grace fills that they be not empty."[367]

W. Meuser interpreted Isaac's division between a *gratia creatrix* which forms the faculties and *gratia adiutrix* which activates them as a clear distinction between the natural and supernatural orders (though framed in Augustinian terms), so that Isaac distinguished

364. Note the equation of *esse* and *essentia* here (1887B), which is also to be found in Sermon 19 (1753C–D).

365. XX (1887B).

366. XXI (1887C).

367. "Vasa ergo que creatrix gratia format ut sint, adiutrix gratia replet ne vacua sint." XXI (1887D). Cf. 1774D.

a grace that is natural from the grace that is identical with the modern concept of supernatural grace.[368] Despite Isaac's use of *natura* in the same context as *gratia creatrix*,[369] Meuser's reading is incorrect, as later students of Isaac, e.g., A. Fracheboud,[370] F. Mannarini,[371] and R. Javelet[372] have shown. The mistake is partly conditioned by the unhistorical viewpoint of Meuser's age which still attempted to project a distinction of the natural and supernatural back upon the thought of Augustine.[373] It is clear from the text of Isaac that he cannot be read in this fashion. Though the *facultates* are *ex natura*, *natura* is used here in a general and not in a special sense, the special theological sense being relative to a concept of *supernatura* lacking in Isaac. *Gratia adiutrix* is not the divine gift above and beyond the nature of man, not owed to it in any way; but is the divine gift necessary for all activity: "nevertheless the know-

368. *Op. cit.,* pp. 43–5: "Die Unterscheidung Natur und Gnade findet bei unserem Autor schon starke Betonung, aber die Begriffsfassung ist von heute geläufigen etwas verschieden, zumindest in ihrer Nuancierung . . . Es ist zu unterscheiden eine 'gratia creatrix oder prima,' die Schöpfergnade, in der Gott die Welt und ihre Gesetze schuf (sie ist identisch mit der 'natura') und eine 'gratia adiutrix, die helfende Gnade,' welche uns zu dem Geschenk der Schöpfung noch hinzugegeben wird; *sie ist die Gnade im engeren Sinne und deckt sich mit unserem heutigen Gnadenbegriff.* . . . Die Schilderung beweist deutlich, dass die Illumination nicht ein natürlicher Vorgang ist, sondern übernatürlichen, gnadenhaften Charakter trägt; sie ist ein Geschenk der 'gratia adiutrix' und bringt uns die übernatürliche 'Erfüllung' und Vollendung natürlicher Anlagen."

369. ". . . facultates et quasi instrumenta cognoscendi et diligendi habet *ex natura* . . ." XXI (1887D). Compare with 1775B.

370. "L'Influence de S. Augustin sur le Cistercien Isaac de l'Étoile," pp. 7–11. "La *gratia adjutrix,* dirions-nous, bien que supérieure à la *gratia creatrix,* ne fait qu'actuer naturellement ce dont celle-ci lui donne la puissance¸' (p. 9).

371. *Op. cit.,* pp. 141, 144. Mannarini's explanations are confused by his constant use of later theological terminology to interpret Isaac, but he would agree on the issue in question.

372. "La vertu . . . ," pp. 264–65, especially n. 96 (though I could scarcely agree with the statement, "La grâce créatrice fait l'image; la grâce adjutrice opère la ressemblance. . . ."); and *Image et Ressemblance,* I, 123–4, 323, 330–1.

373. A work instrumental in overcoming this viewpoint was H. de Lubac's *Surnaturel,* first published in 1946. Cf. the revised English version, *The Mystery of the Supernatural* (New York, 1967).

ledge of truth and the order of love can be had in no way except through grace."[374] Isaac here considers historic man; his thought knows nothing of later Scholastic distinctions, and his concepts of *natura* and *gratia* are to be viewed in terms of the Platonic world of forms and the Dionysian world of ascents.[375]

The examples that follow of illumination demonstrate the same point. The eye has the capacity to see, but can never actually exercise vision without the benefit of an exterior light; in the same way, the rational spirit, from creation fit to know the truth and love the good, has need of the interior light to illuminate the mind and fire the heart. The source of this passage, as well as the parallel one in Sermon Nine, is Augustine's doctrine of illumination as contained in his Thirty-fifth *Tractatus in Joannem*.[376] The Augustinian context becomes even clearer in the following example, the comparison between the sun which cannot be seen apart from the ray of light identical with itself that it sends forth, and the true divine light which can only be seen in the light that it sends into the *intelligentia*.[377]

Isaac's next passage leads into one of the major morasses of Augustinian scholarship: "thus, remaining in God, the light which departs from him illumines the mind, so that first of all it may see that very blazing forth of light without which nothing can be seen, and in that, it may see other things."[378] Does this mean that man

374. ". . . cognitionem tamen veritatis et ordinem dilectionis *nequaquam* habet nisi ex gratia," XXI (1887D).

375. The treatment of man in terms of *gratia creatrix* and *gratia adiutrix* was fairly popular in the twelfth century, though the uses are divergent. It is found in St Bernard, *De Gratia et Libero Arbit.* VI, 16 (*ed. Leclercq,* III, p. 178); in Hugh of St Victor, *De Sac.* I, 6, 17 (*PL* 176, 273C–D); and in Richard of St Victor, *Liber Except.* II, 1 (*ed. Châtillon,* p. 114), though in different senses than with Isaac.

376. XXI (1887D–88A). Compare with 1775C; both passages are dependent on Augustine, *In Joan.* XXXV, 3 (*CC* 36, pp. 318–19).

377. *Ibid.* Compare with the almost identical passage in 1775C–D, based on *In Joan.* XXIV, 4 (*CC* 36, pp. 312–13). Parallel to these passages is one in 1795A.

378. ". . . ita manens in Deo lux que exit ab eo, mentem irradiat, ut primum quidem ipsam coruscationem lucis sine qua nil videret, videat, et in ipsa cetera videat." Cf. 1775D.

must have direct contact with the divine nature in order to know creatures in any way? The key here is what we mean by "know." Though the poverty of Isaac's epistemology makes it difficult to answer with certainty, if we understand "know" in the general sense of any kind of knowledge, the answer is probably not. Note that the Abbot is talking here about the upper part of the soul, the *mens,* or *intelligentia,* not about the lower powers of *ratio, imaginatio,* and *sensus* directed to the things below and capable of achieving only *scientia.* On the higher levels of the soul, directed to *sapientia* and *veritas* (and not just the formation of general concepts), illumination from God is necessary by the very nature of the objects involved. The phrase *"et in ipsa cetera videat"* causes no major problem, for it includes not only souls and angels, the objects of *intellectus,* but also the *truth* of sensible natures, i.e., their character as created participations of the divine nature, and not just as general concepts existing in sensibles. This is the doctrine of Isaac, and without attempting to enter into a complex and perhaps insoluble debate on the nature of illumination in Augustine, it has similarities to a commonly accepted interpretation of the thought of the African doctor.[379]

Themes of Ascension and Illumination

The following brief paragraph (XXII) has already been mentioned in the course of our commentary because of its succinct presentation of the dynamic aspect of the connection of all things on the chain of being. There is movement from below, the phantasms that rise into the imagination, but not beyond; as well as movement from above, the theophanies that descend upon the *intelligentia.*[380] This highlights the dimension of the soul as the center of the universe— its need of the *spiritus vitalis* below to give life to body, and of the

379. E.g., E. Gilson, *The Christian Philosophy of St Augustine,* pp. 77–105 and Fracheboud. *op. cit.,* pp. 11–13.

380. XXII (1888B). On *theophania,* cf. Chenu, *La théologie au douzième siècle,* pp. 304–7.

divine actuation from above to attain to wisdom. All five powers of
rationabilitas contribute to this microcosmic function.[381] Brief
though the passage may be, it reminds us that themes of ascension
are among the most frequent and characteristic of Isaac and of
many contemporary writers.[382] Symbols of ascension—flight,
mountain, ladder, etc.—are common in human society from the
primitive to the most advanced levels. M. Eliade's study of "Sym-
bolisms of Ascension" from the point of view of comparative
religion[383] finds that "images of 'flight' and of 'ascension,' so
frequently appearing in the worlds of dream and imagination,
become perfectly intelligible only at the level of mysticism and
metaphysics, where they clearly express the ideas of freedom and
transcendence."[384] That this is true in Isaac will become more manifest as we turn to the final part of his *Epistola*, the treatment of
intelligentia, the highest point of the soul. Since the theme of
intelligentia is such a significant one for Isaac, we will comment
only on some of the implications of the text here, and leave for
Chapter IV a full treatment of the origins of the schema of ascent
culminating in *intelligentia*.

At the beginning of XXIII, *intelligentia* is defined in terms of the
connections demanded by the chain of being: "it is that power of
the soul which immediately suggests God, just as the *phantasticum
animae* suggests the body, or as the *sensualitas carnis* suggests the

381. *Ibid.*
382. E.g., St Bernard, cf. J. Leclercq, *The Love of Learning and the Desire for
God*, pp. 61–2; and W. Hiss, *Die Anthropologie des Bernhards von Clairvaux*,
p. 9. On ascent and descent themes in Hugh of St Victor's important work,
In Cael. Hier., cf. R. Roques, *Structures Théologiques*, pp. 320–6, 354–62.
Ascent themes are also strong in Richard of St Victor, e.g., *Benj. Min.*,
Chaps. 22, 75–8 (*PL* 196, 15B–16A, 53D–56A); *Benj. Maj.*, II, 6; V, 2 (*PL*
196, 169D–171C; 83D–85A). On the importance of ascensional themes in
Romanesque art, cf. G. de Champeaux and S. Sterckx, *Le monde des symboles*,
pp. 161–4; and M.-M. Davy, *Initiation à la Symbolique Romane*, pp. 63–89.
The best theological treatments are in Chenu, *Le théologie au douzième siècle*,
pp. 384–5; and H. de Lubac, *Éxegèse Médiévale*, I, 2, Chap. 10, "Anagogie
et Eschatologie," pp. 621–43.
383. *Myths, Dreams and Mysteries* (London, 1960), pp. 99–122.
384. *Op. cit.*, p. 122.

lowest point of the soul."[385] The problem that Isaac confronts is reminiscent of the *Sermones in Sexagesima*: how does the knowledge of God attained by *intelligentia* relate to the three Persons of the Trinity? In the Trinity all three Persons are equal and work as one, yet, returning to a theme mentioned in the Seventh Sexagesima Sermon (1768D–72A), Isaac asserts that: "nevertheless the Holy Spirit seems to be closer to the creature in a certain sense, as he who proceeding from both is the gift and the power."[386] The "munus" gives us the clue; the Hilarian triad signifying participation is behind this statement, every enjoyment of divinity comes from the *munus naturale* which is the Holy Spirit.[387] We are brought even closer to the Sexagesima Sermon by the repetition of a familiar triad from St Augustine's *Soliloquies* I, 8, 15: *lux, lucere, illuminare* as an analogy for the Trinitarian processions.[388] The light which enables *intelligentia* to acknowledge the truth and the heat which inflames *affectus* to love the good are the effects in us of the Holy Spirit, the Illuminating Power of the Splendor, who is the Son sent forth from the Father, the Inaccessible Light beyond all.[389] Whatever deficiencies the light analogy may have from the viewpoint of later Scholasticism, in the world of symbolic theology it is of the utmost moment.

The Trinitarian entry into the world of anagogy and participation reaches a crescendo as the *Epistola* concludes. The ascending and descending process noted earlier in the case of *phantasiae* and

385. ". . . ea vis anime est que immediate supponitur Deo, sicut phantasticum anime supponitur corpori, vel sicut sensualitas carnis supponitur infimo anime," XXIII (1888B).

386. "creature tamen quodammodo quasi proprior esse videtur Spiritus Sanctus, quippe qui de utroque, munus est virtusque," XXIII (1888C). I prefer the *lectio difficilior* "virtusque," supported by the manuscripts, to the "utriusque" of the *Patrologia* text. On the Holy Spirit in the work of Redemption, cf. Gaggero, *op. cit.*, pp. 34–35, and the magnificent Sermon 45 (1841B–45B).

387. *Ibid.*

388. *Ibid.* and 1770C–D are almost verbal equivalents in many places. Moreover, the whole context of the passages is the same, e.g., the stress on participation, the use of Hilary's triad, etc. For another appearance of *lux, lucere, illuminare* in Isaac, cf. 1776A.

389. XXIII (1888D).

theophaniae is here given a deeper meaning: "just as divine gifts descend to us from the Father, through the Son and the Spirit, or in the Spirit . . ., so through the Spirit to the Son, and through the Son to the Father, human gifts ascend."[390]

The Christological Dimension

Perhaps it may seem that the Trinitarian dimension has been introduced by sleight-of-hand to give a Christian appearance to what is really a Platonizing psychological treatise. We may make the problem more precise by asking what the place of Christ is in all of this. Is he really necessary at all in the golden chain of being? This is where I think the properly theological nature of Isaac's enterprise becomes clear, because the introduction of the Trinitarian dimension, and especially Christ active in his Spirit in the world, is not an afterthought, but is at the heart of the system. Resuming a number of hints scattered along the way, we can summarize Christ's role as that of the supreme link which restores the chain of being broken by sin. If, as the passage at the end of Sermon Fifty-four (1875A) stressed, disobedience had destroyed the link between God and the created spirit, and concupiscence that between the spirit and the flesh, and the curse of servility that between the flesh and the world, then Christ by his obedience unto death, his birth as perfect man without concupiscence, and the promise of the new heaven and new earth contained in his resurrection, rebuilt the chain of being and restored man.[391] As R. Javelet aptly

390. "sicut ad nos a Patre per Filium et Spiritum, vel in Spiritu, divina descendunt . . . , ita per Spiritum ad Filium, et per Filium ad Patrem humana ascendunt," XXIII (1888D–89A). The question still occurs—do the lower levels rise into the higher? We know that the line between matter and spirit is never transgressed; and, given the Boethian background, this confirms the assertion that the lower levels of rationality do not ascend beyond their places. In a hierarchical world the lower cannot act upon the higher. The higher, however, does act upon the lower: God in restoring man draws up all things to himself. The *humana* ascend because the *divina* have first descended.

391. A succinct expression of this may be found in *Sermon 9* (*ed. Hoste*, p. 218, 1722D): "De Adam qui concupiscentiam generatus carnaliter, ad Christum qui per gratiam spiritualiter regenerat; et per ipsum ad Patrem, qui regeneratum tamquam Filium feliciter haeredat"

remarks: *"L'Incarnation est un cas exemplaire de concaténation et l'homme-microcosme récapitule en lui le problème qu'elle pose."*[392] He is the link connecting all, because as the perfect man he fulfills in himself the true microcosmic pattern lost by sin, and as personally uniting God and man he achieves a more efficacious link than the descent of theophanies alone could ever create.[393]

Within such a theology of the Incarnation and Redemption we can see how all the values which we have discovered as facets of the central symbol become explanatory principles for Christ's work in the world. R. Javelet remarked that, in an inverse manner from today's concern with the Incarnation as incorporation of the divine in the material and temporal, Isaac, and twelfth-century writers in general, tended to stress the Incarnation as an ascension, an anagogic movement from matter to the Godhead.[394] Not only the themes of joining together and ascension, but those of image and exemplar are also a part of this generalized Platonic soteriology based upon the anagogic world of the Pseudo-Dionysius.[395] Paragraph IV of the *Epistola* had stressed Christ as the exemplar of the virtues,[396] as Paragraph XXI had the necessity for Divine Illumination, which, given its Augustinian background, must be identified with the activity of the Second Person of the Trinity.[397] These forms from on high which fill the rational and affective nature of the created spirit and give it the power to reach the goal come through the Son, their Exemplar. Isaac's symbolic master image allows for a comprehension of the centrality of Christ, decidedly different from that of the thirteenth-century Scholastics, but with a

392. *Image et Ressemblance,* I, 153.

393. This is well brought out by Javelet, *op. cit.,* I, 235, 302, 304-5, 320-1; II, p. 153, n. 131.

394. *Op. cit.,* I, 312. Cf. also pp. 374-6 and 453 on anagogy.

395. Cf. R. Roques, "Connaissance de Dieu et théologie symbolique," pp. 345-6, for the background in Dionysius.

396. "Dominus autem Iesus cuius omnes anime vires indute sunt virtute ex alto, plenus spiritu sancto, plenus quoque gratie et veritatis, et fortasse solus de cuius plenitudine omnes accepimus" (1887D). Cf. Javelet, *op. cit.,* I, 108-10.

397. XXI (1888A).

distinctive and rich character of its own. Whatever the problems inherent in a theology built upon the symbolic implications of Platonic modes of thought, there is an undeniable grandeur to it.

One final implication of this comprehensive viewpoint achieved through the symbol of the *catena aurea* appears at the end of the *Epistola*. The closing words of the text tell us:

> For upon the departure of the Son the Spirit is sent that he might unite the body to the head, that is, to Christ, and Christ himself might unite it to God, as it is written: "Man is the head of woman, Christ of man, and God of Christ." Therefore the Spirit rules, consoles, instructs, and leads the Church to Christ who offers it, without spot or blemish, as the kingdom to his God and Father. May the glorious Trinity deign to fulfill this in us. Amen.[398]

The theology of the Church as body united to Christ as head through the power of the Holy Spirit that appears so strongly here is a good illustration of Isaac's position in twelfth-century theological reflection. Basing himself upon texts from the Pauline Epistles, Augustine had made much of the body image as a means of explaining the relations between Christ, the Church, and the Eucharist. This side of Augustine's doctrine was not popular in the early medieval period; it was, however, developed in significant fashion in the thirteenth century, particularly by Thomas Aquinas. E. Mersch in his important work on the history of this doctrine, *Le Corps mystique du Christ*, was the first to draw attention to the fact that it is Isaac of Stella, along with William of St Thierry, who is the most important witness to the theology of the Mystical Body

---

398. "Ipso namque abeunte Filio mittitur paraclitus Spiritus, qui corpus capiti uniat, id est, Christo, et ipse, Deo; sicut scriptum est: 'Caput mulieris vir, viri Christus, Christi Deus,' Spiritus igitur regit, et consolatur, et erudit, et perducet ecclesiam ad Christum, quam ipse simul sine macula et ruga offeret regnum Deo et Patri. Quod in nobis adimplere dignetur gloriosa Trinitas. Amen." XXIII (1889A), The Cambridge MS., followed by Tissier, includes the interesting covering letter to Alcher which enabled Mlle Debray-Mulatier to date the *Epistola*. It is a curious testimony to the twelfth-century fascination with signs, and the optimism that Lovejoy asserted as one of the hallmarks of the Great Chain of Being.

in the twelfth century.[399] Since the appearance of Mersch's book, a number of studies have discussed this aspect of Isaac's theology;[400] hence it is not necessary to go into a full study of his thought in this matter, particularly since most of his development occurs in Sermons outside our chosen texts of concentration.[401] The only question that must be broached is the source of Isaac's interest and creativity on this question. His wide knowledge of Augustine is undoub edly a factor; but many twelfth-century theologians knew Augustine as well as the Abbot of Stella did. I think it possible that the drive toward unified thought through controlling images that we have found to be central to Isaac's theology is also at work here. In true symbolic fashion, it is synthesis, even of disparate elements, rather than careful analysis, which is operative. In this sense the *catena aurea poete* finds its fitting completion in the *corpus Christi mysticum*. They are both aspects of the same reality—the total historical order of God's creation of which Isaac had such a strong sense. The Abbot of Stella's attitude toward the whole Christ, then, far from being an afterthought, unassimilated into his complex Platonic world, is very much in harmony with it. It was the essence of his relation to Christ, as he put it in one of the Sermons: "O fortunate soul, which never forgets nor loses the child Jesus! More

399. *Le Corps mystique du Christ* (Paris, 1933), II, 142–48. Mersch remarked apropos of Isaac: "Il est étonnant que cet homme remarquable ait été relativement peu étudié" (p. 143).

400. H. de Lubac, *Corpus Mysticum* (Paris, 1944), esp. pp. 121–2, 131; A. Piolanti, "De nostra in Christo solidarietate praecipua Isaac de Stella testimonia," *Euntes Docete,* II (1949), 349–68 (Italian translation in *Palestro del clero* [1956], #7, pp. 1–18); J. Beumer, "Mariologie und Ekklesiologie bei Isaak von Stella," *Münchener Theologische Zeitschrift,* V (1954), 48–61. This important study notes: "Kein anderer hat im 12. Jahrhundert so sehr sein Interesse gerade der Einheit im mystischen Leibe Christi zugewandt und diese so lebendig zur Darstellung gebracht wie Isaac von Stella" (pp. 54–5). Cf. also L. Bouyer, *The Cistercian Heritage* (Westminster, 1958), pp. 179–81; R. Collini, *Studi su Isaaco della Stella* (Milan, 1956–57; unpublished thesis), I, 117–25; L. Gaggero, *op. cit.,* pp. 32–34 (explains Isaac's doctrine of Redemption on the basis of our solidarity in Christ) and A. Hoste, *Sermons* I, "Introduction, pp. 49–50; and pp. 344–5.

401. Especially *Sermons 9, 11, 15, 42, 51,* and the *Sermo in Dedicatione Ecclesie.*

fortunate, which always meditates on the great Jesus; most fortunate of all, which contemplates forever the immense Jesus."[402]

On this note, we can bring to a close our commentary on the structure and development of the *Epistola de Anima*. One thing remains to be considered before we can attempt to summarize Isaac's place as one of the most significant Cistercian thinkers of the century. The Abbot's treatment of the fivefold ascent of the rational power culminating in *intelligentia* is an ideal illustration of the transforming power of his particular symbolic mode of theology upon the materials he inherited. It is to this question that we turn in the final chapter.

402. "O beata anima, quae numquam obliviscitur, nec dimittit puerum Jesum! Magis beata, quae semper meditatur grandem Jesum; maxime beata, quae contemplatur semper immensum Jesum." *Sermon 7*, 15 (ed. Hoste, pp. 188–90; 1715C–D).

THE HIGHER DIMENSION OF THE SOUL
IN ISAAC OF STELLA

T HE THEOLOGICAL QUESTION that Isaac's use of the five stages of the ascent of the intellectual power in man introduces us to is a characteristic problem of the mixing of Hellenic and scriptural anthropologies. This forms the context in which Isaac's works must be read. The desire to bridge the gap caused by the division of the world into the spheres of the necessary and the contingent, the real world of pure forms and the shadow world of appearances, led to emphasis on the soul as the source of contact with the divine, because it alone in man was in touch with the world of the real. It was only in and through the soul that the body and the material universe could share in the reconciliation of all things. As the sense of separation between the transcendent other-ness of the First Principle and the material world increased, the mediating realities tended to multiply—a process to which we have already adverted on several occasions.

The soul itself as the intermediate reality bringing the disparate realms together was influenced by the same process; this is evident as early as Plato's transition from the unitary view of the soul in the early *Dialogues* to the divided view of his later works. One of the most important aspects of this differentiating process in the Platonic tradition was the question of the higher dimension of the soul, that part or function above the ordinary operations of reason where immediate contact was made with God. In any period when Platonism was strong we find this an object of concern, not least in the twelfth century. Isaac of Stella's discussion of *intelligentia* is one of the most notable contributions of the twelfth century to this long tradition. In order to appreciate the importance of the Abbot's views on this question, the background and sources of the higher dimension of the soul will be discussed before turning to his own treatment. At the end of the chapter we shall also survey the influence of Isaac's views.

THE GREEK AND PATRISTIC BACKGROUND TO THE HIGHER DIMENSION OF THE SOUL

The higher dimension of the soul has its roots in the Greek process of differentiation which first made it possible to think of the soul as distinct from the body and then of the soul itself as distinguishable into parts. Hesiod held that certain men were immortalized after death as *daemons* (*Works and Days*, lines 121 sqq.; 255 sqq.), a doctrine which seems to have influenced Heraclitus.[1] E. R. Dodds pointed out that Empedocles distinguished between *psyche*, the firesoul which is not immortal, and the immortal "*daemon* [which] is . . . the carrier of man's potential divinity and actual guilt."[2] This process of extruding a higher region of the soul out of the undifferentiated spirituality which the Greek genius had uncovered was conditioned by the increasing stress on the transcendent character of the First Principle which played such a notable role in the history of Greek thought. If man possesses something divine within him, then as the divine comes to be more and more transcendently viewed (e.g., the conception of Anaxagoras and Diogenes concerning God as *nous*[3]), the soul tends to be seen in a

1. Kirk and Raven, *The Presocratic Philosophers*, (Cambridge, 1966), pp. 209–10.
2. *The Greeks and the Irrational* (Berkeley, 1963), p. 153. Kirk and Raven (pp. 351–61) have a detailed description of Empedocles's doctrine on the soul, especially the contrast between the migrating soul and the physical consciousness (pp. 359–61). They indicate that Dodd's division may be too simple.
3. W. Jaeger, *The Theology of the Early Greek Philosophers* (Oxford, 1967), pp. 162-4, 170–1. Cf. Onian's suggestions on the original sense of νους νόος in *The Origins of European Thought* (Cambridge, 1951), pp. 82-3.

fashion that will encourage the specification of a part, faculty, action of the soul, which is somehow superior to its ordinary operations and ways of knowing. This incipient differentiation began in the Presocratics and was continued by Plato; even if he identified the immortal nature of man with the *psyche*, in the late and all-important *Timaeus* he introduced distinctions which were of great importance for the medieval formulation of the higher power of the soul. In 41d we find the Demiurge, or "God, the founder of the universe," as Chalcidius puts it, instructing the lower gods to see to the forming of a mortal body for the immortal and heavenly part of the soul: "I will make a sowing of this whole race and I will hand it over to you; it is your task to do the rest, so that from without you surround the immortal and heavenly nature with a mortal covering and command it to be born."[4] Resuming one of the possible terms for the incipient distinction between the divine and the non-divine soul available to him from the Presocratic tradition, in 90a d this divine and immortal soul is identified with the rational part seated in the head, and is significantly described by the use of the term *daemon*.[5] *Nous*, another possible differentiating term available from the tradition, also made its entry into the *Timaeus*, though not in any systematic fashion. Plato was using *nous* in the general sense of the product of intellectual activity, and not as a division of the soul, in a passage in 51e where he contrasted opinion and true knowledge of the Forms: "which is so because every man shares in correct opinion, but *intellect* is proper to God and to but a few of the learned among men."[6] His stress on the

4. "Huius ego universi generis sementem faciam vobisque tradam; vos cetera exequi par est, ita ut immortalem caelestemque naturam mortali textu extrinsecus ambiatis iubeatisque nasci . . ." (*ed. Waszink*, p. 36).

5. Not a part of the Chalcidius translation, which only went as far as 53c, this passage is still an important witness to Plato's strong acceptance of the differentiating tendency here resulting in disparate souls. Though not directly known to the medievals, such a passage was influential in many indirect ways, e.g., Chalcidius's *Comm.* 139 (*ed. Waszink*, pp. 179–80). On this passage in Plato, cf. F. M. Cornford, *Plato's Cosmology*, Liberal Arts Paperback (New York, 1957), pp. 352–5; Dodds, *op. cit.*, pp. 213–14.

6. "Quid quod rectae opinionis omnis vir particeps intellectus vero Dei proprius et paucorum admodum lectorum hominum" (*ed. Waszink*, p. 50.,

200   *The Golden Chain*

nous as what is properly divine and shared by only a few men, however, made this text a possible source for speaking of various higher regions of the soul above the ordinary operations and in direct contact with the divine. The passage was frequently cited in this sense in the twelfth century. Chalcidius significantly has no fixed Latin equivalent for *nous*, but uses *intellectus*,[7] *intelligentia*,[8] or *mens*[9] —all terms that at one time or another were to be used for the summit of the soul. Plato was not the direct source for the patristic and medieval theories on this question; but just as he provided the intellectual framework within which the religious world of Late Hellenism expressed itself, the possibilities and complexities of his thought offered fertile ground for the creation of the speculative symbols which manifested this dimension of mystical experience in antiquity and the Middle Ages.

In Plotinus the dualistic implications of Plato's view of the divine and earthly parts of man are enhanced by the repeated assertion of a clear distinction between the upper and lower man. Only the upper man, the soul that lives on the level of *nous*, or the Intellect, the first emanation from the One, can truly be called man.[10] At times Plotinus seems to introduce a further differentiation, for his emphasis on the two faces of the soul, one that is directed below to the changeable realities of this world, and the other whose gaze is directed to the intelligible realities above, and his placing of discursive reason as a mediating ground between these two,[11] imply that man's opening to the world of the divine transcends the

---

ll. 9–10). "καὶ τόν μὲν πάντα ἄνδρα, μετέχειν φατέον, νόυ δὲ θεούς, ἀνθρώπων δὲ γένος βραχύ τι."

7. 30b (ed. *Waszink,* p. 23, ll. 5–6); 46d (p. 43, ll. 16–19); and the passage cited above.

8. 47e–48a (p. 45, ll. 9–13).

9. 39e (p. 32, l. 18). Cf. *Indices* in Waszink, p. 368.

10. *Enn.* I, 1, 7; II, 1, 5; II, 3, 9; III, 8, 5; IV, 1, 1; IV, 8, 4; VI, 7, 5. In many of these texts the upper man is identified with the reasoning part, but taken in a general sense.

11. *Enn.* II, 9, 2; V, 3, 3; V, 9, 1–2. Cf. A. H. Armstrong, "Plotinus," *Cambridge History of Later Greek and Early Medieval Philosophy,* pp. 224–5.

merely rational. While Plotinus for the most part avoids the mythic presentation of the story of the soul that later Neoplatonists were to indulge in, the mystical goal of his philosophical speculations—the "flight of the alone to the Alone"—the ecstatic union with the Unknowable One as expressed in the metaphors of ascent, interiorization and return to origins,[12] and above all, the fact that the possibility of this union is grounded in something super-rational in man, necessitate the kinds of striking images to which he so frequently has recourse to convey his meaning. Can the mystic experience be brought to speech in any other way?

The view of man as a mixture of diverse elements, the highest part (the true man) as something that was to be placed in the sphere of the divine, and the fact that this highest part was sometimes thought of as beyond the range of the operations of reason, the opening that this approach gave to the thematizing of mystic experience—all these themes were assumed and developed by the Christian Fathers. In general, two types of formulas were used: *a schema of interiorization*, where God is to be found by going within, where that which opens out to God is expressed as the deepest ground of the soul; and *a schema of ascent*, where man moves up through the ascending levels of his being to that point at the height of the soul which impinges on the divine. Neither of these schemas is mutually exclusive; we are frequently told that to go within is really to ascend above; but they provide a useful tool for determining the general emphasis and symbolic implications of the thought of the writers we shall discuss. The ascent schema, for instance, has affinities for cosmological symbolism which the interiorization schema alone lacks.

Although St Augustine made use of the symbolism of ascent to describe the progress of the soul to the beatitude that is God,[13] it is primarily as the great exponent of the mysticism of introversion

12. Cf. Paul Henry, "Plotinus' Place in the History of Thought," in *Plotinus: The Enneads*, trans. by Stephen MacKenna (London, n.d.), pp. xlv–li.

13. E.g., *De Quan. An.*, 33 (PL 32, 1073–7); *De Doc. Christ.* II, 7, 9–11 (PL 34, 39–40); *Conf.* IX, 10 (*ed. cit.*, pp. 332–5).

that he is remembered. Augustine recognized the necessity of maintaining in some way the unity of man composed of body and soul, but he experienced considerable difficulty expressing this in the kind of Neoplatonic framework in which he worked. What is most evident in the drive of his thought, however, is his desire to highlight the spirituality and substantiality of the soul which provided the ground for the introspective analysis of the thinking subject that leads man to God. Beginning with the reflections on *memoria* (what today we would call psychological consciousness) in the Tenth Book of the *Confessions*,[14] this reached its culmination in the Fourteenth and Fifteenth Books of the *De Trinitate*, where the image of the Trinity in man is found to lie in that special presence of memory to itself for which Augustine coined the terms *abstrusior memoriae profunditas* and the *principale mentis*.[15] When we reach this inmost part of the soul the introspective task is complete:

> For if we betake ourselves to the inner memory of the mind by which it remembers itself, and to the inner understanding by which it understands itself, and to the inner will by which it loves itself, where these three are always together at the same time, and always have been together at the same time . . . , then the image of that Trinity too will be seen to belong to the memory alone. . . . But we have finally arrived at that point in our discussion where we begin to consider the principal part of the human mind, by which it knows or can know God.[16]

14. *Conf.* X, 7–27 (*ed. cit.*, pp. 359–92).

15. "abstrusior memoriae profunditas," *De Trin.*, XV, 21, 40 (*ed. cit.*, II, 532); "Principale mentis," *De Trin.* XIV, 8, 11 (*ed. cit.*, II, 372). On the psychological and mystical terminology of Augustine, cf. L. Reypens, "Âme . . . ," *op. cit.*, pp. 436–41; Gilson, *The Christian Philosophy of St Augustine*, pp. 44–55, and especially pp. 269–70, n. 1 and M. Schmaus, *Die Psychologische Trinitätslehre des Heiligen Augustinus, passim*.

16. *De Trin.* XIV, 7, 10–11 (trans. of S. MacKenna, *St Augustine: The Trinity* [Washington, 1963], pp. 424–5) (*ed. cit.*, II, 370–2): "Nam si nos referamus ad interiorem mentis memoriam qua sui meminit, et interiorem intelligentiam qua se intelligit, et interiorem voluntatem qua se diligit, ubi haec tria simul semper sunt, et semper simul fuerunt ex quo esse coeperunt, sive cogitarentur, sive non cogitarentur; videbitur quidem imago illius trinitatis et ad solam memoriam pertinere. . . . Nunc vero ad eam jam per-

Augustine's introspective achievement, one of the high points of patristic speculation, is capable of development in two directions: on the one hand, as the rational self-appropriation of the conscious subject, it transcends the symbolic level of expression in the sense that we are using the term and provides an important stimulus for Aquinas's reflections on the nature of the interior word;[17] on the other, within the symbolic context of twelfth-century theology and in much late medieval mysticism it is an important source for the images of the center of the soul, the *fundus animae*, one of the primary symbols in which mystic experience took place.

While it may be an oversimplification, I believe that it is nonetheless true to assert that it is primarily the *hierarchical schema of ascent* which comes to the fore in the writings of Boethius and in the Dionysian corpus. In a famous passage in the *De Consolatione Philosophiae*, Boethius tells us:

> Likewise *sensus, imaginatio, ratio,* and *intelligentia* consider man himself in different ways. For *sensus* judges the figure as it is established in the matter that underlies it, but *imaginatio* the figure alone without the matter. *Ratio*, however, transcends this and examines by its universal consideration that species which exists in singular things. Finally, the eye of *intelligentia* is yet higher, for surpassing the whole of creation it gazes upon that simple form itself by the clear point of the mind.[18]

Can the *intelligentia* here be said to be Boethius's equivalent of the

---

venimus disputationem, ubi principale mentis humanae, quo novit Deum vel potest nosse, considerandum suscepimus, ut in eo reperiamus imaginem Dei."

17. Cf. Bernard Lonergan, *Verbum: Word and Idea in Aquinas* (Notre Dame, 1967), pp. vii–xv.

18. "Ipsum quoque hominem aliter sensus, aliter imaginatio, aliter ratio, aliter intelligentia contuetur. Sensus enim figuram in subiecta materia constitutam, imaginatio vero solam sine materia iudicat figuram. Ratio vero hanc quoque transcendit speciemque ipsam quae singulariter inest universali consideratione perpendit. Intelligentiae vero celsior oculus exsistit; supergressa namque universitatis ambitum ipsam illam simplicem formam pura mentis acie contuetur," *De Cons. Phil.* V, prosa 4, lines 82–91 (ed. Rand, p. 388).

summit of the soul? The question is controverted,[19] but there are indications that it can. In his poetic summary of the *Timaeus* in Book III, metrum 9, Boethius repeats in general fashion the myth of the divine origin of the human soul and uses the term *mens* both for this part of the soul and for the forming mind which is the Platonic Demiurge.[20] If we remember that *intelligentia* was, along with *mens* and *intellectus*, one of the terms used to translate the Greek *nous* in Chalcidius, and if we advert to the fact that *intelligentia* in Book V is described as pertaining to the divine nature, just as reason pertains to the human,[21] then there seems to be good reason for asserting that *intelligentia* is man's share in the divine nature, conceived in a broadly Platonic fashion. It is the source of his return to the Primal Good, as is made clear in a later passage: "Wherefore, let us be lifted up if we can to the summit of that understanding, for

19. K. Bruder, *Die Philosophischen Elemente in den Opuscula Sacra des Boethius* (Leipzig, 1928), Chap. II, "Die Erkenntnislehre," pp. 11–33, claims that there are two ways of knowing in man, according to Boethius: one (*sensus, imaginatio, ratio*) empirical, though a mixture of Platonic and Aristotelian elements; the other (*intelligentia*) basically *a priori*, Neoplatonic, and deeply influenced by Augustine's theories of illumination. V. Schurr, on the other hand, in *Die Trinitätslehre des Boethius im Lichte der "skythischen Kontroverse,"* (Paderborn, 1935), pp. 46–50, claims that there is no *a priori* form of knowledge in Boethius, because *intelligentia* is not a human form of knowing at all. The controversy would seem to be clarified by three questions: (1) Is the object of *intelligentia* divine? (2) Is the source divine? and (3) In what sense may it be spoken of as a faculty of man? Both Bruder and Schurr would seem to agree on (1); Schurr feels that Bruder would answer no to (2); which would seem to be an incorrect reading of Boethius. Finally, the weakness of Schurr's approach is his cavalier treatment of (3), because in some way *intelligentia* must be said to enter into the condition of man, if only as a gift, and this would mean that there are two faces to man's knowing, according to Boethius. *Intelligentia* is the divine faculty of knowing *in* man.

20. The divine Mind: "pulchrum pulcherrimus ipse mundum *mente* gerens," lines 7–8; the human soul: "Da pater augustam *menti* conscendere sedem," line 22 (*ed. Rand,* p. 264).

21. "ratio vero humani tantum generis est sicut intelligentia sola divini," *De Cons. Phil.* V, 5, 17–18 (*ed. Rand,* p. 394). Even where the knowledge of *intelligentia* is described as including things below the sphere of the divine (V, 4, 92–104), it is described in the manner of a knowledge of them as they are known in the Highest Principle (to know them as God knows them, in traditional theological terminology).

there reason will be able to see what it cannot behold in itself,"[22] i.e., the mystery of divine foreknowledge. The clarity of the Boethian schema, its close relationship with his useful classifications of human knowledge,[23] and the peculiar cast given it by its weight of mythic and poetic content were to make it extremely important in the twelfth century.

The absolute unknowability of God as above all being and knowledge has rarely been stressed with more power than in the writings of the Pseudo-Dionysius; yet, despite this unknowability, the corpus of these mysterious and obscure writings is carefully organized to lead the faithful soul back to that Highest Principle by means of an intricate ascent that begins with the Symbolic theology, proceeding from the material world to the intelligible, and moves on to the Negative (Apophatic) theology to end in the Mystical theology that goes beyond the intelligible sphere to reach the unknowable. Despite the presence of introspection or introversion in places in the Pseudo-Dionysius,[24] it is clearly hierarchical ascent by means of this carefully worked out theory which is his dominant mode of thought. The difficulty of these writings (especially in the translations of John Scotus Eriugena), and the fact that there is little speculation in them on the parts of the soul and which of these parts might be the faculty by which man is united with the divine,[25] should not blind us to their significance, for they not only provided a comprehensive framework within which the scattered Biblical and Classical symbols of ascent could organize themselves, but also stressed, more strongly than ever

22. "Quare in illius summae intelligentiae cacumen, si possumus, erigamur; illic enim ratio videbit quod in se non potest intueri," *De Cons. Phil.* V, 4, 50–3 (*ed. Rand*, p. 396).

23. Cf. the classification of divisions of knowledge according to the three-fold pattern in *De Trin.* II, 5–21 (*ed. Rand*, p. 8) and *In Isagogen Porphyrii Commenta Prima* I, 3–4 (*ed. Brandt*, p. 7–12).

24. *De Div. Nom.* IV, 9 (*Dionysiaca* I, 190–4), on the three motions of the soul.

25. The Pseudo-Dionysius is more inclined to speculate on the classes of beings and the fact that man has something in common with each, e.g., *De Cael. Hier.*, IV (*Dionysiaca* II, 802–4). This will be important for the assimilative aspect of the theme we are investigating.

before, that union with God was something taking place in an instant of ecstasy where all forms of knowledge are surpassed.[26]

This survey of the Hellenic and patristic background for the twelfth-century development makes it evident that the problem of man's opening out to God had already received considerable treatment before it was taken up by the medievals. Whether we consider the introspective categories of Augustine with their ambiguous stance between the symbolic and the critically reflective, or whether we turn to the anagogic and image-laden approach of Boethius and the Pseudo-Dionysius, we are still in a world where men are striving by the creation of symbolic forms of experience to find those tools which will enable them to be seized by a direct, unmediated contact with the divine and to communicate to others the framework within which such a contact can take place. Such modes seek to organize and express what in the life of man of its very nature goes beyond what can be organized on the level of ordinary experience and is capable of rational understanding and expression; hence what in these modes we find most difficult to grasp—namely, their imprecision, mutability, interactions, contradictions, nuances, in short, their synthetic power to include rationally diverse materials into congeries that suggest the dimension of unknowability in the very mystery of their immediately striking, convincing manifestation—is also the true secret of their genius.

Symbols, like words, can live or die. Individuals, groups, organizations, whole centuries and cultures can continue the proliferation of the symbolic modes of a former age, but the dry bones have no life in them. That which is closest to the marrow of the symbol, its ability to manifest the unknown but present dimensions of ultimate reality at the same time and within the frame-

26. "per quam [power of the Spirit] ineffabilibus et ignotis, ineffabiliter et ignote, conjungimur secundum meliorem nostrae rationalis et intellectualis virtutis et operationis unitatem. Universaliter itaque non audendum dicere neque intelligere quid de superessentiali et occulta Divinitate praeter divinitus nobis ex sacris eloquiis expressa. Ipsius enim super rationem et *intelligentiam* et essentiam superessentialitatis, ipsa superessentiali scientia reponendum," *De Div. Nom.* I, 1 (trans. of Eriugena, Ph. Chevallier; *Dionysiaca*, I (Paris, 937), 6–8).

work of an experience and expression of the known, can be eviscerated to the vanishing point. Simple criteria for distinguishing between living symbolism—that which really nourishes man and gives him a reference within which to organize his experience—and an atrophied dead symbolism that is the unlived legacy of the past cannot be determined with facility. I would suggest that within the categories of a symbolic mode of thought itself, abstracting from the hermeneutics that moves toward philosophical appropriation of the truth-value of the symbol, that is within the understanding of symbols in the symbols themselves,[27] there are certain indications which point the way toward a symbolism that is alive and authentic. The first of these indications would be the power of *combination*, for where the symbolic expression of an era shows the power to combine and synthesize, to present within a convincing whole, elements frequently disparate and sometimes contradictory in the inherited agglomerate there is evidence of continued creativity in the symbolic mentality. Along with the power of combination, comes the power of *interaction*, for these newly combined elements will not come together in mere juxtaposition if the symbolic mode is still alive, but will influence each other in manifold ways, so that in the complex net of symbolic expressions no one mode will remain quite what it was in previous expressions. Finally, such combinations and interactions will produce both *transvaluations* of the old symbols and sometimes the *creation of new symbolic modes* to organize and express those factors in the life of the age which cannot be contained within the framework inherited from the past. Transvaluation, by which I mean the absorption of the expressive content of the old reference into a new cultural milieu wherein it serves as a correlative that is at once objective and subjective for styles of life, expressions of self-understanding, and political, social, and religious forms that mark a departure from the past, is obviously the more frequent occurrence, and it is possible that in the case of twelfth-century anthropology we shall not get beyond this horizon; outright creation, where new primary images are formed that then build up a whole new world of symbolic expression, is a rarer

27. Cf. P. Ricoeur, *The Symbolism of Evil*, p. 353.

phenomenon, since it involves the kind of break with tradition and clarity and force of creation not common in the history of cultures and of individuals.

It is possible to view the absorption by twelfth-century theology of the patristic and Platonic handling of the question of the higher dimension of man in these categories. The manner of expression of this particular central problem was extremely varied: some of the solutions are no more than repetitions and modernizations of one of the dominant patristic motifs (e.g., Aelred of Rievaulx's neo-Augustinianism as seen in his *De Anima*); others upon careful study reveal themselves as original re-symbolizations of a highly convincing nature (e.g., William of St Thierry's profound discussions of the interpenetrability of love and knowledge); but one mode which stands out with great prominence and provides a convincing illustration of the originality of twelfth-century symbolic thought is the speculation regarding *intelligentia* as the highest power of the soul, that from which the opening out to the divine takes place.

INTELLIGENTIA AND THE FIVEFOLD SCHEMA

Intelligentia, as we have seen, was one of the common psychological terms found in the inherited materials available to the twelfth-century authors. It is, of course, very frequently found in the generic sense of the act of understanding, and in this regard contributes nothing of importance to our study; but *intelligentia* as a power of the soul is of greater significance. We have seen it used in Chalcidius's *Timaeus* as one translation of *nous*, thus indicating its connection with the intellectual mysticism of Hellenistic philosophy; it was also one of the terms used for that highest power of the soul by which man returns to God in Latin translations of late Classical texts, such as the Hermetic *Asclepius* and Porphyry's *De Regressu Animae*.[28] The word is found in Augustine, sometimes as

28. "dicebam enim in ipso initio rerum de coniunctione deorum, qua homines soli eorum dignatione perfruuntur—quicumque etenim hominum tantum felicitatis adepti sunt, ut illum *intelligentiae* divinum perciperent sensum, qui sensus est divinior in solo deo et in *humana intelligentia*." *Asclepius*,

indistinguishable from *mens*, his most generally employed term for the higher aspect of the soul, and therefore as capable of important contributions to the twelfth-century formulation; but considering the variety of meanings given it by Augustine,[29] he can scarcely be the direct source for the views we will examine. Likewise, the uses of *intelligentia* in Eriugena are too general and diffuse to be seen as the direct source for the twelfth-century development.[30]

II (*edd. A. D. Nock and A.-J. Festugière*), p. 303. ". . . ad Deum per virtutem *intelligentiae* pervenire paucis dicis esse concessum," Porphyry, *De Regressu Animae* (*ed. Bidez*, p. 37*, lines 11–16, as cited in *De Civ. Dei*, X, 29).

29. The term *intelligentia* is frequently used in Augustine, but in rather diverse senses. It is often used for the act of understanding itself, e.g., *De Trin.* XIV, 7, 10 (*ed. cit.*, II, 370): "Hanc autem nunc dico *intelligentiam*, qua intelligimus cogitantes, id est, quando eis repertis quae memoriae praesto fuerant, sed non cogitabantur, cogitatio nostra formatur. . . ." Cf. also *De Trin.* XV, 21, 40 (*ed. cit.*, II, 531–2). In other places *intelligentia* seems to be placed above reason, e.g., *De Civ. Dei*, XI, 2 (*ed. cit.*, II, 322) and is sometimes used as a synonym for *mens* itself, e.g. *Liber de Div. Quaest.* 46, 2; 83, 7 (PL 40, 31; 100); *De Lib. Arbit.* I, 1, 3 (PL 32, 1223) and *In Ioan.* XXIV, 6 (*ed. cit.*, pp. 246–47). Augustine was not really concerned with the terminology involved, since he never intended to create a strict classification of the powers of the soul. That part of the *mens* which is superior to *ratio* is frequently identified with *intellectus*, which we are told is the same as the *intelligentia* (*Enarr. in Ps. 31*, 9; PL 36, 263–4) and in a significant passage in the *De Gen. ad Litt.* he even asserts that *ratio*, *mens*, and *intelligentia* are merely different names for the same reality in which the image of God in man is to be found: "ut videlicet intelligamus in eo factum hominem ad imaginem Dei, in quo irrationalibus animantibus antecellit. Id autem est ipsa ratio, vel mens, vel intelligentia, vel si quo alio vocabulo commodius appelatur." (*De Gen. ad Litt.* III, 20, 30; PL 34, 292). Clearly, Augustine cannot be the source for the precise formulation of *intelligentia* as the specific name for the highest power in man, but the appearance of the term in his writings will re-enforce and enrich the nuances of the term.

30. The extent of possible influence from the Pseudo–Dionysius and Eriugena is difficult to determine. Eriugena uses *intelligentia* twenty-two times in the course of his translations of the *Corpus Dionysiacum*. It is his characteristic term to translate the generic νόησις of the Pseudo–Dionysius, and as such maintains much of this general sense in his translation. Cf. G. Théry, "Scot Érigène, traducteur de Denys," p. 271. The Ideas in the Mind of God are referred to as *intelligentiae* (*DN* VII, 1; *CH* XIV; cf. *Dionysiaca* I, 382; II, 982) and *intelligentia* is also used to describe the divine understanding given to the angels (*CH* XV; *Dionysiaca* II, 1006, 1031). The passage that is closest to the developed twelfth-century usage is found in *DN*. VII, 2 (*Dionysiaca* I, 404):

The influence of Boethius is what is decisive here. Not only as the logician and creator of theological terminology, but as the Platonic seer and master of the theory of the soul, his fame in the twelfth century was immense.[31] The traditional fourfold Boethian schema of *sensus, imaginatio, ratio, intelligentia*, as seen in the *De Consolatione Philosophiae*, was common in the twelfth century, as its appearance in such writers as William of Conches, John of Salisbury, Godfrey of St Victor, Aelred of Rievaulx, Clarenbald of Arras, Hugh of St Victor, and William of St Thierry, and in anonymous works like the *Liber Alcidi* indicates.[32] Nor is this use merely an empty repetition, for we find it absorbing and assimilating other symbolic modes such as that of the microcosm theme,[33] seeking clarification of its role as the source of divine knowledge in man, and gradually being modified, transformed, and transvalued in a manner that manifests its living relation to the intellectual and religious context in which it found itself.

The most significant transformation of the Boethian schema crowned by *intelligentia* was its development into a more organized, assimilative mode based upon a fivefold pattern of ascent of *sensus, imaginatio, ratio, intellectus, and intelligentia*. Hugh of St Victor and possibly Thierry of Chartres, two of the most influential thinkers and teachers of the first half of the twelfth century, are at the origin of this development.

"Per quam [pax] animae largissimas suas rationes intelligentes, et ad unam intellectualem congregatae puritatem, progrediuntur propria sibi via et ordine, *et immaterialem et simplicem intelligentiam*, in unitatem super intellectum." In his own *De Divisione Naturae*, when Eriugena speaks in terms of a threefold division of man's powers of knowing, he always uses the terms *intellectus, ratio* and *sensus* (e.g., *PL* 122, 787A); but when he speaks in a general fashion, at times he uses *intelligentia* for *intellectus* as the power superior to *ratio* (e.g., *PL* 122, 735A–B; 750B). Thus it appears impossible for the Dionysian-Erigenean strain to have been more than a contributory factor.

31. Cf. "Aetas Boetiana," M.-D. Chenu, *La Théologie au 12ᵉ Siècle*, pp. 142–58.

32. M.-T. d'Alverny, *Alain de Lille* (Paris, 1965), pp. 170–6; E. Bertola, "Di una inedita Trattazione Psicologica Intitolata: *Quid Sit Anima*," *Rivista di Filosofia Neo-Scolastica*, LVIII (1966), 571–5.

33. E.g., Godfrey of St Victor, *Microcosmos*, I, 19 (*ed. Delhaye*, p. 46).

Leaving aside the *De Unione Corporis et Spiritus* which in general follows the fourfold schema and whose ascription to Hugh has recently been questioned, we can follow Hugh's modifications of the traditional formula in his *Didascalicon*. The source of the modification is partly rooted in two corresponding texts of Boethius himself, for in his *In Isagogen Porphyrii Commentum Primum*, when discussing the powers of the soul activated in the divisions of philosophy that correspond to the grades of being, he speaks of both *intellectus* and *intelligentia*, although here giving *intellectus* the higher role,[34] while in another discussion of the parts of speculative philosophy in the *De Trinitate* he indicates three higher activities in man, though once again speaking of the highest as exercised *intellectualiter*.[35] When we recall that both *intellectus* and *intelligentia* were used for translating the *nous* of the *Timaeus*, and when we reflect on their interchangeability with each other and with *mens* in Augustine, this variation appears significant for the later medieval development. In commenting on the passage from the *In Isagogen Porphyrii* in his *Didascalicon*, Hugh significantly reverses the roles of the two highest powers, so that now *intellectus* deals with the intelligible world and *intelligentia* with the highest, or *intellectible*, world.[36] There are still inconsistencies in the schematization of the *Didascalicon*, particularly the fact that the object of the knowledge of *intelligentia* includes things other than God;[37] but if we can accept the fragment of Hugh's teaching found in the *Miscellanea I*,

34. *In Isagogen Porphyrii Commentum* I, Liber I, 3 (ed. Brandt, pp. 8–9).

35. *De Trin.* II (ed. Rand, p. 8). Cf. M.-T. d'Alverny, *op. cit.*, pp. 171–4.

36. "intelligibile autem quod ipsum quidem solo percipitur *intellectu*, sed non solo intellectu percipit, quia imaginationem vel sensum habet, quo ea quae sensibus subiacent comprehendit . . . cum vero ab hac distractione [being pulled down into the world of sense] ad puram *intelligentiam* conscendens in unum se colligit, fit beatior *intellectibilis substantiae* participatione." *Didascalicon* II, 3 (ed. Buttimer, p. 17).

37. "est igitur, ut apertius dicam, intellectibile in nobis id quod est *intelligentia*, intelligibile vero id quod est imaginatio; intelligentia vero est de solis rerum principiis, i.e., Deo, ideis, et hyle, et de incorporeis substantiis, pura certaque cognitio," *Didascalicon* II, 5 (ed. Buttimer, p. 29).

Chap. 15, as authentic, then some time around the year 1130,[38] Hugh had organized the data into a clear fivefold pattern:

> There are five progressions of knowledge: the first is in *sensus*, the second is in *imaginatio*, the third in *ratio*, the fourth in *intellectus*, the fifth in *intelligentia*. Through *sensus*, knowledge is in the visible things and according to them; through *imaginatio* it is not in them, but it is according to them; through *ratio* it is neither in them nor according to them, but it is in intelligible realities which exist after the manner of visible things; through *intellectus* it is not in intelligible realities, but it is from them; through *intelligentia*, it is neither in intelligible realities nor from them.[39]

Thierry of Chartres's three Commentaries on Boethius's *De Trinitate* also exhibit interesting variations on the fourfold schema. If we can accept the authenticity and dating for these three works as proposed by Nicholas Häring,[40] then in the first Commentary, sometimes known as the *Librum hunc*, for which a date around 1135 is suggested,[41] we find a stage analogous to that of the *Didascalicon*, that is, no clear new schematization, but a preference for the

38. Cf. D. van den Eynde, *Essai sur la succession et la date des écrits de Hugues de Saint Victor* (Rome, 1960), pp. 194 and 224, and Tableau Synoptique suggests 1125–1131. M.-T. d'Alverny suggests a date close to that of the *Didascalicon*, also in the late 1120's, *op. cit.*, p. 174. The *Miscellanea* are a compilation of Victorine materials in which Books I–II are basically Hugonian; the later books contain some material from Richard; cf. J. Châtillon, "Autor des 'Miscellanea' attribués à Hugues de Saint-Victor," *Mélanges Marcel Viller, RAM*, XXV (1949), 299–305.

39. "Quinque sunt progressiones cognitionis. Prima est in sensu; secunda in imaginatione; tertia in ratione; quarta in intellectu; quinta in intelligentia. Per sensum est in istis, et secundum ista; per imaginationem non est in istis, sed secundum ista; per rationem, neque in istis est neque secundum ista, sed est in illis et de illis quae sunt secundum ista; per intellectum non est in illis, sed de illis; per intelligentiam, *nec in illis nec de illis*." *Miscellanea*, I, 15 (PL 177, 485BC).

40. N. Häring, "Commentary on Boethius' *De Trinitate* by Thierry of Chartres," *AHDL*, XXXI (1956), 260–2.

41. M.-T. d'Alverny suggests Peter Elias as the author, which would place it after 1145; cf. *op. cit.*, p. 176, n. 62.

term *intelligentia* to describe the highest power of the soul at work in the science of theology;[42] whereas in the later *Lectiones in Boethii Librum De Trinitate* (c. 1140–45), there is a fivefold arrangement:

And it must be known that in physics, mathematics, and theology different powers and comprehensions of the soul are used to understand the universe as it is subject to these three parts of speculative philosophy. For in theology *intellectibilitas* or *intelligentia* is used; but in mathematics *intellectus* which is discipline; in physics *ratio, sensus* and *imaginatio* which understand whatever they understand in matter.[43]

In the last Commentary, the *Glosse super Librum Boethii De Trinitate* (c. 1145–50), the term *intelligibilitas* is preferred for this highest operation of the soul, and *intelligentia* is relegated to the position of the faculty of mathematical knowledge in the fivefold schema.[44]

Thus, by the middle of the twelfth century, both the traditional Boethian schema and a new five-stage variant were in existence. Mlle d'Alverny has pointed out the richness of these schemas, which could be used in a didactic sense to indicate the divisions of philosophy, a cosmological sense to manifest the similarity between the stages of man's knowledge and the degrees of being and a

42. *Commentum super Boethium de Trinitate*, II, 6, 9, 16; cf. N. Häring, "Two Commentaries on Boethius by Thierry of Chartres," *AHDL*, XXXV (1960), 92–5. In #6 we find *intelligentia* substituted for the *intellectus* (*nous*) of *Timaeus* 51c: "Haec vero comprehendendi vis suo nomine vocatur 'intelligentia.' Quae solius quidem Dei est et admodum paucorum hominum" (*op. cit.*, p. 92).

43. *Lectiones in Boethii De Trinitate*, II, 30, in N. Häring, "The Lectures of Thierry of Chartres on Boethius' *De Trinitate*," *AHDL*, XXXIII (1958), 162: "Et sciendum quod diversis animae viribus et comprehensionibus in physica, mathematica, theologia utendum est ad comprehendendum [am] universitatem ut subiecta est his tribus speculativae partibus. Nam in theologia utendum est *intellectibilitate sive intelligentia;* in mathematica vero *intellectu* qui est disciplina; in physica *ratione, sensu et imaginatione* quae circa materiam comprehendunt quicquid comprehendunt."

44. *Glossa super Librum Boethii De Trinitate* II, 3–10; cf. N. Häring, "A Commentary on Boethius' *De Trinitate* by Thierry of Chartres," pp. 279–80.

mystical sense to specify the stages of contemplation;[45] but it is
only by studying their mode of operation at its richest in Isaac of
Stella that we can observe how the fivefold schema can include all
this and more besides, harnessing the anagogic possibilities of the
Dionysian world, and even absorbing the symbolic side of Augustinian introspection.

The appearance of the schema in Paragraph VIII of the *Epistola de
Anima* and its later explanation in the remainder of the treatise is
fuller and more detailed than any of the texts we have seen thus far:

> Therefore one speaks of sense knowledge, imagination, reason,
> discernment, understanding. All of these in the soul are neverthe-
> less nothing other than the soul. . . . Therefore just as the visible
> world is directed upward by a certain fivefold ordering—earth,
> water, air, aether, or the firmament, and the supreme heaven
> which is called the empyrean—so also there are five stages to
> wisdom for the soul as it makes its pilgrimage in the world of
> its body: sense, imagination, reason, discernment, understanding.
> For the power of reason is aroused to wisdom by five steps, just as
> the affective power is to love by four; so that in these nine
> stages the soul journeying into itself on the internal feet of
> rational and affective power, as it were, lives in the spirit, may
> walk in the spirit, even to the seraphim and cherubim. that is,
> the fullness of wisdom and the fire of love.[46]

A variety of theories have been advanced concerning the origin
of this schema and the significance of *intelligentia* in Isaac. It may be
well to outline these briefly before giving the reasons for our own

45. M.-T. d'Alverny, *op. cit.,* p. 173; cf. also E. Bertola, *op. cit.,* pp. 573–6.
46. "Dicitur ergo sensus corporeus, imaginatio, ratio, intellectus, intelligentia. Hec tamen omnia in anima non aliud sunt quam anima. . . . Sicut ergo
sursum versus quinquepertita quadam distinctione mundus iste visibilis
gradatur: terra, aqua, aere, ethere sive firmamento, ipso quoque celo supremo
quod empyreum vocatur; sic et anime in mundo sui corporis peregrinanti
quinque sunt ad sapientiam progressus: sensus, imaginatio, ratio, intellectus,
intelligentia. Quinque etenim progressionibus rationabilitas exercetur ad
sapientiam, sicut quatuor affectus ipse ad caritatem, quatenus in novem istis
progressibus in semetipsa proficiens anima, sensus et affectus quasi internis
quibusdam pedibus, que spiritu vivit, spiritu ambulet, usque ad cherubin et
seraphin, id est, plenitudinem scientie et rogum caritatis." (1880AB)

structuring of its antecedents. The possible theories of origin may be reduced to four:

(1) *St John Damascene.* In an early article, E. Bertola cited a text of John Damascene quoted by O. Lottin as a possible source for Isaac's pattern.[47] He did not discuss the possibilities of this contact, and has himself abandoned it in later articles.[48]

(2) *Proclus.* An interesting, if controversial, theory was proposed by E. von Ivánka.[49] Beginning with Thomas Gallus (†1246), he traced the history of the classification back through Alfredus Anglicus, Alan of Lille, the *De Spiritu et Anima*, and finally to Isaac. For von Ivánka the most important feature of the schema is the sharp contrast between *intellectus* and *intelligentia*;[50] on this basis, he rejects the usual Boethian explanation, since he feels that it does not provide for such a sharp separation. The last source that he finds for the separation is a text from Proclus's *De Providentia et Fato*.[51] The contrast is assuredly present; but among other difficulties, the text

47. "La dottrina psicologica di Isaaco della Stella," p. 304. The text is found in Lottin, *Psychologie et morale au XII et XIIIe siècles*, I, 397: "Oportet scire quoniam anima nostra duplices habet virtutes, has quidem cognoscitivas, illas vero zoticas. Et cognoscitivae quidem sunt intellectus, mens, opinio, imaginatio, sensus."

48. E.g., "Di una inedita Trattazione . . . ," pp. 571-75.

49. "Zur Überwindung des neuplatonischen Intellektualismus in der Deutung der Mystik," *Scholastik*, XXX (1955), 185-94; *Plato Christianus*, pp. 352-63.

50. *Op. cit.*, p. 189.

51. "Quartam autem adhuc tibi et hoc simpliciorem intelligendum nostram cognitionem, quam non adhuc methodis utentem et resolutionibus aut compositionibus aut divisionibus aut demonstrationibus, sed epibolis (id est adiectionibus) simplicibus et velut autopticis (id est per se visivis) entia speculantem collaudant qui secundum ipsam operare possunt, intellectum iam et non scientiam ipsam veneranter dicentes. . . ."

"Quintam etiam post has omnes cognitionis intelligentia volo te accipere, qui credidisti Aristotile quidem usque ad intellectualem operationem sursumducenti, ultra hanc autem nichil insinuante; assequentem autem Platoni et ante Platonem theologis, qui consueverunt nobis laudare *cognitionem supra intellectum* et maniam et vere hanc divinam divulgant: *ipsam aiunt unum anime*, non adhuc intellectuale excitantem et hoc coaptantem uni." *Procli Diadochi Tria Opuscula* (ed. H. Boese; Berlin, 1960); *De Providentia et Fato*, 30, 1-7; 31, 1-7 (pp. 139-40).

P

was not known in the twelfth century[52]—most of it survives only through a thirteenth-century translation of William of Moerbeke; furthermore, von Ivánka denies any possibility of indirect transmission of the schema through the Pseudo-Dionysius, Maximus the Confessor, Eriugena, or the *Liber de Causis*.

(3) *The Pseudo-Dionysius and Scotus Eriugena.* Another possible explanation was hinted at by two competent investigators in the area of twelfth-century intellectual history, although in the long run both hold to the Boethian source theory. A. Fracheboud, in speaking of the influence of the Dionysian concept of hierarchy on Isaac, makes mention of the *De Caelesti Hierarchia.* He finds Isaac's combining of the five levels of cognition with the four levels of affectivity, and the equating of the nine stages with the nine choirs of angels,[53] a sure sign of Dionysian influence.[54] M.-D. Chenu also drew attention to the Dionysian-Erigenean corpus as a major source of twelfth-century interest in man as microcosm,[55] and mentions a passage from the *De Caelesti Hierarchia*, IV, I[56] which presents a four-stage system known to Alan of Lille and Simon of Tournai. Various other microcosmic texts in the Pseudo-Dionysius and Eriugena compare man with the four or five levels of being,[57] particularly Eriugena's *Commentary* on the passage from the *De Caelesti Hierarchia.*[58]

52. E.g., J. T. Muckle, "Greek Works Translated Directly into Latin before 1350," *Medieval Studies,* V (1943), 114.

53. VIII (1880B).

54. Cf. A. "Le Pseudo-Denys . . . parmi les sources du . . . Isaac de l'Étoile," pp. 28–29: "Le chiffre neuf emprunté aux hiérarchies célestes et applique aux étapes de l'âme en est une garantie, Denys ayant été le premier a distribuer les anges en neuf choeurs subordonnés."

55. "Spiritus: le vocabulaire . . . ," pp. 220–22.

56. Given as the underlined lemma in the text from the *Commentary* in note 58 below.

57. Pseudo-Dionysius, *DN*, 1, 4; V, 3 (*Dionysiaca*, I, 42–44, 327–31). Eriugena, *De Div. Nat.* II, 24 (*PL* 122, 580D–81A) for a five-fold comparison similar to that in the *Commentary* (compare with IV, 6 in 755B); in III, 37 (733A) there is a four-fold microcosmic pattern.

58. "*Sequitur: Existentia igitur omnia esse eius participant; esse enim omnium est super esse divinitas; viventia autem eadem super omnem vitam vivifica virtute;*

(4) *Boethius*. The most popular and convincing explanation for the source of Isaac's schema is to be found in Boethius. This suggestion seems to have been made first by W. Jansen on the basis of the famous passage from *De Consolatione Philosophiae* V, 4.[59] It was easy to see that this passage portrayed a fourfold plan, rather than Isaac's five-stage one. W. Meuser was the first to suggest that the answer to this problem was in terms of the ambiguities and interchangeability of *intellectus* and *intelligentia* in Boethius's terminology.[60] The Boethian origin has been generally accepted by the historians of medieval thought, e.g., B. Geyer,[61] E. Gilson,[62] P. Michaud-Quantain,[63] M.-D. Chenu,[64] A. Fracheboud,[65] P. Künzle,[66]

---

rationalia et intellectualia eadem super omnem et rationem et intellectum per se perfecta et ante perfecta sapientia. Clarissime brevissimeque totius universalis creature quadripartitum modum pronuntiat. Omne siquidem quod divinam bonitatem participat, aut solummodo est, aut est et vivit, aut est et vivit et ratiocinatur, aut est et vivit et rationis et intellectus capax. Ubi notandum quod, *dum ceteri auctores utriusque lingue quinquiformem universitatis condite dividunt modum:* omne enim quod creatum est, aut solummodo est, aut est et vivit, aut est et vivit et sentit, aut est et vivit et sentit et rationis capax, aut est et vivit et sentit et rationis capax et intellegit: eo enim modo humanam segregant et angelicam naturam, humanae quidem rationem, angelice vero distribuentes intellectum; iste magister quadripartitum diffinit modum, attribuens videlicet irrationabilibus animantibus sensum, qui tamen, quoniam communis est et rationabilibus et irrationabilibus animantibus, suum ceteris auctoribus in divisione nature locum optinere videtur." H. Dondaine, "Les *Expositiones super Ierarchiam Caelestem* de Jean Scot Érigène, texte inédit, d'après Douai 202," *AHDL,* XXV–XXVI (1950–51), 263–4.

59. *Der Kommentar des Clarenbaldus von Arras zu Boethius De Trinitate* (Breslau, 1926), discussed the twelfth-century use of *intelligentia* with great erudition (pp. 56–68).

60. *Op. cit.,* p. 67.

61. *Die Patristische und Scholastische Philosophie* (Berlin, 1928), p. 259.

62. *A History of Christian Philosophy in the Middle Ages,* p. 169.

63. "La classification des puissances de l'âme au XIIe siècle," p. 25.

64. *La théologie* . . . , p. 126; "Spiritus: le vocabulaire . . . ," p. 228, n. 66; "Notes de Lexicographie philosophique: Disciplina," *RSPT,* XXV (1936), 691–92.

65. "L'Influence de S. Augustin . . . ," p. 13, n. 6.

66. *Das Verhältnis der Seele* . . . , p. 66.

R. Baron,[67] R. Javelet,[68] and F. Mannarini;[69] but it was not until the researches of Mlle M.-T. d'Alverny and N. Häring uncovered the early history of the twelfth-century variations on the Boethian passage by Hugh of St Victor and Thierry of Chartres that the lines of the transmission and transformation were clarified.

It is obvious that the question of origin is a complex one; even the insufficient theories have something to contribute to the dialectic of the problem. E. von Ivánka's thesis, for instance, has the value of demonstrating the startling parallels that can be found in the permutations of Neoplatonic themes; but his hypothesis of a no longer extant translation of Proclus's *De Providentia et Fato* as Isaac's source is an attempt to explain the obscure through the unknown, particularly in the light of more recent research on the history of Boethius in the twelfth century. The extent of the influence of the Pseudo-Dionysius as known through the translations and commentaries of Scotus Eriugena provides us not so much with a source—the textual differences are obvious—as with explanation for some of the symbolic accretions of the Boethian image. Thus, the passage from the *De Caelesti Hierarchia* IV,1, occurs within a context stressing the participation in the Divine Nature and the necessity for illumination of the human soul (*theophaniae*) which are also important themes in Isaac's use of his schema in the *Epistola*; but the differences are even greater; e.g., the absence of the term *intelligentia*, and the fact that the *quinqueformis modus* mentioned in the *Commentary* stops short of the sphere of the divine.

The theories of origin demonstrate one fundamental truth. The

67. "L'Influence de Hugues de S. Victor," *RTAM*, XXIII (1955), 71, n. 96.

68. "Thomas Gallus et Richard de St Victor mystiques," *RTAM*, XXIX (1962), 212–18, "Intellectus—intelligentia," sees the distinction between the two terms in Richard of St Victor as still fluid, and therefore earlier than that of Isaac. For Richard's use of the pair, e.g., *Benj. Maj.* III, 9; V, 9 and the *Adnotatio in Ps.* 2 (PL 196, 118D–19A; 178C–79A; 266D). Now cf. also *Image and Ressemblance*, II, 138–9. Richard's use of *intelligentia* provides the most interesting comparison with Isaac, though the differences argue to independent development. A comparison between the two understandings would make a valuable study.

69. "La Grazia in Isaaco di Stella," *COCR*, XVI (1954), 143, n. 7.

variations on Boethius may be the central source, but the use of the dynamic pattern of *rationabilitas* in the *Epistola* shows that Isaac is not merely a passive receptacle for the tradition. The relationship of a creative thinker in the twelfth century to his sources is more complex, much more of an interchange. M. Eliade has remarked: "One cannot insist strongly enough that the search for symbolic structures is not a work of reduction but of integration. We compare or contrast two expressions of a symbol not in order to reduce them to a single, pre-existent expression, but in order to discover the process whereby a structure is likely to assume enriched meaning."[70] This is eminently true of Isaac's use of *intelligentia*.

Even in comparison with the passages from Hugh of St Victor and Thierry of Chartres which were probably his immediate sources, Isaac's text from Paragraph VIII has a comprehensiveness which makes it quite distinctive.[71] An important new element, the one which gives the ensemble its anagogic power, is the influence of the ascensional themes discussed in Chapter III. The Dionysian ramifications of the transformed Boethian four powers are obvious in the ninefold ascent recalling the choirs of angels in the *De Caelesti Hierarchia*.[72] The passage also indicates some, though not all, of the other symbolic themes which Isaac's image could incorporate. First, the cosmological implications are richer than the traditional Boethian arrangement; not only does the passage place man squarely in the material universe by the comparison of each stage of the ascent to one of the five elements or regions of the universe given by Chalcidius,[73] but it also provides a cosmological symbol to manifest the union of body and soul, a problem which we have noted was of particular importance in the twelfth century. Isaac's

70. "Methodical Remarks on the Study of Religious Symbolism," *History of Religions: Essays in Methodology*, p. 97.

71. We are not concerned here with the interesting minor variations evident from later passages, e.g., for Thierry *mathematica* belongs to the sphere of *intellectus* (*Lectiones in Boethii De Trin.* II, 30; *ed. Häring*, p. 162), while for Isaac it is the *scientia* of *ratio* (XVI, 1884C).

72. E.g., *CH* VII (*Dionysiaca* II, 835–68).

73. *Comm.* 129 (*ed. Waszink*, pp. 171–2).

theory of the union of body and soul has meaning only within a hierarchical vision of the world where all things ascend to God in such a way that in the necessary passage from the lower to the higher there will always be points of convergence at the extremities. This is true of the *sensualitas carnis* and the *phantasticum animae* in which the body and soul of man are united; it is also true of the union of man with God effected by the action of the divine *theophaniae* on the *intelligentia*. Man is one because he ascends to God; the body must have a place in the dialectic of ascent. The Pseudo-Dionysius himself had said of the Divine Wisdom that its task was "always connecting the ends of one set of things with the beginnings of the next set and making a single beautiful organization and harmony."[74]

There are other aspects to the fusion of the Dionysian and Boethian worlds taking place here. The Dionysian framework allows for an infusion of affective power into the more intellectualist background of Boethius. Isaac does not accomplish this in a completely satisfactory fashion (the full ninefold pattern is only mentioned, while the intellectualist pattern is the one developed), but his constant assertion that it is always by both *sensus* (*ratio*) and *affectus* that we return to God indicates the presence of the new dimension. The Dionysian world itself does not remain unaffected in the new symbolic mode, but undergoes changes of its own. The most important for the assimilative power of the symbol is the interiorization of the Dionysian hierarchies suggested by the metaphor of the soul journeying within itself.[75] The whole system then becomes capable of receiving a symbolic increment from the interiorization categories of Augustine (though not the heart of the Augustinian program itself), and thus being able to be tied in with Augustinian illumination towards the end of the *Epistola*. Isaac's schema of *intelligentia* then is the expression of a systematized mystical theology peculiar to the twelfth century. The concurrence

74. "et semper fines priorum connectens principiis secundorum, et unam universitatis conspirantiam et harmoniam pulchram faciens." *DN* VII, 3 (*Dionysiaca* I, 407–8).

75. VIII (1880B).

of Augustinian and Dionysian elements building upon an original Boethian substratum is meant to provide a symbolic system in which man can live as the being who has access to God. Thus, Isaac is influenced by both major forms of symbolism available in the twelfth century, the subjective aspect of the Augustinian *signum*, where the meaning is in the knower, and the objective Dionysian *symbolum*, where meaning is centered in the objective theophany.[76]

THE INFLUENCE OF ISAAC'S SCHEMA

The later history of Isaac's schema is of considerable interest. It served as an important symbol for a whole body of psychological and mystical treatises in the latter part of the century whose history we can only briefly sketch here. There is considerable variation in the use of the schema, and a degree of obscurity due to the fact that so many of the treatises are anonymous, but the reappearance of similar assimilative and combinatory aspects argues for the grouping of these texts into a general, if loosely defined, movement which seems to have been most active within the Cistercian order.[77]

The most important of these treatises is the enigmatic *Liber de Spiritu et Anima*. This distressingly eclectic *mélange* of texts from Augustine, Cassiodorus, Gennadius, Isidore of Seville, Anselm, Bernard, Hugh of St Victor, and Isaac, among others, was current in the late twelfth and thirteenth centuries as a work of St Augustine;[78] Aquinas himself after some initial hesitation was able to recognize the falsity of this ascription from internal evidence,[79] but modern historical criticism has thus far been unable to solve the problem of its true author with any degree of certainty. The

76. Chenu, *La Théologie* . . . , pp. 174–8.

77. Cf. E. Bertola, "Di alcuni trattati psicologici attribuiti ad Ugo di San Vittore," *Rivista di Filosofia Neo-Scholastica,* LI (1959), 455; G. Webb, *An Introduction to the Cistercian De Anima* (Aquinas Paper 36; London, 1962).

78. It appears in Migne under Augustine, *PL* 40, 779–832.

79. G. Théry, "L'authenticité de *De Spiritu et Anima* dans S. Thomas et Albert le Grand," *RSPT*, X (1921), 373–7.

usual ascription to Alcher of Clairvaux, the recipient of Isaac's *Epistola de Anima*, has been shown to be based on insufficient evidence by Gaetano Raciti, but Raciti's own suggestion that Peter Comestor is the author is also unconvincing.[80] What we may be certain of is that this treatise is posterior in date to Isaac's letter; the appearance of Isaac's fivefold schema, sometimes in almost word-for-word dependence, is clear enough proof for that (Chap. IV, c. 782; Chap. XI, cc. 786–87); but there are other elements of Isaac present, too, such as the stress on the identity of the soul and its powers, and the manner of explanation of the union of body and soul (Chap. XIII, cc. 789–90). What in Isaac had been a carefully organized treatise capable of combining diverse modes of patristic thought in new ways, in the *De Spiritu et Anima* has broken down into a string of unrelated excerpts; but the aura of authenticity given it by its ascription to Augustine endowed it with an importance in the history of medieval thought far beyond that of Isaac's *Epistola*. To reflect on what in the treatise made possible the acceptance of this ascription gives us a significant insight into the thought of the twelfth century. What led to the vast popularity of the text was the juxtaposition of so much traditional Augustinian material with elements and themes from other sources, foreign to the thought of the African doctor. This made it the ideal exemplar of an amorphous thought-world which was suited to absorb new intellectual currents, particularly the Aristotelian and Avicennan ideas becoming available by the end of the century, and to involve itself in psychological questions, like the careful enumeration of the powers of the soul, which were foreign to the intent of Augustine, without nevertheless appearing to depart from the authoritative figure of the great Father of the Western Church.[81] As Pierre Michaud-Quantain has pointed out in discussing the influence of this text: *"La notion d'une classification 'augustinienne' des puissances de l'âme,*

---

80. G. Raciti, "L'Autore del *De Spiritu et Anima,*" *Rivista di Filosofia Neo-Scolastica,* LIII (1961), 385–401. Cf. M.-T. d'Alverny, *Alain de Lille,* p. 178, n. 9.

81. E. Bertola, "Di una inedita trattazione . . . ," pp. 576–9.

analogue et comparable à celles, inspirée de la pensée d'Aristote, qu'affraient au moyen âge les auteurs arabes ou même Jean Damascene, est quelque chose d'iréel, une illusion."[82] Illusion though this may have been from the standpoint of fidelity to Augustine, the category of *intelligentia* as the culmination of a classification of powers of *rationabilitas* had a wide influence through the *De Spiritu et Anima* on the latter twelfth century. While rarely attaining the powers of symbolic organization which it demonstrated in Isaac of Stella, probably because the channel of its influence was itself so eclectic and confused, it frequently displayed similar cosmological, didactic, medical, ascensional, and even new scriptural dimensions, if only in isolated and programmatic fashion.

To return to a problem left unsolved in the earlier stages of our investigation, while most students of Hugh of St Victor consider the treatise *De Unione Corporis et Spiritus* to be authentic, E. Bertola has suggested that its mixture of psychological and medical material argues for a date after the middle of the century and thus places it within the context of the movement represented by Isaac and the author of the *De Spiritu et Anima*.[83] There are many affinities with Isaac present in this treatise, notably the Dionysian description of the union of soul and body (285A–D). Since Hugh was one of the main proponents of Dionysian influence in the early twelfth century through his *In Hierarchiam Caelestem Sancti Dionysii Commentariorum*,[84] it is tempting to see him as the author and an important source for Isaac, a view that is corroborated by the lack of organization in the numbering and naming of the stages of ascent to

82. P. Michaud-Quantain, "Une division 'augustinienne' des puissances de l'âme au moyen âge," *Revue des études augustiniennes*, III (1957), 235–48, cf. p. 248.

83. *PL* 177, 285–94. E. Bertola, "Di alcuni trattati psicologici attribuiti ad Ugo di San Vittore," *Rivista di Filosofia Neo-Scolastica*, LI (1959), 452–4; R. Baron, however, says that it is definitely a work of Hugh, see "Hugues de St Victor: Contribution à un nouvel Examen de son Oeuvre," *Traditio*, XV (1959), 249.

84. *PL* 175, 923–1145. Cf. R. Roques, "Connaissance de Dieu et théologie symbolique d'après l'*In Hierarchiam Caelestem sancti Dionysii* de Hugues de Saint Victor," *Structures Théologiques*, pp. 294–364.

intelligentia (288D–89A) which makes the probability of reverse influence unlikely.[85]

In its more developed form, however, the schema appears in a number of anonymous texts that are undisputedly from the latter part of the century. Most of these are brief and of a second-rate nature;[86] a few possess greater interest, such as the *Quinque Digressiones Cogitationis*, a commentary on the original formulation in Hugh of St Victor's *Miscellanea*;[87] the *Quid sit Anima*, which attempts to inject some incipient Aristotelian and Avicennan influence into what was by then regarded as a formula consecrated by Augustine himself;[88] and the *Distinctiones* of a Paris manuscript that show the direct influence of Isaac.[89] The same schema is taken up by Hugh of Honau; Simon of Tournai uses it in his *Sententiae*, drawing out the Erigenean and Dionysian content in explaining the angelic orders.[90] We find it in both the *De Anima* and the *De Processione Mundi* of Dominic Gundissalinus.[91]

The most important author to adopt the formula, however, was Alan of Lille, the noted Paris master who ended his life as a Cistercian in 1202. Alan, at once poet and theologian, is the ideal figure to demonstrate once again the manifold combinations of which this symbol was capable. His theology has a much wider base than that of any of the other authors who used the schema; his powers of symbolic and poetic creation are almost unique among the theologians of his era. Perhaps as a result of this we find considerable variation in

85. The same may perhaps be said for the interesting treatise *De Septem Septennis*, falsely ascribed to John of Salisbury in *PL* 199, 945–64; cf. M.-D. Chenu, "Une definition pythagorienne de la verité," *AHDL*, XXXVI(1961). Here the fivefold schema, outlined in a general way, is combined with *mens* and *opinio* (951–4).

86. E.g., Treatises in Arras, ms. 981, ff. 85v–95v; Paris, Bib. Nat. ms. lat. 18172, ff. 19v–23; cf. M.-T. d'Alverny, *Alain de Lille*, pp. 182–3, n. 87.

87. Edited in M.-T. d'Alverny, *op. cit.*, pp. 313–17.

88. Edited in E. Bertola, "Di una inedita trattazione . . . ," pp. 581–3.

89. Cf. M.-T. d'Alverny, *op. cit.*, pp. 182–3, n. 87.

90. Edited in M.-T. d'Alverny, *op. cit.*, pp. 307–12.

91. *De Anima* X (ed. Muckle, p. 99); *De processione mundi* (ed. Bülow, pp. 2–3).

the use he makes of the fivefold ascent. In the *Distinctiones Dictionum Theologicalium*[92] and in the first book of the *Contra Haereticos*[93] he explicitly cites Augustine's *Perisichen*, that is, the *De Spiritu et Anima*, and uses the material in a rather standardized fashion; but in the *Summa Quoniam Homines*[94] and the *Regulae de Sacra Theologia*[95] he makes use of the three highest stages of *ratio*, *intellectus*, and *intelligentia* (*intellectualitas* in the *Regulae*) to introduce new classifications of theology (thus re-assuming the didactic concerns of Isaac), and to stress the divine, apophatic, ecstatic character of the highest stage and the ascensional process that leads up to it. In the *Sermo de Sphaera Intelligibili*[96] Alan seems to lean more heavily upon the fourfold pattern in constructing a rich treatment of man's return to God that includes a wealth of Hermetic and Neoplatonic material; but in works like the *Liber Sententiarum*[97] and the *Sermo in Die Epiphaniae*,[98] the three highest powers of the fivefold schema take on new symbolic dimensions in being applied to the senses of Scripture:

The historical sense since it concerns transitory things that are destined to die is symbolized through the myrrh which is applied to the bodies of the dead. *Ratio* offers this because its perception is concerned with the things that take place in history. The tropological or moral sense which is concerned with the customs and instruction of men is symbolized through the incense which bears a marvelous fragrance . . .; *intellectus* offers this, since its gaze is turned toward the pure forms. Anagogy, that is, the contemplation of heavenly things, is symbolized through gold, because as gold has the first place among metals, anagogy is king among the ways of understanding. Anagogy, as it were, is that which leads above. The highest power of the soul, the

92. *PL* 210, 819D; 922A–B.
93. *PL* 210, 330C.
94. *Summa Quoniam Homines* (ed. Glorieux, p. 121).
95. *PL* 210, 673–74.
96. Edited in d'Alverny, *op. cit.*, pp. 297–306.
97. *PL* 210, 236B–C.
98. Edited in d'Alverny, *op. cit.*, pp. 242–43.

intelligentia, which contemplates only divine things, offers this gift.[99]

It would be beyond our scope to trace the history of *intelligentia* in such thirteenth-century authors as Alfred of Shareshal, Ralph of Longchamps, John of La Rochelle, Alexander of Hales, and the indirect influence on Thomas Gallus and the great Bonaventure himself; rather it is time to ask the question of the meaning of *intelligentia* within the context of the twelfth century.

When we reflect upon this analysis of the different strands present in Isaac of Stella's use of the fivefold schema and those of his followers as well, we find that the work of analysis does not recapture the secret of the whole. The reason for this, of course, is that analysis is our mode of dealing with the relation of this schema to the patristic context; synthesis was the mode of its creation. It would be an illusion to think of the creators of this symbolic mode as deliberately trying to reconcile or to collate divergent aspects of tradition; their effort was rather along the lines of attempting to manifest within the limits of a body of inherited material, elastic enough in its symbolic aspects to allow for the expression of experiences of life considerably different from those of the patristic era, their understanding of man's place in God's world. The sudden growth of new religious orders, especially the Cistercians, had given impetus to a generation many of whose noblest representatives were obsessed with the question of the possibility of man's direct experience of God in this life and of the problem of the relationship of this experience to other forms of human knowing and to man's place in the physical universe. As an indication of this

99. "Per myrram, que cadaveribus mortuorum apponitur, historia figuratur, quia ipsa circa res caducas et transitorias vertitur . . . hanc offert ratio, quia circa historialia eius versatur consideratio. Per thus, quod miram parit fragrantiam figuratur tropologia sive moralitas, que circa mores et hominum informationes vertitur . . . hanc offert intellectus, quia circa formas eius versatur intuitus. Per aurum significatur anagoge, id est celestium consideratio, quia, sicut aurum inter metalla prerogativam retinet, sic anagoge inter intelligentias monarchiam retinet. Unde anagoge quasi sursum ductiva. Hanc offert superior anime potentia, id est intelligentia, que sola contemplatur divina" (*ed. d'Alverny,* p. 243).

obsession there remains to us not only the institutional, economic, and political records of the growth of religious orders, but also the human and spiritual records of the forms which these men adopted for the expression and organization of their world of meaning. The symbolic schema of *intelligentia* and the stages leading to it allowed twelfth-century man to experience his being as at once a part, and yet in a most important way not a part, of the world about him. Its striking use in Isaac of Stella and its important posterity in the history of twelfth-century theology show it to be a significant expression of the century's symbolic understanding of man.

THE PLACE OF ISAAC OF STELLA IN CISTERCIAN THOUGHT

A N EXTENDED JOURNEY not infrequently leads in directions rather different from those intended in setting forth. Perhaps that is the feeling that may have stolen over the reader during the long discussions of the background to Isaac of Stella's thought. The history of this study is a partial explanation for such a feeling and for the historical approach that has produced it. My interest in Isaac of Stella grew out of an acquaintance with the thought of some of the better-known Cistericans, particularly Bernard of Clairvaux and Aelred of Rievaulx. Seen from this perspective, the thought of Isaac of Stella had appeal as an important Cistercian contribution which had not as yet received the attention which it deserved. The attempt to substantiate the importance of Isaac's intellectual claims, however, gradually moved this study away from more direct confrontation of Isaac's thought with that of his contemporaries among the Cistercians in the direction of an interpretation in the light of a much wider tradition, because it is here alone that the full significance of his thought, even for the Cistercian movement itself, may be seen.

The theology of the Abbot of Stella cannot be understood unless it is seen as a twelfth-century re-symbolization of certain questions and answers inherent in the long history of the mixture of Platonic and Christian categories of thought. As has been suggested in

Chapter III, the symbolic form of theology was an integral part of
the theological effort of this vibrant era, the essential correlative to
the disciplined march of the logical mentality that ordered and
differentiated the theological heritage through the development of
the Scholastic method. When we come to describing and explicating
what kind of re-symbolization Isaac was trying to create, we find
its most immediate and obvious affinities with the traditions of the
School of Chartres and the School of St Victor. Significantly
enough (considering the antipathy of Bernard and William of St
Thierry to Chartres), no matter how much Isaac is indebted to
Hugh of St Victor—and the debt was certainly great—he is still
just as close in spirit to that optimism toward Platonic thought
which was so characteristic of the School of Chartres.

This is not to deny that the other Cistercian theologians of the
period did not share in the same Platonic tradition. Much of what
both Bernard and Isaac accepted as true doctrine had been revealed
at the Academy rather than at Jerusalem. But while Bernard felt
the necessity of condemning Plato and Aristotle in relation to the
truth revealed in the Scriptures, Isaac sensed no such obligation.
Prepared as he was to assert in unequivocal fashion the ultimacy of
the Word of God who was the man Jesus—the *immensus Jesus*—
Plato always remains for him the *magnus theologus gentium*.

This optimism toward the Platonic tradition, and the extent of
his knowledge of its sources gained during his years in the Schools,
are major factors distancing the Abbot of Stella from his contemporaries in the Order of Cîteaux. It was the explication and demonstration of these factors that was at the source of our lengthy discussions of the Platonic background and context of the Abbot's
thought.

Isaac's significant differences from the other major figures in the
early Cistercian movement (among whom Bernard and William
of St Thierry must be given pride of place) at first glance might
seem to cast his thought in such an exceptional role that it has little
to tell us about specifically Cistercian concerns. This, though,
would be a superficial reading; rather, the untypical character of
Isaac's thought itself raises a deeper question about the nature of

the Cistercian intellectual effort which may provide a new perspective on some old questions and the ground for proposing new ones. The distance of Isaac of Stella from men like Bernard, William, and Aelred of Rievaulx may be the most significant thing about him as a Cistercian, for if this distance is a personal appropriation of a specifically Cistercian interest, the thought of the Abbot of Stella will take on a new and important dimension in the history of Cistercian theology. Before the implications of this statement can be explored, however, it will be useful to summarize the relations of Isaac to the other contemporary schools of theology, as the means of framing the problem of his relation to the other Cistercians.

The affinities of the Abbot with the interests of the School of Chartres must be mentioned first. The attitude toward the Platonic tradition which we have already pointed out, and the wide knowledge of its major available monuments, particularly the *Timaeus* itself, Chalcidius's *Commentary*, the *Commentary on the Dream of Scipio* of Macrobius, and the works of Boethius were the heritage which he shared with thinkers like Thierry of Chartres, William of Conches and Clarenbald of Arras. It is not the knowledge of these thinkers alone (a common ground, after all, of so much theological effort of the century), but the extent of that knowledge and the depth of its influence which tie him so closely to the Masters of Chartres. Numerous suggestions of more precise points of contact have been made in the course of this work and are present elsewhere in the works of our Abbot, particularly in the *Sermones in Sexagesima*. Some of these are themes of general interest to many of the early twelfth-century theologians, such as a theology of creation that builds upon both the *Book of Genesis* and Plato's *Timaeus*. While the details of Isaac's treatment of this question are heavily dependent on St Augustine, the general tenor of his attempt is closest to that of the Chartrains among his contemporaries. Other themes, especially the speculation on God as *unitas*, or the One, and the central symbol of the *catena aurea poete* which binds the many themes of his theological anthropology together, are so distinctively Chartrain, with explicit appearance

first in texts of Thierry and William of Conches, that they admit
of no other explanation than Isaac's wide acquaintance with this
tradition. Finally, the Abbot's knowledge of Aristotle, particularly
the use of substance, accident, and abstraction, does not go beyond
the Boethian Aristotle of the *Categories* and *Commentaries on the
Isagoge of Porphyry*, which were popular at Chartres.

The other major influence of the early twelfth-century Schools
on Isaac's development came from Hugh of St Victor. The breadth
of the theology of the great Victorine and the deeply Augustinian
character of his thought gave him a central position among the many
divergent theological strands of the first four decades of the century.
Hugh rarely showed the daring and subtle insights that we come to
expect in Abelard or Gilbert of Poitiers, but he compensates for this
by an awareness of contemporary problems and a sense of balance
in dealing with them that were distinctive among twelfth-century
theologians. One of the difficulties in determining the extent of
Hugh's influence on Isaac is that both men are so steeped in
Augustine that ideas and concepts found in each can frequently be
explained in terms of their common source in Augustine just as
easily as in terms of a more immediate contact. Fortunately, there
are a number of significant themes, largely in Isaac's theology of
man, which bring him strongly within Hugh's sphere of influence.
Many of these themes are common to other Cistercian writers, but
Isaac's treatment tends to adopt a Victorine posture rather than one
closer to Bernard or William.

The Platonic category of man as the image and likeness of God
was indispensable to all medieval theologians; Isaac does not
develop his theology of *imago et similitudo* in terms of Bernard's
thoughts on man's freedom as the image, but rather in terms of an
understanding that links *imago* to intellectual powers and *similitudo*
to affective ones. While this was a fairly common piece of theological furniture, it is Hugh of St Victor whose treatment is
closest to Isaac's. Similarly, *gratia creatrix* and *gratia adiutrix* appear
in both Hugh and St Bernard, but Hugh's use seems closer to
Isaac's explanation. There are also a number of themes common to
the tradition—such as *sensus* and *affectus* as the two fundamental

Q

powers of the soul, the doctrine of the two directions of knowledge, the Augustinian explanation of original sin, and the image of the eye of the soul—which Isaac could have received from any number of predecessors, but which in their nuances and terminology suggest an origin in Hugh. Two of the cornerstones of the Abbot's theological anthropology are also Hugonian. The all-important five stages of the ascent of rationality, despite the possibility of influence from Thierry of Chartres, must be seen as largely dependent on Hugh's reworking of the schemata from Boethius. Lastly, the concern with *imaginatio* and its place in dealing with the problem of the union of body and soul in the *Epistola de Anima* suggest that Hugh's *De Unione Corporis et Spiritus* was a work with which Isaac was very familiar. If Isaac's theology of the divine nature is close to Chartrain interests, his theology of man is strongly Hugonian.

The concern with the problem of the joining together of disparate realities, the theme of concatenation which pervades the Abbot of Stella's work from the general symbol of the *catena aurea* to the particular examples such as the question of *imaginatio*: raises one final question with regard to Hugh's influence on Isaac: was Hugh the mediator of Isaac's knowledge of the Pseudo-Dionysius? The question admits of no completely satisfactory answer. While Hugh was the great popularizer of the Dionysian writings in the 1130's, the Dionysian-Erigenean tradition was present in other circles, too, viz., at the School of Laon and with Honorius Augustodunensis. Hugh may have provided the occasion for Isaac's acquaintance with this theological tradition; but the Abbot's interests here, concentrating on the divisions of theology and the application of its negative function, are not those of the Victorine. This side of Isaac's theology seems to be a personal development springing from his own reading of the Pseudo-Dionysius and John Scotus Eriugena.

Some mention should also be made of Isaac's relation to the other major figure of the Victorine School, Richard. Almost exact contemporaries, these two exiles to the continent, one from England, the other from Scotland, show striking similarities. Both were deeply influenced by Hugh, but both created original theologies in which Hugonian themes interacted with a rich mixture of traditional and contemporary concerns. Due to his abandonment of the Schools, Isaac's theology is both narrower in scope and more fragmentary in survival than that of the Prior of St Victor; but in areas of common concern, especially in the theory of divine nature and in the stages of the ascent of the human soul to God, they are independent, but comparable, developments from the same general background.

Chartres and St Victor were the two major moments in Isaac's theological background, but they were not in any sense the only contacts that he had with contemporary thought. There were, to be sure, theological Schools and figures with whom Isaac appears to have little acquaintance. Thus, despite the presence of Chartres and the interest in Boethius, the Abbot's thought has little to do with that of Gilbert of Poitiers. To the best of my knowledge, there is also little connection with Peter Lombard and his followers that a common background in Augustine cannot explain. Two other cases are more significant. In the *Sermones in Sexagesima* we find interesting similarities between Isaac's method of theological discourse and that of St Anselm of Canterbury. Further similarities in dealing with the problem of proving God's existence also argue for the Abbot's extensive knowledge of at least the *Monologion* and probably the *Proslogion* among the writings of the Archbishop. The absence of any significant comparable influence on Isaac's theology of man indicates a less extensive role for Anselm's influence than a consideration of the *Sermones* alone would imply. The case of Peter Abelard and his School is less easy to deal with. Abelard's early theology of creation is strongly Platonic; some of his logical theories, and his interest in negative theology are further possible sources of influence on the Abbot of Stella. But once again the influence in the question of anthropology is much slimmer, and the formulations in the areas of common interest between the two men are sufficiently general to make it difficult to determine any strong direct connections. Two important themes connect Isaac with works from the early Abelardian School of the 1140's: the *unum*, *simplex, et immobile* triad of the essential attributes of God that we find in the Sexagesima Sermons hints of a passage in the *Sententiae Parisienses* (though Isaac's treatment is so extensive that he may be fully independent); and the *ratio, memoria, ingenium* classification of rationality seems to go back to the *Ysagoge in Theologiam*. These connections with Anselm and the Abelardian School demonstrate with increasing force Isaac's openness to a wide variety of the theological speculation of his era, though they do not negate the preponderance of Chartres and St Victor.

This survey of Isaac's relations with contemporary theology raises anew the problem of his place in the Cistercian movement of the twelfth century. Despite the differences of attitude toward the variety of contemporary theology which separate Isaac from his great contemporaries among the Cistercians, it is most important to note that he shared a concern with them for the creation of a new theory of man's return to God which can be seen as the theological expression of the Cistercians' institutional reform of traditional monasticism. This theological effort felt itself to be both a response to a new historical situation and a reaffirmation of the pure springs of tradition, just as, from the viewpoint of monastic history, the Cistercians were both a return to the pristine monasticism of the Rule of St Benedict and a "New Model" for the men of the twelfth century. The paradoxical tension of these two concerns is reflected in the theological thought of the major Cistercian figures—Bernard, William, and Isaac. The theology that these men created assumed much from the patristic past, and yet was also capable of organizing and combining this legacy in ways that made it able to be the intellectual form of a new religious situation. The immense popularity and success of the Cistercian movement in the middle decades of the twelfth century are sufficient witness to this. The unity of the program involved not only the desire to re-symbolize the patristic legacy, but also the fact that the basic interest of this theology turned toward the question of the nature of man and the possibility of his access to the sphere of the divine. It was St Bernard's recognition of the religious needs of his age that enabled him to mold the Cistercian Order into such a potent force and to place the problem of the theology of man and man's ascent to God at the center of the Order's intellectual interests.

Bernard's own reflections on the nature of free will and conscience, his organization of the degrees of love and their path to God, his ability to project his own religious experiences in these terms, are justly the most famous creations of this movement. Within recent years, the depth of the theological anthropology of Bernard's close friend, William of St Thierry, has begun to receive the attention it deserves. Due to his training in the Schools, his speculative interests, and his powers of synthesis, William is in some ways a more interesting theologian than Bernard himself, though as an historical figure his importance cannot be compared to that of the Abbot of Clairvaux. The insight that went into his account of the Trinitarian structure of the soul's ascent to God is unsurpassed among Cistercian theologians. Isaac of Stella's *Epistola de Anima* shows him to be very much a part of this concern with theological anthropology. His theological achievement is comparable to that of Bernard and William in this area; but the significant differences that we have found in Isaac, particularly his more positive relation to a wide spectrum of contemporary and traditional theology, give him a unique status within the Cistercian movement.

Isaac does share many specific points of theological development with his two major Cistercian contemporaries. Some of the themes which the Abbot of Clairvaux had made popular among the brethren, such as the necessity for self-knowledge, the description of original sin in terms of the *regio dissimilitudinis*, appear in the Abbot of Stella in a more or less Bernardine fashion. William of St Thierry, however, is the Cistercian to whom Isaac bears the closest resemblance. For example, the Abbot of Stella's concern with the problem of the relation of body and soul led him to an interest in microcosmic theory and an awareness of the medical and physiological material being made available in translation in the eleventh and twelfth centuries. This side of his thought has analogies with Chartres; but the combination of medical interest, microcosmic themes, and a theology concerned with organizing and systematizing the stages of the ascent to God, brings Isaac much closer to the *De Natura Corporis et Animae* of William than to any of the treatises emanating from Chartrain circles.

William shows a concern for classifying the powers of the soul which, though not strong in Bernard, was implicit in the impetus towards a theological anthropology which the Abbot of Clairvaux had fostered in the Order of Cîteaux. "Know yourself," in its character as a permanent key to Cistercian theology, moved from Bernard's concern with the problems of grace and free will toward a more systematically oriented attempt to deal with the body, the soul, and the powers and the relations of each, in William's *De Natura Corporis et Animae*. The medical and physiological material that we encounter in this treatise are among the hallmarks of any systematic theology of man that builds upon a largely Platonic basis. Aelred of Rievaulx's *De Anima* shows a similar concern for system, but uses a narrower base of a more strictly Augustinian nature. Isaac's *Epistola de Anima* is in many senses the culmination of this side of Cistercian theological anthropology. The history of its influence proves that it was known and used by later members of the Order, not only through its influence on *De Spiritu et Anima* (through which Isaac's fivefold schema under the disguise of Augustine was known to many Scholastics such as Alan of Lille, Philip the Chancellor, and Alexander of Hales), but also through the recovery of such texts as the *Quid sit Anima* and the *Distinctiones* of Paris Bib. Nat. ms. lat. 3389. The anonymity of these tracts makes a definitive judgment concerning their provenance impossible, but everything about them suggests a source in Cistercian circles.

While it is evident that Isaac of Stella was intimately involved in this major theological program in his Order, the manner in which he appropriated this program is distinctive. The great difference between Isaac on the one hand, and Bernard and William on the other, as has been pointed out, is in their attitude toward the theological currents of the day. Bernard is far from being a theological obscurantist: his knowledge of Origen and aspects of the Greek tradition, his favorable attitude toward Hugh of St Victor and Peter Lombard, and his own achievement are proof enough of this. William's training at Laon and the quality of his theology demonstrate the same. Nevertheless, both show a real hesitation toward the full spectrum of contemporary theology which the Abbot of Stella does not share. Bernard's theological jousts against Abelard, William of Conches, and Gilbert of Poitiers are important not so much for the issues involved, as for the attitude they reveal. Bernard's questionable political manoeuvres in several instances during these disputes only serve to heighten the anxiety, the feeling of being threatened, which even such an intelligent man as the Abbot of Clairvaux felt in the face of this new, and sometimes radical, theological thought. William of St Thierry, due perhaps in part to the strong effect which Bernard's personality had upon him, shared this reaction, as his involvement in the struggles against Abelard and William of Conches indicates. While Bernard and William were justified in some of their protests, the antipathy toward the new speculation they exposed in these events can only be described as retrograde in the light of the history of theology.

This is where Isaac of Stella has his special place in the creative era of Cistercian theology. He managed to keep open to both sides of his heritage. His training in the Schools was not the sole cause of the positive views he retained towards the new currents of speculation. A Geoffrey of Auxerre, for example, could totally renounce his Scholastic background and upon entering the monastery become the most intemperate of the Cistercian protestors against the new theology. Isaac's sense of balance and his active curiosity about the deepest theological problems prevented him from adopting such a stance. His position is expressed in the *Apologia* of Sermon Forty-eight, but the fruits of this option are to be found in the wide-ranging receptivity and deep insight that are so evident in both the *Sermones in Sexagesima* and the *Epistola de Anima*, the twin peaks of Isaac's theology. It is true that the Abbot's theological horizon was largely formed by the great theologians of the generation of 1120–1150, so in a sense his writings of the 1160's have a slightly old-fashioned ring. This in no way negates their quality as an original rethinking and transformation of some of the deepest concerns of twelfth-century theology, nor does it lessen the

Abbot's optimism in the face of the theological tensions of his age.

The Cistercians were the spiritual elite of their time. The effect they had in the twelfth century upon the Church and society can only be compared with that of the Mendicants in the thirteenth century and the Jesuits in the sixteenth in the history of the Catholic Church. Formed at the same time as the nascent Universities, like them a response to a changed social and intellectual context, the new Order achieved at best an ambiguous stance in relation to the new intellectual world growing up around it. Could this stance have been more positive? That a more intimate relation with the new theology might have entailed major changes in the conception of monasticism cannot be denied, but the thought of Isaac of Stella demonstrates that bridges could be built between the vital religious force of the Cistercian Order and the more experimental facets of the theology of the Schools, bridges that were not present in the other representatives of early Cistercian theology. This, coupled with the attraction that the Cistercians exercised on some of the most prominent minds of the century (Thierry of Chartres, Peter Cantor, and Alan of Lille all ended their lives in Cistercian monasteries), argues to the fact that along with the economic, social, and political failures which have been pointed out in the Cistercian movement in the latter part of the twelfth century, it is possible to argue that there was an intellectual failure as well.

Isaac of Stella's significance in the light of the history of the Cistercian movement in the latter part of the century is then that of an option which was not followed up. Perhaps it could not have been within the framework of monasticism. Despite the influence of the *Epistola de Anima*, the attitude embodied in Isaac's theology was not developed to any great extent in the twelfth- and thirteenth-century Cistercians. The founding of a house for Cistercians at the University of Paris in the thirteenth century did not produce major Cistercian theologians. To say what the history of Cistercian theology would have been if Isaac's attitude had been more influential than that of Bernard and William would be to write historical fiction. It is sufficient for the historian of thought to know that the option existed in Isaac, Abbot of Stella.

APPENDIX

THE *CATENA AUREA* IN WILLIAM OF CONCHE'S GLOSS ON MACROBIUS'S *COMMENTARIUM IN SOMNIUM SCIPIONIS*[1]

Secundum hoc ergo. Quandoquidem *togaton* genuit *noyn, noyc* animam, anima creavit corpora, et in terrenis talis est ordo qualem prediximus, ergo si quis perspicaciter intueri velit inveniet quandam connexionem creaturarum inter se, connex-
5 ionem etiam coniunctam ipsi deo. Anima enim est deo coniuncta in multis, utpote quod immortalis est et incorporea, intellectu et ratione et in multis aliis. Similiter et angelis, his iterum coniuncta est in ratione, brutis vero animalibus in sensu et vegetatione, bruta animalia herbis et arboribus in
10 vegetatione, herbe et arbores corporibus inanimatis in existentia. *Unus fulgor.* Quicquid fulgoris et pulchritudinis inest homini, ex anima inest corpori. Sed ne aliquis putaret hoc esse mirum vel impossibile quod una et eadem anima in diversis esset corporibus, ostendit non esse mirum. *Ut in multis speculis*
15 *usque ad ultimam rerum creaturam: Usque ad ultimam rerum creaturam* quia nulla est creatura que cum deo non obtineat aliquam similitudinem qualemcumque, et hec est rerum coniunctio. *Aurea catena Homeri.* Ad hanc enim coniunctionem rerum figurandam ait Homerus Iovem dimittere quandam
20 catenam a celo deorsum usque ad terras continuam pendere, et hec est etiam scala quam sompniavit Iacob.

1. See above Chapt. II, note 103.

CRITICAL APPARATUS

K f. 66v, U f. 82v. 1. Secundum: De U/ 1–2. *togaton*—corpora: deus ex se mentem genuit, ex deo autem et mente nascitur anima, et omnia humana corpora habent existere, ex his vero terrena U/ 3. qualem prediximus: qualis est predictis U// 4. quandam: add. rerum K// 5. coniunctam: earumdem U/ 5–6. coniuncta est deo: trans. U/ 6–7. in—ratione: om. U//7. in: om. U/ 7. et similiter: trans. U//8. coniuncta: corr. ex coniunctus KU//9. bruta: enim add. U// 10. herbe et arbores: herbis et arboribus K/ arbores: et add. K//9. in:om. U// 10–11. existentia: Una connexio et nunquam interrupta. Quia noyc ex una parte brachii tenet togaton et uno animam et fac istam connexionem in circulo ibi unumquodque amplectitur duo altrinsecus posita invenietur dico cum hac constantia cum deus genuerit mentem, mens animam, anima corpora. Omnia que sequuntur que sunt inferioris dignitatis. Corpora enim que creavit sunt inferiora dignitate, ideo "sequitur" posuit pro "inferiore" quia inferior persona sequitur maiorem. add. K.// 13. vel: et U/ quod: quia U// 14. ostendit: subiungit a simili U// 15. creaturam: fe [*sic*] U/ scilicet post fe add. U/ rerum (2): et villiorem U//16. quia: om. U/ est: enim add. U/ cum: alia qualem et cum ipso add. U/ 17. qualemcumque: quamtalacunque U/ est: scilicet add. U//18. coniunctio: est add. U/ Homeri: om. U// 19. figurandam: significandam U// 21. et: om. U.

BIBLIOGRAPHY

SOURCES

ISAAC OF STELLA

Manuscript Sources (for *Epistola de Anima*):
Cambridge: University Library, KK I.20, ff. 3r–7v.
Paris: Bibliothèque Nationale, Ms. lat. 1252, ff. 5v–13v.
Rome: Bibliotheca Angelica, Ms. 70 (A.7.9), ff. 40b–42c.

Printed Sources:
Isaac Abbas de Stella. *Opera.* PL 194, 1689–1876. Reprinted from Bertrand Tissier, *Bibliotheca Patrum Cisterciensium*, VI, 1–83; 104–7. Bonnefontaine: 1662.
Isaac de l'Étoile. *Sermons* I. Edd. Anselm Hoste and Gaston Salet. *Sources Chrétiennes* 130. Paris: 1967.
Leclercq, Jean. "Nouveau sermon d'Isaac de l'Étoile." RAM, XL (1964), 277–88.
Raciti, Gaetano. "Isaac de l'Étoile et son siècle." *Cîteaux*, XII (1961), 281–92 [Sermon 48].

TWELFTH CENTURY

Manuscript Sources:
Copenhagen: Kongelige Bibliotek, GI, Kgl. S.1910.
Rome: Vatican Library, Urbinus lat. 1140.

Printed Sources:
Absalon of St Victor. *Sermones.* PL 211, 11–294.
Achard of St Victor [?]. *De discretione animae, spiritus, et mentis.* Nicholas Häring, "Gilbert of Poitiers, Author of the *De discretione animae, spiritus et mentis* commonly attributed to Achard of St Victor." *Medieval Studies*, XXII (1960), 148–91.
Adelhard of Bath. *Quaestiones Naturales.* Martin Müller, *Die Quaestiones Naturales des Adelhardus von Bath.* BGPM, XXXI, 2 (1934).
Aelred of Rievaulx. *De Anima. Mediaeval and Renaissance Studies: Supplement I,* ed. C. H. Talbot. London: 1952.

241

——. *Sermones inediti Beati Aelredi Abbatis Rievallensis,* ed. C. H. Talbot. *Series Scriptorum Sacri Ordinis Cisterciensis* I. Rome, 1952.

Alan of Lille. *Opera.* PL 210.

——. *Alain de Lille: Textes inédits,* ed. M.-T. d'Alverny, Études de Philosophie Médiévale LII. Paris: 1965.

——. *Summa quoniam homines.* P. Glorieux, "La Somme 'Quoniam homines' d'Alain de Lille." AHDL, XX (1954), 113–364.

Alberic of Trois-Fontaines. *Chronica.* MGH SS, XXIII, 629–950.

Alexander III, *Litterae et Diplomata.* PL 200, 9–89.

Annales de Wintonia. Rolls Series, 36, 3.

Annales Reichespergenses. MGH SS, XVII, 443–76.

Anonymous. *De Anima.* E. Bertola, "Il 'De Anima' del Vat. Lat. 175," *Rivista di Filosofia Neo-Scholastica,* XLV (1953), 253–61.

Anonymous. *De cognitione humane conditionis.* PL 184, 485–508.

Anonymous. *De erectione animae mentis in Deum.* PL 177, 171–90.

Anonymous. *De interiori domo seu de conscientia aedificanda.* PL 184, 507–52; PL 177, 165–70.

Anonymous. *De spiritu et anima.* PL 40, 779–832.

Anonymous. *De statibus hominis interioris.* M.-T. d'Alverny, "Les pérégrinations de l'âme dans l'autre monde d'après un anonyme de la fin du XIIe siècle." AHDL, XV–XVII (1940–42), 239–99.

Anonymous. *Liber Alcidi (Altvidius de immortalitate animarum).* E. Garin, *Studi sul Platonismo Medievale.* Florence: 1958, pp. 239–99.

Anonymous. *Quid sit Anima.* E. Bertola, "Di una inedita Trattazione psicologica intitolata Quid sit Anima," *Rivista di Filosofia Neo-Scolastica,* LVIII (1966), 564–83.

Anonymous. *Quinque digressiones cogitationis.* M.-T. d'Alverny, *Alain de Lille: Textes inédits,* 313–17.

Anonymous. *Tractatus de conscientia (Petis a me).* PL 213, 903–12; PL 184, 551–60.

Anselm of Canterbury. *Opera Omnia,* ed. Francis Schmitt. 6 vols. Edinburgh: 1938–61.

Anselm of Laon. *De animabus hominum.* G. Lefévre, *Anselmi Laudunensis et Radulphi Fratris eius Sententias excerptas.* Milan: 1895, pp. 5–9.

Arnold of Bonneval. *De paradiso animae.* PL 189, 1515–70.

Bernard of Clairvaux. *Sancti Bernardi opera,* edd. J. Leclercq, C. H. Talbot, H. M. Rochais. Vols. I–VI. Rome: 1957–70.

Bernardus Silvestris. *De mundi universitate libri duo,* edd. Carl S. Barach and Johann Wrobel. Innsbruck: 1876.

Chronicon Clarevallense. PL 185, 1247–52.

Cistercii Statuta Antiquissima, ed. Joseph Turk. Rome: 1949.

Clarenbald of Arras. *Tractatus super Librum Boethii De Trinitate.* N. Häring, *Life and Works of Clarenbald of Arras.* Toronto: 1965, pp. 63–186.

——. *Tractatulus super Librum Genesis. Op. cit.,* 225–49.

Dominicus Gundissalinus. *De anima.* J. T. Muckle, "The Treatise 'De Anima' of Dominicus Gundissalinus," *Mediaeval Studies,* II (1940), 23–103.

——. *De immortalitate animae.* Georg Bülow, *Des Dominicus Gundissalinus Schrift von der Unsterblichkeit der Seele.* BGPM, II, 3 (1897).

. *De immitate or into.* PL 65, 1075 78.

——. *De processione mundi.* G. Bülow, *Des Dominicus Gundissalinus Schrift "Von dem Hervorgange der Welt" (De processione mundi).* BGPM, XXIV, 3 (1925).

Epistolae ad Abbatem Pontiniacensem de Fundatione Abbatiae Reae. Thesaurus Novus Anecdotorum. Edd. E. Martène and U. Durand, III, 1242. Paris 1717.

Garnier of Rochefort. *Sermones.* PL 205, 555–828.

Gervase of Canterbury. *Chronicle.* Rolls Series, 75, 2 Vols.

Gilbert of Poitiers. *The Commentaries on Boethius by Gilbert of Poitiers,* ed. N. Häring. Toronto, 1966.

Godfrey of St Victor. *Microcosmos.* P. Delhaye, *Le Microcosmos de Godefrey de Saint Victor. I. Étude théologique. II. Texte.* Lille, 1951.

Helinand of Froidmont. *De cognitione sui.* PL 212, 721–36.

Helmhold. *Chronica Slavorum.* MGH SS, XXI, 1–99.

Hermes Trismegistus (Pseudo). *Liber Hermeticus Mercurii Triplicis de VI rerum principiis.* Ed. T. Silverstein, AHDL, XXII (1956), 217–301.

——. *Liber XXIV Philosophorum.* C. Baeumker, *Das Pseudo-Hermetische Buch des 24 Meister.* BGPM, XXV, 1–2 (1928).

Hildegard of Bingen. *Liber de operibus dei.* PL 197, 742–1038.

Honorius Augustodunensis. *Opera.* PL 172.

Hugh Eterianus. *Liber de anima corpore iam exuta.* PL 202, 167–226.

Hugh of Fouilloy. *De claustro animae.* PL 176, 1017–1182.

——. *De medicina animae.* PL 176, 1183–1202.

Hugh of Ribodimonte. *Epistola de essentia animae et peccato.* PL 166, 833–36.

Hugh of St Victor. *Opera omnia.* PL 175–77.

——. *Didascalicon,* Ed. Charles H. Buttimer. Washington, 1939.

John of Salisbury. *Opera.* PL 199.

——. *Historia pontificalis.* Ed. Marjorie Chibnall. London, 1956.

——. *Metalogicon Libri IV.* Ed. Clemens C. I. Webb. Oxford, 1929.

Joachim of Fiora. *Concordia novi ac veteris testamenti.* Venice, 1519.

Materials for the History of Thomas Becket. Edd. J. C. Robertson and J. B. Sheppard. Rolls Series 67. 7 Vols. London, 1875–85.

Nicholas of Clairvaux. *Epistolae.* PL 202, 491–513.

Peter Abelard. *Opera.* PL 178.

——. *Logica ingredientibus.* Bernhard Geyer, *Peter Abelard's philosphische Schriften.* BGPM, XXI, 1 (1933).

Peter of Celle. *Liber de conscientia.* PL 202, 1083–98.

Peter Lombard. *Liber IV sententiarum.* 2 vols. Quaracchi, 1916.

Peter of Poitiers. *Sententiae.* PL 211, 783–1280.

Recueil des Actes de Henri II . . . concernant les provinces Française et les affaires de France. Edd. Leopold Delisle and Elie Berger. Paris, 1916.

Regesta Pontificium Romanorum. Edd. P. Jaffé, S. Loewenfeld, et al. Vol. II. Leipzig, 1888.

Richard of St Victor. *Opera.* PL 196.

——. *De statu interioris hominis.* J. Ribaillier, "Richard de Saint-Victor. De Statu interioris hominis," AHDL, XXXIV (1967), 7–128.

——. *De Trinitate.* Ed. J. Ribaillier. Paris, 1958.

Roger of Hoveden. *Chronicle.* Rolls Series 51. 4 Vols.

Sacrorum conciliorum nova et amplissima collectio. Ed. J. D. Mansi. 31 Vols. Venice, 1759–93.

Sententie Parisienses. A. Landgraf, *Écrits Théologiques de l'École d'Abelard,* 1–60. Louvain, 1934.

Simon of Tournai. *Disputationes.* Joseph Warichez, *Les Disputationes de Simon de Tournai.* Louvain, 1932.

——. *Sententiae.* (partial ed.) M.-T. d'Alverny, *Alain de Lille: Textes inédits.* Paris, 1965, 307–12.

Statuta Capitulorum Generalium Ordinis Cisterciensis ab anno 1116 ad annum 1786. Ed. J.-M. Canivez. Vol. I, Louvain, 1933.

Summa sententiarum. PL 176, 41–154.

Thierry of Chartres. *Commentum super Boethium De Trinitate (Librum Hunc).* N. Häring, "Two Commentaries on Boethius by Thierry of Chartres," AHDL, XXXV (1960), 65–136.

——. *Librum hunc.* W. Jansen, *Der Kommentar des Clarenbaldus von Arras zu Boethius De Trinitate,* 3*–25*. Breslau, 1926.

——. *De septem diebus.* N. Häring, "The Creation and the Creator of the World according to Thierry of Chartres and Clarenbald of Arras," AHDL, XXII (1955), 137–216.

——. *Glossa super Librum Boethii De Trinitate.* N. Häring, "A Commentary on Boethius' 'De Trinitate' by Thierry of Chartres," AHDL, XXXI (1956), 257–325.

——. *Lectiones in Boethii Librum de Trinitate.* N. Häring, "The Lectures of Thierry of Chartres on Boethius' 'De Trinitate'," AHDL, XXX (1958), 112–226.

William of Champeaux. *De origine animae.* PL 163, 1043–44.

William of Conches. *De philosophia mundi.* PL 172, 39–102. (also in PL 90, 1127–8).

——. *Dragmaticon. Dialogus de substantiis physicis,* ed. G. Grataroli. Strasbourg, 1567.

——. *Glosae super Platonem.* Ed. E. Jeauneau. Textes Philosophiques du Moyen Âge XIII. Paris, 1965.

William of St Thierry. *Opera.* PL 180.

——. *Enigma Fidei.* M.-M. Davy, *Deux Traités sur la Foi: Le Miroir de la Foi. L'Énigme de la Foi.* Paris, 1959, pp. 92–179.

Ysagoge in Theologiam. A. Landgraf, *Écrits théologiques de l'École d'Abelard,* pp. 61–285. Louvain, 1934.

OTHER SOURCES

Aelius Aristides. *Quae supersunt omnia.* Ed. Bruno Keil. Vol. II. Berlin, 1898.

Alcuin. *De ratione animae ad Eulaliam virginem.* PL 101, 639–47.

Ambrose. *In Hexaemeron.* CSEL 32, 1, 3–261. Ed. C. Schenkl. Vienna, 1896.

——. *Isaac vel de anima.* CSEL 32, 2, 641–700. Ed. C. Schenkl. Vienna, 1897.

Anonymous. *De mundi coelestis terrestrisque constitutione.* PL 90, 881–910.

Aristotle. *Opera omnia.* Loeb Classical Library.

Augustine. *Opera omnia.* PL 32–46.

——. *Confessiones.* Ed. P. H. Wangnereck. Turin, 1962.

——. *De civitate dei.* CC 47–48, edd. B. Dombart and A. Kalb. Turnhout, 1955.

——. *De natura et origine animae.* CSEL 60, 303–420, edd. C. Urba and J. Zycha. Vienna, 1913.

——. *De origine animae.* CSEL 44, 545–84, ed. A. Goldbacher. Vienna, 1904.

——. *De Trinitate. Bibliothèque Augustinienne* 15–16, edd. M. Mellet and T. Camelot; P. Agaësse and J. Moingt. Paris, 1955.

——. *Tractatus in Evangelium Ioannis.* CC 36, ed. R. Willems. Turnhout, 1954.

Benedict of Nursia. *Sancti Benedicti Regula.* CSEL 74, ed. R. Hanslik. Vienna, 1960.

Boethius. *Opera.* PL 63–64.

——. *In Isagogen Porphyrii Commenta.* CSEL 48, edd. C. Scheipss and S. Brandt. Vienna, 1906.

——. *The Theological Tractates and the Consolation of Philosophy.* Edd. H. F. Stewart and E. K. Rank. Loeb Classical Library. Cambridge (Mass.), 1962.

Cassiodorus. *Magni Aurelii Cassiodori Senatoris Liber de Anima.* Ed. James W. Halporn. *Traditio,* XVI (1960), 39–109.

Chalcidius. *Timaeus a Chalcidio translatus commentarioque instructus.* Ed. J. H. Waszink. *Corpus Platonicum Medii Aevi: Plato Latinus IV.* London, 1962.

Cicero. *Opera omnia.* Loeb Classical Library.

Claudianus Mamertus. *De statu animae.* CSEL 11, ed. A. Engelbrecht. Vienna, 1885.

Costa-ben-Luca (Constabulinus). *De differentia animae et spiritus.* C. S. Barach. *Excerpta a libro Alfredi Anglici "De Motu cordis." Item Costa-ben-Lucae "De differentia animae et spiritus."* Innsbruck, 1878.

Dionysius Areopagita (Pseudo). *Dionysiaca (Opera omnia).* Ed. P. Chevallier. 2 Vols. Paris, 1937.

——. *La Hiérarchie Céleste.* Edd. R. Roques, G. Heil, and M. de Gandillac. *Sources Chrétiennes* 58. Paris, 1958.

Gennadius of Marseilles. *Liber de ecclesiasticis dogmatibus.* PL 58, 979–1000.

Gregory the Great. *Homeliae in Ezechielem Prophetam.* PL 76, 785–1072.

——. *In Evangeliorum Homeliae XL.* PL 76, 1075–1314.

Gregory of Nyssa. *De imagine, vel de opificio hominis.* PL 67, 347–408 (trans. of Dionysius Exiguus). M. Cappuyns, "Le 'De Imagine' de Grégoire de Nysse traduit par Jean Scot Érigène," RTAM, XXXII (1965), 205–62.

Hermes Trismegistus (Pseudo). *Asclepius.* Edd. A. D. Nock and A.-J. Festugière, *Corpus Hermeticum.* Vol. II, 296–401. Paris, 1960.

Isidore of Seville. *Differentiarum libri duo.* PL 83, 9–98.

——. *Etymologiae.* PL 82, 73–728.

John Scotus Eriugena. *Opera.* PL 122.

——. *Expositiones super Ierarchiam caelestem III-VII, XV.* Ed. H. Doandine. AHDL, XVIII (1951), 245–302.

Macrobius. *Ambrosii Theodosii Macrobii Commentarii in Somnium Scipionis.* Ed. Jacobus Willis. Leipzig, 1963.

Martianus Capella. *De nuptiis Mercurii et Philologiae.* Ed. A. Dick. Leipzig, 1925.

Nemesius of Emesa. *Nemesii Episcopi Premnon Physicon.* Ed. C. Burkhard. Leipzig, 1917.

Plato. *Opera omnia.* Loeb Classical Library.

Plotinus. *Enneads I-III.* Ed. A. H. Armstrong. Loeb Classical Library. Cambridge (Mass.), 1966-67.

——. *Plotin: Ennéades.* Ed. E. Brehier. 7 Vols. Paris, 1924-28.

Plutarch (Pseudo). *De vita et poesi Homeris. Plutarchi Operum:* Vol. V, *Spuria et Fragmenta,* 100-64. Ed. J. Friedrich. Paris, 1855.

Porphyry. *De regressu animae.* J. Bidez, *Vie de Porphyre le philosophe neo-platonicienne,* 27*-44*. Gand, 1913.

Proclus. *Elements of Theology.* Ed. E. Dodds. 2nd Edition. Oxford, 1963.

——. *Procli Diadochi in Platonis Timaeum Commentaria.* Ed. Ernst Diehl. 3 Vols. Leipzig, 1903-6.

——. *Procli philosophi Platonici opera inedita.* Ed. Victor Cousin. Paris, 1864.

——. *Procli Diadochi Tria Opuscula.* Ed. H. Boese. Berlin, 1960.

Rabanus Maurus. *De universo.* PL 111, 9-614.

——. *Tractatus de anima.* PL 110, 1109-20.

Ratramnus of Corbie. *De diversa et multiplici animae ratione.* PL 125, 933-52.

——. *De natura animae.* A. Wilmart, "L'Opuscule inédit de Ratramne sur la nature de l'âme," *Revue Bénédictine,* XVIII (1931), 207-33.

SECONDARY LITERATURE

WORKS RELATING SPECIFICALLY TO ISAAC OF STELLA

Note: The last general bibliography on Isaac of Stella was done by M. R. Milcamps in 1958. Since Milcamps missed some items, and since a good number of studies have appeared in the last eleven years, it seems worthwhile to devote a separate section to Isaac as a way of providing a new general bibliography up to 1969.

Balic, C. *Testimonia de Assumptione Beatae Maria Virginis.* Vol. I. Rome, 1948.

Baron, Roger. "L'Influence de Hugues de Saint-Victor." RTAM, XXII (1955), 56-71.

Barre, Henri. "Marie et l'Église dans la pensée médiévale." *La vie spirituelle,* XCI (1954), 124-41.

——. "Marie et l'Église du Venerable Bede à Saint Albert le Grand." *Marie et l'Église I. Études Mariales* IX (1951), 59-125.

——. "Saint Bernard, Docteur marial," *Analecta Sacri Ordinis Cisterciensis,* IX (1953), 92-113.

Baumgartner, Matthias. *Alanus de Insulis.* BGPM, II, 4 (1896).

Bernhart, Josef. *Philosophische Mystik des Mittelalters*. Munich, 1922.

Bernareggi, Adriano. "Isaaco di Stella." *Enciclopedia Ecclesiastica*, V, 103–4. Milan, 1953.

Bertola, Ermengildo. "Di alcuni Tratti Psicologici attribuiti ad Ugo di San Vittore." *Rivista di Filosofia Neo-Scolastica*, LI (1959), 436–55.

———. "Di una inedita Trattazione psicologica intitolata 'Quid sit Anima'." *Rivista di Filosofia Neo-Scolastica*, LVIII (1966), 564–83.

———. "Il Socratismo Christiano nel XII secolo." *Rivista di Filosofia Neo-Scolastica*, LI (1959), 252–64.

———. "La dottrina psicologica di Isaaco di Stella." *Rivista di Filosofia Neo-Scolastica*, XLV (1953), 25–36.

———. *San Bernardo e la Teologia Speculativa*. Padua, 1959.

Beumer, Johannes. "Die Parallele Maria-Kirche nach einem ungedruckten Sermo des Gottfried von St Victor." RTAM, XXVII (1960), 248–66.

———. "Mariologie und Ekklesiologie bei Isaac von Stella." *Münchener Theologische Zeitschrift*, V (1954) 48–61.

Bliemetzrieder, F. "Eine unbekannte Schrift Isaaks von Stella." *Studien und Mitteilungen aus dem Benediktiner und dem Cistercienser-Orden*, XXIX (1908), 433–41.

———. "Isaac von Stella. Beiträge zur Lebensbeschreibung." *Jahrbuch der Philosophie und spekulativen Theologie* (*Divus Thomas: Freiburg*), XV (1904), 1–34.

———. "Isaac de Stella: Sa Speculation théologique." RTAM, VI (1932), 132–59.

Bourgain, Louis. *La chaire française au XIIᵉ siècle*. Paris, 1879.

Bouyer, Louis. *The Cistercian Heritage*. Westminster, 1958.

Boyle, Charles W. *De Officio Missae. The Epistle of Isaac of Stella to John Bishop of Poitiers. Translation and Commentary*. Master's Dissertation. Department of Religious Education, Catholic University of America. Washington, 1963.

Brady, I. C. "Isaac of Stella." *The New Catholic Encyclopedia*. VI, 663. New York, 1967.

Burch, George Bosworth. *Early Medieval Philosophy*. New York, 1951.

———. *The Steps of Humility by Bernard, Abbot of Clairvaux*. Notre Dame, 1963.

Ceillier, Dom Remy. *Histoire générale des auteurs sacrés et ecclésiastiques*. XIV, 2. Paris, 1863.

Châtillon, Jean. "Cordis affectus au moyen âge." DS, II, 2288–2300. Paris, 1953.

Chenu, Marie-Dominique. *La théologie au douzième siècle*. Paris, 1957.

———. "Spiritus, le vocabulaire de l'âme au XIIᵉ siècle." RSPT, XLI (1957), 209–32.

Collini, R. *Studi su Isaaco della Stella*. Unpublished dissertation. 2 Vols. Università Cattolica del Sacro Cuore. Milan, 1956–57.

Congar, Yves. "L'Ecclesiologie de Saint Bernard." *Analecta Sacri Ordinis Cisterciensis*, IX (1953), 136–90.

Courcelle, Pierre. *La Consolation de Philosophie dans la Tradition littéraire: Antécédents et Posterité de Boèce*. Paris, 1967.

R

——. *Les Confessions de Saint Augustin dans la Tradition littéraire: Antécédents et Posterité.* Paris, 1963.

——. "Tradition Néo-platonicienne et Traditions Chrétiennes de la 'Région de Dissemblance." AHDL, XXXII (1958), 5–33.

d'Alverny, Marie-Thérèse. *Alain de Lille: Textes inédits.* Études de Philosophie Médiévale LII. Paris, 1965.

——. "Les pérégrinations de l'âme dans l'autre monde d'après un anonyme de la fin du XIIe siècle." AHDL, XV–XVII (1940–42), 239–301.

Davy, Marie-Madeleine. *Initiation à la Symbolique Romane (XII siècle).* 2nd edition. Paris, 1964.

de Bruyne, Edgar. *Études d'esthétique médiévale.* Vol. II. Bruges, 1946.

de Contenson, P.-M. "Avicennisme latin et vision de Dieu au debut du XIIIe siècle." AHDL, XXVI (1959), 29–97.

de Ghellinck, J. *L'essor de la littérature latine au XIIe siècle.* 2nd edition. Paris-Brussels, 1955.

de Lubac, Henri. *Catholicisme.* Paris, 1938.

——. *Corpus Mysticum: L'Eucharistie et L'Église au moyen âge.* Paris, 1944.

——. *Exégèse Médiévale: Les quatre sens de l'Écriture.* 2 Vols. in 4 parts. Paris, 1959–64.

——. *Meditation sur l'Église.* Paris, 1953.

de Vaux, R. *Notes et textes sur l'avicennisme latin aux confines des XIIe et XIIIe siècles.* Bibliothèque Thomiste, XX. Paris, 1934.

de Visch, Charles. *Bibliotheca Scriptorum Sacri Ordinis Cisterciensis.* Cologne 1656.

de Wulf, Maurice. *Histoire de la philosophie médiévale.* Vol. I, 6th edition. Paris, 1934.

Debray-Mulatier, J. "Biographie d'Isaac de Stella." *Cîteaux,* X (1959) 178–98.

del Pra, Mario. *Scoto Eriugena.* Milan, 1951.

Dreux-Duradier, Jean-François. *Histoire littéraire du Poitou.* Vol. II. Niort, 1849.

Dumontier, M. *Saint Bernard et la Bible.* Paris, 1953.

Engelhardt, Georg. *Die Entwicklung der dogmatischen Glaubenspsychologie in der Mittelalterlichen Scholastik vom Abaelardstreit (um 1140) bis zu Phillip dem Kanzler (gest. 1236).* BGPM, XXX, 4–6 (1933).

Espenberger, Johannes N. *Die Philosophie des Petrus Lombardus und Ihre Stellung im zwölften Jahrhundert.* BGPM, III, 5 (1897).

Fabricius, Johannes Albertus. *Bibliotheca Latina mediae et infimae Aetatis.* Vol. III/IV. Florence, 1858.

Fairweather, Eugene R. "Isaac of Stella." *The Encyclopedia of Philosophy,* Vol. IV, 219. New York, 1967.

Forest, Aimé, F. Van Steenberghen, and M. de Gandillac. *Le mouvement doctrinal du XIe au XIVe siècle.* Vol. XIII. Fliche-Martin, *Histoire de l'Église.* Paris, 1956.

Fracheboud, André. "Denys l'Aréopagite: en occident." DS, III, 329–40. Paris, 1957.

——. "Divinization: Auteurs monastiques du 12ᵉ siècle." DS, III, 1399–1413. Paris, 1957.

——. "Isaac de Stella à l'Université de Naples." COCR, XIV (1952), 278–81.

——. "Isaac de l'Étoile et l'Écriture Sainte." COCR, 19 (1957), 133–45.

——. *Les premiers spirituels cisterciens.* "Pain de Citeaux," XXX. Chambaroud en Raybon, 1967.

——. "L'Influence de Saint Augustin sur le Cistercien Isaac de l'Étoile." COCR, XI (1949), 1–17; 264–78; XII (1950), 5–16.

——. "Le Pseudo-Denys l'Aréopagite parmi les sources du Cistercien Isaac de l'Étoile." COCR, IX (1947), 328–41; X (1948), 19–34.

François, Jean. *Bibliothèque générale des écrivains de l'Ordre de Saint Benoit.* Vol. II. Paris, 1777.

Franz, Adolph. *Die Messe im deutschen Mittelalter.* Freiburg-im-Breisgau, 1902.

Gaggero, Leonard. "Isaac of Stella and the Theology of Redemption." COCR, XXII (1960), 21–36.

Gallia Christiana in provincias ecclesiasticas distributa (Dionysius de Sainte-Marthe). Vol. II, 1352–56 (Series abbatum B. M. de Stella). Paris, 1720.

Gessner, Jakob. *Die Abstraktionslehre in der Scholastik bis Thomas von Aquin mit besonderer Berüchtsichtigung des Lichtbegriffes.* Inaugural-dissertation zu Freiburg-im-Breisgau. Fulda, 1930.

Geyer, Bernhard. *Die Patristische und Scholastische Philosophie.* Vol. II of *Grundriss der Geschichte der Philosophie von Friedrich Ueberweg.* Berlin, 1928.

Gilson, Etienne. *A History of Christian Philosophy in the Middle Ages.* New York, 1955.

——. "Les sources gréco-arabes de l'augustinisme avicénnisant." AHDL, IV (1929), 5–107.

Graf, Thomas. *De subjecto psychico gratiae et virtutum.* Vol. I. Rome, 1934.

Häring, Nicholas. "Gilbert of Poitiers, Author of the *De Discretione animae, spiritus et mentis,* commonly attributed to Achard of St Victor." *Medieval Studies,* XXII (1960), 148–91.

Hergenröther, Josef, and Franz Kaulen (edd.). *Wetzer und Weltes Kirchenlexicon.* Vol. VI, 937. Freiburg-im-Breisgau, 1889.

Heurtebize, B. "Isaac de l'Étoile." DTC, Vol. VIII, 14. Paris, 1924.

Histoire littéraire de la France. 12 vol. (A. Rivet). IX, 190; XII, 678–83. Paris, 1733–63.

Hoste, Anselm. "Une thèse inédite sur Isaac de l'Étoile." COCR, XXV (1936), 256–7.

——. Review of Milcamps' Bibliography. *Cîteaux in de Nederlanden,* IX (1958), 302.

——. "Introduction au texte latin." *Isaac de l'Étoile: Sermons* I, 69–81. Paris, 1967.

Hurter, H. *Nomenclator Literarius Theologiae Catholicae,* II. Innsbruck, 1906.

Jansen, Wilhelm. *Der Kommentar des Clarenbaldus von Arras zu Boethius De Trinitate.* Breslau, 1926.

Javelet, Robert. "Au XIIᵉ siècle, L'Écriture Sainte servante de la mystique?" *Revue des sciences religieuses,* XXXVII (1963), 345–69.

———. "Intelligence et amour chez les Auteurs spirituels du XIIe siècle." RAM, XXXVII (1961), 273–90, 429–50.

———. *Image et Ressemblance au douzième siècle.* 2 Vols. Paris, 1967.

———. "La vertu dans l'oeuvre d'Isaac de l'Étoile." *Cîteaux,* XI (1960), 252–67.

———. "Thomas Gallus et Richard de Saint-Victor mystiques." RTAM, XXIX (1962), 206–33; XXX (1963), 88–121.

Jugie, M. *La mort et l'assomption de la Sainte Vierge.* Rome, 1944.

Käpelli, Thomas M. "Eine aus frühscholastischen Werken exzerpierte Bibelkatene." *Divus Thomas (Freiburg),* IX (1931), 309–19.

Künzle, Pius. *Das Verhältnis der Seele zu ihrem Potenzen.* Freiburg (Schweiz), 1956.

Landgraf, Artur M. *Dogmengeschichte der Frühscholastik.* 4 Vols. in 8 parts. Regensburg, 1952–55.

———. "Isaac von Stella." *Lexicon für Theologie und Kirche,* V, 614–15. Freiburg-im-Breisgau, 1933.

Laurentin, R. *Jésus au Temple.* Paris, 1966.

Leclercq, Jean. *The Love of Learning and the Desire for God.* New York, 1961.

———. "Nouveau sermon d'Isaac de l'Étoile." RAM, XL (1964), 277–88.

———. *Otia Monastica: Études sur le vocabulaire de la contemplation au moyen âge.* Rome, 1963.

———. "St Bernard et la théologie monastique du XIIe siècle." *Analecta Sacri Ordinis Cisterciensis,* IX (1953), 7–33.

———. Vandenbroucke, F., and Bouyer L, *La spiritualité du moyen âge.* Paris, 1961.

Leff, Gordon. *Medieval Thought: St Augustine to Ockham.* Baltimore, 1962.

Lepin, M. *L'Idée du Sacrifice de la Messe d'après les théologiens depuis les origines jusqu' à nos jours.* Paris, 1926.

Lewicki, M. L. "Une double thèse de philosophie sur Alcher de Clairvaux et Isaac de l'Étoile à l'Université de Lublin (Pologne)." COCR, XVIII (1956), 161–64, 247–53.

Lottin, Odon. *Psychologie et morale au XIIe et XIIIe siècle.* 6 Vols. Louvain, 1942–60.

Mannarini, Franco. "La Grazia in Isaaco di Stella." COCR, XVI (1954), 137–44, 207–14.

Mersch, E. *Le corps mystique du Christ.* Vol. II. Paris, 1933.

Merton, L. "Isaac of Stella: An Introduction to Selections from his Sermons." *Cistercian Studies,* II (1967), 243–251.

Meuser, Wilhelm. *Die Erkenntnislehre der Isaak von Stella. Ein Beitrag zur Geschichte der Philosophie des 12ten Jahrhunderts.* Inaugural-Dissertation, Freiburg-im-Breisgau. Botttrop, 1934.

Michaud-Quantain, Pierre. "La classification des puissances de l'âme au XIIe siècle." *Revue du moyen âge latin,* V (1949), 15–34.

Mikkers, E. "Isaac de Stella." *Theologisch Woordenboek,* 2431–2.

Milcamps, M. R. "Bibliographie d'Isaac de l'Étoile." COCR, XX (1958), 175–86.

O'Brien, Robert. "A Commentary of the Canticle of Canticles attributed to Isaac of Stella." *Cîteaux,* XVI (1965), 226–8.

Ortuzar, Martin. "El ser y la accion en la dimension humana (Pedro Abelardo, 1097–1142), y su gruppo." *Éstudios (Madrid)*, XIII (1957), 219–48, 431–63.

Ostler, Helnrich. *Die Psychologie des Hugo von St Viktor. Ein Beitrag zur Geschichte der Psychologie in der Frühscholastik.* BGPM, VI, 1 (1906).

Ott, Ludwig. "Isaak von Stella." *Lexikon für Theologie und Kirche,* V, 777–8. Freiburg-im-Breisgau, 1960.

Oudin, Casimir. *Commentarium de Scriptoribus Ecclesiasticis.* II, 1485–6. Leipzig, 1722.

———. *Supplementum de Scriptoribus vel Scriptis Ecclesiasticis a Bellarmino omissis ad annum 1460.* Paris, 1686.

Piolanti, Antonio. "De nostra in Christo solidarietate praecipua Isaac de Stella testimonia." *Euntes Docete,* II (1949), 349–68.

———. "Isaaco della Stella." *Enciclopedia Cattolica,* VII, 234. Vatican City, 1951.

———. "La nostra solidarietà soprannaturale nel pensiero di Isaaco della Stella." *Palestro del Clero,* VII (1956), 1–18.

———. "Maria et Ecclesia. Quaedam inter utramque relationes a Scriptoribus marianis saeculi XII illustratae." *Euntes Docete,* VI (1951), 324–38.

———. "Mater unitatis. De spirituali Virginis maternitate secundum nonnullos saeculi XII scriptores." *Marianum,* II (1949), 423–39.

Raciti, Gaetano. "Isaac de l'Étoile et son siècle." *Cîteaux,* XII (1961), 281–306; XIII (1962), 18–34, 133–45, 205–16.

———. "L'Autore del 'De Spiritu et Anima'." *Rivista di Filosofia Neo-Scolastica,* LIII (1961), 385–401.

———. Review of J. Leclercq, "Nouveau Sermon d'Isaac de l'Étoile." COCR, XXVII (1965), 337–9.

Reypens, L. "Âme (son fond, ses puissances, et sa structure d'après les mystiques)." DS, I, 442–5. Paris, 1937.

Ritter, Heinrich. *Geschichte der Christliche Philosophie.* III. Hamburg, 1844.

Ruidor, Ignacio. "Maria mediadora y madre del Christo místico en los escritores eclesiásticos de la primera mitad del siglo XII." *Éstudios eclesiásticos,* XXV (1951), 181–217.

Salet, Gaston. "Introduction générale." *Isaac de l'Étoile: Sermons* I, 7–63. Paris, 1967.

Sarton, George. *Introduction to the History of Science,* II. Baltimore, 1931.

Schneider, Artur. *Die Abendländische Spekulation des 12ten Jahrhunderts in ihrem Verhältnis zur Aristotelischen und Jüdisch-Arabischen Philosophie.* BGPM 17, 4 (1915).

Siebeck, Hermann. *Geschichte der Psychologie.* Gotha, 1884.

Spicq, Ceslaus. *Esquisse d'histoire de l'exégèse latine au moyen âge.* Paris, 1944.

Stegmüller, Friedrich. *Repertorium Biblicum Medii Aevi,* III. Madrid, 1951.

Stinglhamber, L. "Predicateurs au moyen âge." *Nouvelle Revue théologique,* LXIX (1947), 651–64.

Stöckl, A. *Geschichte der Philosophie des Mittelalters,* I. Mainz, 1865.

Talbot, C. H. "Introduction." *Aelred of Rievaulx: De Anima. Mediaeval and Renaissance Studies. Supplement I.* London, 1952.

van den Bosch, Amatus, and de Ganck, Rogier. "Isaak van Stella in de weten-schappelijke literature." *Cîteaux in de Nederlanden,* VIII (1957), 203–18.
van Ivánka, Endre. "L'Union à Dieu. La structure de l'âme selon S. Bernard." *Analecta Sacri Ordinis Cisterciensis,* IX (1953), 202–8.
———. *Plato Christianus.* Einsiedeln, 1964.
Vandenbroucke, F. *La Morale monastique du XIᵉ au XVIᵉ siècle. Analecta Mediaevalia Namurcensia,* XX. Louvain-Lille, 1966.
Vanni-Rovighi, Sofia. "Notes sur l'influence de Saint Anselme au XIIᵉ siècle." *Cahiers de Civilization Médiévale,* VII (1964), 423–37; VIII (1965), 43–58.
Vernet, F. *La spiritualité médiévale.* Paris, 1929.
Webb, G. *An Introduction to the Cistercian De Anima. Aquinas Paper* 36. London, 1962.
Wellens, M. Edouard. "L'Ordre de Cîteaux et l'Assomption." COCR, XIII (1951), 30–51.
Werner, Karl. *Der Entwicklungsgang der mittelalterlichen Psychologie.* Vienna, 1876.
Wilmart, A. *Auteurs spirituels et textes devots du moyen âge latin.* Paris, 1932.

OTHER WORKS ON ISAAC

Isaac has been the subject of six theses, listed below. The second part of this section lists works purporting to deal with Isaac which for various reasons, including the possibility that some are bibliographical ghosts, I have been unable to examine personally; hence, I include them here in a separate category.

Theses: Of the six theses devoted to Isaac of Stella, one has been published, and I have been able to examine one other, that of R. Collini. Reports on the unpublished investigations, however, have appeared in the periodical literature.

Collini, R. *Studi su Isaaco della Stella.* Università Cattolica del Sacro Cuore. 2 Vols. Milan, 1956–57. Reported in A. Hoste, "Une thèse inédite sur Isaac de l'Étoile," COCR, XXV (1963), 256–57.
Debray-Mulatier, J. *Isaac de Stella et l'Epistola de Anima.* Position de thèse. École nationale des Chartes. Paris, 1940. Presumably this contributed to Mlle Debray-Mulatier's "Biographie d'Isaac de Stella," *Cîteaux,* X (1959), 178–98.
Lewicki, M. L. *Filozoficzna antropologia Isaaka Stelle.* Lublin, 1955. Reported in the author's "Une double thèse de philosophie sur Alcher de Clairvaux et Isaac de l'Étoile à l'Université de Lublin (Pologne)," COCR, XVII (1956), 161–4, 247–53.
Mannarini, Franco. *La Grazia in Isaaco di Stella.* Dissertazione per la Laurea, Possillipo. Naples, 1952. Summarized in the author's "La Grazia in Isaaco di Stella," COCR, XVI (1954), 137–44, 207–14.

Meuser, Wilhelm. *Die Erkenntnislehre der Isaak von Stella.* The only published thesis; cf. above.

Raciti, Gaetano. Unpublished thesis presented at Università Cattolica del Sacro Cuore. Milan, 1962. Presumably the basis for his articles, "Isaac de l'Étoile et son siècle," *Cîteaux*, XII (1961), 281–306; XIII (1962), 18–34, 133–45, 205–16.

Works on Isaac Not Seen (information frequently incorrect):

Berlière, Ursmer. *L'ascèse bénédictine des origines à la fin du XIIe siècle.* Maredsous, 1927.

Bunderius, J. *Index librorum manuscriptorum totius Belgii.* Litt. I, n. 87.

Cappelletti, Angel J. *Origen y grados del conocimiento segun Isaac de Stella. Philosophia*, XXIV. Mendoza, 1961.

Cheneviere, E. *Nos Pères par eux-mêmes*, III, 97–154.

de Blic, J. *Pour l'histoire de la théologie des dons avant Saint Thomas.*

Dupin, L.-E. *Nouvelle bibliothèque des auteurs ecclésiastiques*, II, 2, 629. Paris, 1699.

Grancolas, J. *Critique abrégée des auteurs ecclésiastiques*, II, 300.

Hermans, V. *Spiritualité monastique.* Rome, 1954.

"Isaac de Stella." *Enciclopedia Universal Illustrada Europeo-Americana*, XXVIII, 2011. Barcelona, 1926.

Le Bail, Anselme. *La spiritualité cistercienne.* Cahiers du Cercle thomiste feminin. Paris, 1927.

Lenssen, Seraphin. *Hagiologium cisterciense*, II, 39. Tilburg, 1949.

Lienhart, G. *Spir. lit. Norbert* (?). 1771.

Pinard, G. *Les hommes célèbres de l'Ordre de Cîteaux*, I, 564–7. Dijon (manuscript?).

Potanick, C. "Simbolizem u razagah rimske masne liturgije (De symbolismo in expositionibus liturgiae romanae)." *Bogosl. Vestn.* VIII (1928), 210–55.

Robinet, Dom. *Abrégé chronologique de l'histoire de l'abbaye et abbés de Pontigny.* Bibliothéque Communale d'Auxerre ms. 222.

Rusca, Roberto (Antonio?). *Breve compendio di alcuni huomini illustri per dignità, santità et dottrina cisterciensi.* Milan (c. 1600).

Thomas, R. *Sermonaire Cistercien.* "Pain de Cîteaux," 3 and 4. Chambaraud en Raybon, 1966.

Thiebault, Dom. *Bibliothèque universelle des auteurs suivant la Regle de S. Benoit.* Besançon ms. 759.

OTHER SECONDARY LITERATURE

(Some well-known works are cited in their more recent printings.)

Allers, Rudolph. "Microcosmos from Anaximandros to Paracelsus." *Traditio*, II (1944), 319–409.

Altaner, Berthold. *Patrology.* 5th ed. Freiburg-im-Breisgau, 1958.

Altmann, Alexander and Stern, S. M. *Isaac Israeli: A Neoplatonic Philosopher of the Early Tenth Century.* Oxford, 1958.

Altmann, Alexander. "The Delphic Maxim in Medieval Islam and Judaism." *Biblical and Other Studies,* 196–232. Cambridge (Mass.), 1963.

Armstrong, A. H. *The Architecture of the Intelligible Universe in the Philosophy of Plotinus.* Cambridge, 1940.

——. (ed.). *The Cambridge History of Later Greek and Early Medieval Philosophy.* Cambridge, 1967.

——, and Markus, R. A. *Christian Faith and Greek Philosophy.* New York, 1960.

——. "Platonic Elements in St Gregory of Nyssa's Doctrine of Man." *Dominican Studies,* I (1948), 113 sqq.

Arnou, R. "Platonisme des Pères." DTC, XII, 2258–2392. Paris, 1925.

Auerbach, Erich. *Literary Language and its Public in Late Latin Antiquity and in the Middle Ages.* New York, 1965.

——. *Mimesis: the Representation of Reality in Western Literature.* New York, 1957.

Baeumker, Clemens. "Der Platonismus im Mittelalter." *Studien und Charakteristiken zur Geschichte der Philosophie insbesonders des Mittelalters,* 139–79. BGPM, XXV, 1–2 (1927).

——. "Mittelalterlicher und Renaissance Platonismus." *Op. cit.,* 180–93.

——. *Witelo, Ein Philosoph und Naturforscher des XIII. Jahrhunderts.* BGPM, III, 2 (1900).

Barber, Richard. *Henry Plantagenet.* London, 1964.

Baron, Roger. "Hugues de St-Victor: Contribution à un nouvel examen de son oeuvre." *Traditio,* XV (1959), 223–99.

——. "La Situation de l'homme d'après Hugues de Saint-Victor." *L'Homme et son destin d'après les penseurs du moyen âge* (Actes du premier Congrès international de Philosophie Médiévale, Louvain-Brussels, 1958), 431–6. Louvain-Paris, 1960.

——. "Note sur le *De Claustro.*" *Sacris Erudiri,* XV (1964), 249–55.

——. *Science et Sagesse chez Hugues de Saint-Victor.* Paris, 1957.

——. "Spiritualité médiévale: le Traite de la contemplation et ses espèces." RAM, XXXIX (1963), 137–51, 294–301.

Beauchet-Filleau, G. (ed. H. Filleau). *Dictionnaire historique et généalogique des familles du Poitou,* II. Niort, 1895.

Bertola, Ermengildo. "Le Fonti Medico-Filosofiche della Dottrina dello 'Spirito'." *Sophia,* XXVI (1958), 48–61.

——. "Le Proebizioni di Aristotele del 1210 e 1215 e il Problema del' Anima." *Rivista di Filosofia Neo-Scholastica,* LVII (1965), 725–51.

Boissard, E. "St Bernard et le Pseudo-Aréopagite." RTAM, XXVI (1959), 214–63.

Boussard, Jacques. *Le Gouvernement d'Henri II Plantagenêt.* Paris, 1956.

Brooke, O. "The Speculative Development of the Trinitarian Theology of William of St Thierry in the 'Aenigma Fidei.'" RTAM, XXVII (1960), 192–211, XXVIII (1961), 26–58.

——. "The Trinitarian Aspect of the Ascent of the Soul to God in the Theology of William of St Thierry." RTAM, XXVI (1959), 85-127.

Brooke, Z. N. *The English Church and the Papacy from the Conquest to the Death of John.* Cambridge, 1952.

Bruder, Karl. *Die Philosophischen Elemente in den Opuscula Sacra des Boethius.* Leipzig, 1928.

Brunner, Fernand. "Deus Forma Essendi." *Entretiens sur la Renaissance du 12e siécle,* edd. M. de Gandillac and J. Jeauneau, 85-116. Paris, 1968.

Bultmann, Rudolph. *Primitive Christianity in its Contemporary Setting.* New York, 1965.

——. *The Theology of the New Testament.* 1 Vol. ed. New York, 1955.

Bultot, R. "Les 'Meditationes' Pseudo-Bernardines sur la connaissance de la condition humaine." *Sacris Erudiri,* XV (1964), 256-92.

Camelot, T. "La théologie de l'image de Dieu." RSPT, XL (1957), 433-71.

Cantor, Norman F. "The Crisis of Western Monasticism." *American Historical Review,* XLVI (1960), 47-67.

——. *Medieval History.* New York, 1963.

Cappuyns, Maieul. *Jean Scot Érigène: sa vie, son oeuvre, sa pensée.* Paris, 1933.

Cassirer, Ernst. *The Individual and the Cosmos in Renaissance Philosophy.* New York, 1964.

Châtillon, Jean. "Autour des 'Miscellanea' attribués à Hugues de Saint-Victor." *Mélanges Marcel Viller.* RAM, XXV (1949), 299-305.

——. "De Guillaume de Champeaux à Thomas Gallus: Chronique d'histoire littéraire et doctrinale de l'école de Saint-Victor." *Revue du moyen âge latin,* VIII (1952), 139-62.

Chenu, Marie-Dominique. "Érigène à Citeaux." *La philosophie et ses problèmes. Receuil d'études de doctrine et d'histoire offert à Mgr Jolivet,* 99-107. Lyon-Paris, 1960.

——. "Histoire et allégorie au douzième siècle." *Festgabe Joseph Lortz: II. Glaube und Geschichte,* 59-73. Baden-Baden, 1958.

——. "Imaginatio." *Miscellanea Giovanni Mercati II. Studi e Testi* 122, 593-602. Vatican City, 1946.

——. "Involucrum. Le mythe selon les théologiens médévaux." AHDL, XXII (1955), 75-79.

——. "Notes de lexicographie philosophique: Disciplina." RSPT, XXV (1936), 686-92.

——. "Platon à Cîteaux." AHDL, XXI (1954), 99-106.

——. "Situation Humaine: Corporalité et Temporalité." *L'Homme et Son Destin,* 23-49. Paris, 1960.

——. "Un vestige du stoicisme." RSPT, XXVII (1938). 63-8.

——. "Une définition pythagorienne de la verité." AHDL, XXXVI (1961), 7-13.

Clerval, A. *Les Écoles de Chartres au moyen âge du Ve au XVIe siècle.* Paris, 1895.

Congar, Yves M.-J. *A History of Theology.* New York, 1968.

Cooper, L. *A Concordance to Boethius.* Cambridge (Mass.), 1928.

Copleston, Frederick. *A History of Philosophy,* I-II. Westminster, 1953-55.

Cornford, Francis M. *Plato's Cosmology.* New York, 1957.

Cottineau, L. H. *Répertoire topo-bibliographique des Abbayes et Prieurés.* 2 Vols. Macon. 1935–37.

Courcelle, Pierre. "Complément au répertoire des textes rélatifs à la region de dissemblance." *Augustinus,* XIII (1968), 135–40.

——. "Interpretations néo-platonisantes du livre VI de L'Enéide." *Recherches sur la Tradition Platonicienne,* 95–136. *Entretiens sur la Antiquité Classique (Fondation Hardt),* III. Geneva, 1955.

——. "L'Âme en Cage." *Parusia: Studien zur Philosophie Platons und zur Problemgeschichte des Platonismus, Festgabe für Johannes Hirschberger,* ed. Kurt Flasch, 103–16. Frankfort, 1965.

——. "La posterité chrétienne du 'Songe de Scipion.' " *Revue des études latines,* XXXVI (1958), 250–34.

——. "Le corps-tombeau." *Revue des études anciennes,* LXVIII (1966), 101–22.

——. *Les lettres grécques en Occident de Macrobe à Cassiodore.* 2nd ed. Paris, 1948.

——. "Les Pères de l'Église devant les enfers virgiliens." AHDL, XXX (1955), 5–74.

——. " 'Nosce teipsum' du Bas-Empire au Haut Moyen Âge. L'Heritage profane et les developpements Chrétiens." *Il Passagio dall' Antichità al Medioevo in Occidente. Settimane di Studio del Centro Italiano di Studi sull' Alto Medioevo,* IX, 265–95. Spoleto, 1962.

——. "Traditions Platoniciennes et chrétiennes du corps-prison." *Revue des études latines,* XLIII (1966), 406–43.

Coutourier, Charles. "La structure metaphysique de l'homme d'après Saint Augustin." *Augustinus Magister,* I, 543–50. Paris, 1954.

Cullmann, Oscar. "Immortality of the Soul or Resurrection of the Body?" *Immortality and Resurrection,* ed. Krister Stendhal, 9–53. New York, 1965.

d'Alverny, Marie-Thérèse. "Le cosmos symbolique du XIIe siècle." AHDL, XX (1953), 31–81.

Daniélou, Jean. *Platonisme et théologie mystique: doctrine spirituelle de Saint Grégoire de Nysse.* 2nd ed. Paris, 1953.

Daubercies, P. "La théologie de la condition charnelle chez les Maîtres du haut moyen âge." RTAM, XXX (1963), 5–54.

de Champeaux, Gerard, and Sébastien Sterckx. *Introduction au Monde des Symboles.* Paris, 1966.

de Ghellinck, J. "L'entrée d'essentia, substantia, et autres mots apparentés dans le latin médiéval." *Archivum Latinitatis Medii Aevi,* XVI (1942), 77–112.

——. *Le mouvement théologique de XIIe siècle.* Paris, 1948.

de Gandillac, M. "Le platonisme au XIIe–XIIIe siècles." *Actes du Congrès Budè: Congrès de Tours et Poitiers, 1953,* 266–85. Paris, 1954.

de Lubac, Henri. *The Mystery of the Supernatural.* New York, 1967.

de Vogel, C. J. "Amor quo coelum regitur." *Vivarium,* I (1963), 2–35.

——. "On the Neoplatonic Character of Platonism and the Platonic Character of Neoplatonism." *Mind,* LXII (1953), 43–64.

Déchanet, J.-M. "Guillaume et Plotine." *Revue du moyen âge latin,* II (1946), 241–60.

Dekkers, E. *Clavis Patrum Latinorum. Sacris Erudiri,* 3. 2nd ed. Bruges-The Hague, 1961.

Delhaye, P. "Dans le sillage di S. Bernard, trois petits traités 'de conscientia'". *Cîteaux in de Nederlanden*, V (1954), 92–103.

———. "L'organisation scolaire au XIIe siècle." *Traditio*, V (1947), 211–68.

———. *Une controverse sur l'âme universelle au IXe siècle. Analecta Mediaevalia Namurcensia* I. Namur, 1950.

Dimier, Anselme. *L'art cistercien*. La-Pierre-qui-Vire (Yonne), 1962.

———. "Les premiers cisterciens étaient-ils ennemis des études?" *Los Monjes y los Estudios*, 119–46. Poblet, 1963.

Dodds, E. R. *The Greeks and the Irrational*. Berkeley and Los Angeles, 1963.

———. "Numenius and Ammonius." *Les Sources de Plotin*, 1–61. *Entretiens Hardt*, V. Geneva, 1957.

———. *Pagan and Christian in an Age of Anxiety*. Cambridge, 1965.

———. "The Parmenides of Plato and the Origin of the Neoplatonic 'One'." *Classical Quarterly*, XXII (1928), 129–42.

Dondaine, H. "Cinq citations de Jean Scot Érigène chez Simon de Tournai." RTAM, XVII (1950), 303–11.

———. *Le Corpus Dionysien de l'Université de Paris au XIIIe siècle*. Rome, 1953.

Dörrie, Heinrich. "Das fünffach gestufte Mysterium. Der Aufstieg der Seele bei Porphyrios und Ambrosius." *Mullus: Festschrift Theodor Klauser, Jahrbuch für Antike und Christentum, Ergänzungsband* I, 79–93. Münster, 1964.

Duchesne-Guillemin, Jacques. *The Hymns of Zarathustra*. New York, 1963.

Duhem, Pierre. *Le Système du monde*, III–IV. Paris, 1915–16.

Durand, Gilbert. *L'Imagination Symbolique*. Paris, 1964.

Ebner, Joseph. *Die Erkenntnislehre Richards von St Viktor*. BGPM, XIX, 4 (1917).

Edelstein, Ludwig. "The Golden Chain of Homer." *Studies in Intellectual History dedicated to Arthur O. Lovejoy*, 48–66. Baltimore, 1953.

Eichrodt, Walther. *Man in the Old Testament*. London, 1951.

———. *Theology in the Old Testament*, I. London, 1961.

Eliade, Mircea. *Cosmos and History: The Myth of the Eternal Return*. New York, 1959.

———. *Images and Symbols*. London, 1961.

———. "Methodological Remarks on the Study of Religious Symbolism." *History of Religions: Essays in Methodology*, edd. M. Eliade and J. M. Kitagawa, 86–107. Chicago, 1959.

———. *Myths, Dreams and Mysteries*. London, 1960.

———. *Patterns in Comparative Religion*. New York, 1958.

Fabro, Cornelio. *La nozione metafisica di particepazione secondo San Tommaso d'Aquino*. 3rd ed. Turin, 1963.

Festugière, André-Jean. *La révélation d'Hermès Trismégiste*. 4 Vols. Paris, 1944–53.

———. *Personal Religion among the Greeks*. Berkeley, 1960.

Fliche, A., Foreville, R. et Rousset, J. *Du premier Concile du Latran à l'avènement d'Innocent III (1123-1198)*. Vol. IX of the Fliche-Martin *Histoire de l'Église*. Paris, 1953.

Fontaine, Georges. *Pontigny, abbaye cistercienne*. Paris, 1928.

Foreville, R. L'église et royauté en Angleterre sous Henry II Plantagenet. Paris, 1943.

Frankfort, Henri, et al. Before Philosophy: The Intellectual Adventure of Ancient Man. Baltimore, 1951.

Friedländer, Paul. Plato: An Introduction. New York, 1964.

Galbraith, V. H. "Monastic Foundation Charters of the 11th and 12th Centuries." Cambridge Historical Journal, IV, 3 (1934), 206–21.

Garin, Eugenio. "Per la storia della tradizione platonica medioevale." Giornale critico della Filosofia Italiana, XXVIII (1949), 125–50.

——. Studi sul Platonismo Medievale. Florence, 1958.

Gelin, André. The Concept of Man in the Bible. Staten Island, 1968.

Gilson, Etienne. Being and Some Philosophers. 2nd ed. Toronto, 1952.

——. "La technique du sermon médiéval." Les idées et les lettres, 93–154. Paris, 1932.

——. The Christian Philosophy of St Augustine. New York, 1967.

——. The Mystical Theology of St Bernard. London, 1940.

——. The Spirit of Medieval Philosophy. New York, 1940.

Glorieux, P. "Pour révaloriser Migne: Tables rectificatives." Mélanges de Science Religieuse 9: Cahier Supplementaire. Lille, 1952.

Grabmann, Martin. Die Geschichte der Scholastischen Methode. 2 Vols. Freiburg-im-Breisgau, 1909–11.

Grant, Robert. Gnosticism and Early Christianity. New York, 1966.

Gregory, Tullio. Anima mundi. La Filosofia di Guglielemo di Conches e la Scuola di Chartres. Florence, 1955.

——. "L'idea della natura nella scuola di Chartres." Giornale critico della Filosofia Italiana, XXXI (1952), 433–442.

——. "Note e testi per la storia del platonismo medievale." Giornale critico della Filosofia Italiana, XXXVI (1955), 346–84.

——. "Note sul platonismo della scuola di Chartres. La dottrina delle specie native." Giornale critico della Filosofia Italiana, XXXII (1953), 358–62.

——. "Nuove note sul platonismo medievale. Dall' anima mundi all' idea di natura." Giornale critico della Filosofia Italiana, XXXVI (1957), 37–55.

——. Platonismo medievale. Studi e Ricerche. Istituto Storico Italiano per il Medio Evo. Studi Storici. fasc. 26–27. Rome, 1958.

Grundmann, Herbert. "Zur Biographie Joachims von Fiore und Rainer von Ponza." Deutsches Archiv für Erforschung des Mittelalters, XVI, 2 (1960), 437–546.

Grunwald, Georg. Geschichte der Gottesbeweise im Mittelalter bis zum Ausgang der Hochscholastik. BGPM, VI, 3 (1907).

Guthrie, W. K. C. "Plato's Views on the Nature of the Soul." Recherches sur la Tradition Platonicienne, 3–22. Entretiens Hardt, III. Geneva, 1955.

Häring, Nicholas M. "The Case of Gilbert de la Porée, Bishop of Poitiers (1142–54)." Medieval Studies, XIII (1951), 1–41.

——. "The Cistercian Everard of Ypres and his Appraisal of the Conflict between St Bernard and Gilbert of Poitiers." Medieval Studies, XVII (1955), 143–72.

——. "Notes on the Council and Consistory of Rheims." *Medieval Studies*, XXVIII (1966), 39–60.

——. "The Writings against Gilbert of Poitiers by Geoffrey of Auxerre." *Analecta Cisterciensia* (*Analecta Sacri Ordinis Cisterciensis*), XXII (1966), 3–83.

Hartman, Louis (ed.). *Encyclopedic Dictionary of the Bible*. New York, 1963.

Haskins, Charles H. *Studies in the History of Medieval Science*. Cambridge (Mass.), 1924.

——. *The Renaissance of the Twelfth Century*. New York, 1927.

Heer, Friedrich. *The Medieval World: 1100–1350*. New York, 1963.

Hill, Bennett. *English Cistercian Monasteries and their Patrons in the Twelfth Century*. Urbana, 1968.

Hirschberger, Johannes. "Platonismus und Mittelalter." *Philosophisches Jahrbuch*, LXIII (1954), 120–30.

Hiss, Wilhelm. *Die Anthropologie des Bernhards von Clairvaux*. Berlin, 1964.

Hödl, Ludwig. *Von der Wirklichkeit und Wirksamkeit des dreieinen Gottes nach der appropriativen Trinitäts-theologie des 12. Jahrhunderts. Mitteilungen des Grabmann-Instituts*. Heft 12. Munich, 1965.

——. "Zur Entwicklung der frühscholastischen Lehre von der Gottebenbild-lichkeit des Menschen." *L'Homme et Son Destin*, 347–59. Paris, 1960.

Holmes, U. T. "The Idea of a Twelfth-Century Renaissance." *Speculum*, XXVI (1951), 643–51.

Hourlier, Jacques. *Le Chapitre Général jusqu'au moment du Grand Schisme: Origines-Developpement-Étude juridique*. Paris, 1936.

Hubert, M. "Aspects du latin philosophique aux XIIe et XIIIe siècles." *Revue des études latines*, XXVII (1949), 211–33.

Huizinga, Johan. *Men and Ideas: History, the Middle Ages, the Renaissance*. New York, 1959.

Jaeger, Werner. "The Greek Ideas on Immortality." *Immortality and Resurrection*, 97–114. New York, 1965.

——. *The Theology of the Early Greek Philosophers*. Oxford, 1967.

Janauschek, Leopold. *Originum Cisterciensium*, I. Vienna. 1877.

Jaspers, Karl. *The Origin and Goal of History*. New Haven, 1953.

Javelet, Robert. *Psychologie des auteurs spirituels du XIIe siècle*. Strasbourg, 1959.

Jeauneau, Édouard. "Gloses de Guillaume de Conches sur Macrobe: Note sur les Manuscrites." AHDL, XXXV (1960), 17–28.

——. "L'usage de la notion d'integumentum à travers les Gloses de Guillaume de Conches." AHDL, XXXII (1957), 35–100.

——. "Macrobe, source du platonisme chartrain." *Studi Medievali*, 3rd Series, I (1960), 3–24.

——. "Mathématiques et Trinité chez Thierry de Chartres." *Die Metaphysik im Mittelalter. Miscellanea Mediaevalia*, II, 289–95. Berlin, 1963.

——. "Note sur l'école de Chartres." *Studi Mediaevali*, 3rd Series, V (1964.), 821–65.

——. "Un représentant du platonisme au XIIe siècle, maître Thierry de Chartres." *Mémoires de la Société archéologique d'Eure-et-Loir*, XX (1954), 1–10.

Jonas, Hans. *The Gnostic Religion*, Boston, 1958.

Kantorowicz, Ernst H. "Plato in the Middle Ages." *Selected Studies*, 184–93. New York, 1965.

Kemmerer, E. *Histoire de l'île de Ré*, II. La Rochelle, 1888.

King, Archdale A. *Cîteaux and her Elder Daughters*. London, 1954.

Kirk, G. S. and Raven, J. E. *The Presocratic Philosophers: A Critical History with a Selection of Texts*. Cambridge, 1966.

Kleinz, J. *The Theory of Knowledge of Hugh of St Victor*. Washington, 1944.

Klibansky, Raymond. *The Continuity of the Platonic Tradition during the Middle Ages. Outlines of a Corpus Platonicum Medii Aevi*. London, 1939.

——. "Plato's Parmenides in the Middle Ages and the Renaissance: A Chapter in the History of Platonic Studies." *Mediaeval and Renaissance Studies*, I, 2 (1943), 281–330.

——. "The School of Chartres." M. Clagett *et al.*, *Twelfth-Century Europe and the Foundations of Modern Society*, 3–14. Madison, 1966.

Knowles, David. *The English Mystical Tradition*. London, 1961.

——. *The Evolution of Medieval Thought*. London, 1962.

——. *From Pachomius to Ignatius*. Oxford, 1966.

——. *Great Historical Enterprises. Problems in Monastic History*. London, 1963.

——. *The Historian and Character*. Cambridge, 1963.

——. *The Monastic Order in England*, 940–1216. 2nd ed. Cambridge, 1963.

Koch, J. *Platonismus im Mittelalter*. Akademische Festrede gehalten am 26 Mai, 1948, zur Universitätsgründungsfeier (Köln). Krefeld, 1951.

Kremer, Klaus. "Das 'Warum' der Schöpfung: 'quia bonus' vel/et 'quia voluit'? Ein Beitrag zum Verhältnis von Neuplatonismus und Christentum an Hand des Prinzips 'bonum est diffusivum sui." *Parusia*, 241–64. Frankfort 1965.

Kristeller, Paul Oskar. *Latin Manuscript Books before 1600*. 3rd ed. New York, 1960.

——. *Renaissance Thought*. New York, 1961.

Ladner, Gerhart B. *The Idea of Reform*. Cambridge (Mass.), 1959.

Landgraf, Artur. *Einführung in die Geschichte der theologischen Literatur der Frühscholastik*. Regensburg, 1948.

——. "Zum Lehre von der Gotteserkenntnis in der Frühscholastik." *The New Scholasticism*, VI (1930), 261–88.

Langer, Susanne K. *Philosophy in a New Key*. 2nd ed. New York, 1951.

Lebreton, M. M. "Recherches sur les principaux thèmes théologiques traités dans les sermons du XIIᵉ siècle." RTAM, XXIII (1956), 5–18.

Leclercq, Jean. *Études sur Saint Bernard et le texte de ses écrits. Analecta Sacri Ordinis Cisterciensis*, IX, 1–2 (1953).

——. "Le genre épistolaire au moyen âge." *Revue du moyen âge latin*, II (1946), 63–70.

——. "Les écrits de Geoffrey d'Auxerre." *Revue Bénédictine*, LXII (1952), 257 sqq.

——. "Recherches sur d'anciens sermons monastiques." *Revue Mabillon*. XXXVI (1946), 1–14.

——. "St Bernard et ses secrétaires." *Revue Bénédictine*, LX (1951), 208–29.

———. "Table pour l'inventaire des homeliaires manuscrits." *Scriptorium,* II (1948), 195–214.

Leisegang, Hans. "La connaissance de Dieu au miroir de l'âme et de la nature." *Revue d'histoire et de la philosophie religieuses,* XVII (1937), 145–71.

Lekai, L. J. *The White Monks.* Okauchee (Wisconsin), 1953.

Lenssen, P. S. "A propos de Cîteaux et de S. Thomas de Cantorbéry. L'abdication du bienheureux Geoffrey d'Auxerre comme abbé de Clairvaux." COCR, XVII (1955), 98–110.

Lewis, C. S. *The Discarded Image.* Cambridge, 1967.

Lloyd, G. E. R. *Aristotle: The Growth and Structure of His Thought.* Cambridge, 1968.

Lonergan, Bernard. *De Deo Trino.* 2 Vols. Rome, 1959–61.

———. *Insight: A Study of Human Understanding.* New York, 1958.

———. "St Thomas' Thought on Gratia Operans." *Theological Studies,* II (1941), 290–323; III (1942), 69–87, 375–400.

———. *De Verbo Incarnato.* 2nd ed. Rome, 1961.

———. *Verbum: Word and Idea in Aquinas.* Notre Dame, 1967.

Lossky, V. "La théologie negative dans la doctrine de Denys L'Aréopagite." RSPT, XXVIII (1939), 204–21.

Lovejoy, Arthur O. *The Great Chain of Being.* New York, 1965.

Luscombe, D. E. *The School of Peter Lombard.* Cambridge, 1969.

McIntyre, John. *St Anselm and his Critics: A Reinterpretation of the Cur Deus Homo.* London-Edinburgh, 1954.

McKenzie, John L. *Dictionary of the Bible.* Milwaukee, 1965.

McKeon, Richard. "Medicine and Philosophy in the 11th and 12th Centuries: The Problem of the Elements." *The Thomist,* XXVI (1961), 211–56.

———. "Poetry and Philosophy in the 12th Century. The Renaissance of Rhetoric." *Modern Philology,* XLIII (1946), 217–34.

———. "Rhetoric in the Middle Ages." *Speculum,* XVII (1942), 1–32.

McNally, Robert E. *The Bible in the Early Middle Ages.* Westminster, 1959.

Mahn, J. B. *L'Ordre Cistercien et son gouvernement des origines au mileau du XIIIe siècle (1098–1265).* 12th ed. Paris, 1951.

Maitland, Frederic William. "Henry II and the Criminous Clerks." *Roman Canon Law and the Church of England,* 132–47. London, 1898.

Manrique, Angel. *Cisterciensium seu verius ecclesiasticorum annalium a condito Cistercio,* II. Lyon, 1642.

Maréchal, Joseph. *Studies in the Psychology of the Mystics.* London, 1927.

Mariétan, Joseph. *Problème de la classification des sciences d'Aristote à S. Thomas.* Paris, 1901.

Martin, R. M. "Pro Petro Abelardo, Un Plaidoyer de Robert de Melun contre S. Bernard." RSPT, XII (1923), 308–33.

Mathon, G. "Jean Scot Érigène, Chalcidius et le problème de l'âme universelle." *L'Homme et Son Destin,* 361–75. Paris, 1960.

Maurer, Armand A. *Medieval Philosophy.* New York, 1964.

Mazzantini, C. *Il Platonismo della Scuola di Chartres.* Turin, 1958.

Merlan, Philip. *From Platonism to Neoplatonism.* 3rd ed. The Hague, 1968.

———. "Neo-Platonism." *Encyclopedia of Philosophy,* V, 473–6. London, 1967.

Michaud-Quantain, P. "La psychologie dans l'enseignement au XIIe siècle." *L'Homme et Son Destin*, 407–15. Paris, 1960.
——. "Notes sur le vocabulaire psychologique de St Anselme." *Spicilegium Beccense I; Congrès Internationale du IXe Centenaire de l'arrivée d'Anselme au Bec*, 23–31. Paris, 1959.
——. "Une division 'augustinienne' des puissances de l'âme." *Revue des Études augustiniennes*, III (1957), 235–48.
Minio-Paluello, Lorenzo. "The Genuine Text of Boethius' Translation of Aristotle's Categories." *Mediaeval and Renaissance Studies*, I, 2 (1943), 151–77.
Mitterer, S. "Die Cistercienser im Kirchenstreit zwischen Papst Alexander III und Kaiser Friedrich I." *Cistercienser-Chronik*, XXXVI (1922), 1–8, 21–6, 35–40.
Moltmann, Jürgen. *Theology of Hope*. New York, 1967.
Mork, Wulfstan. *The Biblical Meaning of Man*. Milwaukee, 1967.
Morrison, Karl F. "Church, Reform, and Renaissance in the Early Middle Ages." *Life and Thought in the Early Middle Ages*, 143–59. Minneapolis, 1967.
Morson, John. "Les traités cisterciens De Anima." COCR, XXIV (1962), 377.
Muckle, J. T. "Greek Works Translated Directly into Latin before 1350." *Medieval Studies*, IV (1942), 33–43; V (1943), 102–15.
Mulligan, R. "Ratio Superior and Ratio Inferior: The Historical Background." *The New Scholasticism*, XXIX (1955), 1–32.
Nitze, W. A. "The So-called 12th Century Renaissance." *Speculum*, XXIII (1948), 464–71.
Norris, Richard A. *God and World in Early Christian Theology*. New York, 1965.
O'Connell, Robert J. *St Augustine's Confessions*. Cambridge (Mass.), 1969.
——. *St Augustine's Early Theory of Man, AD 386–91*. Cambridge (Mass.), 1968.
O'Connor, W. *The Concept of the Soul according to St Augustine*. Catholic University of America. Washington, 1921.
O'Donnell, J. R. "The Meaning of Silva in the Commentary of the Timaeus of Plato by Chalcidius." *Medieval Studies*, VII (1945), 1–20.
O'Meara, John J. *The Young Augustine*. London, 1965.
Onians, Richard Broxton. *The Origins of European Thought about the Body, the Mind, the Soul, the World, Time and Fate*. Cambridge, 1951.
Ostler, Heinrich. *Die Psychologie des Hugos von St Viktor*. BGPM, VI, 1 (1906).
Ott, Ludwig. "Die Platonische Weltseele in der Theologie der Frühscholastik." *Parusia*, 307–31. Frankfort, 1965.
Ottaviani, Carmelo. *Riccardo di San Vittore, la vita, le opere, il pensiero. Memorie della Romana Accademia dei Lincei*, VI (1933), 411–541.
Otto, Stephan. *Die Funktion des Bildbegriffes in der Theologie des 12. Jahrhunderts*. BGPM XL, 1 (1963).
Panofsky, Erwin. "Renaissance and renascenses." *Kenyon Review*, VI (1944), 201–34.
Paré, G., Brunet, A., and Trembley, P. *La renaissance du XIIe siècle. Les Écoles et l'Enseignement*. Paris-Ottawa, 1939.

Parent, J. M. *La doctrine de la création dans l'école de Chartres.* Paris-Ottawa, 1938.

———. "Un nouveau témoin de la théologie dionysienne au XII⁰ siècle." *Aus der Geisteswelt des Mittelalters,* 289–309. *Festschrift Martin Grabmann.* BGPM, Supplement III. Münster, 1935.

Peghaire, Julien. "L'Axiome 'Bonum est diffusivum sui' dans le néoplatonisme et le thomisme." *Revue de l'Université d'Ottawa,* I (1932), Section Spécial, 5*-30*.

Pegis, Anton C. *At the Origins of the Thomistic Notion of Man.* New York, 1963.

Pieper, Josef. *Scholasticism: Personalities and Problems of Medieval Philosophy.* New York, 1960.

Poole, A. L. *From Domesday Book to Magna Carta: 1087–1216.* 2nd ed. Oxford, 1964.

Poole, Reginald Lane. *Illustrations of the History of Medieval Thought.* 2nd ed. London, 1920.

———. "The Masters of the Schools of Paris and Chartres in John of Salisbury's Time." *English Historical Review,* XXXV (1920), 321–42.

Portalie, Eugène. *A Guide to the Thought of St Augustine.* Chicago, 1960.

Pouzet, P. *L'anglais Jean dit Bellesmains (1122–1204?) évêque de Poitiers (1162–82), pius archevêque de Lyon (1182–93).* Lyon, 1927.

Preiss, Martin. *Die politische Tätigkeit und Stellung der Cisterizienser im Schisma von 1159-1177.* Historische-Studien 248. Berlin, 1934.

Puech, H.-Ch. "La Ténébre mystique chez le Ps.-Denys l'Aréopagite et dans la tradition patristique." *Études Carmélitaines,* XXIII (1938), 33–53.

Raby, F. J. E. "Nuda Natura and 12th Century Cosmology." *Speculum,* XLIII (1968), 72–7.

Raven, J. E. *Plato's Thought in the Making.* Cambridge, 1965.

Reypens, Leonce. "Dieu (Connaissance Mystique)." DS, III, 883–929. Paris, 1957.

Rich, Audrey. "The Platonic Ideas as the Thoughts of God." *Mnemosyne,* Series IV, 7, 2 (1954), 123–33.

Ricoeur, Paul. "Hermeneutique des Symboles et Réflexion philosophique." *Archivio di Filosofia* (1961), 51–73.

———. *The Symbolism of Evil.* New York, 1967.

Rivière, Jean. "Theologia." *Revue des sciences religieuses,* VIII (1936), 47–57.

Robertson, James Craigie. *Becket, Archbishop of Canterbury.* London, 1859.

Robilliard, J. A. "Les six generes de contemplation chez Richard de Saint-Victor et leur origine platonicienne." RSPT, XXVIII (1939), 229–33.

Robinson, John A. T. *The Body: A Study in Pauline Theology.* London, 1952.

Rohde, Erwin. *Psyche: The Cult of Souls and Belief in Immortality among the Greeks.* 2 Vols. New York, 1966.

Roques, René. *L'Univers Dionysien. Structure Hiérarchique du monde selon le Ps-Denys.* Paris, 1954.

———. *Structures Théologiques de la Gnose à Richard de Saint-Victor.* Paris, 1962.

Rosán, Laurence Jay. *The Philosophy of Proclus.* New York, 1949.

S

Rutledge, Denys. *Cosmic Theology: The Ecclesiastical Hierarchy of Pseua-Denys, An Introduction.* Staten Island, 1964.

Sanford, E. M. "The 12th Century: Renaissance or Proto-Renaissance." *Speculum,* XXVI (1951), 635–42.

Schedler, P. M. *Die Philosophie des Macrobius und ihr Einfluss auf die Wissenschaft des christlichen Mittelalters.* BGPM, XIII, 1 (1916).

Schipperges, Heinrich. "Die Schulen von Chartres unter dem Einfluss des Arabismus." *Sudhoffs Archiv für Geschichte der Medizin und der Naturwissenschaften,* XL (1956), 193–210.

———. "Einflüsse arabischer Medizin auf die Mikrokosmos-literatur der 12. Jahrhunderts." *Miscellanea Mediaevalia. Vol. I. Antike und Orient im Mittelalter,* 129–53. Cologne, 1962.

Schmaus, Michael. *Die Psychologische Trinitätslehre des heiligen Augustinus.* Münster, 1927

Schmidt, Margot. "Regio dissimilitudinis." *Freibürger Zeitschrift für Philosophie und Theologie,* XV (1968), 63–108.

Schmidt-Kohl, Volker. *Die Neuplatonische Seelenlehre in der Consolatio Philosophiae des Boethius.* Meisenheim, 1965.

Schurr, Viktor. *Die Trinitätslehre des Boethius im Lichte der 'skythischen Kontroverse."* Paderborn, 1935.

Siegmund, A. *Die Überlieferung der griechischen christlichen Literatur in der lateinischen Kirche bis zum 12ten Jahrhundert.* Munich, 1949.

Sikes, J. G. *Peter Abailard.* New York, 1965.

Silverstein, Theodore. "Guillaume de Conches and Nemesius of Emesa: On the Sources of the 'New Science' of the 12th Century." *Harry Austryn Wolfson Jubilee Volume,* II, 719–34. Jerusalem, 1965.

———. "Hermann of Carinthia and Greek: A Problem in the 'New Science' of the 12th Century." *Medioevo e Rinascimento II. Studi in Onore di Bruno Nardi,* 681–99. Florence, 1956.

Smalley, Beryl. *The Study of the Bible in the Middle Ages.* Notre Dame, 1964.

Snell, Bruno. *The Discovery of the Mind: The Greek Origins of European Thought.* New York, 1960.

Southern, R. W. *The Making of the Middle Ages.* New Haven, 1963.

Squire, Aelred. *Hugh of St Victor: Selected Spiritual Writings.* London, 1962.

Stahl, William Harris. *Macrobius' Commentary on the Dream of Scipio.* New York, 1966.

Sulowski, J. F. "Studies in Chalcidius, Anthropology, Influence and Importance." *L'Homme et Son Destin,* 153–61. Paris, 1960.

Taylor, Jerome (ed.). *The Didascalicon of Hugh of St Victor: A Medieval Guide to the Arts.* New York, 1961.

Theiler, Willy. "Antike und christliche Rückkehr zu Gott." *Mullus: Festschrift Theodor Klausner,* 352–61. Münster, 1964.

———. *Porphyrios und Augustin. Forschungen zum Neuplatonismus,* 160–251. Berlin, 1966.

Théry, G. "Contribution à l'histoire du procès d'Eckhart: Bref aperçu sur l'histoire de la théologie negative." *Vie Spirituelle: Supplément,* XIV (June, 1926), 46–55.

——. "L'authenticité du 'De Spiritu et anima' dans S. Thomas et Albert le Grand." RSPT, X (1921), 373–77.

——. "Notes indicatrices pour s'orienter dans l'étude des traductions médiévales." *Mélanges J. Marechal*, II, 297–315. Louvain, 1950.

——. "Scot Érigène introducteur de Denys." *The New Scholasticism*, VII (1933), 91–108.

——. "Scot Érigène traducteur de Denys." *Bulletin Du Cange*, VI (1931), 185–278.

Thorndike, Lynn. *A History of Magic and Experimental Science*, II. New York, 1923.

van den Eynde, Damien. *Essai sur la succession et la date des écrits de Hugues de Saint Victor*. Rome, 1960.

van der Meer, Frederic. *Atlas de l'Ordre Cistercien*. Amsterdam, 1965.

Van Steenberghen, Fernand. *Aristotle in the West*. Louvain, 1955.

Vanneste, J. *Le Mystère de Dieu: Essai sur la structure rationelle de la doctrine mystique du Ps-Denys*. Brussels, 1959.

Verbeke, Gerard. "Spiritualité et immortalité de l'âme chez S. Augustin." *Augustinus Magister*, I, 329–34. Paris, 1954.

Voegelin, Eric. *Israel and Revelation*. Louisiana State University Press, 1956.

Wallace-Hadrill, D. S. *The Greek Patristic View of Nature*. London, 1968.

Walzer, R. "Arabic Transmission of Greek Thought to Medieval Europe." *Bulletin of the John Rylands Library*, XXIX (1945–46), 160–83.

Weisweiler, H. "Die Ps.-Dionysiuskommentare des Skotus Eriugena und Hugos von St Viktor." RTAM, XIX (1952), 26–47.

Whitehead, Alfred North. *Symbolism: Its Meaning and Effect*. New York, 1927.

Williams, Michael E. *The Teaching of Gilbert Porreta on the Trinity as found in his Commentaries on Boethius*. Analecta Gregoriana 56. Rome, 1951.

Wolfson, Harry A. "Immortality and Resurrection in the Philosophy of the Church Fathers." *Immortality and Resurrection*, 54–96. New York, 1965.

——. "Negative Attributes in the Church Fathers and the Gnostic Basilides." *Harvard Theological Review*, L (1957), 145–56.

Woolsey, R. B. "Bernard Silvester and the Hermetic *Asclepius*." *Traditio*, VI (1948), 340–44.

Zaehner, R. C. *Mysticism Sacred and Profane*. Oxford, 1957.

——. *The Dawn and Twilight of Zoroastrianism*. New York, 1961.

INDEX OF NAMES

267

ANALYTIC INDEX

271

Laus tibi Christe

CISTERCIAN FATHERS SERIES

Under the direction of the same Board of Editors as the CISTERCIAN STUDIES SERIES, the CISTERCIAN FATHERS SERIES seeks to make available the works of the Cistercian Fathers in good English translations based on the recently established critical editions. The texts are accompanied by introductions, notes and indexes prepared by qualified scholars.